Entrepreneurship
and Small Business Management

Earl C. Meyer, Ph.D.
Teacher Educator—Marketing Education
Eastern Michigan University
Ypsilanti, Michigan

Kathleen R. Allen, Ph.D.
Assistant Professor of Clinical Entrepreneurship
The Entrepreneur Program
University of Southern California
Los Angeles, California

Glencoe
McGraw-Hill

New York, New York   Columbus, Ohio   Woodland Hills, California   Peoria, Illinois

Photography

Arizona Biological Control 201; Arndt Brothers Industries Inc. 245; Arnold and Brown Photographers vii, viii, ix (2), 1, 49, 78, 91, 94, 102, 140, 143, 146, 149, 150, 156, 163, 166, 172, 174, 176, 180, 195, 196, 197, 198 (2), 199, 209 (4), 220, 227, 231, 236, 250, 259, 266, 269, 271, 328, 332, 333, 334, 336, 340, 346; Barefoot Press 321; L. L. Bean 9; Ben and Jerry's 344; Pat Berrett/Bone Deco 112; Big City Comics Inc. 66; Bio Dynamics, Ltd. 88; Melanie Bishop 50; Bonecutter Trading 188; Boston Trolley Tours 175; Randy Brandon/Third Eye Studio 343; Charles William Bush/AEGIR, 352; Cal Corn Inc. 132; The Coca-Cola Company 11; John Coletti/The Picture Cube v, 16; Comstock, Inc. cover (TL, BR); Culver Pictures 8 (3); Welton B. Dolby III/The Answer Temps. Inc. 270; Laima Druskis Photography vi, 18, 33, 34 (2), 54, 84, 87, 100, 108, 113, 114, 118, 121, 125, 128, 130, 131, 137, 160, 171, 180, 203, 206, 211, 223, 260; Ethnic Reams, Rolls, and Bags Plus Inc. 123; Cathy Ferris 148; Henry Ford Museum and Greenfield Village (Archive # 92-757) 4; Golf USA, Inc. 353; Greylag Artist Multiples 228; Harden Industries 144; Ellis Herwig/The Picture Cube 86; Walter Hodges/ Westlight 29, 70; Inky Fingers 162; K. B. Kaplan/ The Picture Cube 40; Kentucky Fried Chicken Corporation 11; Pierre Kopp/Westlight cover (TR); Long Photography/Mrs. Gooch's 73; D & I Macdonald/The Picture Cube 89; McDonald's Corporation 11, 98 (3); Old Parr's Carousel Animals 212; Pelton & Associates, Inc./Westlight cover (BL); Photo Network 75; Alon Reininger/ Unicorn Stock Photos 192; Rhode Island Tourism Division 7 (L); M. Richards/Photo Edit 309; Charles Steck/Simple Machines Records 294; Superstock 3, 30, 32, 34 (L), 83, 265; Topps Custom Floral Designs 101; Vans Inc. 331; Lorenzo Vega 20; Vermont Teddy Bear Company 257; Wave Rave 286; Wendy's Inter-national Inc. 35; Dana C. White/ Dana White Productions x, 122, 276, 278, 280, 283, 290, 292, 296, 297, 298, 302, 316, 320, 323, 325, 350, 354 (3) 356, 357; Martin Wong/Comic Connection 312; Yale University Art Gallery 7 (R)

Illustrations

R.J. Miyake Illustration 21, 22, 23, 25, 37, 42, 43, 44, 45, 46, 47, 56, 59, 60, 61, 62, 65, 72, 76, 96, 104, 111, 120, 134, 135, 142, 152, 159, 169, 182, 185, 186, 187, 213, 214, 215, 216, 225, 229, 232, 239, 240, 241, 242, 243, 244, 252, 253, 254, 255, 272, 284, 285, 293, 304, 305, 307, 310, 311, 319

Glencoe would like to thank the following for their generous assistance in providing locations for some of the photography listed above:

Conrad Johnson; Martin Minkardo; Mt. Olive Pre-School; Pavilion's Market; Pets on Wilshire; Santa Monica High School; Southern California Edison; Sun Computers; Venice Family Clinic; Wherehouse Records; Natalie, Michael, and Andrew White.

Glencoe/McGraw-Hill

A Division of The **McGraw·Hill** Companies

Send all inquiries to:
Glencoe/McGraw-Hill
21600 Oxnard Street, Suite 500
Woodland Hills, CA 91367

ISBN 0-02-675119-4 (Student Edition)
ISBN 0-02-675121-6 (Teacher's Annotated Edition)

8 9 10 11 12 13 14 15 16   027   04 03 02 01 00 99 98

About the Authors

Earl C. Meyer has extensive experience in both business and education. He is currently the teacher educator for marketing education at Eastern Michigan University. He has been a base coordinator and faculty member for Southern Illinois University's Vocational Education Studies Military Program and a high school marketing education teacher-coordinator in Rome, Georgia. While working at the secondary level, he taught entrepreneurship for 8 years. For 16 years prior to moving into education, he was involved with the operation and management of retail and service businesses, including his own golf enterprise.

Meyer has been the project director for two entrepreneurship education curriculum guides. He has also authored articles, held workshops, and made numerous conference presentations on teaching entrepreneurship. Presently he serves as the Michigan representative to the International Entrepreneurship Education Consortium.

Meyer has a B.A. in Distributive Education from the University of South Florida. His M.A. and Ph.D. in Vocational and Career Development (with an emphasis in marketing education) are both from Georgia State University.

Kathleen R. Allen is a recognized researcher and consultant in venture creation strategies and feasibility. She joined the faculty of the Entrepreneur Program at the University of Southern California in the fall of 1990, after 15 years of high school and college-level teaching.

In addition to her teaching and research responsibilities, Allen is also the project administrator of *"Marketplace" in the Schools*, an audio-cassette program designed to teach high school students how global economics affects their daily lives. Based on the highly acclaimed "Marketplace" program broadcast on public radio, *"Marketplace" in the Schools* also encourages students to use entrepreneurship as a way to take charge of their lives and contribute something to society.

As an entrepreneur herself, Allen has co-founded three businesses, including a new technology-based manufacturing venture. She has also served as a consultant to private investors, real estate developers, banks, and city governments.

Allen holds masters degrees in both foreign languages and business administration. She has a Ph.D. in Higher, Adult, and Professional Education (with a research emphasis in entrepreneurship) from the University of Southern California.

Acknowledgments

Dr. Meyer wishes to thank his graduate assistant, Maria Weisenberger, for her research work on the text.

Dr. Allen wishes to express her appreciation to Dr. Jon P. Goodman, Director of the Entrepreneur Program at the University of Southern California, for her support. She also wishes to thank her faculty assistant, Jeffrey J. Trojan, for his research efforts.

Reviewers

Kay Baker
Area Supervisor—Business and
   Marketing Education
Vocational and Technical Education Division
Arkansas State Department of Education
Little Rock, Arkansas

Katherine L. Cole
President
Private Ventures, Inc.
Flint, Michigan

Gayle Flowers
Tech-Prep Manager
Northwest Louisiana Tech-Prep Consortium
Shreveport, Louisiana

J. Scott Harris
Technology Education Teacher
Logan Senior High School
Logan, Utah

Douglas A. Haskell
Associate Director
Greater Cincinnati Center for
   Economic Education
University of Cincinnati
Cincinnati, Ohio

Jayne W. James
Business/Marketing Teacher
Temescal Canyon High School
Lake Elsinore, California

Marlene Cusaac Johnson
Marketing Education Teacher-Coordinator
Lee County Vocational School
Bishopville, South Carolina

A. E. Mozisek
Marketing Education Teacher-Coordinator
Winston Churchill High School
San Antonio, Texas

Kathy A. White
Business Education Teacher
J. Everett Light Career Center
North Central High School
Indianapolis, Indiana

Table of Contents

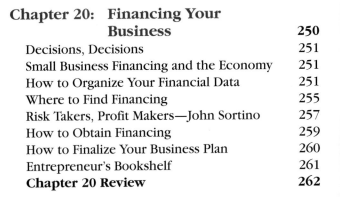

UNIT ONE

The Role of Small Business in the U.S. Economy

Chapter 1:
Our Entrepreneurial Heritage

Chapter 2:
Economic Forces

Chapter 1
Our Entrepreneurial Heritage

Objectives

After completing this chapter, you will be able to

- explain what entrepreneurs do,
- describe the role of entrepreneurs in our country's development,
- list the trends that will shape the future of entrepreneurship, and
- identify entrepreneurial opportunities that are of special interest to you.

Terms to Know

entrepreneur
venture
entrepreneurship
entrepreneurial
niches

Decisions, Decisions

It's hard to believe I'm a junior already. In just two years, I'll be out on my own.

I don't know exactly how I'm going to support myself, but I do have a few things in mind. First, there's nursing—easy choice. I say "easy" because I'm taking health occupations courses right now in school. Of course, I'd have to work awhile to afford nursing school.

That's where Petland comes in. That's where I work now after school and on weekends. Carl, my boss, is really encouraging. He thinks I've got the makings of a store manager (I'm really organized and good with people). Petland's a national chain, so there's plenty of opportunity.

My third choice, though, is the one that really gets me going. I could start my own business. What kind? I'm not sure. I just know that my uncle and my grandad have their own businesses, and they get such a charge out of it. Whenever they visit, that's all they talk about—the things customers do, bargaining with suppliers, all the financial stuff. They seem to thrive on it.

How about a business taking care of animals? That would be good for me, wouldn't it? There must be tons of possibilities there—although off the top of my head I can't name them. Or what about starting up something in health care? I'm not as sure about that. I don't think too many health care workers are self-employed, are they? Oh, there must be possibilities there. In fact, there must be possibilities all over the place. The question is, How do I find out what they are?

What Is an Entrepreneur?

Most people at one time or another in their lives think about going into business for themselves. The purpose of this book is to prepare you to succeed if and when that thought occurs to you.

When you put thoughts of self-employment into action, you become an **entrepreneur**. By definition an entrepreneur is a person who undertakes the organization and ownership of a business with the intent of making a profit. He or she assumes the risks and responsibilities associated with the **venture**.

In our discussions in this book, we will also frequently use the terms *entrepreneurship* and *entrepreneurial*. **Entrepreneurship** is the process of getting into and operating your own business. **Entrepreneurial** means of or having to do with an entrepreneur or entrepreneurs.

Entrepreneurs in American History

The history of America is the history of its entrepreneurs. Since the earliest days of our nation, the American ideals of opportunity and freedom have attracted immigrants and inspired citizens who have an entrepreneurial spirit. These individuals have created the enterprises that have formed the economic backbone of our society. They have also had a profound impact on our social and political development.

Colonial Merchants

Entrepreneurship was a way of life for the settlers of the original thirteen colonies. Nearly all were farmers who used their surplus crops for trade. By trading among themselves and with England, many colonists made enough money to start small businesses. They raised rice and tobacco for export, built ships, fished, and set up lumber and fur-trading companies. These early entrepreneurial efforts set the pattern for generations of Americans to come.

As the 1700s unfolded, American merchant entrepreneurs developed an extensive cottage industry system. Merchants distributed raw materials to farm families and paid them to turn those materials into finished products, such as furniture and clothing. This system, combined with expanding markets, created the largest increase in average personal income the world had seen up to that time.

During the Revolutionary War, the colonial army experienced transportation, supply, and financial problems that could have meant defeat. To solve these problems, they called upon the talents of some prominent entrepreneurs—Jeremiah Wadsworth and Robert Morris. Wadsworth was a banker, investor, and manufacturing pioneer. He procured supplies and organized supply lines, earning himself the title of Quartermaster of the Revolution. Morris was the best-known merchant of the day. He almost single-handedly financed the war by pledging his personal fortune and encouraging others to do so. In tribute to men like these, it was said the British did not lose so much to American generals as to American entrepreneurs.

Entrepreneurial Inventors

In the late 1700s, an enterprising young mechanic named Samuel Slater emigrated from England to America. He brought with him the plans for a spinning machine. Slater used those plans to establish the first factory in America—a cotton mill using water-powered spinning machines. A few years later, Francis Cabot Lodge added the concept of specialization—having factory workers focus on just one or two tasks. With these innovations, the Industrial Revolution came to America. The nation began to harness its great natural resources and move into the age of power-driven machinery.

During this era, many entrepreneurs were also inventors. Their genius lay in their ability to see the potential of the new technology. John Deere and Cyrus McCormick developed machinery that greatly increased farm production. Eli Whitney's cotton gin had a similar effect in the textile industry. Elias Howe's sewing machine revolutionized the production of clothing.

In the early 1800s, other entrepreneurs found opportunities in opening the territory beyond the Allegheny Mountains to settlement. Robert Fulton designed the steamboat to take advantage of rivers as transportation routes. Other entrepreneurs imported the concept of the railroad and developed toll roads and canals. Samuel Morse invented the telegraph to provide a communications link to the nation's new frontiers. These innovations in transportation and communication opened the West and dramatically enlarged the nation's economy.

Captains of Industry

After the Civil War, population and personal income grew rapidly. Entrepreneurs had to find new approaches to serve these large, new national markets.

In response, many industrial entrepreneurs created enormous organizations. John D.

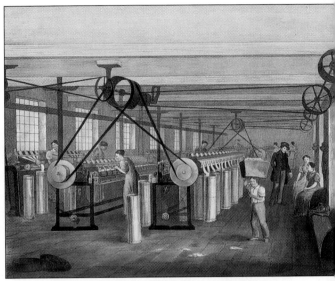

Samuel Slater built and ran America's first machine-powered cotton mill (left) at Pawtucket, Rhode Island. Judging from the interior view of such a mill (above), how were its machines powered?

Rockefeller eliminated competitors in the oil industry by aggressively cutting costs and prices. Andrew Carnegie did the same in the steel industry. Jay Gould and Edward Harriman expanded the nation's railroads sixfold. In banking, J. P. Morgan promoted corporate mergers that created companies like AT&T, General Electric, and U.S. Steel.

Merchandising entrepreneurs also tried new approaches. John Wanamaker brought several retail operations under one roof to create the first department store. Aaron Montgomery Ward began widespread distribution of goods in rural areas through mail order.

The paths pioneered by these and other business innovators set the pattern for many present-day businesses. In the process, they helped the American economy become the most productive in the world.

Molders of Modern Life-style

Entrepreneurial inventors continued to have a major impact on America well into the twentieth century. People like Alexander Graham Bell and Thomas Edison created products that profoundly changed the life-style of average Americans. So great was the influence of their work that today it is hard to imagine life without their principal inventions—the telephone and the electric light.

The two inventions that had the greatest impact, however, were in the field of transportation. The first was Henry Ford's Model T. It brought the automobile within the financial reach of almost everyone. In the process, it also made mobility a major characteristic of American life.

The second transportation innovation was the airplane. It was developed by a pair of bicycle shop owners, the Wright brothers. Perhaps more than any other invention, it changed our perception of the world by making it a smaller place. Consider this fact: At the turn of this century, it took a week to reach Europe by ship. Today it takes a mere three hours by supersonic jet!

Entrepreneurial inventors have had a major impact on America throughout its history. Can you identify these famous entrepreneurs and their contributions to modern American life?

World War II presented modern American entrepreneurs with many of the same challenges that faced their colonial counterparts. Both were asked to meet unparalleled demands for war equipment and supplies. Twentieth-century entrepreneurs, however, had to provide technically sophisticated weapons. What's more, they had to do it with a largely untrained work force.

Despite the difficulties, they succeeded. They converted factories from domestic to military production, developed new technology, and trained tens of thousands of new workers—all in record time. The result was a record output of ships, planes, guns, and other war matériel.

After the war, entrepreneurs adapted many of the wartime innovations in technology to meet pent-up demand for consumer goods. The increased production of automobiles, houses, appliances, and similar products created an era of prosperity that lasted two decades.

It is too soon to assess the overall impact of entrepreneurial efforts on our nation since the end of the 1970s. What can be said with certainty is that the efforts of entrepreneurs continue to

Risk Takers, Profit Makers

L.L. Bean

When in 1912 Leon L. Bean found a way to make hunting easier with improved footwear, he didn't just bag more deer. He also started a new business and captured an untapped market.

Bean was running his brother's dry-goods store when he came up with the idea for the Maine Hunting Shoe. As a hunter himself, Bean needed a dry, lightweight hunting boot. Such boots didn't seem to exist, so Bean designed a pair for himself and had them made. They had the rubber soles of galoshes and the leather uppers of boots—and they kept his feet dry. Suspecting he might have a product worth selling, Bean decided to go into business for himself.

Bean set up shop in the basement of his brother's store. He bought a mailing list of people holding Maine hunting licenses and created a three-page advertising brochure. Soon, the orders started coming in.

Bean's first efforts at large-scale production were not exactly successful. Of the first 100 pairs of boots he sold, 90 were returned. The problem? The rubber soles separated from the leather uppers.

This experience taught Bean a valuable lesson. Never again would he sell a product without first testing it extensively in the field. Bean refunded his customers' money, but he didn't give up on his business. Instead, he perfected his boots, took out patents on their design, and continued to sell them through his brochure-turned-catalog.

Bean was careful not to expand his business too rapidly. He added other outdoor products to his catalog—but only things he believed in and would use himself. He gradually enlarged his mailing list and the amount of his advertising. Mainly, though, he relied on product quality and customer satisfaction to build a loyal base of repeat customers. By 1924, 12 years after Bean

founded the company, his entire staff consisted of just 25 employees. They did everything—cut and stitched boots, filled orders, and maintained the books. Sales totaled $135,000.

When L. L. Bean died in 1967, his grandson, Leon Gorman, took over the firm. Gorman enlarged the store and enhanced the mail order business by employing modern technology, like computers and toll-free telephone lines. Today L. L. Bean has approximately 3,000 employees and sends out over 20 different catalogs a year. Sales have reached the $600 million mark.

Clearly, Gorman faces business challenges far more complex than those that L. L. Bean faced when he began his enterprise. The company is many times larger than when it originated. Retail competition is stiff and ever increasing. Yet the company continues to run according to Bean's underlying philosophy: "Sell good merchandise at a reasonable profit, treat your customers like human beings, and they'll always come back for more."

shape our lives as well as respond to changes in them.

In the 1970s, for example, economic changes created the need for two-income families and forced many homemakers into the workplace. At the same time, people became more concerned with the quality of their lives. Entrepreneurs reacted quickly to both trends. They saw that the average person's life was becoming more crowded, complex, and fast-paced, and that this was creating a whole new range of personal needs. Present-day entrepreneurs like Tom Monaghan (Domino's Pizza) and Mary Anne Jackson (My Own Meals, Inc.) created services designed to simplify working couples' lives. Others, like Arthur Jones (Nautilus Equipment) and Steven Jobs (NeXT Computer), offered high-tech ways to improve health and fitness, recreation, and education. In the process, all have reshaped today's life-styles.

Directions for Entrepreneurship

In recent years more and more Americans have been going into business for themselves. According to the Internal Revenue Service, the number of self-employed people has grown from under 6 million in 1970 to over 12 million in 1988. The number will continue to increase as individuals like you take advantage of the opportunities that the future holds.

One Analyst's View

No one can say for sure exactly what your entrepreneurial opportunities will be or where they will come from. You can, however, get some idea by looking at current and projected trends.

John Naisbitt is a respected trend analyst with a remarkable record of accuracy in predicting social and economic developments. Among the trends he has identified are several likely to affect entrepreneurial opportunities in this decade:

- *We are well into a shift from an industrial to an informational society.* Manufacturing businesses have declined sharply. On the other hand, businesses that process information (mass communication, data processing, etc.) and those that deal in information (banking, finance, insurance, etc.) will continue to see dramatic increases.

- *We are moving toward a balance between high tech and "high touch."* Technology has been a good area for entrepreneurs for some time and will continue to present all sorts of opportunities. Consumer dissatisfaction with technology that is impersonal, however, will cause an important shift in the direction of this trend. Technology-oriented entrepreneurs who understand the need for people to deal with people will have the best chance for success.

- *We are moving from a national to a world economy.* Trade barriers are falling throughout the world. Countries that in the past have had government-run economies are switching to market-based economies. For the individual entrepreneur, the global economy will present both challenges and opportunities. The challenges will be in the form of competition for limited resources and customers. The opportunities will involve expansion into international markets and foreign operations. Future entrepreneurs will be affected by the global economy no matter what business they are in.

- *Global life-styles and cultural nationalism are surfacing.* Food, music, and clothing styles from other countries are becoming increasingly popular in the major cities of every country. At the same time, there are strong feelings in many countries about the importance of maintaining national values and traditions. Both have implications for entrepreneurship.

- *We are becoming a multiple-option society.* For much of our history consumers have had

The move toward a global economy is apparent on the streets of any major city in the world. Where are each of these streets, and what evidence do you see of this key trend?

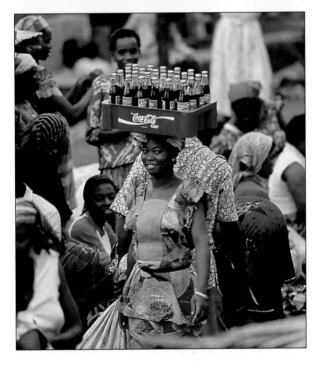

simple either/or choices—Ford or Chevy, chocolate or vanilla, etc. Now consumers can choose from a variety of models, styles, and colors in almost every product line. This continuing trend toward diversity of choice will open a multitude of **niches**—or suitable places—for entrepreneurial ventures.

- *There is a move toward private companies taking over government services.* Government services at the national, state, and local levels are very expensive. It is becoming apparent in the United States, as well as in other countries, that private-sector entrepreneurs can deliver these services more cheaply and better.

- *The Pacific Rim countries are becoming a major economic force.* The countries and states that border on the Pacific Ocean represent an enormous share of the world's geography, population, and production. They present a huge market as well as a source of supply for potential entrepreneurs.

Entrepreneurial Areas and Opportunities

ARTS AND HUMANITIES

Foreign language interpreter/translator, graphic artist/illustrator, manufacturing jeweler, music instructor, photographer, piano tuner, sign painter, writer.

BUSINESS AND OFFICE

Accountant, copy shop owner, desktop publisher, mail receiving service owner, messenger service owner, shorthand reporter, tax preparer, temporary service owner, word-processing service owner.

CONSTRUCTION

Air conditioning/heating/refrigeration/solar energy technician, architect, contractor, floor covering installer, painter/paperhanger, plumber, surveyor, welder.

GENERAL MARKETING

Advertising agency owner, appraiser, food distributor, fund raiser, independent insurance agent, public relations consultant, real estate broker, retail store owner, trade show manager.

HEALTH

Chiropractor, dental laboratory technician, dentist, dispensing optician, family doctor, massage therapist, pharmacist, physical therapist, speech-language pathologist.

HOME ECONOMICS

Caterer, child care provider, clothing decorator, dietician, dry cleaner, housekeeping service owner, interior designer, nanny placement service owner.

HOSPITALITY AND RECREATION

Bed-and-breakfast owner, health club owner, personal trainer, pool-cleaning service owner, restaurant owner, tour operator, travel agency owner, valet parking service owner.

PERSONAL SERVICE

Career counselor, cosmetologist, event planner, financial planner, funeral director, image consultant, personal service provider.

PLANTS AND ANIMALS

Dog trainer, farmer, fish farmer, horse trainer, interior landscape specialist, landscaper, nursery owner, pet groomer, veterinarian.

PROTECTIVE AND SOCIAL SERVICES

Bodyguard, locksmith, private investigator, security service owner, sign language interpreter.

SCIENCE AND TECHNOLOGY

Appliance repairer, computer programmer, consulting engineer, hazardous waste management consultant/firm owner, photo finishing lab owner.

TRANSPORTATION

Airplane/helicopter pilot, auto detailing service owner, auto repair/maintenance service owner, bicycle shop owner, boat yard owner, car/truck dealership owner, gasoline station owner, limousine fleet owner, moving service owner, truck driver.

Figure 1–1   Entrepreneurial opportunities exist in every field. Study the possibilities shown here. Which could be pursued part-time by individuals? How?

- *Our population is aging.* More than half of our population is either in or nearing the over-45 age group. Millions of these Americans are 65 or older. Entrepreneurs who can develop new products and new marketing strategies that appeal to this group will have a big advantage.

Some Additional Trends

Naisbitt's trends are not the only ones that might affect entrepreneurship in the future. Other authorities have their own opinions. From these sources an additional list of commonly cited trends can be compiled:

- *In recent years, there has been a reduction in government regulations that restrict business and discourage new ventures.* In addition, government at all levels has actively encouraged the creation of new businesses as a way to spur economic growth. Grants, conferences, and economic development councils have all been used to help entrepreneurs start enterprises.
- *Support for women and minorities who wish to start new businesses has been increasing.* There are now special advisory and assistance programs sponsored by the Small Business Administration (SBA) and other government agencies. Private sector programs also exist.
- *Small business ventures have increasingly taken customers from larger corporate competitors.* Small enterprises are often able to respond more quickly and creatively to consumer needs.
- *Downsizing of large corporations has resulted in fewer jobs and opportunities for advancement in that setting.* Also, many individuals find corporate work limiting or lacking in personal satisfaction. Self-employment, on the other hand, offers opportunity and challenge as well as the potential for greater personal and monetary rewards.

Areas of Entrepreneurial Opportunity

As fascinating as trends are, they are not the only indicators of where future entrepreneurial opportunities will be. Those opportunities exist and will continue to be found in all areas.

Often it is not the newness of an idea that counts. Rather, success comes from having the right idea, at the right time, and in the right place. It is also important for the beginning entrepreneur to enjoy what he or she is doing.

Figure 1-1 shows some areas of entrepreneurial opportunity and specific examples of businesses you might go into in each area. Read through these carefully. As you do, note any options that are appealing to you. Also, note any possibilities that are not listed but which the entries suggest to you.

As you consider your entrepreneurial options, remember that most ventures start small. Some even start as part-time ventures and grow into full-fledged businesses. Also, consider that many businesses have been started by entrepreneurs while they were in high school.

Entrepreneur's Bookshelf

To learn more about the subjects discussed in this chapter, consider reading these books:

- *The Wealth Creators: An Entrepreneurial History of the United States* by Gerald Gunderson (© 1989)
- *Megatrends 2000: Ten New Directions for the 1990s* by John Naisbitt and Patricia Aburdene (© 1990)

Chapter 1 Review

Recapping the Chapter

- Entrepreneurship is a career option for everyone.
- Entrepreneurs are people who organize and develop their own business.
- Entrepreneurs have played a major role in shaping the history of America.
- Current and projected trends favor entrepreneurship as a career option.
- Opportunities for entrepreneurial ventures are available in every field.

Reviewing Vocabulary

1. *Venture* is not defined in the chapter. Look the word up, and write an explanation of why it would be used to describe new business start-ups.
2. Write five sentences using one of the following vocabulary terms in each:

   - entrepreneur
   - venture
   - entrepreneurship
   - entrepreneurial
   - niches

Checking the Facts

1. What is meant by the term *cottage industry*?
2. What role did entrepreneurs play in winning the Revolutionary War? in winning World War II?
3. Summarize in a phrase the contributions of each of the following people to America's economic development:

   - Samuel Slater
   - Francis Cabot Lodge
   - John Wanamaker
   - Aaron Montgomery Ward
   - Alexander Graham Bell

4. What characteristics did each of these entrepreneurs share—Robert Fulton, Henry Ford, and the Wright brothers?
5. List a half dozen trends that are likely to create market opportunities for entrepreneurs in this decade.
6. For each area of entrepreneurial opportunity listed in this chapter (see Figure 1–1), suggest one business venture a person could undertake.

Thinking Critically

1. If you had been a trend analyst in the latter half of the nineteenth century, in what directions would you have seen entrepreneurship moving?
2. Describe the opportunities that might be available to you as an entrepreneur because of the trend toward a global economy.
3. Consider the other trends presented in the chapter. Then suggest at least one product an entrepreneur could provide to take advantage of each.
4. Does the growth of entrepreneurship now mean that there will be fewer opportunities in the future? Why or why not?

Discussing Key Concepts

1. Which of the trends affecting entrepreneurship do you think is most important? Why?
2. If it were 20 years from now and you were looking back at the role today's entrepreneurs had in shaping the country, what would you say about them?

Chapter 1 Review

3. If you were to go into business for yourself, would it be really important to you that you enjoy what you were doing? Why or why not?

4. On the basis of the trends listed in the chapter, would you say that the climate is favorable for you to go into business for yourself? Explain.

Using Basic Skills

Math
1. The number of entrepreneurs increased from under 6 million to over 12 million in the past 20 years. If they increased at the same rate over the next 20 years, approximately how many entrepreneurs would there be at that time?

Communication
2. Read a current magazine article featuring a successful entrepreneur. Write a summary of the article, and draw some conclusions about how this person's business affected (or was affected by) modern life-styles and the economy.

Human Relations
3. You have scheduled an appointment with a local entrepreneur to get advice on going into business for yourself as a career option. The person was on the telephone when you arrived, and now—25 minutes later—he or she is still talking. During that time there have been interruptions to deal with two employees and a vendor. What should you do?

Enriching Your Learning

1. Arrange an interview with a local entrepreneur. In your interview, try to get answers to the following questions:

   - Why did you decide to go into business for yourself?
   - What was involved in setting up your business?
   - What have been the high points of your venture? the low points?
   - What plans do you have for expansion of your business?
   - What advice would you give to someone planning to go into business for him- or herself?

2. If you are currently employed, select three products your company sells that were developed by small business people. (If you are not aware of any such products, ask experienced employees or your manager.) Research each product to determine the following:

   - Identity of the product developer
   - How that person got the idea
   - What was involved in getting the product off the ground
   - Company's record of success selling the product

3. From Figure 1–1 select a category of self-employment that appeals to you. Then refer to a Sunday newspaper from a large metropolitan area. Using the classified ads, locate and list all of the businesses you can find that fall into your selected category.

Economic Forces

Objectives

After completing this chapter, you will be able to

- illustrate the importance of entrepreneurship in the U.S. economy,
- define economics in its most basic terms,
- explain the relationship between political and economic systems,
- tell how free enterprise works, and
- summarize the special contributions of entrepreneurs to a free market economy.

Terms to Know

economics
goods
services
factors of
  production
capital
scarcity
opportunity cost
profit
elastic
inelastic
principle of
  diminishing
  marginal utility
equilibrium price
balance of trade
exports
imports

Decisions, Decisions

Boy, talk about being in a bind! I have exactly $20 to my name, and I've got to make it last till the end of the week. That'll take a miracle.

First of all, my car's running on fumes, so I'm going to need some gas to get around. Then I've got to pay my drama club dues. (I owe for three months.) To make matters worse, this morning I remembered that my mom's birthday is tomorrow. Of course, I haven't gotten her present yet. And there's this new CD I've been wanting for weeks. I figure I need at least $40 to cover all that.

You know how all those TV economists are always talking about supply and demand? Well, when it comes to my wallet, I've got lots of demand and very little supply! I tried to get around that by asking for more hours at the sub shop where I work. But since the auto factory dropped its second shift, there just isn't enough business.

Well, I guess I'm going to have to make some serious choices—you know, necessities first. Big help—they're all necessities to me. Who designed this system anyway? I wonder if it's just me or does everyone have a hard time with stuff like this?

Entrepreneurship in Today's Economy

As you learned in Chapter 1, the United States is becoming a more entrepreneurial, globally oriented country. At present, 38 percent of our Gross National Product (the total value of the goods and services we produce nationally each year) is supplied by small businesses. These small, but growing, enterprises have also provided virtually all of the new jobs created in the United States since the 1960s.

Peter Drucker, perhaps the most widely read writer on the management of modern organizations, believes that we are fast moving from a managerial economy to an entrepreneurial economy. We are shifting from mega-corporations to smaller, more adaptable and efficient companies.

But even smaller, more adaptable companies are subject to the forces of economics. They must compete for everything from raw materials and workers to customers. They must do so in bad times as well as good. They must operate in a marketplace that increasingly is not just local or national but global.

None of this is easy. It would be impossible, however, without at least a minimal grasp of economics. You can get only so far in business on luck. You can accomplish only so much by muddling through. After that, you have to know what you are doing. You have to understand the economic environment in which you are operating.

Economics—Making Choices

Economics is the study of the decisions (or choices) that go into making, distributing, and consuming products. To appreciate what entrepreneurs do for and in our economy, you need to know some basic economics.

If that sounds intimidating to you, it shouldn't. You're already familiar with many of the concepts that will be discussed in this chapter. That's because you experience them every day in your role as a consumer.

Goods and Services

Think about what you did yesterday. Did you take a bus to school? After school did you stop off at a fast-food restaurant for a snack? Did you go to your favorite music store and buy a CD? If you stopped at the music store, while you were there did you purchase tickets to an upcoming rock concert?

If you did any of these things, you have used or purchased goods and services. Goods and services are the products that our economic system produces to satisfy our wants.

Goods are tangible (or physical) products. They are of two types. Industrial goods are those used in the manufacture of other goods. (Plastic to produce toys would be an example.) Consumer goods are those purchased by you for your own needs.

Services are intangible (or conceptual) products. They represent the largest, fastest-growing segment of the small business economy. Physicians, accountants, theaters, barbers—all provide services.

Factors of Production

To purchase goods and services, you use your personal resources. Usually this means spending money. If you work for your money, it can also mean spending a certain amount of time and effort.

To produce the goods and services that people want, businesses also use resources. Their resources, however, are given a special name—**factors of production**. There are four types of factors:

- *Land.* In economic terms, land is all the natural resources upon and beneath the earth's surface.

Products consist of goods and services. Which does this small business produce? Explain.

It includes not only geographic territory but also air, water, trees, minerals, and crude oil.

- *Labor.* Labor refers to the human effort used to produce goods and services. Labor is comprised of full- and part-time workers as well as management.
- *Capital.* **Capital** consists of the equipment, factories, tools, and other goods needed to produce a product. It also includes money used to buy these things.
- *Entrepreneurship.* This factor consists of the ideas and decisions of the business owner, or entrepreneur. He or she is the initiator, the one who brings together all the other factors of production to create value in the economy. (Right now you might not understand what the term *value* means in this context. Have patience—we'll come back to it at the end of the chapter.)

Scarcity

All of us, consumers and businesses alike, must make choices about how we use our resources. Why? Because even after the bills are paid, there's always that emergency, that forgotten event, that little reward we've been promising ourselves for weeks. Our wants, in other words, are unlimited—but our resources are not.

This concept is called **scarcity**, and it's more than just a matter of money. Land, labor, and capital are all scarce.

Because resources are scarce, we sometimes have to sacrifice one thing in order to get another. This sacrifice is called an **opportunity cost**. When you choose to save the money you earn instead of purchasing a car, you have made a choice that has an opportunity cost attached to it. You have given up personal transportation for something you believe to be more important—savings.

Entrepreneurs must also contend with opportunity costs. The owner of a new restaurant, for example, may decide to forego a costly decor in order to have more money to put into staff or kitchen equipment.

Political Systems and Economics

The way that countries allow their citizens to consume and do business depends largely on the political systems they have. These permit varying degrees of economic freedom.

Communism

In a communist country, the government sets all economic goals or priorities. It owns the means of production (all the factories) and the means of distribution (all the sales outlets and the transportation systems by which goods reach them). The result is that citizens of communist countries have little to say about what goods are available and how much they cost.

Democracy

In a democratic nation such as ours, it is the market (or buyers and sellers interacting) that determines what is produced, how, and for whom. If consumers want a particular product, someone will see the opportunity and produce it. If the producer satisfies consumer wants, the new business will thrive, and others will be attracted to the field. If the producer offers an inferior or otherwise unsatisfactory product, the business will fail. The overall result of such a system is an ample and varied supply of quality products.

Democratic Socialism

Democratic socialist nations fall somewhere between communist and democratic societies in what they permit economically. The government makes the economic decisions for major or essential industries, such as transportation and health care. In all other areas, however, individuals and businesses are free to operate according to market principles.

Risk Takers, Profit Makers

Lorenzo Vega

Lorenzo Vega turns rags to riches—literally. He stitches together patchwork ties from leftover strips and scraps of silk. His designs mix his colorful Colombian heritage with traditional American quilting and modern design theory. That combination has made the young New York designer a premiere figure in high fashion.

A native Colombian, Vega arrived in the United States for schooling when he was 17. He planned to study architecture but soon discovered his talent for fashion.

At first, Vega did quite well designing evening and bridal gowns. Then a client asked him to make a tie for her husband. In the process, Vega made a discovery—that ties were an undervalued element of men's fashion. With the correct tie, he found, you could upgrade a suit, assert individuality, and have some fun.

Vega's first ties appeared in 1989. They were floral prints, and they shocked the conservative tie market.

Vega never even thought of patchwork ties until his second year of business. The idea grew out of what he saw as an intolerable waste—garbage bags full of expensive silk scraps. The scraps were what was left after patterns were cut from bolts of fabric. They became the stuff of Vega's most distinctive designs.

Vega's seamstresses had reservations about his first efforts. Somehow they looked too busy. Vega's solution? He used larger pieces of fabric. When the prototype was finished, Vega knew he had something unique.

Today, so do the men who wear Vega's ties. Each pattern is sold in only limited quantities to small boutiques. This practically guarantees wearers that they will never run into someone wearing the same tie.

Vega also pampers the wearer. His latest ties have a pocket built into the back and a small chain to keep the panels together. And if a Lorenzo Vega tie is damaged, he fixes it free of charge.

Vega's selling points don't end with exclusivity, conservation, and style. A shrewd marketer, he caters to retailers. Because he offers only a limited number of each design, retailers purchase ties by the unit instead of by the dozen. That way, they don't buy far in advance or in bulk, which saves them space and minimizes their risk. Vega also emphasizes speed. He ships out a new collection every 6–8 weeks.

As a result of his imagination and entrepreneurial skill, Vega's business is booming. Following the success of his patchwork ties, the designer has expanded his collection to include an entire line of menswear. In the fickle world of fashion, Vega's designs look as though they're around—necks, that is—to stay.

How Free Enterprise Works

The economic system most characteristic of democratic nations goes by a variety of names. These include free enterprise, capitalism, and a market economy. Fundamental to such a system is the right of economic choice:

- People can choose what products to buy.
- People can choose to own private property.
- People can choose to start a business and compete with other businesses.

The Profit Motive

Free enterprise has as its primary incentive the profit motive. **Profit** is what is left after all the expenses of running a business have been deducted from income. It is one way of measuring success in a free enterprise system.

Of course, the possibility of making a profit is only one side of the coin. The other side is the risk of failure. This risk, however, serves a positive function in a free enterprise system. As noted earlier, it encourages the production of quality products that truly meet the needs of consumers.

The Role of Competition

A business's attempt to get customers in the face of other businesses' selling the same or similar products is called competition. Competition is essential to the success of a market economy. It forces companies to become more efficient in order to survive. This, in turn, keeps prices down and quality up.

Businesses compete on the basis of both price and non-price factors. For example, in a mature industry such as electronics, the focus is on getting prices down. An established firm can do this. It is likely to have large plants and an experienced work force, unlike a small firm just setting up its first production line. Revenues lost to lower prices can be made up through higher volume

(a larger number of sales). The success of discount stores is based on the same principle.

In other industries non-price factors such as quality, service, and reputation are more important. The auto industry provides an example of this approach. For most people, a car is a long-term purchase requiring regular after-sale service. For this reason, people are often willing to pay more for a make or model that has a good repair history or a better warranty.

The Laws of Supply and Demand

In a free enterprise system, the price of a product is determined in the marketplace. There consumers and producers interact in response to the laws of supply and demand.

DEMAND. According to the law of demand, price is inversely related to demand. In other words, as price goes up, the quantity demanded goes down.

The demand curve in Figure 2-1 shows the number of CDs that would be purchased at specific prices. Notice that more CDs would be bought at $15 than at $25. This is because more people could afford the disks at the lower price.

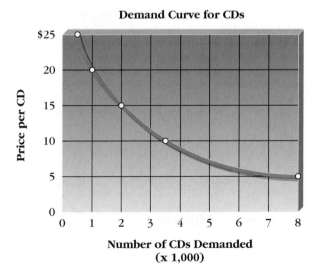

Demand Curve for CDs

Figure 2–1   This curve shows that fewer items will be purchased at higher prices than at lower ones. Which price increment reduces demand the most?

Some products respond more readily to the law of demand than others. If a small change in the price of an item causes a significant change in the quantity demanded, we say that the demand for the item is **elastic**. In contrast, if a change in price has little or no effect on the quantity demanded, we say that demand for the item is **inelastic**.

For example, demand for products like milk and bread that are considered necessities is typically inelastic. We generally continue to buy them in approximately the same quantities despite moderate price increases. On the other hand, demand for luxury items like ice cream is elastic. If the price goes up two dollars a half gallon, we are likely to take that item off our shopping lists. We may miss it, but we don't need it to survive.

In general, demand tends to be inelastic in these circumstances:

- No acceptable substitutes are available.
- The price change is small relative to buyer income.
- The product is a necessity.

Thus, demand for butter tends to be elastic because a lower-priced substitute, margarine, is available. There is no substitute for milk, on the other hand, and so demand for it tends to be inelastic.

You should take care not to extend the law of demand's reach too far. If a product's price is low, that does not mean that people will keep buying it indefinitely. At a certain point, they will stop. They will not, for example, buy more than they can reasonably use. This effect is known as the **principle of diminishing marginal utility**. It establishes that price alone does not determine demand. Other factors (like income, taste, and the amount of product already owned) play a role as well.

SUPPLY. The amount of a good or service that producers are willing to provide is called supply. Producers are more willing to supply products in greater amounts when prices are

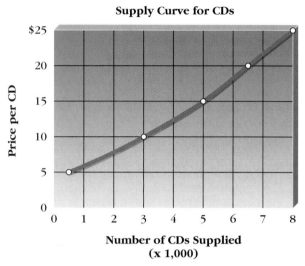

Supply Curve for CDs

Figure 2–2   This curve reveals a direct relationship between price and the number of items produced. Describe the effect on supply of tripling the selling price from $5 to $15.

high. They are less willing to do so when prices are low.

Figure 2–2 depicts a supply curve for CDs. Notice that supply is directly related to price. As price goes up, the quantity supplied goes up.

SURPLUS, SHORTAGE, AND EQUILIBRIUM. Supply and demand are dynamic in the marketplace—that is, they are continually shifting. This creates surpluses, shortages, and equilibrium.

Consider the CD example that we've been using. On the release of a new CD, fans flock to music outlets. They buy up every copy of the album at the high initial price and still ask for more. A shortage develops. Stores have waiting lists of customers for their next shipments. Eventually, though, the excitement passes. Soon those same stores find that they have more copies of the CD on hand than fans will buy at the marked price. In other words, they now have a surplus. To solve this problem, they reduce the album's price. In a short time a modest discount of 20 percent clears the excess copies from their shelves. They have achieved equilibrium.

The principles underlying this situation are illustrated in Figure 2-3. It shows the demand and supply curves we've been studying, together, in

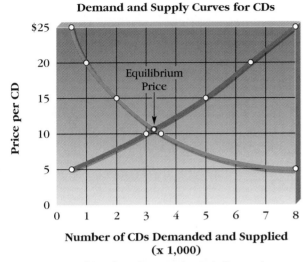

Demand and Supply Curves for CDs

Number of CDs Demanded and Supplied
(x 1,000)

Figure 2–3 Merging the supply and demand curves into a single graph allows you to locate the equilibrium point or price. What is the equilibrium price for CDs? At that price approximately how many will consumers demand?

the same graph. The point at which the two curves meet represents the **equilibrium price**. It is the price at which consumers will buy all that is supplied, leaving neither a surplus nor a shortage.

The Role of Marketing

Supply and demand graphs can be a bit misleading. They seem to suggest that where demand exists supply just follows, that the two just spring into existence and interact. It's not quite that simple.

For businesses to respond to consumer demand, they must know about it. For consumers to make purchases, they must be aware of what is available. How do businesses learn what consumers want? How do consumers find out what businesses have to offer? The answer in both cases is the same—marketing.

IMPORTANCE IN BUSINESS. Business in a free enterprise system has two principal functions. The first is producing goods and services. The second is marketing those products. Marketing involves determining consumer wants on one

hand and then satisfying those wants on the other through the exchange process. (The exchange, of course, is the exchange of goods or services for money.)

Viewed in this light, marketing encompasses an extremely broad range of activities. To learn specifically what consumers want (and how much they would be willing to pay for it), businesses conduct marketing research. Once they have developed products based on that research, they engage in promotion. They advertise. They offer free samples, coupons, and contests. They call attention to their products with eye-catching packages and in-store displays. They lure customers with special discounts and woo them with personal sales pitches. In other words, through marketing activities, businesses arrange for consumers to see their products, to hear about them, to recognize that they fulfill a want, and finally to buy them.

IMPACT ON CONSUMERS. While used by companies to bring in business, marketing clearly offers much to consumers. First and most obvious, marketing makes it possible for consumers to learn what products are available. Radio, TV, and print ads identify products by name and briefly describe their features and benefits. Package labels and personal sales pitches provide more information. Finally, samples and trial sizes let consumers try products at little or no cost.

Marketing also makes products easier for consumers to obtain. Through its distribution function, it enables consumers to find the products they've heard about. It ensures that those products will be available where and when consumers can get to them.

Ultimately, marketing even makes it possible for consumers to afford products. By enabling businesses to appeal to larger numbers of potential buyers, marketing allows firms to take advantage of volume sales. Recall from earlier in the chapter that this translates into lower prices for consumers. Marketing activities like advertising and promotion also increase competition. This, too, helps lower prices.

SIGNIFICANCE FOR THE ECONOMY. In the end, then, marketing is mutually beneficial to consumers and businesses. Their increased ability to purchase goods and services helps consumers to raise their standard of living. Their purchases, in turn, tell businesses that they are on the right track, that they are indeed satisfying genuine consumer wants. Businesses can then use this knowledge to improve their existing products—and to develop new ones. For businesses, that means more profits. For consumers, it means new life-style possibilities. And for the economy, it means more growth.

The Business Cycle

Because businesses are a part of our economy, they cannot help but be affected by events in that economy. In ideal circumstances, an economy would continue to grow forever. In reality, however, that does not happen. Economies alternately grow and contract in what are called business cycles.

A business cycle has four stages:

- *Peak.* This is a period of prosperity characterized by high employment, high demand for goods and services, and continuous growth of GNP. The 1940s, fueled by the military spending of World War II, provides an example.
- *Contraction.* During this stage, the economy begins to slow down. This development is often called a recession. People cut back on their spending. In response, businesses cut back on their production and eventually lay off workers. This results in increased unemployment. The early 1990s provides a recent example.
- *Trough.* This stage marks the low point of a contraction. If the contraction has been mild, this stage can also be characterized as a recession. If the contraction has been severe, however, this stage may be called a depression. In a depression, the downward slide in the GNP becomes extreme. People tend to buy only necessities. Widespread unemployment

and poverty become the norm. The 1930s offers an example of the worst depression in modern times.

- *Expansion.* This stage signals a turnaround in the economy. It is a period of recovery. Demand for goods and services begins to rise. As new jobs are created, unemployment declines. Soon people have more money to spend, and there is a subsequent rise in GNP.

Figure 2–4 illustrates this sequence of events.

International Trade

Our economy also does not operate in a vacuum. It is part of a larger world economy driven by trade among nations.

The principal measure of how any nation (ours included) is doing in the world economy is called **balance of trade**. It compares **exports** (what we sell to other nations) and **imports** (what we buy from other nations). If our businesses sell more abroad than we buy there, we have a positive balance of trade. More money flows into our nation than leaves it, more jobs are created, and we prosper. If our businesses sell less abroad than we buy there, the opposite occurs.

In recent years, the United States has been running a negative balance of trade. Government is looking to the creativity and energy of American entrepreneurs to help turn that situation around.

What Entrepreneurs Contribute

Recall that early in this chapter we stated that entrepreneurs "create value" in the economy. Now you can understand what that means. Consider their contributions in the light of what you have learned in this chapter:

- *Entrepreneurs are the mechanism by which our economy turns demand into supply.* It is

The Business Cycle

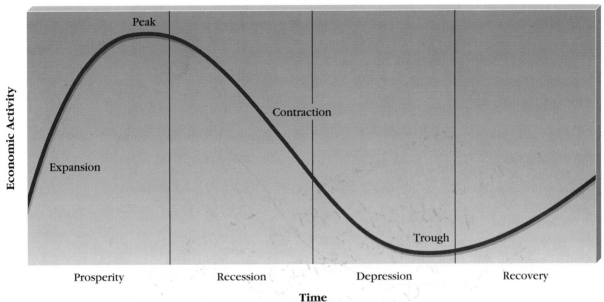

Figure 2–4   *Economies expand and contract in a series of stages. Why are these called the business* cycle?

entrepreneurs who recognize consumer wants and see the economic opportunities in satisfying them.

- *Entrepreneurs are a principal source of venture capital.* As part of the process of planning and setting up a new business, entrepreneurs gather resources. Money is one of the most important of these. Entrepreneurs usually start with their own funds and then seek out contributions from private investors.
- *Entrepreneurs provide jobs.* This is a natural outcome of their organizing resources to produce goods and services. They spend the capital they raise on setting up a place of business and hiring workers. When they do this, they provide for not only their own financial security but also for the financial security of others.
- *The most successful entrepreneurs change society.* Consider the example of Steven Jobs and Steven Wozniak. In 1976 they set out to create the first personal computer. In less than five years, they had created a whole industry comprised of hundreds of related businesses and thousands of new jobs. Today it is hard to

imagine a workplace or a home without at least one personal computer.

Ironically, then, entrepreneurs start out by responding to society's wants and end up by changing that society and creating even more wants. In this sense, entrepreneurs are more than just one of the driving forces in our economy. They are the initiators in the cycle of progress.

Entrepreneur's Bookshelf

To learn more about the subjects discussed in this chapter, consider reading these books:

- *Friends or Strangers* by George J. Borjas (© 1990)
- *Innovation and Entrepreneurship* by Peter F. Drucker (© 1986)
- *What Is Economics?* by Jim Eggert (© 1987)

Chapter 2 Review

Recapping the Chapter

- Economics deals with the choices that go into making, distributing, and consuming products.
- The way a nation allows its citizens to do business depends on its political system. For example, democracies (which grant their citizens political freedom) usually grant them a high degree of economic freedom.
- A market, or free enterprise, system allows people to buy what they wish, to own private property, and to start their own businesses.
- In such a system, the primary reason people go into business is to make a profit.
- Competition is the means by which free enterprise ensures that businesses will be run efficiently, thus enabling them to keep quality up and prices down.
- Entrepreneurs create value in our economy by recognizing wants and bringing together the resources to satisfy them. In the process, the most successful entrepreneurs change society.
- In the United States, nearly 40 percent of GNP and virtually all new jobs are created by small (or entrepreneurial) businesses.

Reviewing Vocabulary

1. Study each pair of terms. Then in your own words describe how they are related to each other. (*Hint:* Are they the same? Are they opposites? Are they both? Is one part of the other? Is one the result of the other?)

   - goods—services
   - factors of production—capital
   - scarcity—opportunity cost
   - elastic—inelastic
   - economics—diminishing marginal utility

2. Define the terms *profit* and *equilibrium* by using equations that consist of words rather the numbers.

Checking the Facts

1. How are industrial goods different from consumer goods?
2. What are the four factors of production?
3. Who decides what will be produced, how, and for whom in a communist state? in a democracy? in a democratic socialist state?
4. What role does profit play in a free enterprise system?
5. How is price related to the demand for a product? How is it related to the supply of that product?
6. Under what circumstances does demand tend to be inelastic?
7. Name the stages of the business cycle, and describe each with a short phrase.

Thinking Critically

1. Name three goods and three services not discussed or used as examples in this chapter.
2. Describe a recent situation in which you made a choice that had an opportunity cost attached to it. What was the reasoning that led to your decision?
3. Explain why you agree or disagree with each of the following statements:

Chapter 2 Review

- Start a business in a free enterprise system, and you'll be guaranteed a profit.
- If your business has the lowest prices, that's it—you get all the customers!
- Scarcity will always be with us.

4. Consider the last five products you bought. For which was demand elastic? For which was it inelastic? Explain.

Discussing Key Concepts

1. Do you believe that formerly communist countries can change over immediately to market economies? Why or why not?
2. Assume you are going to start a business. What have you learned from this chapter about market economics that should help you in making a profit?

Using Basic Skills

Math
1. Silhouettes is an upscale women's clothing store. The cost of the goods it sold last year was $600,000. Its expenses (including employee wages and administrative costs) were $300,000. Its sales revenues were $850,000. Did the store have a profitable year or not? Explain.

Communication
2. Choose a business with whose advertising you are familiar, and analyze the way it competes with other businesses. (Does it use a price or non-price approach?) Then write a print or radio ad for the firm employing that same approach. Target your ad to young people in their late teens or early twenties.

Human Relations
3. You are a salesperson for an auto dealership.

- *You sell American cars.* A customer you approach explains that she's leaning toward buying a foreign car. She admits it might cost more, but she believes the import is better built. How would you use basic economic principles to convince her of the wisdom of buying American?
- *You sell foreign cars.* A customer you approach explains that he's leaning toward buying an American car. He's sure he can get a much better deal on a domestic rather than an import. How would you use basic economic principles to convince him of the wisdom of buying a foreign car?

Enriching Your Learning

Interview an entrepreneur in your community to learn more about competitive strategy. Specifically, ask the following:

- Who are your firm's main competitors?
- How do they compete? (Do they use a price or non-price strategy?)
- How do you handle surpluses and shortages?

Prepare a written report on your findings.

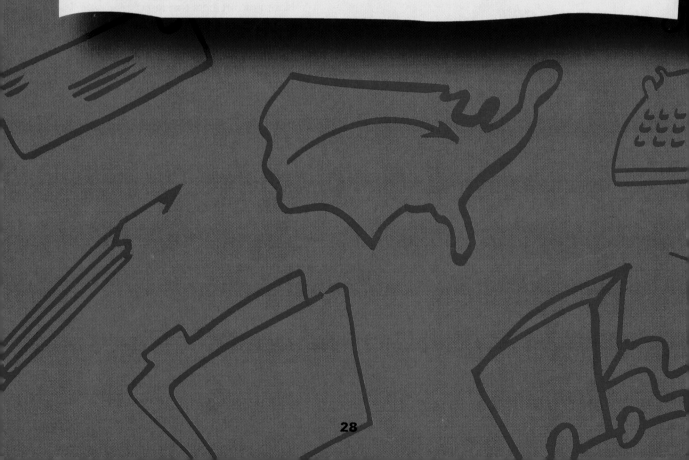

UNIT TWO

What It Takes to Be an Entrepreneur

Chapter 3:
Your Potential as an Entrepreneur

Chapter 4:
Business Communication

Chapter 5:
Math for Entrepreneurs

Chapter 6:
Decision Skills

Chapter 3
Your Potential as an Entrepreneur

Objectives

After completing this chapter, you will be able to

- explain the advantages and disadvantages of being an entrepreneur,
- discuss what is known about the background of entrepreneurs,
- list the personal characteristics of entrepreneurs,
- determine how to get the most out of your own entrepreneurial potential, and
- identify the skills needed to be an entrepreneur.

Terms to Know

assessment
investment
role models
persistent
inquisitive
profile
foundational skills

Decisions, Decisions

I always enjoyed my entrepreneurship class—until today. Mr. Miller, our teacher, gave us something he called an entrepreneurship **assessment**. It's like a test to see how entrepreneurial you are—you know, whether you're cut out to run your own business or not. When we were done, he went over each item and told us how entrepreneurs would've answered. Then he asked us to compare our answers with theirs. Well, after I finished, I felt really dismal. Only a few of my answers matched.

Mr. Miller went on with the lesson, but I couldn't concentrate. All I could think about was that assessment. What it said basically was that I was wasting my time taking the class. I just don't have what it takes to be an entrepreneur.

Not that that's surprising. No one in my family owns a business, and I'm no great student. I get mostly C's, except for math (I've gotten a few D's there).

I seem to do my best at things that don't count. For example, I'm on the track team. I'm no star, but I've never missed a practice or a meet. I also have a job at Fast-Fried Chicken, and I do pretty well there. I'm good at keeping my cool when things get hectic. For me it's sort of a challenge. You know, see how many people you can serve in ten minutes. See if you can keep the lines down to a few customers each.

Gees, I like working so much. I think I'd really enjoy having my own place. I wonder if you can *develop* entrepreneurial traits? I wonder if you can *learn* to be an entrepreneur?

Why Be an Entrepreneur?

When most people think about entrepreneurs, they picture a highly successful business owner with a large house, an expensive car, and an opulent life-style. While that description may fit some entrepreneurs, it does not fit the vast majority. In fact, for the majority, the greatest satisfactions of entrepreneurship are not material at all.

The Advantages of Entrepreneurship

For most entrepreneurs, the main advantages of owning a business are intangible. They involve such things as independence, personal satisfaction, and prestige. Specifically, they include the following:

- *Being your own boss.* This is the advantage that most entrepreneurs put at the top of their lists. The reason is obvious—it gives them the freedom to make their own business decisions. They have the final word on all aspects of their operations, from hours of business to products offered to new directions for expansion.

- *Doing something you enjoy.* An entrepreneurial endeavor typically starts with a business or personal activity that the entrepreneur enjoys. Someone who takes pleasure in cooking for others starts a catering business. Someone who likes tinkering with old cars goes into auto restoration. In cases like these, the enjoyment is compounded by the satisfaction the new business owner derives from creating and developing the enterprise.

- *Having the opportunity to be creative.* Most people who work for others merely follow procedures; entrepreneurs make them. In other words, entrepreneurs can shape a business in ways that employees cannot. This is especially true where daring or creative ideas are concerned. Such ideas suggested by an employee might be lost or compromised beyond recognition as they moved up a chain of command. When such ideas originate with an owner, however, they are far more likely to be acted upon.

- *Having job security.* As long as an owner-operated business is a going concern, the owner has job security. Put another way, if you're the owner, no one can fire you!

The financial rewards of being an entrepreneur usually far outpace those of being an employee. Why?

- *Making more money.* People who work for others are normally paid wages or a salary. If they work especially hard or if the company does especially well, they may get a raise. This is not certain, however. Nor is it certain that the amount of any raise will be commensurate with the effort expended. That, after all, is a matter of opinion—someone else's opinion, usually a manager's. An owner's earnings, however, are limited only by the potential of his or her business.

- *Being recognized within the community.* Business ownership carries with it a certain amount of prestige. Entrepreneurs, after all, have done something that many others would like to do—something that takes hard work, daring, and know-how. What's more, in the process they have made an economic contribution to the community.

The Disadvantages of Entrepreneurship

If being an entrepreneur is so wonderful, you might ask, why doesn't everyone do it? Clearly, the advantages tell only one side of the story. In an economy where competition is the rule, business ownership can be a difficult endeavor. There is a downside, a list of disadvantages that must also be considered:

- *Working long hours.* Long hours are the norm for entrepreneurs, especially during the start-up period of a business. During this time survival often depends on daily decisions, and there is little in the way of paid help. Most entrepreneurs respond by devoting most of their waking hours to their endeavor, often working seven days a week.

- *Having an uncertain income.* As a rule, owners make more money than employees—but only when business is good. When business is bad, earnings can be low or even nonexistent. Business owners do not get a regular paycheck.

In an emergency, the owner of a business is often the "employee" of last resort. In what sense?

- *Being fully responsible.* The owner of a business is responsible for more than just decision making. He or she must see that everything gets done—from sweeping the floors to paying the bills to making any repairs. Ultimately, there is no one else to see to these things. The success or failure of the venture in all its aspects, large and small, rests entirely on the owner.
- *Risking one's investment.* Undoubtedly, the biggest disadvantage of being in business for oneself is the risk of losing one's **investment**. To reach the stage where the earnings potential of a business is unlimited, an entrepreneur must first get his or her enterprise up and running. An entrepreneur who fails to do this can lose all the money he or she put into the endeavor.

What Do We Know About Entrepreneurs?

Because entrepreneurs are so important to our nation's economy, there is a great deal of interest in them. They are featured in magazine and newspaper articles. Best-sellers are written about them. Some who have become celebrities do talk shows and build ad campaigns for their products around themselves.

In recent years, entrepreneurs have even been the subject of research. Several studies have been done to determine what, if any, traits or experiences they have in common. Ultimately, the object of such studies has been to learn whether entrepreneurs are born or made.

Background and Life Experiences

What kinds of people choose to become entrepreneurs? A surprising variety. Research reveals a wide spread of ages, educational backgrounds, and personal histories. It also reveals a few common life experiences that may incline people toward entrepreneurship.

Here is a summary of what the research shows:

- About a third of entrepreneurs (35 percent) are under age 30 when they start their businesses; 11 percent are over age 50.
- A large proportion of entrepreneurs (40 percent) have a high school diploma or less; only 20 percent have a college degree.
- Many entrepreneurs were independent from an early age, often because they were orphans or came from broken homes.
- Half of all entrepreneurs had parents who owned a business.
- Many entrepreneurs were influenced early in life by **role models** whose attitudes and achievements they tried to duplicate.
- Approximately one out of six entrepreneurs has participated in a high school vocational education program.

Personal Characteristics

Studies have also been done of the personal characteristics of entrepreneurs. These are the distinctive traits needed to set up an owner-operated business and run it successfully. Listings vary but usually include these ten items.

- **Persistent.** Entrepreneurs are willing to work until a job is done, no matter how long it takes. They are tenacious in overcoming obstacles and pursuing their goals.
- *Creative.* Entrepreneurs continually look for new ways to solve old problems.
- *Responsible.* Entrepreneurs don't "pass the buck." They take responsibility for their decisions and actions.
- **Inquisitive.** Entrepreneurs want to know as much as possible about anything that might affect their ventures. When they uncover a problem, they study it thoroughly.
- *Goal-oriented.* Entrepreneurs decide where they want to go and then set out to get there.
- *Independent.* Entrepreneurs want to set their own agendas and schedules. They want to make their own decisions.
- *Demanding.* Entrepreneurs have high expectations of themselves.
- *Self-confident.* Entrepreneurs believe in themselves and act accordingly.

- *Risk-taking.* Entrepreneurs like to take risks, but they are not reckless. They do not deliberately put themselves in no-win situations. Rather, they seek opportunities that offer both challenge and a reasonable chance of success.
- *Restless.* Once entrepreneurs achieve their goals, they begin looking for new challenges.

What's Your Entrepreneurial Potential?

The research findings about the background and characteristics of entrepreneurs are often misinterpreted. People assume that if they haven't had experiences similar to those of the typical entrepreneur or if they don't already have strong entrepreneurial characteristics, they can't succeed as entrepreneurs. Neither assumption is correct.

Certain personal characteristics might be called "the right stuff" for entrepreneurs. Which are illustrated here?

Risk Takers, Profit Makers

R. David Thomas

If there is such a thing as a typical entrepreneur, then R. David Thomas, founder of Wendy's Old-Fashioned Hamburgers, must be it. In fact, Thomas seems almost to have been destined from birth to become a success in the restaurant business.

Thomas was orphaned when he was six weeks old. His adoptive family moved around the country a great deal, which had disadvantages. "With all the moving," explained Thomas, "I didn't get a chance to know kids. I guess that's why work became my constant companion." By the age of 12, Thomas had already entered the restaurant business, working behind a lunch counter.

After a few more years of work, Thomas decided he was capable of living on his own. He found himself a room at the YMCA and dropped out of the tenth grade in order to work full time as a busboy. Later, at 18, he joined the army and attended the army's cook and baker school.

One of the greatest influences on Thomas was Colonel Harland Sanders, founder of Kentucky Fried Chicken. In 1962, Thomas was given the opportunity to turn around four failing KFC franchises. To do this, he cut back on the number of menu items and focused on selling chicken and salads. He also used radio advertising to stimulate business. At age 35 Thomas sold the franchises back to the company—for $1.5 million! His success brought him a position as a regional operations director for KFC and a personal acquaintance with Sanders.

Thomas started his own restaurant in 1969, shortly after leaving Kentucky Fried Chicken. To project a homey image, he named the restaurant Wendy's, after his daughter.

In the beginning, Thomas promoted Wendy's mainly by word-of-mouth. Later, when Wendy's

had grown to a chain, he began running television ads. They were to prove crucial to Wendy's success.

In 1977 Wendy's went national with its advertising. The company's "Hot 'n Juicy" campaign stressed on-the-spot preparation of food made to each customer's order. A half dozen years later, Wendy's classic "Where's the beef?" ad appeared. The ad was so effective that it earned a Cleo Award, the advertising industry's highest honor. It also brought Wendy's tremendous national attention.

Despite all of this success, Thomas continues to work to improve his company. In fact, he believes this is the secret to his success. "Just work hard and apply yourself," he advises simply. That kind of commitment, Thomas believes, leads inevitably to the top.

Putting the Research in Perspective

From what is known about the background of entrepreneurs (page 33), it is possible to draw two kinds of conclusions—the obvious and the not-so-obvious. Here are the obvious conclusions:

- If you share any of the experiences listed, it increases the likelihood that you'll become an entrepreneur.
- The more experiences you share, the more likely you are to start your own business.

Such conclusions can and should be reassuring to someone who fits the background **profile** of the typical entrepreneur.

What if you don't fit the profile, however? You shouldn't let that stop you from pursuing any entrepreneurial aspirations you might have. Why? Because it's possible to draw other, less obvious conclusions from the research data. Consider the fact that 50 percent of entrepreneurs had parents who owned a business. That also means that 50 percent had parents who didn't!

What the research really shows is that everyone has the potential to become an entrepreneur. Entrepreneurs come from all kinds of economic circumstances. They have varying levels of education and begin their enterprises at virtually any point in their lives. What this means is that background isn't everything. A can-do attitude and a genuine desire to go into business for yourself are far more important.

Strengthening Your Entrepreneurial Traits

The personal characteristics described on page 34, on the other hand, *are* essential to people who are going to set up and run their own enterprises. Persistence, creativity, independence, self-confidence—they are what it takes to get the job done.

You should understand that everyone has these traits. True, they are stronger in some individuals than in others. Even a small measure of a trait, however, is enough to build on. It just takes commitment, a willingness to work at strengthening what needs development.

THREE STEPS TO FOLLOW. How can you become more entrepreneurial? The process involves three steps:

- *Step 1—Determine the current strength of your entrepreneurial characteristics.* You can use the Entrepreneurial Characteristics Assessment shown in Figure 3–1 to do a self-evaluation.
- *Step 2—Make a conscious effort to think of entrepreneurial characteristics as habits that can be changed.* It would probably never occur to you that you couldn't eat less junk food, watch less television, or get up earlier each morning—*if you wanted to.* These are all things that you feel are within your control. You can change them. Entrepreneurial traits are no different. You can change them, too.
- *Step 3—Work on developing the characteristics in which you feel weak.* How? Practice. Throughout each day concentrate on acting as though you have the traits you want to develop. After a while, you will find that those traits become part of your makeup. You won't be acting, and you won't have to concentrate. Being entrepreneurial will come naturally.

ACTIVITIES TO DO. There are also activities you can do to strengthen your entrepreneurial characteristics. They include the following:

- Reading articles and books about entrepreneurs and entrepreneurial activities
- Watching films about businesspeople, athletes, or others who are achievement oriented
- Writing about individuals who overcame obstacles to achieve success
- Working through case studies that involve goal-oriented behavior, creativity, and moderate risk taking

While entrepreneurial characteristics can be strengthened through such activities, you should recognize that the process takes time—and practice. In fact, repetition is the key to success. That

Entrepreneurial Characteristics Assessment

Directions: Each of the statements below represents a characteristic helpful to entrepreneurs. Read through the list, and on a separate sheet of paper record your reactions. If you feel a particular statement describes you very accurately, write 5. If you feel it doesn't describe you at all, write 1. If you feel it only partially describes you place yourself somewhere between these two extremes by writing a number from 2 to 4.

1 2 3 4 5	1. You stay with a task despite difficulties.
1 2 3 4 5	2. You're creative.
1 2 3 4 5	3. You take responsibility for your actions.
1 2 3 4 5	4. You want to know about things.
1 2 3 4 5	5. You set goals for yourself and work toward them.
1 2 3 4 5	6. You like to work on your own schedule.
1 2 3 4 5	7. You set high standards for yourself.
1 2 3 4 5	8. You believe in yourself and in what you're doing.
1 2 3 4 5	9. You like a challenge, but you're not a gambler.
1 2 3 4 5	10. You're never completely content.

Figure 3–1   The circled figures in the assessment are a kind of scale representing the strength of each characteristic illustrated. If you had to use words instead of numbers to describe each level, which terms would you choose?

is what transforms uncharacteristic behavior into habit. That is what can make entrepreneurial behavior a part of anyone's makeup.

What Skills Do Entrepreneurs Need?

In addition to desire and the characteristics already discussed, entrepreneurs need to be skilled in some basic areas like communication, math, and problem solving. They need not be experts in these areas, but they must develop as much competence as their enterprises require for successful operation.

For example, entrepreneurs must be competent enough writers to turn out whatever correspondence their businesses require on a regular basis. They must be able to do whatever math calculations their businesses utilize each day. They must be able to set goals for not only

themselves and the ventures they head but for their employees as well. Because of their importance to the process of setting up and running a new enterprise, **foundational skills** like these will be explored over the next three chapters.

Entrepreneur's Bookshelf

To learn more about the subjects discussed in this chapter, consider reading these books:

- *Making It on Your Own* by Paul Edwards and Sarah Edwards (© 1991)
- *Fundamentals of Creative Thinking* by John S. Dacey (© 1989)

Chapter 3 Review

Recapping the Chapter

- There are both advantages and disadvantages to being an entrepreneur.
- Some personal traits and life experiences seem to incline people toward entrepreneurship, but entrepreneurs come from all sorts of backgrounds.
- Certain characteristics are needed to organize and operate a business, but these characteristics can be developed if you don't have them.
- Entrepreneurs must have a certain level of skill in basic areas like communication, math, and problem solving in order to set up and run a new enterprise.

Reviewing Vocabulary

Use context clues from the chapter to develop definitions of your own for each of these terms:

- assessment
- investment
- role models
- persistent
- inquisitive
- profile
- foundational skills

Checking the Facts

1. What do most entrepreneurs consider to be the biggest advantage of being in business for themselves?
2. Name the biggest risk involved in being in business for yourself.

3. Give the percentage of entrepreneurs who have a high school diploma or less.
4. List five of the personal characteristics needed by entrepreneurs.
5. What skills do entrepreneurs need to set up and run their enterprises?

Thinking Critically

1. Would you say that the advantages of being an entrepreneur outweigh the disadvantages or vice versa? Why?
2. How might being influenced early in life by a role model be critical to someone's success as an entrepreneur?
3. Do you agree with the idea that everyone has the potential to become an entrepreneur? Why or why not?
4. Of the personal characteristics needed by an entrepreneur, which do you feel are the most important? Explain.
5. Describe some situations in which an entrepreneur would need the foundational skills listed in the chapter.
6. You have a friend who wants to go into business for herself. She does not fit the profile of a typical entrepreneur, and her foundational skills need work. Still, she does have some strong entrepreneurial characteristics. What advice would you give her?

Discussing Key Concepts

1. Identify some entrepreneurs who are familiar to you. How would you describe their life-styles?

Chapter 3 Review

2. Think of the advantages and disadvantages of working for someone else. How do they compare with the possible risks and rewards of entrepreneurship?
3. Why do you think some people become entrepreneurs while others don't?
4. The personal characteristics needed by entrepreneurs are necessary for success in *any* career—do you agree or disagree with this statement? Explain.
5. What personality traits do you think would interfere with someone's becoming an entrepreneur?

Using Basic Skills

Math
1. Refer to the research findings on the background and life experiences of entrepreneurs (page 33) and calculate the following figures:

   - Percentage of entrepreneurs who were between the ages of 30 and 50 when they started their businesses
   - Percentage of entrepreneurs who do not have a college degree

Communication
2. Do an oral or written book report on a biography of a successful entrepreneur. As you read, note incidents or observations that illustrate entrepreneurial characteristics at work. Make these the focus of your report.

Human Relations
3. You are discussing your plans to go into business for yourself with your uncle. He makes it clear that he doesn't think you're the "entrepreneurial type." He insists that someone like you—not very organized, not much of a "people person," and not likely to finish what you start—will never get the venture off the ground let alone up and running successfully. How would you handle the encounter?

Enriching Your Learning

1. Consider the strength of your entrepreneurial characteristics as measured by the assessment shown in Figure 3-1 (page 37). For each area in which you rated moderate or low, identify situations in your daily life where you could strengthen those characteristics by practicing them. Keep a daily log in which you note the opportunities you used to become more persistent, creative, etc.
2. Begin a collection of original stories about people who are achievement oriented. Write a one-page story about a fictional person who overcomes personal and/or other obstacles to reach a goal. In the story, describe how your main character felt and what he or she thought. Throughout the remainder of the semester, add at least one new story a week to your collection.
3. Make a list of your long-term goals. Then select the three or four goals that are most important to you. For each of these, list all the activities you could do to reach that goal. Refer to these lists daily, and do one activity (or one step in an activity) that will advance you toward one of your goals.

Chapter 4
Business Communication

Objectives

After completing this chapter, you will be able to

- explain the importance of effective communication to a business,
- produce the most commonly used types of business correspondence,
- present strategies for effective oral communication in situations ranging from telephone use to negotiation,
- demonstrate good listening technique, and
- discuss some of the communication challenges presented by a global economy.

Terms to Know

concrete word
abstract word
buffer
negotiation
feedback

Decisions, Decisions

Yesterday I think I bit off more than I can chew. My business teacher asked if anyone in the class knew an entrepreneur who might be willing to come in and talk to us about starting up a new business. Well, my dad knows this woman who has her own space-planning business. What she does is floor plans for stores. You know, she chooses the display cases, orders the lighting fixtures, and stuff like that.

I thought she'd be a great speaker, so I volunteered. Now my dad tells me that he doesn't think she'll have the time. He says she's always out overseeing jobs and spends tons of time on the phone—and when she is in, she needs that time to do plans. He's afraid she'll feel obligated to say yes because it's for a friend even though she'd rather not. He doesn't like putting her on the spot like that, and he wishes I'd mentioned it to him first.

But—I didn't. Now I have to write her a letter and get her to say yes without making her feel pressured and embarrassing my dad. How in the world am I going to do that?

The Importance of Good Communication Skills

The value of good communication skills in business cannot be overstated. All business activity involves speaking, listening, reading, or writing to some extent. No matter what career you choose to enter or what type of business you choose to start, you will need good communication skills to have the best chance for success.

Think how costly mistaken communication can be. Suppose a company does a telephone survey based on questions so confusingly worded that no one knows how to answer them. What value would the results of such a survey have? What about a business that regularly sends out letters that are either ungrammatical or filled with misspelled words? What kind of image does that project? What about a store that advertises a sale—on the *wrong* day or of the *wrong* merchandise? What kind of goodwill does that generate—and what potential legal problems?

Considered in this light, effective comunication is more than just desirable. It's positively profitable. It can save you time, money, and reputation. It can bring in customers and keep them coming back. It can suggest ways to improve a business and avoid pitfalls. With that kind of potential, why would any entrepreneur ignore it?

This chapter assumes that you recognize a good thing—and an important tool—when you see one. The chapter is not built around grammar, spelling rules, or the like. (That's what your English course is for.) Rather, it's designed to help you learn to use speaking, writing, and listening to your *business* advantage.

Business Correspondence

The most common form of writing for small businesses is correspondence, mainly letters. These are sent to people outside the company.

Internal correspondence (if the business is large enough to require it) usually takes the form of memos.

Basic Principles of Business Writing

To make the most effective use of either kind of correspondence, you should have an understanding of the basic principles of business writing. There are five of these. If you can put them into practice, you will be well on your way to communicating effectively.

FOCUS ON THE READER.   Take a look at a letter you have written recently and circle all of the times you said *I* or *me* or *we*. Surprised? In general, people do not realize how much they focus on themselves when they speak and write. They don't understand what a difference it makes to include the reader in the communication.

Study the following paragraph. Notice how *I/we*-oriented it is.

> *I* am very pleased that you applied for credit with *our* store. *We* are sure that *we* can satisfy your needs. When it comes to electronics, *we* offer the greatest selection in town. Come in soon. *We* are here to serve you.

What feeling do you think a potential customer would get from this paragraph? Does it sound as though the store is patting itself on the back? Does it sound as though the store is more interested in itself than the customer? That's what happens when the focus is not on the reader. The wrong message is sent.

Now read the revision. Notice that when the focus is shifted to the reader, the feeling is one of genuine concern or interest in the customer.

> Thank you for your application for credit, which is now being processed. When it comes to electronics, you will find that Zap's has everything you need. Come in soon.

SHOW THE READER A BENEFIT.   Business letters need to convey two things—(1) what you or your company can do for the reader and (2) how it will benefit the reader to do what you want. Does this sentence show a reader benefit?

> Please fill out the enclosed form with your correct address and phone number.

This type of request is not going to get an immediate response from very many people. Most people want to know *why* they are being asked to do something.

The same is true when you are trying to sell something. Customers want to know why they should buy. They want to know what the product can do for them. Figure 4–1 presents a letter that describes a reader benefit.

Letter Based on Reader Benefit

University of the South
Financial Aid Office

September 10, 19--

Tom Glazer
555 Quincy Drive
Mobile, Alabama 36617

Dear Tom:

So that you can promptly receive the latest information on available scholarships, please fill out the enclosed form with your current address and telephone number.

Every week we receive notices of newly established grant, award, and scholarship programs. The sooner that information is sent to you, the sooner you can take advantage of the financial aid that is out there.

Be sure to return the form in the enclosed envelope. We look forward to helping you fund your college education.

Sincerely,

Helen Miyake

Helen Miyake
Financial Aid Officer

Enclosure

Figure 4–1   A reader benefit can be used to entice the recipient of a letter to take action the sender desires. What does the sender of this letter want the receiver to do? What benefit does she offer in return?

Positive vs. Negative Language

Negative	Positive
We cannot give you credit at this time.	When you have worked in the same job for one year, you will receive...
Your order will not arrive on June 5 as you requested.	Your order will arrive by June 10.
You did not sign the contract, so we cannot...	When you have signed the contract, we will...

Figure 4–2 Favoring positive over negative constructions helps you put the best face on an unfortunate outcome from the viewpoint of the recipient. Of the positive statements shown here, which do you think would be most effective? Which would be least effective? In each case, explain why.

BE POSITIVE. In any business correspondence, stress the positive. Just about anything you need to say can be said in a more positive way. Look at the examples in Figure 4–2.

Learn to use positive words. Avoid terms like *regret, unfortunately, trouble,* and *inconvenience.* Remember, if you tell readers what you can do (not what you can't do), they are more likely to be cooperative.

BE SURE EVERYTHING IS CORRECT. As a businessperson, you should understand that the way you write doesn't just reflect on you. It reflects on your business as well. If what you write contains errors—misspelled words, poor grammar, nonstandard English—you may be sending an unintended message. By being careless about your correspondence, you may be implying that your business is careless about the quality of the work it does.

Accuracy is another area of concern. If facts and figures included in your correspondence are not carefully checked, you could find yourself forced to act against your own interests. For example, suppose you agree to sell your product to a customer for $35. When you do the invoice, however, you accidentally write in a price of $25. Having committed yourself in writing, you might actually have to sell at the lower figure. That would mean incurring a $10 loss.

If you believe that you are weak in the mechanics of writing, you should have someone else proofread your correspondence before you send it out. This is especially important when you are dealing for the first time with someone critical to your business's success. (This person might be a client, customer, banker, or supplier.) Making a good first impression through carefully written correspondence is often the first step in establishing a valuable, long-term business relationship.

BE CLEAR AND CONCISE. The last basic principle is to make certain that your writing is clear and concise. In your English classes, you may have been encouraged to write in rich, descriptive language. That is one style of writing. However, in business writing, ideas need to be presented as quickly and concisely as possible.

The reason for the difference in style is that most businesspeople are busy. They don't have the luxury of spending hours composing a letter or memo or even a short report. They must be able to get their ideas on paper quickly, clearly, and coherently.

In business writing, the main points of a document should stand out. Also, the sentences should flow logically from beginning to end. To accomplish this, choose words that are short and familiar and give a clear image of what you are trying to say.

Consider the following examples:

Unclear
Pursuant to the above-referenced letter, I am forwarding for your perusal a copy of the subject invoice.

Revised
As you requested, I am sending you another copy of the invoice.

Notice how much easier it is to understand the revised version. It uses familiar words and is written in a simple and direct manner.

Concrete vs. Abstract Words

Abstract	Concrete
The project has received many awards.	The project has received three first-place awards.
Your order will reach you soon.	You will receive the chair on Saturday, June 4.
You did a good job on the report.	The report was concise and to-the-point.

Figure 4–3   Fuzzy language may indicate fuzzy thinking—or worse. What unfavorable inferences might people read into the examples of abstract language given here?

It is often said that in business time is money. That is why it is important for others to be able to understand what you have written the first time they read it.

To accomplish this, use concrete rather than abstract words. A **concrete word** has a very clear meaning, while an **abstract word** is one that can take on many meanings. For example, words like *many, few, good*, and *bad* are abstract. When someone says, "Our company produces many products," do you really know what *many* means? Does the firm produce 5 products or 25 or 100? You don't know. Likewise, what is good (or bad) to one person may not be to another.

To ensure that your reader understands what you are saying, then, you need to be concrete and specific. Study Figure 4-3, and note how much easier it is to grasp things written in specific terms.

Steps to Effective Correspondence

Companies send and receive correspondence from customers, suppliers, dealers, and attorneys, to name just a few. With all of these letters going back and forth, it is important to cut down on the time and cost of writing them. The process can be made easier by following five simple steps.

DETERMINE THE PURPOSE.   The first step is to identify the reason you are writing the letter. Usually this is to send good news, to send bad news, or to persuade the reader to do something. Identifying the purpose allows you to choose the proper approach for your letter.

UNDERSTAND THE RECEIVER.   The more you know about the people to whom you are writing, the better you will be able to communicate with them. Some of the characteristics that are helpful to know are age, education level, culture, and geographic location. Having such information can help you see things from your readers' point of view. This, is turn, will help you gear your correspondence to their needs.

CHOOSE THE MAIN IDEAS.   Once you know why you are writing and to whom, you are ready to decide what the main points in the letter will be. Start by brainstorming all of the ideas you think should be included. Then rank them in order of importance. It is usually better to limit the number of points presented to no more than three or four. This will keep the letter as brief as possible.

Present your ideas from most to least important. That way, if the recipient does not read the entire letter (always a possibility with busy people), you will still get your message across. Research has found that the first and last paragraphs of letters are the ones most easily remembered. You should, therefore, present your most important ideas in the first paragraph. (As you will shortly learn, you should reserve your last paragraph to request specific action.)

CHOOSE AN APPROACH.   Business letters usually employ one of two approaches—the direct or the indirect. In the direct approach, you tell the reader in the first paragraph what you want. This approach is used for presenting good news, requesting information, or ordering something.

In the indirect approach, you lead up to the main point, which usually appears in the second or third paragraph. Why the delay? Most likely because your main point is negative or something your readers will resist (like spending money).

Using the indirect approach allows you time to warm your readers up to the idea.

ORGANIZE, WRITE, AND REVISE. Organizing and writing business letters may be difficult at first. You may have to revise what you write several times before it is ready to send out. Nonetheless, you should persevere. In time the process will become familiar and the principles of business writing habitual.

Types of Business Letters

As already noted, the type of business letter you write will depend on your purpose in writing. That purpose, in turn, will determine the approach you take. For example, if your purpose is to convey good news, you will be direct—not so if you are conveying bad news.

Figure 4-4 provides an overview of the four basic letter formats. The next few pages will detail how to organize and write such letters and present examples.

Basic Letter Formats

Par.	Good News	Bad News	Persuasive
1	Present the request or good news.	Start with something positive or at least neutral.	Get the reader's attention.
2	Give details and explanations.	Give a buffer, then the bad news, then another buffer.	Build interest.
3	Request action and close.	Suggest action and close.	Build desire by giving details and support related to par. 2.
4			Request action and close.

Figure 4–4   Most business correspondence falls into the three categories shown here. What features do all of the formats share?

Good-News Letter

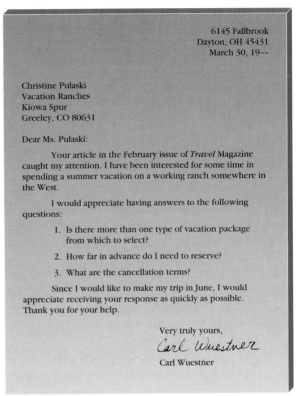

6145 Fallbrook
Dayton, OH 45431
March 30, 19--

Christine Pulaski
Vacation Ranches
Kiowa Spur
Greeley, CO 80631

Dear Ms. Pulaski:

Your article in the February issue of *Travel* Magazine caught my attention. I have been interested for some time in spending a summer vacation on a working ranch somewhere in the West.

I would appreciate having answers to the following questions:

1. Is there more than one type of vacation package from which to select?

2. How far in advance do I need to reserve?

3. What are the cancellation terms?

Since I would like to make my trip in June, I would appreciate receiving your response as quickly as possible. Thank you for your help.

Very truly yours,

Carl Wuestner

Carl Wuestner

Figure 4–5   A letter that asks for information follows the good-news format. Track the content of this letter by identifying the purpose of each paragraph.

GOOD-NEWS LETTERS. If the reason you are writing is to

- ask for information,
- order a product,
- present a claim,
- issue an invitation, or
- send good news,

you should use the good-news format. It has three paragraphs and employs a direct approach.

The first paragraph includes the main idea, or what you want in one or two sentences. The second paragraph contains the explanation in some detail of the letter's purpose. The third and final paragraph tells what action the reader should take and courteously closes the letter. An example of this type of letter is presented in Figure 4-5.

BAD-NEWS LETTERS. If the purpose of your letter is to convey something your reader does not want to hear, you should use the bad-news format. Examples of bad-news situations include

- turning down a request for credit,
- refusing a claim,
- rejecting a job application, or
- telling the reader you cannot supply a good or service.

The bad-news format employs an indirect approach. It buries the bad news in the middle of the letter. This is done to take advantage of the fact that people tend to remember mainly first and last paragraphs.

The first paragraph includes a positive, or at least neutral, beginning. It should say something agreeable relating to the subject of the letter. You must be very careful, however, not to mislead the reader into thinking that you are going to grant his or her request.

The second paragraph has three parts. It begins with a **buffer**, or statement designed to soften the blow of the bad news. Often the buffer offers an explanation for the bad-news decision. (The belief is that if readers understand the logic behind your decision, they will not be so surprised when they actually read it.) The buffer is followed by the decision itself, which can be stated directly:

> Therefore, we cannot give you credit at this time.

The decision can also be implied by what is said:

> Our credit terms require that you have an income of at least $25,000.

After the decision comes another buffer that offers some hope. It gives the reader advice on how to get a positive response the next time.

Like its good-news equivalent, a bad-news letter closes with an action paragraph. This time, however, the action is gently suggested rather than requested. An example of a bad-news letter is shown in Figure 4–6.

Bad-News Letter

Vacation Ranches
Kiowa Spur
Greeley, CO 80631

April 10, 19--

Carl Wuestner
6145 Fallbrook
Dayton, OH 45431

Dear Mr. Wuestner:

We appreciated receiving your letter of inquiry about our vacation ranch program and have enclosed the information you requested.

Vacation Ranches has been in business for ten years, and with each year the program has grown tremendously. This year for the first time we had to cut off reservations for the summer program as of April 1 because we were booked solid. We suggest that should you wish to try us again next year, you contact us in January to ensure your choice of time slot.

You might also consider our fall program that runs during September and October. It is a beautiful time of year here and less crowded. Please let us know if we can help you plan an unforgettable vacation.

Sincerely,

Christine Pulaski

Christine Pulaski
Program Director

Figure 4–6   A bad-news letter employs an indirect approach. Which statements in this example serve as bad-news buffers? How?

PERSUASIVE LETTERS. When the purpose of your letter is to sell someone on an idea or a product or to get them to do something they may not want to do, you will need to use the persuasive format. Persuasive letters are generally longer than other types. This is because they must cover everything and anticipate all of the reader's questions.

The basic persuasive letter contains four paragraphs. Each deals with one of these elements, in order: attention, interest, desire, action. You can remember this sequence by using the name *AIDA*.

The first paragraph grabs the reader's attention and gets him or her interested in reading the rest of the letter. Some of the ways that you can do this are through humor, a compliment, a question, or a visual image.

After you have the reader's attention, build interest in what you have to say. In the second paragraph, use description and emphasize any benefits to the reader. For example, suppose you are asking for contributions to a fund for young entrepreneurs. You might explain that by helping students become entrepreneurs, your reader would be helping the local economy. (This is a philanthropic, or charitable, benefit.)

Once the reader is interested, he or she will have many questions. In the third paragraph, you anticipate those questions. You also give specific facts and figures to support the claims made in the previous paragraph. This is called building desire. Let's say your goal is to entice an entrepreneur to come and speak to your class. In the desire paragraph, you would give the person all the details—when, where, what time, for how many people, and so on.

The action paragraph is important because in it you tell the reader what you want him or her to do. Be sure to include deadlines, how you can be contacted, and a confident statement about the reader's willingness to do what you are asking. An example of a persuasive letter appears in Figure 4-7.

Memos

Memos differ from letters in several respects:

- They are for internal use—that is, within an organization only.
- They are usually less formal than letters.
- They are often typed on a form that contains a preprinted heading with spaces for the names of the sender and recipient, the subject, and the date.
- They are initialed rather than signed.

Figure 4-8 gives an example of a typical memo.

Persuasive Letter

Forest View High School
20500 Merton Avenue
San Diego, CA 92110

October 21, 19--

Sharon Powell
CCV Enterprises, Ltd.
10313 Rialto Vista Boulevard
San Diego, CA 92127

Dear Ms. Powell:

I am a senior at Forest View High School and am studying entrepreneurship. I recently saw an article in the newspaper about your new product and was fascinated by the story of how you got started.

To help us really get a feel for what entrepreneurs do, my teacher often asks local entrepreneurs to visit the classroom and tell their stories. The students love to hear from people who are out there already, doing what we are learning about in school. For all of us, visitor's day provides the best class of the week.

I was given an assignment to find a local entrepreneur and ask him or her to speak to the class. The date and time of this talk would be Friday, November 6 at 10:00 a.m. in room 110. We could arrange to have any necessary equipment, such as an overhead projector, available for the presentation.

We've never had a speaker from your field before, so it would be a thrill for us to hear from you. Please consider joining us on November 6 and telling us about your success. I look forward to hearing from you soon. You may reach me at 555-8467.

Sincerely,

Mercedes Alonzo

Mercedes Alonzo

Figure 4–7   A persuasive letter follows the AIDA formula, paragraph by paragraph. How does this letter get attention? arouse interest? build desire?

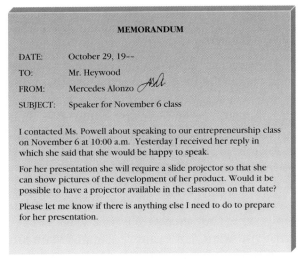

MEMORANDUM

DATE: October 29, 19--

TO: Mr. Heywood

FROM: Mercedes Alonzo

SUBJECT: Speaker for November 6 class

I contacted Ms. Powell about speaking to our entrepreneurship class on November 6 at 10:00 a.m. Yesterday I received her reply in which she said that she would be happy to speak.

For her presentation she will require a slide projector so that she can show pictures of the development of her product. Would it be possible to have a projector available in the classroom on that date?

Please let me know if there is anything else I need to do to prepare for her presentation.

Figure 4–8   A memo is a less formal kind of letter used within a company. What elements usually found in a letter are dispensed with or condensed in a memo?

Oral Communication

Thus far this chapter has focused on written communication. However, your ability to communicate orally, or with the spoken word, is equally important. This section will concentrate on two critical areas of oral communication for businesspeople—the use of the telephone and negotiation.

Telephone Technique

The telephone is certainly one of the most important modes of communication in business. Nevertheless, it is often not used effectively. As a result, time and effort are wasted.

To ensure that the calls you make accomplish what you want them to, try to do the following:

- Jot down in advance the questions you intend to ask or the main points you want to cover.
- Make sure that your tone of voice is clear and friendly.
- If the person you are calling is not available, ask when the best time to call back might be.
- Avoid calling right before lunch or at the end of the work day.

Negotiation

The process of persuading someone to agree with your point of view in such a way that both of you win is called **negotiation**. Effective negotiation is a communication art that takes time to master. However, you can begin practicing immediately in your dealings with other people, provided you know the basic principles.

KNOW YOUR BACKUP STRATEGY. Before you begin to negotiate for anything, you need to know what your alternatives are if you can't get what you want. For example, suppose you are negotiating to buy a car and the dealer holds firm to a price you don't want to pay. Your backup strategy may be to go to another dealer and purchase your second-choice car. If you go into a negotiation knowing what will happen if things don't go your way, you will be in a much stronger position to get the best deal.

DON'T REACT. The people with whom you are negotiating will be expecting a certain reaction from you when they present their position. If you respond the way they expect, you are giving them more power in the negotiation.

Suppose you are negotiating with your parents for a later curfew. You tell them that you want to stay out till 1 A.M. because all of your friends do. Your parents know that in the past when they have not given you what you wanted, you have argued and stomped out of the room. They are expecting this and know that the reaction will end the negotiation. If instead you calmly and logically explain why you deserve a later curfew, it will come as a surprise. Faced with this unexpected reaction, your parents will be more likely to listen to your reasons.

LISTEN, LEARN, AND QUESTION. The best negotiators do more listening than speaking. By carefully listening to the other person and asking clarifying questions, you soon learn the real reasons why they do not want to agree with you.

Sometimes those reasons have nothing to do with the issue at hand. Consider the curfew example again. In listening and asking questions of your parents, you may find their resistance has nothing to do with your maturity level. Their real concern may be for your safety.

CREATE A FAVORABLE ENVIRONMENT. How? By making it easy for the other person to say yes. One way to do this might be to show a benefit from this response. Another way might be to ask problem-solving questions that require more than a no answer. Questions that begin with *why, what if,* and *how* achieve this end. Problem solving (which will be covered in Chapter 6) works toward a solution that will take care of everyone's needs.

In short, to negotiate successfully for something you want, consider the other person's needs as well as your own. Then incorporate them into the negotiation.

Listening

How many times have you caught yourself thinking about something else while someone was speaking to you? Was it embarrassing when that person then asked you a question and you couldn't answer? Clearly, communication fails when listening does not take place.

Listening is not the same as hearing. Hearing is something you do with your ears. Listening engages your mind as well.

To listen, you must first focus on the speaker. You should not be thinking about yourself. You must put aside any personal problems, any reservations you have about the subject matter, any discomfort you feel with the surroundings.

Next, you must concentrate on understanding what the speaker is saying. Don't interrupt unless you've been invited to do so as a condition of the presentation. Also, avoid mentally composing any responses you might have while the speaker is making his or her points.

Finally, you should give feedback. **Feedback** consists of both the verbal and nonverbal messages you send speakers to let them know your reaction to their words. It could be anything from asking a question for clarification to nodding your head in agreement. In fact, simply paying attention or taking notes is a form of feedback.

Assume you are a speaker, and this is your audience. Judging from their feedback, how are you doing? Explain.

Risk Takers, Profit Makers

Melanie Bishop

Kids call Melanie Bishop the Lizard Lady. But her skin isn't scaly, her blood isn't cold, and she definitely doesn't have a tail that snaps off. However, when she's at work, these same descriptions fit more than a few of her business associates.

Work for Bishop is a party. For a fee, she educates, engrosses, and entertains at childrens' parties—with more than a dozen live reptiles.

Bishop had never kept a reptile until a friend asked her to baby-sit some snakes in 1987. The Los Angeles teacher accepted and, on a whim, took the snakes to her preschool class for show-and-tell. Her students responded enthusiastically. Bishop, who was looking for new ways to earn money, saw an opportunity and went into business.

First, she went to the library to research reptiles. Then, she borrowed some animals from an exotic pet store and tested her routine at a friend's party. Once again, Bishop enthralled the young audience with her presentation. Confident in her plan, she invested $4,000 in animals and cages, created a press kit, and bought advertising space in a local magazine.

In her first month, Bishop booked four parties. All were hits. Since then, continued advertising, television exposure, and word-of-mouth have kept her consistently busy. Now she averages 14 parties a month. (In one particularly busy month in 1990, she booked 40!) She also talks at summer camps, schools, and community events.

One major reason for Bishop's success is her background as a preschool teacher. While competitors may mimic her reptile routine, Bishop finds that her experience with children sets her apart. So does her content. Bishop includes far more factual information in her presentations than her competitors.

Ever conscious of her joint role as teacher and entertainer, Bishop is careful to stress environmental concerns in her presentations. She also practices what she preaches. A portion of every fee she receives goes to save the rain forests.

Ironically, the biggest problem Bishop faces is finding someone to look after her own youngsters while she entertains at other children's parties. Because most parties fall on weekends, day care centers are closed when she needs them. Although her older daughter now serves as an assistant, friends usually take care of her younger daughter.

Five years after her first party, Bishop remains delighted with her business. She has even furnished her sister-in-law in San Francisco with her routine and some animals. For Bishop, the Age of the Reptiles didn't die with the dinosaurs. It's just beginning.

Showing interest in these ways increases your chances of understanding the speaker's message. It also makes it easier to resolve any differences that might subsequently arise. For example, if you have listened carefully or taken notes, you can check your understanding of what the speaker has said by restating it in your own words.

Cross-cultural Communication

Today most businesspeople need to think globally. They need to realize that to a greater degree their competition is coming from abroad. Consequently, entrepreneurs in the 1990s will have to take more time to understand foreign cultures.

Often what we consider normal business practice in the United States is unacceptable in other countries. For example, Americans tend to make decisions rather quickly compared to the Italians or the French. Even slower are the Japanese, who rely on group decision making and mutual consent. Individuals not aware of these differences could grow impatient with the deliberate pace at which business is conducted in these cultures.

In face-to-face contacts, even more basic misunderstandings can occur because of cultural differences. Take the issue of personal space. Americans typically see people as surrounded by a more generous "space bubble" than many other nationalities do. Latin Americans, for example, stand much closer together when they talk. This often makes Americans feel uncomfortable. They tend to look upon this "closeness" as an invasion of their private space.

In Asian cultures, touching often presents similar problems. For a Japanese or Chinese person, much of the social touching that Westerners engage in is unacceptable among people who are only casually acquainted. In such circumstances,

even a gesture of greeting like shaking hands may pose a problem. Before you extend your hand, you should know whether the practice is acceptable to those you are dealing with.

Eye contact is another area in which cultural standards vary. Americans tend to expect it as a courtesy. When someone addresses you, you expect that person to look at you and perhaps even to smile. Many Asians, however, look away as a form of deference. In fact, where rank is involved (as student to teacher), they may even position themselves a few steps back and out of view. This can make carrying on a conversation while walking a neck-wrenching experience. As for smiling, some Asian cultures regard it as out of place in business situations.

To avoid offending anyone or sending the wrong message when doing business abroad, you should try to learn all you can about other cultures. At the very least, read about communication practices in other lands. If possible, participate in cultural exchange programs, either locally or abroad.

Entrepreneur's Bookshelf

To learn more about the subjects discussed in this chapter, consider reading these books:

- *Successful Business English* by Lois J. Bachman, Norman B. Sigband, and Theodore Hipple (© 1987)
- *Managing Cultural Differences* by Philip R. Harris and Robert T. Moran (© 1987)
- *The Complete Negotiator* by Gerard I. Nierenberg (© 1986)
- *Getting Past No* by William Ury (© 1991)

Chapter 4 Review

Recapping the Chapter

- Effective business communication is important because it can bring in customers, save time and money, and present a favorable image.
- In all business writing you should focus on the reader, show a benefit to that reader, be positive, be sure everything is correct, and be clear and concise.
- The steps involved in producing business correspondence are (1) determine your purpose in writing; (2) understand the receiver; (3) choose your main ideas; (4) choose an appropriate approach; and (5) organize, write, and revise.
- To make the most efficient use of the telephone, write down your main points in advance and call at the most opportune time.
- Negotiation is the process of persuading someone to agree with your point of view in such a way that both of you win.
- Good listening technique involves focusing on the speaker, concentrating on what he or she is saying, and providing feedback.
- Doing business across cultural barriers may require entrepreneurs to adjust to different communication practices.

Reviewing Vocabulary

Explain in a sentence or two how each of the following vocabulary terms relates to effective communication.

- concrete word
- abstract word
- buffer
- negotiation
- feedback

Checking the Facts

1. In business writing, what does it mean to "focus on the reader"?
2. Explain the difference between the direct and indirect approaches to writing business letters.
3. What do the letters *AIDA* stand for, and how are they used?
4. What is the purpose of "knowing your backup strategy" in a negotiation?
5. How does listening differ from hearing?
6. What sorts of communication difficulties can businesspeople have as a result of cultural differences?

Thinking Critically

1. Evaluate the following bad-news paragraph, noting what was done well and what should be corrected.

   We are unable to give you credit for the item you returned to us. We noticed that the warranty period has expired. Therefore, the item is no longer covered by the original warranty provisions. May we suggest that you take it to the authorized repair center in your area.

2. You are going to ask your boss for a raise. How will you prepare yourself to negotiate?
3. You would like to export your product to Japan. To this end, you are going to meet next week with some Japanese businesspeople. What sorts of things should you know so that you can communicate effectively?
4. You have to write the following letters. Explain which format you will use for each and why.

Chapter 4 Review

- Ms. Powell's appearance before your entrepreneurship class (see Figure 4–7) must be canceled because fire damage to the building has resulted in a shortage of classroom space.
- Ms. Powell was such a stimulating speaker that your teacher would like her to appear with a panel of other entrepreneurs as part of a parents' night program.

Discussing Key Concepts

1. During a classroom discussion, a student makes the following comment: "I'm not worried about writing skills. I'm going to have a secretary to take care of things like that." Is this attitude reasonable? Why or why not?
2. What do you believe are the key characteristics of an effective communicator?
3. What do you intend to do to ensure that you will be an effective communicator when you enter the business world?
4. The United States is part of a growing global community of nations doing business with each other. How is it possible to deal effectively with so many different cultures?

Using Basic Skills

Math

1. Calculate a Gunning Fog Index to evaluate the readability level of your own writing. Using a sample that contains at least 100 words, do the following:

- *Find the average sentence length.* Divide the number of words by the number of sentences.
- *Calculate the percentage of difficult words.* Count the number of words that have three or more syllables. Then divide

the number of these difficult words by the total number of words in the sample. Convert this decimal number to a percentage by moving the decimal point two places to the right.
- *Calculate the readability level.* Add the average sentence length to the percentage of hard words, and multiply by .4.

A reading level between 8 and 12 is ideal for business writing.

Communication

2. Do a revised version of the paragraph you critiqued in Critical Thinking item 1.
3. Write a direct-request letter asking for information about a good or service in which you are interested.
4. You want to convince your classmates to join your favorite club. Prepare an oral presentation to persuade them using the AIDA format.

Human Relations

5. You're ready to purchase your first car. You go to the nearest dealership to negotiate the deal. Using a car that you would like to buy, describe your negotiation strategy.

Enriching Your Learning

1. Choose a country that interests you, and research cultural differences that might create communication problems. Prepare an oral report using visual aids and/or demonstration to describe these.
2. Arrange for a friend to watch a particular television show at home. Watch the same show yourself at home, but turn the sound off and write your impressions of what is going on during the program. Compare your impressions with what your friend heard. Write a brief report (2–3 pages) summarizing your findings.

Math for Entrepreneurs

Objectives

After completing this chapter, you will be able to

- calculate basic business measurements such as profit and loss, break-even point, and stock turnover rate;

- describe how math is used in various kinds of sales transactions;
- define and calculate pricing markup and markdown; and
- demonstrate the basic procedures involved in operating a cash register.

Terms to Know

income statement
operating expenses
net income
inventory
cost of goods sold
general expenses
break-even point
principal
stock turnover rate
purchase order
invoice
markup
markdown
discount

Decisions, Decisions

I never liked math. I always found it boring in school, and so I never paid much attention.

Now, though, I've got this job as a salesclerk at Swim World, and I'm having second thoughts. Every day I watch Marcia—she's the store's owner—and I realize how important math is when you run a business.

For example, Marcia's always doing POs. (Those are purchase orders for new merchandise.) She usually orders swimsuits in different styles and in different quantities, and that means juggling lots of different prices, totals, and subtotals.

Marcia also verifies the paperwork on all our deliveries. What she's checking for, among other things, are overcharges. She also figures any discounts she can take. She does that a lot more now. She says she's trying to make up for what she lost when we started taking credit cards. I don't completely understand what she meant by "lost," but I know Marcia has the figures to prove it.

Then there's pricing. That's part math and part judgment call. Marcia's figured the markup she needs to cover all her expenses. It's a percentage she applies to everything. Until she does the math, though, we can't tag any merchandise.

The store usually closes at 5:30. The other clerk and I go home, but Marcia stays to balance the register. If there's a discrepancy between the register tape and what's in the cash drawer, she has to figure out where the problem is. Marcia also tracks the inventory and at least once a month figures her profit. That's to keep tabs on how she's doing.

Can you see what I mean now? When you have a business—at least a retail business— you do math day in and day out. Frankly I wish I'd realized that earlier. How am I going to become a math expert now?

Using Math in Business Management

The fact is you don't have to be a "math expert" to run your own business. You need only be competent in two basic kinds of computations:

- A fairly large number of simple computations that you'll use in your daily operations
- A limited number of more complex computations that you'll need to evaluate your business's performance

This chapter will introduce computations of both types and give you a chance to practice them.

In this section you will focus on computations that are used in *all* types of businesses, whether manufacturing, retail, or service. You will learn how to calculate profit and loss, break-even point, and stock turnover. (Such figures are often used to evaluate an enterprise's performance.) You will also learn how to compute interest and keep payroll records.

Later you will concentrate on retail math. You will learn the basics of pricing and cash register management. You will also review the computations involved in sales transactions.

Profit and Loss

Recall from Chapter 2 that profit is what is left after all the expenses of running a business have been deducted from income. The way an owner knows how much he or she has earned (or lost) during a year is by preparing a profit and loss statement. This document is also called an **income statement.**

SERVICE BUSINESSES.   Profit is simplest to calculate for a service business. You just subtract operating expenses from sales revenue. **Operating expenses** are those you incur in operating a business. Here they include such things as payroll, rent, and supplies.

For example, suppose your business earned $50,000 in revenues during the year and paid out $35,000 in expenses. Your profit, or **net income**, would be calculated as follows:

> Revenue – expenses = net income
> $50,000 – $35,000   = $15,000

Net income is an important figure because it is the amount of earnings on which a business pays taxes. Once those taxes have been figured and deducted, the amount remaining is the *actual* profit a business earns.

RETAIL/WHOLESALE BUSINESSES.   When a business sells goods instead of services, the cost of purchasing those goods must be considered in computing profit or loss. Merchandise purchased for resale is called **inventory**, or stock on hand. The inventory of a shoe store, for example, would consist of different styles of shoes, each in a range of sizes.

The cost of that portion of inventory sold during a given year is found by doing a two-step computation. First you add the value of beginning inventory to the cost of inventory purchased during the year. Then, from this figure, you subtract the value of inventory left at the end of the year. The result is the **cost of goods sold**:

> Beginning inventory
> + Purchases
> ———
> Total inventory
> – Ending inventory
> ———
> Cost of goods sold

Subtracting the cost of goods sold from revenues gives the *gross* profit. From the gross profit, the operating expenses are subtracted to arrive at the *net* profit. The term *net profit* is just another way of saying net income before taxes.

> Revenues
> – Cost of goods sold
> ———
> Gross profit
> – Expenses
> ———
> Net profit/income

Figure 5–1 shows how this formula works in an actual income statement for a retail firm.

Swim World
Income Statement

Year Ended December 31, 19--

Revenue		
Sales		$450,000
Cost of goods sold		250,000
Gross Profit		$200,000
Operating Expenses:		
Salaries	$70,000	
Advertising	12,000	
Rent	14,000	
Utilities	3,600	
Loan interest	1,200	
Insurance	1,500	
Miscellaneous	1,000	
Total Expenses		103,300
Net Profit (before taxes)		$96,700

Figure 5–1   *An income statement for a business shows how much it earned after paying all of its expenses. Suppose Swim World had paid $30,000 more each for inventory and salaries, double the rent and utilities, and $5,000 apiece more for advertising and miscellaneous expenses. What would its earnings have been?*

MANUFACTURING BUSINESSES. A business that makes goods goes through a similar set of calculations. While the same elements appear to be involved, their makeup is a little different.

Take cost of goods sold, for example. In this case, it reflects the purchase of things the firm uses to make its products. These could be either raw materials (like iron ore) or components (like computer chips). Likewise, expenses are of two kinds. Operating expenses are those directly related to the manufacture and distribution of the product. They include the wages of production line workers, utility costs for the production process, and charges for shipping finished goods to customers. **General expenses** are those connected with the running of the business. They would include such administrative costs as office supplies, office rent, and secretarial salaries.

Practice 1

Sylvan Nursery had sales revenues last year of $229,000. They purchased and sold plants and gardening supplies worth $67,000. Rent for their two locations came to $26,000; salaries, $86,000; utilities, $12,000; and miscellaneous expenses, $4,000. How much did the firm earn before taxes?

Break-even Point

To make a profit, a business first needs to break even. This means bringing in at least enough money to cover the costs of producing and distributing the good or service it sells. In other words, the business must reach the point where its revenues equal its expenses.

Computing its **break-even point** allows a business to know in advance how many units it must sell before it begins to make a profit. Consider an example. A business manufactures calculators at a cost of $8.50 each. It plans to make 150,000 units and sell them for $12.50 each. How many calculators would the firm have to sell at that price to begin making a profit? To find out, you divide the cost of producing the calculators by the selling price:

$$\frac{\text{Total production costs}}{\text{Selling price}} = \text{break-even point}$$

$$\frac{\$8.50 \times 150,000}{\$12.50} = 102,000$$

To break even and begin to make a profit, the manufacturer must sell a minimum of 102,000 calculators at a price of $12.50.

Practice 2

Calculate the break-even point for a cycling shop that buys bikes for $177 a unit and sells them for $239. The owner plans to sell 100 bikes a month. How many will he have to sell in the course of a year before he makes a profit?

Interest

Business owners borrow money for many reasons. In the start-up stage of an enterprise, they may need funds to construct a building or purchase essential equipment. Later, they may need money to cover operating expenses while they wait for revenues.

The amount borrowed is called the **principal**. The money paid for use of the principal is called interest. Interest is calculated as a percentage of principal according to this basic formula:

Interest = principal ($) x rate (%) x time (in years)
or
i = prt

The interest rate is assumed to be an annual rate, unless otherwise stated.

For example, suppose you borrowed $10,000 at 8 percent interest for three years. At the end of the loan's term, here is how much interest you would have paid:

$$i = prt$$
$$i = \$10,000 \times .08 \times 3$$
$$i = \$2,400$$

Notice the way the annual interest rate interacts with the term of the loan, or time. The 8 percent of the principal is not paid just once. It is paid *three times*. That is what makes borrowing such a significant business expense.

Practice 3

Charlie needs $7,000 to set up his hair-cutting salon, Crazi-Cuts. The best terms he can get are 12.5 percent on a four-year loan. How much will the loan cost him?

Stock Turnover

Inventory management is critical to any retail business because it helps control costs. A store that manages its inventory efficiently keeps just enough stock on hand to satisfy customers' wants. To keep more means tying up a great deal of money that could be better used elsewhere. (Besides the cost of the inventory itself, there could be charges for storage, insurance, and taxes.)

One way to measure how efficiently you are managing your inventory is to calculate the **stock turnover rate**. This is the frequency with which the inventory has been sold and replaced over a particular period of time. A business can use the rate to compare its performance against either previous periods or other businesses.

The stock turnover rate is found by dividing total net sales for a period by average inventory on hand for the same period. Consider the following example:

	Inventory on Hand	Monthly Net Sales
Jan.	$ 80,000	$ 30,000
Feb.	68,000	27,000
Mar.	75,000	31,000
Apr.	72,000	29,000
May	69,000	27,000
June	71,000	28,000
Total	$435,000	$172,000

$$\text{Average inventory:} \quad \frac{\$435,000}{6} = \$72,500$$

To compute the stock turnover rate, apply the following formula:

$$\frac{\text{Total net sales}}{\text{Average inventory on hand}}$$

$$\frac{\$172,000}{\$72,500} = 2.37$$

The stock turnover rate of 2.37 means that, on average, stock was sold and replaced about 2.4 times during a six-month period.

Practice 4

Sound Wave sells consumer electronics. Their total inventory on hand over the last eight months was $388,000. Their total net sales for the same period were $235,000. What was their stock turnover rate based on these figures?

Payroll Records

Businesses use payroll records to do more than just keep track of what is paid to employees. They also use them to calculate federal and state payroll taxes.

Figure 5–2 shows a page from a typical payroll journal. It contains information about a specific employee, including hours worked, earnings, deductions, and net (or take-home) pay.

Payroll Journal

Name	James Murray	Wage rate	$6/hr.
Date of Birth	6-7-72	Date employed	9-1-91
Soc. Sec. No.	123-45-6789	Employee No.	—
No. of Allowances	1	Department	—
Address	753 E. BOND ST.		

Pay Period Ending	Hours							Total Regular	Over-time	Gross Pay	Deductions				Net Pay
	S	M	T	W	TH	F	S				FICA	Federal Income tax	State Income tax	Misc.	
9-14	—	8	8	4	8	8	—	36	0	216	16.52	28.08	5.62	—	165.78
9-21	—	8	8	8	8	8	—	40	0	240	18.36	31.20	6.24	—	184.20
9-28	—	8	8	4	8	8	—	36	0	216	16.52	28.08	5.62	—	165.78

Figure 5–2 *A payroll journal typically devotes one page to each employee. In this employee's records, what accounts for the difference between the figures for 9–21 and 9–28?*

The journal's computations are fairly simple. Look at the figures for the week ending 9-14. To calculate the employee's gross pay, you multiply the hourly rate by the number of hours worked ($6 x 36 = $216). To figure net pay, you must first enter all of the employee's deductions. Typically these include social security (FICA) and federal and state taxes. The government makes it easy to insert these entries by providing tax tables. These eliminate much of the actual math involved. To find the employee's net pay, you merely total the figures pulled from the tables and subtract them from gross pay ($216.00 – $50.22 = $165.78).

Notice that the journal also provides a column in which to mark overtime. Here you would enter any hours worked in excess of 40. Employees are paid 50 percent more for these hours. In other words, they earn time and a half. In the example, this would be $9 ($6 x 1.5).

Practice 5

Figure Nadine's net pay for this week. She worked 32 hours at $9.40 per hour. She has deductions for FICA ($23.01), federal taxes ($30.34), state taxes ($12.92), and medical insurance ($4.25).

Now suppose Nadine worked 47 hours. If FICA is 7.65 percent of gross pay and all other deductions remain the same, what was her net pay?

Using Math for Sales Transactions

Most entrepreneurs find themselves involved with sales transactions in some form on almost a daily basis. If they are not selling their own products, then they are buying the products of others to use in their operations. The differences between such transactions lie mostly in the paperwork. The forms used go by different names—purchase order, sales slip, invoice. The computations, however, are the same.

Purchase Orders

To order goods for use or resale, a business owner fills out a **purchase order**. This preprinted form organizes a purchase so that all essential information is presented simply and clearly.

Notice in Figure 5–3 that separate columns are provided for details like item number, description, size, color, and unit. These entries ensure that the merchandise is fully identified so that the seller can fill the order accurately. Additional columns and entries help with the computations. For example, the unit cost of an item multiplied by the quantity desired determines the item total.

Entries at the bottom of the form remind the purchaser to include sales tax as part of the total amount due. Note, however, that sales tax applies only to those goods purchased for use in the business. Goods purchased for resale are not subject to sales tax. The tax will be paid on them when they are sold at retail to the final customer.

SWIM WORLD
Purchase Order

Invoice and ship to:
Swim World
2785 Ashcroft Avenue
Woodland Hills, CA 91364

Vendor:
Nouveau Swimwear
1509 Lincoln Avenue
Chicago, IL 60644

Purchase Order Number: 2356

Date: Sept. 15, 19--

Item No.	Qty.	Size	Description	Color	Unit	Unit Cost	Total
G4008	5	S	Racer-style swimsuits	Red	Ea.	$7.80	$39.00
"	10	M	" "	"	"	7.80	78.00
"	5	L	" "	"	"	7.80	39.00
G3029	3	S	Two-piece swimsuits	Multi	Ea.	6.40	19.20
"	6	M	" "	"	"	6.40	38.40
"	3	L	" "	"	"	6.40	19.20

Total Amount:	$232.80
Tax:	–
Total Due:	$232.80

Figure 5–3 *A purchase order form is designed to provide slots for all the information needed to fill an order. Why has no sales tax been entered at the bottom of the form?*

NOUVEAU SWIMWEAR
Invoice

INVOICE NO.   G14006

SOLD TO: Swim World
2785 Ashcroft Avenue
Woodland Hills, CA 91364

DATE: 9/25/--

YOUR ORDER NO.	DATE SHIPPED	SHIPPED VIA	FOB	TERMS
2356	9/25/--	UPS	M. KLINE	2/10, N30

ITEM NO.	QTY.	SIZE	DESCRIPTION	COLOR	UNIT	UNIT COST	TOTAL
G4008	5	S	Racer-style swimsuits	Red	Ea.	$7.80	$39.00
"	10	M	" "	"	"	7.80	78.00
"	5	L	" "	"	"	7.80	39.00
G3029	3	S	Two-piece swimsuits	Multi	Ea.	6.40	19.20
"	6	M	" "	"	"	6.40	38.40
"	3	L	" "	"	"	6.40	19.20

Total Amount:	$232.80
Tax:	–
Shipping:	15.55
Total Due:	$248.35

Figure 5–4   *An invoice closely follows the content of the purchase order on which it is based. Account for any differences between this form and the one shown in Figure 5–3.*

Practice 6

You are ordering stationery supplies for the school store. You need four dozen spiral notebooks ($1.30 each), three 12-packs of legal pads ($10.25 each), and two boxes of yellow highlighters ($12.50 each). What would be your purchase order total?

Invoices

When merchandise you ordered is delivered, it should include an **invoice** similar to the one shown in Figure 5-4. An invoice is the seller's record of a transaction initiated by a buyer. It therefore contains much of the same information as the buyer's purchase order. Additional details are limited mainly to shipping information and payment terms.

Because invoices depend so heavily on purchase orders, the two documents should be checked against each other. This process verifies that the order has been filled correctly. It also provides a chance to check the seller's charges and computations.

Practice 7

When the stationery supplies from Practice 6 arrive, you're shocked—at both the size of the order and the size of the bill. By comparing the invoice with your original purchase order, you discover the mistake. You've been sent *12* packages of legal pads. What is the total amount of the overcharge?

Sales Tax

Most retail sales (those to a final customer) involve a sales tax. The tax is paid by the buyer and sent to the state and/or federal government by the seller. In most cases, the seller accumulates the tax revenues over a period of time—say, three months. He or she then sends the total collected to the appropriate agency.

Sales tax rates vary from state to state. The amount may be increased by city and county taxes, as well as federal excise tax (mainly on cars and luxury items). A small number of states (about five) have no sales tax.

Sales tax is calculated on the total price of the item or items being purchased. Assume, for example, that you sell a CD for $15. If the sales tax is 6.5 percent, you would compute the tax as follows:

Purchase total x tax rate = sales tax
$15.00   x   .065   = $ .98

This amount would then be entered on the sales slip and added to the merchandise total.

You should be aware that sales tax is calculated *prior* to adding any shipping or delivery charges. This is because the tax is levied on goods only, not services like shipping.

Practice 8

You sell an item for $19.95. What is the total purchase price if sales tax in your state is 5.75 percent?

Sales Slips

Many entrepreneurs who own retail businesses are often their own salespeople. When acting in this capacity, they fill out sales slips for both cash and credit transactions.

CASH SALES. The most common type of retail sales transaction for a small business is the cash sale. In such a sale the customer uses either actual currency or a check.

Sales Slip (Cash Sale)

SWIM WORLD				
Emp. No. _JM_		Date _9-17_ 19 _--_		
Sold to _Cash_				
Address		_-_		

Cash ☑   Check ☐

Dept.	Qty.	Item	Price	Amount
55	1	GOGGLES	7.95	7 95
41	1	BATHING CAP	5.50	5 50
		Subtotal		13 45
		Sales Tax		91
		Total		14 36

Figure 5–5   A sales slip devotes relatively less space to identifying merchandise and relatively more to computation. Why do you think this is so?

If you use sales slips to record transactions, you simply fill in the information required by the form. The computations involved are identical to those used when filling out purchase orders or invoices. You add merchandise amounts to arrive at a total. You then apply any sales tax rate to this figure and add the computed tax to get an amount due. Figure 5–5 shows a completed sales slip for a cash sale.

CREDIT CARD SALES. The next-most-common type of retail sales transaction is the credit card sale. Because of the popularity of credit cards, more and more businesses are finding it necessary to accept them. For entrepreneurial ventures or small businesses, this can be costly.

To understand why, consider an example. Suppose a customer buys a watch and puts the purchase on his or her VISA or MasterCard. The bank issuing the card pays the merchant and collects from the customer later. The bank does not pay the full amount, however. It deducts a fee for acting as the merchant's collection agent. Thus, if the customer paid $100 and the bank's fee were 3 percent, the merchant selling the watch would receive only $97 ($100 × .03 = $3; $100 − $3 = $97). Since this charge can't be passed back to the watch manufacturer, it must come out of the merchant's profits. This is why offering credit to customers costs businesses money.

A credit card sale is recorded in much the same way as a cash sale. The credit card sales slip, however, has spaces for additional information. There are slots for the credit card number and expiration date and the customer's signature.

There is also room for an authorization code. This is usually obtained by phone or some kind of electronic device. The code indicates that a credit reporting agency has checked the account and found nothing that would keep the card issuer from paying on the transaction.

Using Math for Pricing

Pricing is one of the key decisions that determines a business's profitability. Most of the factors that figure in pricing will be explored in later chapters. In this section, we will focus on the math principles that underlie it.

Markup

Businesses that purchase or manufacture goods for resale use markup pricing. A **markup** is the amount added to the cost of an item to cover expenses and ensure a profit.

Suppose it costs $5 to make a ballpoint pen ($3 for the casing and $2 for the ink refill). The manufacturer will have to charge more than $5 to make a profit—say, $2 more. Together these two figures will determine the pen's price:

$$\text{Cost} + \text{markup} = \text{retail price}$$
$$\$5 \ + \ \ \$2 \ \ = \ \ \ \ \ \$7$$

Once you understand the relationship among these items, you can compute any one if you know the other two. For example, if you know the retail price and the markup, you can figure the cost:

$$\text{Retail price} - \text{markup} \ = \ \text{cost}$$
$$\$7 \ \ \ \ - \ \ \ \$2 \ \ \ = \ \ \$5$$

Or if you know the retail price and the cost, you can determine the markup:

$$\text{Retail price} - \text{cost} = \text{markup}$$
$$\$7 \ \ \ \ - \ \ \$5 \ = \ \ \ \ \$2$$

Business owners do not as a rule decide markup on an item-by-item basis. They do not add $2 to this item and $5 to that item based on whim or "feel." Besides being tedious and inefficient, such an unsystematic approach offers no basis for decision making. Suppose, for example, a firm's profits are not high enough. How would an owner who prices by whim know by how much to increase the amount of each markup in order to earn more?

The fact is that business owners use a system to price. They decide on a standard *percentage* markup. They can arrive at this figure in a number of ways. They can use the average for their industry. They can match their competitors. Finally, they can estimate based on how much they will need per item sold to cover their expenses.

The pen manufacturer discussed above, for example, decided that $2 on a cost of $5 was about right. To convert that figure to a percentage, you would take the dollar amount of the markup and divide by cost. You then change the answer to a percentage by moving the decimal point two places to the right:

$$\frac{\text{Markup}}{\text{Cost}} = \text{percentage markup}$$
$$\frac{\$2}{\$5} \ \ = .4 \text{ or } 40\%$$

The $2 markup on the pen represents a 40 percent markup on cost.

Once a percentage has been decided on, it can be applied to any cost figure to arrive at a retail price. Suppose a jeweler marks up his merchandise 95 percent on cost. Here is how he would price a bracelet that cost him $25:

Cost x markup % = $ markup
$25.00 x   .95   = $23.75

The retail price of the bracelet would be $48.75 ($25.00 + $23.75).

If at some point the jeweler decides he's not making enough profit, he could simply raise his markup 5 or 10 percentage points. All of his prices would be changed systematically and the effect observed over several months. If profits were still not satisfactory, the process could be repeated.

Practice 9

You're sizing up the competition for your new gift shop. An artist friend of yours recently sold a ceramic vase to Tambourine, a successful folk art gallery down the block. Your friend received $40. The vase is now in the gallery's window with an $87 price tag. What is Tambourine's percentage markup on cost?

Markdowns

To reduce their inventories, businesses often mark down their merchandise. This means they lower their retail prices by a certain percentage. (In other words, they have a sale.)

For example, suppose a clothing retailer has some $85 dresses that are just not selling. To get them to move, she decides to mark them down by 30 percent. First, she determines the dollar amount of the **markdown**:

Retail price x markdown % = $ markdown
$85.00   x   .30   = $25.50

Then she computes the sale price:

Retail price – $ markdown = sale price
$85.00   – $25.50   = $59.50

Practice 10

It's six months later, and your friend's vase (Practice 9) still hasn't sold. Tambourine's owner decides to mark it down 25 percent. What will it sell for now?

Discounts

A **discount** is a reduction in the retail or wholesale price of a particular product. Businesses give discounts for a variety of reasons. Some give them as a benefit. Employee discounts are of this type. Others give them to stimulate business. For example, quantity discounts encourage buyers to place larger orders. Seasonal discounts encourage them to buy in advance. Promotional discounts encourage them to advertise, display, or otherwise "push" a product.

You have already encountered one of the most common types of discounts. Look back at Figure 5-4, the seller's invoice. In the box labeled *Terms* appears the notation *2/10, N30*. This means that the seller is offering the buyer a discount of 2 percent if she pays the amount due in 10 days. Otherwise, the whole (or net) amount is due in 30 days. Called cash discounts, such terms are routinely offered to encourage prompt payment.

Discounts are figured in exactly the same way as markdowns. As an example, take the terms given in Figure 5-4. If Swim World's owner decides to take advantage of the discount, here's how much she would save:

Retail price x discount % = $ discount
$232.80   x   .02   = $4.66

Note that the discount applies to the retail price, not the entire amount due. In other words, it does not apply to sales tax or shipping charges. They are computed and added *after* the discount has been subtracted from the merchandise total.

Practice 11

Suppose the terms quoted to Swim World in the invoice (Figure 5-4) had been 3/15, N60. How much would Marcia, the owner, have been able to save by paying early?

Operating a Cash Register

Businesses that sell products typically use a cash register to manage sales transactions. These registers may be so sophisticated that they do all the computations for the people who operate them. Still, such registers must be managed. Many of the skills needed to do this have a math component.

Verifying the Opening Cash Fund

At the start of every business day, the owner or manager must supply the cash register with currency and coins. As this opening cash fund is placed in the cash drawer, it should be counted. The amounts for each denomination should be written down and the overall total verified against the total planned for the register. Figure 5-6 shows the layout of a typical cash drawer.

Practice 12

You normally start the day with $150 in cash in your register drawer. How might this be distributed among the various denominations of bills and coins? Using Figure 5-6 as a guide, do a written tally to verify your drawer's contents.

Cash Drawer

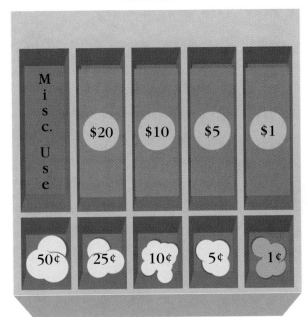

Figure 5–6   A register's cash drawer is typically arranged with the bills at the back and the coins at the front. What items do you think might be placed in the miscellaneous (Misc.) compartment?

Counting Change

When a cash sale is made, the salesclerk should announce key amounts and count aloud. This enables the customer to follow the monetary exchange portion of the transaction.

The exchange of funds begins with a statement of the purchase total:

"That will be $10.60."
The customer hands the clerk $11.
"Out of $11." The clerk places the $11 on the ledge above the cash drawer. He or she begins making change, counting upward from the purchase total.
"That's $10.65 (handing the customer a nickel), $10.75 (handing over a dime), and $11.00 (handing over a quarter)."

Generally, you will want to return as little change as possible to the customer. This means using the largest denominations you can.

Risk Takers, Profit Makers

Guy, David, and Jason Sims

Guy, David, and Jason Sims do not outrace speeding bullets, overpower locomotives, or leap over tall buildings. However, the three native Philadelphians have created a contemporary hero who, in the estimation of many, comes close. Brotherman, Dictator of Discipline, is a rarity—a black comic-book hero. In fact, he is the lead character in the first comic book completely devoted to and created by African-Americans.

The Sims brothers developed the Brotherman character in 1990 to promote their now defunct New Jersey T-shirt business. Since then they have written, drawn, and produced each issue of the comic book totally on their own. The arrangement has guaranteed them complete artistic freedom, something they feel is essential to their portrayal of the black urban American experience. Consider just one example—the residents of Big City, the comic's fictional locale. Unlike their stereotypic counterparts on television, Big City-ites are positive, productive, and knowledgeable.

Like its hero, the *Brotherman* comic book itself is unusual. It comes in an oversized, black-and-white format. Its plots don't involve superhuman powers, rely on violence, or include sexual or racial stereotypes, as traditional comics often do. Still, the publication's artistic and thematic quality allow it to command a slightly higher cover price than its slicker, four-color competition.

Through Big City Comics, Inc., the Simses' own Irving, Texas-based distribution company, *Brotherman* reaches a select and expanding number of stores. Although it requires extra work, the Simses prefer to distribute their quarterly title directly. That way, they know exactly where and how much each issue sells. They also get to know retailers personally and keep in close touch with their audience.

Sales for the athletic, articulate, and intelligent Brotherman have been booming. While *Brotherman* first carved out a niche with urban comic-book vendors and Afrocentric retailers, readers can now find it at stores, stands, and educational outlets worldwide. Circulation has exploded, from 10,000 to 200,000 in the first two years of publication.

Brotherman has also received a great deal of publicity. It started with a wildly successful debut at the Black Expo in New York. Since then the Sims brothers have made numerous personal appearances at bookstores across the country, and there has been regular coverage in the local and national press. (Good word-of-mouth hasn't hurt, either.) As a result, both the enemies of Big City and the readers of *Brotherman* are likely to be kept on the edges of their seats for a long time to come.

Suppose in the transaction described above the customer paid with a $20 bill. To the coins, the clerk would have added (in order) four $1 bills and one $5 bill. He or she would not have used nine $1 bills, unless there was no choice or the customer requested it.

Today most cash registers calculate the amount to be returned to the customer. This eliminates the need for counting backward. If the register says $1.25 in change is due, you would pull out a dollar bill first and then a quarter.

> **Practice 13**
> The purchase total for your customer is $31.18. She hands you two $20 bills. How would you count back her change?

Balancing the Cash Drawer

At the end of each business day, the cash drawer should be balanced. Today's cash registers make this job easier by keeping a running tally of the day's sales on tape. To balance, you simply compare this tape to the contents of the drawer.

You begin by counting all the money in the cash drawer. Then you total and add in all the checks received and all the credit sales. From this overall amount, you subtract any cash refunds. Finally, you subtract the amount of money that was in the cash drawer at the beginning of the day. The result should match your register tape.

Consider an example. Suppose your register tape shows receipts of $1,396.08. You count up the drawer's contents and arrive at these figures:

Cash	$ 574.13
Checks	613.77
+ Credit sales	433.18
Total receipts	$1,621.08
− Cash refunds	75.00
Adjusted receipts	$1,546.08
− Opening cash fund	150.00
Actual receipts	$1,396.08

Since your final total matches the tape total, the cash drawer is balanced.

If the two totals do not match, that means there has been a mistake. If there is more money in the cash drawer, for example, it could mean that a salesclerk has shorted a customer when making change.

> **Practice 14**
> Suppose in the example above the register tape's total were $1,397.33. What would that mean?

Entrepreneur's Bookshelf

To learn more about the subjects discussed in this chapter, consider reading these books and articles:

- *Keys to Business and Personal Financial Statements* by Nicholas Apostolou (© 1991)
- *Entrepreneurship: The Ten Commandments for Building a Growth Company* by Steven C. Brandt (© 1982)
- "Cashless Society May Be Inching Toward Reality" by Amy Dockser, *The Wall Street Journal* (May 9, 1990)
- *How to Really Create a Successful Business Plan* by David E. Gumpert (© 1990)
- *Effective Small Business Management* by Norman M. Scarborough and Thomas W. Zimmerer (© 1991)
- "Arby's Adds Technology to Boost Service" by Cyndee Miller, *Marketing News* (November 12, 1990)
- "How Much Money Does Your New Venture Need?" by James McNeill Stancill, in *The Entrepreneurial Venture*, edited by William A. Sahlman and Howard H. Stevenson (© 1992)

Chapter 5 Review

Recapping the Chapter

- A service business calculates profit (or loss) by subtracting expenses from revenues. A goods business must subtract the cost of goods sold as well to figure its profitability.
- A firm's break-even point is where it sells enough product at a given price to cover its production costs.
- Stock turnover rate tells businesses how often their inventory is sold and replaced over a certain period of time.
- To complete purchase orders, invoices, or sales slips, you add merchandise totals, then multiply the result by the applicable rate to figure any sales tax due.
- A markup is the amount a business adds to the cost of an item to cover expenses and ensure a profit. A markdown is a percentage reduction to help sell merchandise.
- Operating a cash register involves three main duties—verifying the opening cash fund, counting change, and balancing the cash drawer at the end of the business day.

Reviewing Vocabulary

For each of the following terms, write one or two sentences describing how it is used in a business environment.

- income statement
- operating expenses
- net income
- inventory
- cost of goods sold
- general expenses
- break-even point
- principal
- stock turnover rate
- purchase order
- invoice
- markup
- markdown
- discount

Checking the Facts

1. Describe the structure of an income statement.
2. What is the formula for computing interest on a loan? Explain what each element in the formula stands for.
3. How is stock turnover calculated?
4. Who pays sales tax and when? Who collects it and how?
5. How do sales slips for cash and credit transactions differ from each other? How are they alike?
6. If you know the retail price and the cost of an item, how would you determine the markup on it?
7. What does the notation *4/20, N60* mean?
8. Describe how you would balance the cash drawer of a register at the end of a business day.

Thinking Critically

1. Assume that you own a retail business. Trace your income from the enterprise from sales revenues to actual money in your personal bank account.
2. Accepting credit cards costs businesses money. Given this fact, why might you as a business owner consider accepting them?
3. If you wanted to start a business selling a cookie of your own creation, how would you determine how much to charge for it?
4. There is a shortage of a few dollars in the cash drawer at the end of the business day. How would you go about determining where the problem occurred?

Chapter 5 Review

5. Your company, Automotive Motifs, sells jewelry designed around the names, logos, and distinctive features of certain automobiles. It has been in business for one year. Consider the following information, and decide if the company is doing well or not. Justify your answer.

- Revenues for the year were $15,000.
- Cost of goods sold was $5,400.
- Expenses for the year were $10,500.

6. If you do not keep accurate payroll records, who will be affected and in what ways?

Discussing Key Concepts

1. Relate the concept of break-even point to the concept of equilibrium point, which you learned about in Chapter 2. What are the similarities?
2. What are some of the practical ways that the profit motive operates in a business on a daily basis?
3. Based on this chapter, what have you learned about the value to a business of good record keeping?
4. How might the concept of cost of goods sold be applied to a service business? *Hint:* Select a particular service business, and try to define exactly what it is selling. Then consider all the resources that go into the service.

Using Basic Skills

Math

1. During the past year, Mack's Golf Shop sold merchandise that cost $535,000. Mack's markup on cost was 35 percent, and his operating expenses totaled $350,000.

Construct an income statement for Mack to establish his profit or loss.

Communication

2. Write a short script that details a sales transaction for an item that costs $16.95 (plus 6.5 percent sales tax) and for which the customer hands over a $50 bill. Start at the point where the customer approaches the register.

Human Relations

3. You accidentally give the wrong amount of change to a customer, who returns a few minutes later to claim that you still owe her $5. How would you handle this situation?

Enriching Your Learning

1. Interview an owner of a merchandising operation to learn about pricing and stock turnover. Then write a three- or four-page report summarizing what you learned.
2. When you are forced to mark down merchandise to sell it, your markup is reduced. The difference between your cost and your eventual sale price is your *maintained* markup. Assume your clothing store buys some bulky knit sweaters for $30 apiece and marks them up 75 percent.

- What is the initial selling price of the sweaters?
- When the sweaters don't sell, you mark them down one-third. How much do customers pay for them at this point?
- Among the people who buy the reduced sweaters are two of your employees. They make their purchases using their 20 percent employee discount. What do they pay for their sweaters?
- What is your maintained markup on the sweaters your regular customers bought? on the sweaters your employees bought?

Chapter 6
Decision Skills

Objectives

After completing this chapter, you will be able to
- distinguish the two basic approaches to problem solving and decision making,
- list the steps in the formal decision-making process,
- identify two methods of group decision making and explain how they work, and
- suggest some techniques for formulating meaningful and effective goals.

Terms to Know

rational approach
hypothesis
satisficing
brainstorming
criteria
nominal grouping
Delphi technique
consensus

Decisions, Decisions

Today my boss, Marcia, and I ate in for lunch. We're in the middle of inventory right now and couldn't go out. I like brown-bagging with Marcia. She really relaxes then, and I can ask her almost anything about the business. What I did ask her about was this credit card thing that I mentioned before.

She seems to be watching every penny since we started taking credit cards a few months ago. So, I figured it must have been a really tough decision for her. I was wrong. She said she hadn't thought about it much at all. A few of her best customers asked, and she just said yes. Now she wishes she hadn't been so hasty.

In the back of her mind she knew she'd have to pay for their convenience, but she had no idea how much. It's a percentage of every credit purchase. Marcia says that's like discounting her merchandise even when it's not on sale. I sometimes forget that Swim World's just starting to grow. Marcia doesn't, though. I get the feeling that the unexpected discounting really hurt.

Marcia swears that in the future she'll be more careful about those kinds of decisions—no more of this seat-of-the-pants stuff. In the meantime, all she can do is hope that credit cards will bring in new customers (or maybe get the old ones to buy more)—that and cut costs everywhere she can.

Personally, though, I think Marcia did all right. I mean, if your customers want something, what are you going to do? How else would you make a decision like that?

Problem Solving and Decision Making

The average business day is filled with problems that need to be solved and decisions that need to be made. Typically these fall into two categories—routine and nonroutine.

Routine decisions are those that are made regularly, often daily. They seldom involve difficult or complicated matters, and their impact is largely short term. They might include what supplies to order or how to handle a customer complaint.

Nonroutine decisions are those that are made with much less frequency. Usually they deal with complex issues, like whether or not to introduce a new product or enter a new market. Such decisions have long-term consequences for a business. They powerfully affect the future of a company and are often crucial to its success or failure.

Because of their importance, nonroutine decisions require time and thought. Time, however, is something that many business owners do not have in abundance. As a result, they have evolved a dual-approach system for making decisions. They make routine decisions quickly, based largely on previous experience with the particular situation. They put the bulk of their available time where it is needed most—into their nonroutine decision making.

The Rational Approach

When making nonroutine decisions, business owners work systematically. They go through a whole series of steps to ensure that every aspect of the problem or decision is considered. This process is called the **rational approach,** or sometimes the scientific approach.

As its name implies, the rational approach requires a great deal of mental effort. This is because throughout the process the decision maker must respond to new information.

For example, suppose your business is experiencing low sales volume. Before you can fix this situation, you have to figure out what is causing it. Maybe it's poor service. To test this **hypothesis,** you might survey some of your customers. Their responses will tell you if you are right or if something else is the cause. If they don't, you will have to start again, with a new hypothesis. Bear in mind that this is just the *first step* in the process. It is what you have to do to identify your problem.

It should be obvious that such a thorough, painstaking approach is appropriate for only certain kinds of problems or decisions. These would be the large, complex, far-reaching ones that we have already labeled *nonroutine*. Their consequences make the investment of time and effort not only reasonable but also worthwhile.

The Seat-of-the-Pants Approach

For more routine decision making, studies have found that most businesspeople use a much less formal procedure. They rely on personal experience or established procedures or sometimes simply intuition. This method of making decisions is often called the "seat-of-the-pants" approach.

This approach recognizes that decision makers do not always consider all the possibilities in an effort to find the best solution—nor do they have to. Rather, in certain circumstances, they seek a solution that satisfies the moment. This process is called **satisficing**.

For routine decisions made under time pressure, satisficing produces acceptable results. There is no need to do exhaustive research, ponder endless alternatives, or contemplate every conceivable effect. The decisions involved don't warrant that kind of treatment. Their consequences are such that it would be a waste of time and effort to go through a series of decision-making steps. Satisficing, then, is an efficient approach to decision making, one that recognizes the realities of a business owner's day-to-day existence.

Steps in Formal Decision Making

Formal problem-solving and decision-making follow the rational model. In other words, they are based on a series of steps, as shown in Figure 6–1. Let's consider those steps one by one.

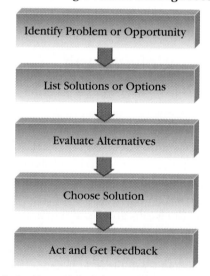

Problem-solving/Decision-making Process

Identify Problem or Opportunity

List Solutions or Options

Evaluate Alternatives

Choose Solution

Act and Get Feedback

Figure 6–1   Formal decision making is very different from the approach used by businesspeople for routine, day-to-day decision making. What is the name of that other approach, and how would you diagram it?

Risk Takers, Profit Makers

Sandy Gooch

Some people see a business need and wait for someone else to fill it. Sandy Gooch saw a need and decided to fill it herself. In 1977 she launched the first of her successful Mrs. Gooch's Natural Foods Markets in the Los Angeles area. Her happy customers have been eating healthier ever since.

In 1974 Gooch began to suffer severe chest pains and seizures. Puzzled doctors could find no cause for her ailment. Fortunately for Gooch, her father was a research biologist and chemist. He discovered that she was having a severe reaction to the artificial additives in her food. Gooch herself later learned that these additives, which routinely find their way into some foods sold in conventional supermarkets, depleted the body's defenses. Some were even toxic. As a result, many people had reactions similar to hers.

Gooch resolved to eat additive-free foods but found that local supermarkets did not have many of the products she needed. She then turned to health food stores but quickly discovered that they were scarce in Southern California and often poorly stocked. In fact, in the mid-1970s, additive-free products were difficult to find anywhere.

To solve her own problem, Gooch became first an expert on natural foods, then a spokesperson for their use. In 1977 she carried her developing interest to its natural conclusion. She opened her first Mrs. Gooch's Natural Foods Market. With the help of Don Volland, an experienced natural foods vender, she created a store that carried a variety of health foods. One year later, she opened a second store. Today, there are seven Mrs. Gooch's Natural Foods Markets in Southern California.

Gooch not only sells health foods. She also promotes health awareness. Her stores carry natural nutritional supplements and environmentally friendly body care products. Each also stocks books on dietary issues, employs a full-time nutritionist, and offers seminars on health-related issues. Employees regularly receive newsletters to update them on the latest health and environmental concerns.

Gooch credits her success to the public's interest in health and ecology. Their continuing interest is apparent. Mrs. Gooch's stores do very little advertising compared to conventional supermarkets. Still, combined annual sales from Gooch's stores have skyrocketed to a whopping $600 million, and they show no signs of faltering.

As more Southern Californians become health conscious about all aspects of their lives, Gooch will probably continue to win new customers. What will they discover in the aisles of her stores? The same thing that Gooch herself discovered years ago—that natural foods are not only healthy but also taste good.

Identify the Problem or Opportunity

Identifying a problem, as indicated earlier, is not as simple as it sounds. Your initial hypothesis may be wrong. You may even have a hard time formulating a hypothesis. Here are some techniques that might help.

LOOK BEYOND SYMPTOMS. Sometimes, what is seen as a problem is really only a symptom. For example, if the "problem" facing your business is high employee turnover, you should realize that the turnover is merely a symptom. The real problem is whatever is *causing* the high turnover. It may be the nature of the job (boring, repetitive); the lack of incentives (low pay, no promotion potential); or any of several other possibilities. Therefore, you must learn to look beyond the obvious, to reduce every potential problem to its root cause. Remember, if you do not solve the cause of a problem, you do not solve the problem.

ANTICIPATE. You must also recognize that your business environment extends far beyond your immediate location and even the boundaries of your community. Problems can come from some quite remote places. Suppose the federal government increased corporate income taxes. Your business, if it were a corporation, would feel the impact. You could quite possibly have a major financial problem on your hands.

You must therefore learn to recognize problems *before* your business is affected. Knowing where problems are likely to come from and watching those areas can help. Anticipation will give you more time to arrive at solutions or devise ways to take advantage of new opportunities.

TAKE A POSITIVE VIEW. Remember always that what is a problem for one company can be an opportunity for another. The problem businesses had getting important papers to clients quickly was the opportunity that launched Federal Express and, much later, the fax machine.

Try, therefore, to look at all problems as potential opportunities. Consider some examples.

Your state enacts a helmet law for motorcyclists. This creates an opportunity for manufacturers and retailers of such equipment. A natural disaster devastates a nearby commercial park. This creates multiple opportunities for those who can help rebuild. Economic conditions weaken demand for expensive clothing. This creates opportunities for discounters and secondhand outlets.

List Solutions or Options

Once you have defined the problem or opportunity you are dealing with, you are ready to think about responses. Since your goal is to find the best solution or option for your purposes, you don't want to rule out any possibilities—at least not at this early stage. One of the best ways to proceed in such circumstances is to employ a technique called **brainstorming**.

The purpose of brainstorming is to generate a large number of ideas in a short period of time. Here's how the technique works. You start with a group of people who have an interest in the problem or decision. To develop potential solutions, you invite participants to volunteer ideas *irrespective of how practical those ideas are*. Criticism or evaluation is discouraged while this is going on. The theory is that statements like "That's crazy," "That'll never work," or "We don't have the money," will stifle creative thinking. That would defeat the whole purpose of using the brainstorming technique in the first place.

Evaluate the Alternatives

At this point, you will probably have generated too many ideas to consider all of them in depth. You'll need to get your list down to something manageable—say, 3–5 options.

How? First, you should eliminate those alternatives that are total impossibilities. These would be the "off-the-wall" solutions, the ideas based

Every problem has within it hidden opportunities for those willing to look for them. What sorts of opportunities are suggested by this common urban problem?

more on wishful thinking than reality. They have served their purpose by encouraging a free-wheeling exchange of ideas. Now, however, is the time to get practical.

SET UP CRITERIA. To narrow your choices further, you should next set up some general **criteria,** or standards, by which to judge the remaining ideas. These criteria will most likely reflect the concerns that made the decision seem nonroutine to you in the first place.

For example, cost might be one of your criteria. What if you have only $1,500 to spend? Toss out any ideas that would be more expensive than that. Personal interests might be another limiting factor. Does any option have an especially negative impact on one group of people who work for you? You might want to pass on that one, too. (If not, then you might consider a compromise to make it more acceptable to the affected workers.) What about risk? If the idea or solution doesn't work out, can you afford the consequences? If it means losing your business, the answer may be no. Recall from Chapter 3 that entrepreneurs are *calculated* risk takers. They are not reckless. They look for solutions that minimize risk, or at least hold it to reasonable levels.

Using criteria like these, you should be able to reduce your options to the necessary few. Just because you have fewer alternatives, however, does not mean that your choice will be easy. In fact, since all the options left will have met your basic standards, you may actually have a harder time choosing. That's when it's time to start writing things down.

WEIGH THE OPTIONS. To make a final decision, you may have to draw fine distinctions among your remaining choices. There are many ways to do this. Two of the most popular depend on weighing the factors favoring each choice.

The first method is the simpler. You just list the pros and cons (or advantages and disadvantages) of each alternative. The sheer number of points in favor of one may result in its standing out from the rest.

Be aware, however, that this procedure has some shortcomings. No option may emerge as the clear winner. Also, this method does not reflect the fact that some advantages may be more important to you than others.

For example, suppose you are trying to decide where to locate a restaurant. You consider an inexpensive building site to be most important. When you tally the pros and cons, one location emerges with the most points in its favor. However, one of those points is *not* its purchase price. The question for you is, Can all of those pros outweigh your preference for a reasonably priced lot?

The second method of evaluating alternatives is more complex but gets around this problem. It does so by setting up a limited number of criteria, which are then weighted. The weights are applied to the options and the results reduced to chart or table form.

Again, consider the restaurant example. You begin by listing your requirements for a location in order of their importance to you. You then assign each requirement a percentage weight that reflects its rank in your list. The first two columns in Figure 6–2 show some possible choices. There cost of land is by far the most important criterion, as reflected in the 60 percent weight assigned to it. Each location is rated by multiplying the dollar value of each criterion by its weight

and adding the results. For example, the rating for City A would be computed as follows:

Land	$5,000 x .60	=	$3,000
Building	6,500 x .20	=	1,300
Advertising	2,500 x .15	=	375
Labor	1,500 x .05	=	75
Total weighted value			$4,750

By quantifying your personal responses to the various sites, the finished table points the way to a decision.

Choose a Solution

What emerges from the evaluation process is the alternative that will give you the outcome you want along with a reasonably high probability of success. In Figure 6–2, this is the location with the lowest weighted costs. Notice that while this city apparently has the lowest land values, it also has the highest costs in other areas. It emerges as the first choice mainly because of the weighting process.

Restaurant Locations Weighing the Options				
Criterion (Cost of:)	Weight (%)	City A	City B	City C
Land	60	$5,000	$9,000	$7,500
Building	20	6,500	4,000	5,000
Advertising	15	2,500	1,000	1,500
Labor	5	1,500	500	2,000
	100	$4,750	$6,375	$5,825

Figure 6–2   Assigning a percentage weight to each criterion allows a decision maker's priorities to be reflected in the weighing process. In this example, if you were simply to add the cost figures, which city would be the choice (that is, have the lowest costs)? When the percentage weights are applied, which city wins out?

Sometimes businesspeople have a great fear of making the wrong decision. This fear may be so great that they choose to make no decision at all. If you go through the decision-making process carefully and thoughtfully, however, you should not feel this way. You can trust your ability to choose the best alternative.

Implement and Get Feedback

No decision can be considered complete until it has been tested in the real world. Therefore, once implemented, most major decisions and solutions go through a further period of evaluation. The feedback received during this period may result in changes. In some instances, it may even uncover a new problem that begins the process all over again.

Group Decision Making

In today's complex business environment, decisions are often made by groups of individuals who have specific areas of expertise. For example, a company that wishes to introduce a new product may bring together a group that includes an engineer, a marketing expert, a financial adviser, and a salesperson. Together they will try to determine if the idea is feasible.

There are several ways to help groups make business decisions. We have already talked about one of these—brainstorming. Now we shall consider two more.

Nominal Grouping Technique

The **nominal grouping** technique derives its name from the fact that each member of the group acts on an individual basis. The process begins with a statement of the problem. In response, individual group members make lists of their own solutions and rank them. They then take turns presenting their ideas while the group leader records them on a chalkboard or flip chart. After all of the ideas have been presented, questions are taken and the various alternatives are clarified. Then each individual makes a new ranked list, this time including all the ideas presented. The last step is to rank all of the ideas based on these new lists to arrive at the top choice.

Delphi Technique

The **Delphi technique** is a more formal procedure. Its goal is **consensus,** or agreement, among group members.

The process is in some respects similar to the nominal grouping technique. With the Delphi method, however, the group members do not meet. In fact, they may not even know who else is participating.

The purpose of this isolation is to keep personalities from influencing the decision-making process. In face-to-face meetings, feelings about a person suggesting an idea can affect how it is received. As a result, it might be accepted or rejected without any real consideration of its merits.

The first step in the Dephi process is the circulation of a questionnaire. It presents the problem and asks group members to suggest potential solutions. The questionnaires are returned to the leader.

In the second step, the results of the various questionnaires are tallied and sent back to the group members along with a more detailed questionnaire. This questionnaire explores the suggested solutions and attempts to clarify any issues they have raised. The members complete these questionnaires and return them to the group leader for tallying. The process continues in this manner until consensus is reached.

The nominal grouping and Delphi techniques are two methods commonly used to promote smooth and effective decision making in a group setting. Which technique is being employed here? How do you know?

Goal Setting

Whether or not you realize it, most of what you have accomplished in your life has been the result of setting goals. Perhaps you set your own goals, like learning to play guitar or getting an after-school job. Perhaps someone else set goals for you, by saying they wanted you to get a certain grade point average or save a certain amount of money. In either case, what you were doing was striving to reach some identified point.

Why Do It?

Setting a goal can be a very positive thing. If you reach the goal you set, you experience a tremendous sense of satisfaction and achievement. This can be a real confidence booster.

Even if you don't reach your goal, however, you still benefit. The very act of setting a goal allows you to measure your performance. This can be an important exercise for someone preparing to set up a business and make it grow.

Businesses regularly set goals for themselves. They may decide to aim for a certain level of sales or market share. They may set a deadline for training new employees. Without goals, a business would lack a sense of direction and would not be able to measure its achievements easily.

What's the Process?

The following steps will ensure that the goals you set will have the best possible chance of being achieved.

- *Put your goals in writing.* By writing down your goals, you symbolically give them importance. Besides, periodically you can look back at them to make sure that you are still on track.
- *Be sure your goals are measurable.* Notice the difference in these two goal statements: "I want to do better in math this semester" and "I want to earn at least a B in math this semester." In the first statement, we don't really know what "better" means. How much better? How will we know when we have achieved better? The second statement, in contrast, is measurable. You will definitely know when you have achieved this goal.
- *Make your goals attainable but challenging.* It is important to set goals that you can honestly achieve within the limits of your abilities. However, be sure that the goals you set are also sufficiently challenging so that you will be motivated to do your best. Select goals that will encourage you and your business to grow.
- *Set deadlines for achieving your goals.* If you don't state a specific time to achieve a goal, you won't be pressed to begin working on it.

Entrepreneur's Bookshelf

To learn more about the subjects discussed in this chapter, consider reading these books and articles:

- *Dynamic Decision-maker* by K.R. Brousseau, Michael J. Driver, and P. Hunsaker (© 1990)
- *Top Decisions: Strategic Decisionmaking in Organizations* by R. J. Butler, D. Cray, D. J. Hickson, G. R. Mallory, and D. C. Wilson (© 1986)
- "Decision-making Behavior in Smaller Entrepreneurial and Larger Professionally Managed Firms" by M. J. Gannon, T. R. Mitchell, and K. G. Smith, *Journal of Business Venturing* (Vol. 3, 1988)
- "The Importance of Work Goals: An International Perspective" by Itzhak Harpaz, *Journal of International Business Studies* (Spring 1990)
- *Crucial Decisions: Leadership in Policy-making and Crisis Management* by I. L. Janis (© 1989)
- "Entrepreneurs: Opportunistic Decision Makers" by Philip D. Olson, *Journal of Small Business Management* (July 1986)
- "Group Decision-making: Approaches to Problem Solving," *Small Business Report* (July 1988)

Chapter 6 Review

Recapping the Chapter

- When problems or decisions will have a significant impact on a business and time is not a consideration, owners typically use a rational, multi-step approach to decide on a course of action. For less important matters or when pressed for time, they use a seat-of-the-pants approach.
- Formal problem solving or decision making involves (1) identifying the problem or opportunity, (2) listing the solutions or options, (3) evaluating the alternatives, (4) choosing a solution, and (5) acting on and evaluating that solution.
- Both the nominal grouping and Delphi techniques bring people together for group decision making. However, nominal grouping brings them together in person, while the Delphi technique brings them together on paper only.
- Effective goal setting involves (1) putting your goals in writing, (2) making sure they are measurable, (3) making sure they are at once attainable and challenging, and (4) setting deadlines for their achievement.

Reviewing Vocabulary

1. The word *hypothesis* is not defined in the chapter. Look the word up in a dictionary. Then write an explanation of why it would be used in the rational approach to decision making.
2. For each of the following vocabulary terms, write a sentence that uses the term in a way that shows you understand its meaning.

   - rational approach
   - satisficing
   - brainstorming
   - criteria
   - nominal grouping
   - Delphi technique
   - consensus

Checking the Facts

1. What type of approach—rational or seat-of-the-pants—would you use to make a routine business decision? Why?
2. What factors make a business decision nonroutine?
3. Why is it important to look for the cause of a problem?
4. You've narrowed down the possible solutions to a problem to three. Describe two commonly used methods of making a final choice.
5. What is the goal of the Delphi technique?
6. When setting goals, why is it important to put them in writing?

Thinking Critically

1. How does the rational approach to problem solving and decision making differ from the seat-of-the-pants approach?
2. Briefly describe a situation in which a formal decision-making process would be appropriate—and one in which it would not be.
3. Suppose you carefully follow the formal decision-making process to solve a problem, and your solution does not work. What will you do?
4. Describe two kinds of problems or two business situations—one for which the nominal grouping technique would be most effective

Chapter 6 Review

and another for which the Delphi technique would give the best results. Explain the reasons for your choice.

Discussing Key Concepts

1. How do *you* determine the amount of risk you are willing to take when you make a decision?
2. Can you think of any other factors that might affect the decision-making process? What are they?
3. Do you believe it is possible to achieve anything of importance without setting a goal? Why or why not?

Using Basic Skills

Math

1. You have saved $5,000 that you want to invest in one of three new businesses. The table below tells you what your expected profit will be after one year for each of the businesses and the probability that you will earn that profit. Based solely on the information given, in which business would you invest and why? (*Hint:* Calculate the expected value for each profit.)

Company	A	B	C
Projected profit after 1 year	$5,000	$10,000	$8,000
Probability	.50	.20	.30

Communication

2. Your new restaurant has been hiring high school students to work part-time, but you are experiencing higher-than-normal turnover. Select five "employees" from among your classmates. Then use one of the group decision-making techniques discussed in this chapter to analyze the problem and come up with a solution.

Human Relations

3. Your assistant has come to you asking for a raise. Unfortunately, your business has been experiencing a slow period, and you don't feel you can spare any money for raises at this time. What would you do?

Enriching Your Learning

1. Using the goal-setting guidelines in this chapter, write a one-page description of three of your goals for the next year.
2. Visit three car dealerships in your community and gather buyer information on three cars that you would like to own. Be sure to obtain price data for both vehicles and any options you desire. Then evaluate your alternatives:

   - Set up criteria for the options and features you want, weighting them according to their importance to you.
   - Set up a table similar to Figure 6–2, comparing the three vehicles.
   - Calculate the weighted cost of each car to identify the best choice for you.

UNIT THREE
Creating Your Small Business

Chapter 7
Selecting Your Field

Objectives

After completing this chapter, you will be able to

- list the steps involved in selecting an area for self-employment,

- recognize sources of self-employment ideas,
- evaluate options for self-employment, and
- apply a decision-making strategy to self-employment options.

Terms to Know

entrepreneurial
  process
unique
trade magazines
specialty
  magazines
trade shows
transferable skills

Decisions, Decisions

Today I attended my first Young Entrepreneurs Club meeting. They had a panel of guest speakers—three people who started their own businesses at home. One of them prints T-shirts. Another has a machine shop in his garage. The third runs a drop-off nursery for parents who need a baby-sitter when they go shopping.

The panel told us how they got started—why they went into business for themselves, what kinds of problems they ran into, how they coped. Every one of them had had some rough times in the beginning, but now they all seem to be doing pretty well.

I know the whole thing was planned to be upbeat and encouraging, but somehow it didn't hit me that way. You see, what impressed me most about all of the people on the panel was how sure they seemed to be. They were sure about themselves, about what they were doing, about entrepreneurship in general. I can't say I feel that way. For instance, they all seemed to know exactly what they wanted to do right off, but I don't. I know I like the idea of being my own boss, but I don't do anything that could be turned into a money maker. I don't make my own clothes. I'm not good with kids. I'm certainly no machinist or anything like that.

What are people like me supposed to do? What if you think you'd like to have your own business, but you're just not sure what that business should be?

Getting Started

With this chapter, you begin the **entrepreneurial process**—the steps involved in creating a business. These steps include planning, gathering information, and making decisions about a whole range of topics.

With the chapters in this Unit as your guide, you will investigate potential markets, business sites, and legal forms of ownership. You will plan for everything from equipment and inventory to employees. You will physically lay out promotional materials, floorplans, and even a record-keeping system. You will develop a clear picture of your financial needs. By the time you are finished, you will know if you can make your business idea a reality.

But we're getting ahead of ourselves. First, you need that idea. You need to decide what business to go into.

Some entrepreneurs choose their field because they already have extensive experience with it. They've worked in a family business or held jobs with other employers. Other entrepreneurs choose their field by a more formal decision-making process. They identify and weigh their options.

This chapter focuses on the second, more formal way to make a choice. It discusses sources of ideas for self-employment and suggests some considerations in evaluating those ideas. It also provides a procedure for arriving at a final decision. *Note:* If you have already settled on a particular entrepreneurial venture, you can use this process to confirm your choice.

Listing Your Options

The first step in selecting your field is to identify all your options. These might be expressed in terms of general interests or specific ideas.

The identification of options will require an active and thorough effort on your part. While you might find some ideas close at hand, others will come to you only after a wider search. Since your ultimate goal is to find just the right endeavor, don't overlook any possibilities.

Consider Your Own Experiences

Self-employment options within your own experience are the easiest to identify. Here are some sources:

IDEAS PAST AND PRESENT. Since you started reading this text, some ideas for entrepreneurial ventures have probably already occurred to you. Before you go any further, write these down (along with any other possibilities you may have thought of in the past). Don't just trust that you will remember them when the time comes to make a choice. Everyone has good ideas, but if they aren't recorded, they tend to drift away.

Keep your list in a small notebook, and keep the notebook with you throughout your research. That way you can write down additional ideas as they come to mind.

HOBBIES. Many hobbies can be turned into successful ventures. Making stained glass, tying fishing flies, knitting, restoring cars—these are just a few pastimes that have such potential.

Step back and try to evaluate your own favorite pastime in terms of its business potential. Be sure to look beyond the obvious (selling any good or service your hobby produces). Consider, for example, the needs of your fellow hobbyists. What equipment, supplies, or special arrangements do they require to pursue their hobby? What kinds of problems or inconveniences do they face on a regular basis? Are there any

Businesses based on hobbies can involve far more than just selling the end product of the activity. What more imaginative approach is shown here?

changes on the horizon that might affect their pastime? Answers to questions like these may suggest a way for you to turn your hobby (or an activity related to it) into a profit-making enterprise.

WORK. If you're working after school, you have another source of ideas for business opportunities. Again, it's a matter of trying to view something familiar—in this case, the company you work for—from a slightly different perspective. Ask yourself: Is there room in the market for a similar business, possibly in a different niche? Are there any gaps in the company's network of suppliers? Are the company or its customers in need of services that aren't being provided? Alternate niches, gaps, unmet needs—all are indicators of potential business opportunities.

If you are not employed, think about casual or summer jobs you may have done, such as baby-sitting or cutting lawns. Could a business be created to fill any of those needs?

AREAS OF INTEREST. Because of your own likes and dislikes, you will probably find that some areas of self-employment are inherently more appealing to you than others. Turn back to Figure 1–1 on page 12, and review the areas of entrepreneurial opportunity and examples listed there. Which catch your imagination? Which do not?

CREATIVE APPROACHES. Entrepreneurs often find their opportunities in **unique** approaches to traditional businesses. The dental hygienist who travels to clients' homes or workplaces to clean their teeth, the delivery service that delivers for several florists out of the same trucks—these are examples of such approaches.

Make a note of any unique approaches that you are familiar with. Think about them. Can they be applied to any businesses you are interested in? If not, can you use them as a jumping-off point for some unique approaches of your own?

succumb to it. To find business opportunities you must keep your focus on that objective. You must constantly remind yourself by asking, What self-employment opportunities does this present to someone with my interests?

TRADE MAGAZINES. **Trade magazines** are periodicals published for specific types of businesses or industries. They often contain articles on new products, services, or business concepts that are expected to do well. But anything in such a publication—a news article, a feature, or even an ad—can trigger an idea for a new venture.

Most trade magazines are available only to those who are already in a particular field, usually through membership in a trade organization. Therefore, you may have to obtain copies from businesspeople or vocational instructors in the field.

SPECIALTY MAGAZINES. Publications targeted to people with interests in sports, camping, fashion, and a variety of other areas can also provide ideas for new business ventures. Articles in such **specialty magazines** won't ordinarily point out opportunities. However, they can help identify interests and needs of potential consumers.

Consult Outside Sources

Additional ideas for entrepreneurial opportunities can be found by using external sources. These are sources outside your usual environment or personal experiences. They include people, places, and things in the business community and the community at large.

Exploring these sources presents one special problem—the tendency to lose sight of your objective. Many of these sources will present you with a wide variety of ideas in exceptionally appealing formats. These may include the glossy pages of a magazine, an attractive storefront, or an eye-catching exhibit with hands-on displays and attentive salespeople. The temptation to browse in these circumstances, sampling everything that momentarily catches your attention regardless of its relevance, will be great. Don't

Trade magazines devote themselves to all aspects of particular industries. What industries would most likely interest readers of these publications?

Risk Takers, Profit Makers

Casey Golden

The wooden tees used by golfers weigh less than half an ounce each. The wooden tees used (and lost or left behind) by golfers *every year* tip the scales at nearly 4.5 million pounds! Thanks to Casey Golden, however, golfers wishing to cut down their handicaps need no longer cut down trees in the process.

At 11, Golden, a Denver native and aspiring professional golfer, developed an alternative. From flour, fertilizer, water, seeds, applesauce, and moss, he perfected a biodegradable golf tee.

Golden began developing his ecologically friendly product in 1989, when he was in the sixth grade. Whenever he and his father played golf, the younger Golden was always required to pick up the tees that littered the course—even if they weren't his. His father, a former greenskeeper, would explain that broken and discarded tees damaged the mowers used to tend the grounds. They also looked bad. Those reasons, however, didn't make the younger Golden's chore any more appealing. He wanted the tees to go away— to just dissolve.

Golden started working on that idea for an after-school class called Creative Analysis. In the family kitchen, he molded, baked, and sanded tees made from a variety of ingredients. (One combination actually exploded in the microwave oven.) Eventually, though, Golden came up with a workable formula. He then standardized the production process by using a caulking gun tip to mold the mixture.

Success was swift. The tee won Golden an award from the Invent America! contest for grade-school students. He received a savings bond and a trip to Washington, D.C. His school received funding for computer equipment. His parents, however, saw the potential for far greater rewards.

The Goldens began consulting course superintendents on the prospects for their son's award-winning tee. They learned, among other things, that the seeds and fertilizer in the tees would taint the meticulously tended teeing areas with foreign grasses. Those ingredients were promptly removed from the formula.

Most of what the Goldens heard, however, was positive. So, with 15 investors they launched Bio-Dynamics, Ltd., to market what was called the BIO*tee*.

Golfers instantly recognized the BIO*tee*'s benefits. Used and broken tees could be simply and safely left behind. Greenskeepers could spend less time tending grounds. Equipment operators would be less prone to injuries from flying tees or tee fragments. They would also spend less time fixing dulled or damaged mower blades. And for everyone there was the satisfaction of using an ecologically sound product.

NEWSPAPERS. Newspapers provide an on-going source of ideas for businesses. Many have business sections which, like other business publications, report on trends and innovations. Beyond the business pages, other sections usually monitor social, political, entertainment, and other events. These also can be a source of ideas.

TRADE SHOWS AND EXHIBITIONS. Nearly every field has national and/or regional **trade shows**. The purpose of these events is to allow vendors and manufacturers to introduce new items and promote established products and services. Exhibits at these shows can be a source of spin-off ideas. So can conversations with vendors, suppliers, and customers willing to talk about their needs.

PERSONAL CONTACTS. Among the adult relatives, co-workers, and friends whose opinions you respect, there are probably some with a knowledge of the local business scene. Their ideas about good (and poor) opportunities for entrepreneurs in your community can provide useful additions to your list of potential options.

VISUAL OBSERVATIONS. A drive around town for the purpose of identifying business opportunities can be very revealing. It should give you some idea of which types of ventures are doing well and which are not. You may also be able to identify needs that are going unmet by existing businesses.

GOVERNMENT AGENCIES. Information regarding specific opportunities as well as trend information can also be obtained from federal agencies. The U.S. Patent Office, for example, can provide information on patents that are available for public use. Names and addresses of organizations that can provide information on any topic are available through the National Referral Service in the Library of Congress. A survey of current business conditions is published by the Bureau of Economic Analysis in the Department of Commerce.

THE INTERNATIONAL SCENE. As noted in Chapter 1, international opportunities are

Trade shows, like trade magazines, can be a rich source of ideas for entrepreneurial ventures. What do these two sources have in common? In what respects might trade shows actually be a superior source of ideas?

becoming increasingly accessible to entrepreneurs. A review of the international trends discussed in that chapter may suggest some ideas to you.

Some SBA offices—particularly those close to Canada, Mexico, and major U.S. export centers—are looking for ways to help small businesses get into international markets. They may be able to provide some very specific ideas. Also, business periodicals and newspapers frequently highlight international opportunities.

Weighing Your Options

The next step in determining what business you should go into is to evaluate each of your options in terms of (1) its soundness and (2) its appropriateness for you. The purpose at this stage is to see how your options stack up against each other. Your final decision should be deferred until all the possibilities have been thoroughly examined.

Is It a Good Idea?

In the process of developing your list of options, the emphasis was on generating sheer numbers of ideas. Practical concerns were brushed aside for the moment in the interest of uncovering every possibility.

Many of the ideas you identified in this process probably represent good business opportunities. Some, however, do not. Asking the following questions about each option will help you sort out those that are sound. (A sound venture is one that has a genuine potential for success and can realistically be undertaken.)

- Would this business have an advantage over existing businesses?
- Would this business require a big change in buyer behavior in order to be successful?
- Would customers be receptive to the business concept (particularly if it is a nontraditional approach)?
- Would customers easily recognize the benefits the business provides?
- Would customers view the business as a way of satisfying their needs?
- Could the business be put into operation in a reasonable period of time?
- Is the business worth doing?

Another indicator of an idea's soundness is the failure rate of businesses in the field. Periodically, business magazines publish articles on the small businesses most likely to succeed (or fail). Businesses on these lists change over time, depending on economic conditions and shifts in consumer tastes. Dun & Bradstreet also publishes an annual report that analyzes business failure rates in specific fields. Checking the most recent Dun & Bradstreet report at your local library can be very helpful in weighing your options.

Is It a Good Idea for You?

By the standards described above, several of your options may qualify as good ideas. All of them, however, may not work well for you. To determine which ones will, you should consider two crucial factors.

YOUR EXPERIENCE. Do you have the necessary experience in the field to succeed as an entrepreneur? How much and what kind of experience is necessary will depend on the nature of the field.

In businesses that are highly technical or complex, you would have a difficult time succeeding without a solid background in the field. For example, suppose you wanted to start a software design firm. You would need to know a great deal about computers and computer programming. You would probably need either a college degree in computer science or years of "hacking." (Hacking refers to hands-on experience experimenting with computers in an informal setting.)

For many businesses, however, experience in almost any field will help you operate a venture effectively. Working as a salesclerk, for example, can provide you with the "people skills" needed to succeed in any business that involves contact with the public. Skills that carry over in this fashion are often called **transferable skills**.

But what if you find yourself strongly attracted to an area in which you have no applicable experience? Keep two things in mind. First, there are relatively uncomplicated businesses (especially in the service area) that can be learned by doing. Running a housekeeping service, copy shop, or mail center fall in this category. Second, it is possible for you to gain experience in a field before you launch your venture. Suppose you've never been a cook or waiter, but you're set on having your own restaurant. Then go to work for a restaurant owner whose establishment you admire. Make the training part of your plan.

THE ENJOYMENT FACTOR. A second key consideration in evaluating your good ideas is whether you would enjoy doing the kind of work involved. Owning your own business requires an enormous commitment of time, energy, and thought. Things don't always go the way you planned. Unexpected problems arise. Bills sometimes come due before the money comes in.

Relating to people in a helpful way is a valuable skill that a salesclerk can use in an entrepreneurial endeavor. What other transferable skills might people with such experience have developed on the job?

Employees quit unexpectedly. Suppliers fail to deliver. If you don't like what you're doing, events like these can quickly overwhelm you. By contrast, if you're excited about your business, you'll be eager and willing to do whatever is necessary to overcome such obstacles. You'll view them as challenges rather than problems. This, in turn, will increase the likelihood of your success.

Making Your Decision

You should try to avoid coming to a final decision while you are in the process of weighing your options. Nonetheless, as you sift through your ideas, some will inevitably begin to rise to the top of your list while others fall. You will want to keep these preferences in mind as you begin making your decision.

During your research, your list of options should have taken on a very specific character.

You might have started out with a list of general fields. By now, though, you should have a list of specific types of businesses. If you haven't been able to narrow your choices in this way, you should go back and do more research. If you have, you're ready to make a decision.

The decision-making process at this point has two steps:

- *Step 1—Narrow your list of options.* Review all your choices and delete any that you have disqualified as a result of the weighing process.
- *Step 2—Rank the remaining items.* Number your first choice one, your second choice two, and so on to the end of your list.

This procedure allows you to view your options clearly in relation to each other. It thus ensures that you will make your best choice. In addition, the procedure guarantees that you will not have to repeat the entire process should it prove impossible for you to pursue your first choice. Your final list identifies your next-best option.

Entrepreneur's Bookshelf

To learn more about the subjects discussed in this chapter, consider reading these books:

- *So You've Got a Great Idea* by Steve Fuffer (© 1986)
- *101 Best Businesses to Start* by Sharon Kahn and the Philip Lief Group (© 1988)
- *Entrepreneur Magazine's 184 Businesses Anyone Can Start and Make a Lot of Money* (© 1990)

Chapter 7 Review

Recapping the Chapter

- The process of deciding what business to go into begins with identifying all the options and then narrowing down the list.
- Many ideas for self-employment lie within a prospective entrepreneur's own experience.
- Self-employment opportunities can also be found by researching the business community and community at large.
- Entrepreneurial options should be evaluated in terms of both their soundness as business opportunities and their appropriateness for the potential entrepreneur.
- Ranking options in order of preference is an effective way to make a final choice of an entrepreneurial venture.

Reviewing Vocabulary

Illustrate the terms below. Name a specific example for each, and explain how and why your choice is appropriate.

- unique
- trade magazines
- specialty magazines
- trade shows
- transferable skills

Checking the Facts

1. What is the first step in selecting a field for self-employment?
2. Why is it important that you write down ideas for entrepreneurial ventures as you think of them or find them?
3. List six external sources of ideas for entrepreneurial ventures.
4. In order to be considered a good business opportunity what would an idea have to have in comparison to existing businesses?
5. Where can an analysis of business failure rates be found?
6. In what types of entrepreneurial ventures would previous experience be crucial?
7. What is one reason why it is important that entrepreneurs enjoy the field of business they choose?

Thinking Critically

1. How could the process of selecting a business venture be applied if the prospective entrepreneur had already made a tentative decision? What value would the process have?
2. Of the two major source areas for entrepreneurial options (your own experience and external sources), which do you think would yield your best ideas for ventures? Why?
3. How could government agencies be of value in identifying entrepreneurial options?
4. Would information about failure rates in a field of business be of value to you if you had only the rates for the past year? Why or why not? How would you use such information?
5. In weighing your options, which consideration should you give more weight—your experience or your potential to enjoy the business? Explain your reasoning.
6. Refer to your own list of entrepreneurial options or Figure 1–1 (page 12).

   - Identify three businesses for which you think experience in the field would be necessary for success.

Chapter 7 Review

- Identify three for which you think no experience would be necessary.

In both cases, justify your choices.

Discussing Key Concepts

1. "Your first thought is always your best." When deciding what business to go into, should entrepreneurs observe this rule? Why or why not?
2. Which factor is most important when weighing your business options—the soundness of the business idea or its appropriateness for you? Explain your choice.
3. What kinds of businesses do you think are needed in your community? Why?
4. What is the best business for anyone to go into? Explain.
5. While ranking your entrepreneurial options in order of preference, you find that you can't decide which should be your first choice among the top three. What should you do?

Using Basic Skills

Math
1. For a business field you are interested in, the Dun & Bradstreet report shows that there were 45 failures per 10,000 concerns last year and 50 the year before. What was the percentage decrease in failures over the year-long period?

Communication
2. Check the trade association directory at your local library for the names and addresses of trade associations representing three business areas of particular interest to you. Write a letter to each requesting information about upcoming national and regional trade shows.

Human Relations
3. The school librarian has been extremely helpful in assisting you in your search for new business ideas. She has helped you locate trade publications and offered to track down some specialty magazines in areas of interest to you. This morning you received a note from her that several issues had arrived. The timing is fortunate because you are supposed to have your list compiled by tomorrow. When you get to the library, however, you find that the librarian had misunderstood and gathered periodicals related to a field of business in which you have no interest. How do you handle the situation?

Enriching Your Learning

1. Interview a business owner or someone whose business judgment you respect. Ask his or her opinion regarding good (and poor) opportunities in your community for entrepreneurs. Write a brief report on the individual's recommendations and comments.
2. Make a visual survey of the businesses or industries in your neighborhood. Look for what seems to be doing well, doing poorly, or doesn't exist. Write up your observations and draw conclusions regarding opportunities for new businesses. Include a brief rationale for each of your conclusions.

Chapter 8
Types of Business Ownership

Objectives

After completing this chapter, you will be able to

- identify three different ways to acquire your own business and describe the advantages and disadvantages of each,

- compare and contrast the various legal forms of business ownership, and
- explain why it is a good idea to consult an attorney prior to starting up a business.

Terms to Know

synergy
goodwill
franchise
franchisee
franchisor
trade credit
sole proprietor
partnership
general partners
limited partners
corporation
stock
equity
dividends

? Decisions, Decisions

I've always dreamed of owning my own business. I like having control over my time and responsibility for what I do. Besides, my family owns a restaurant, so I feel I have a pretty good idea of what it's like to run your own place.

This fall I'll be starting college. I'll be studying business—everything and anything that can help me with my plans. I figure if I live at home, work in the restaurant, and save, I can accumulate enough of a nest egg to go out on my own after graduation.

Naturally, though, my family has other ideas. They want me to join them at the restaurant as assistant manager. They're counting on me to take over after they retire.

What they don't seem to understand is that I'm as committed to "my business" as they are to their restaurant. You see, for years I've been tossing around this idea in my mind for a kind of personalized catering company. It would prepare gourmet meals for customers and bring them to their homes, table settings and all. I think I have the know-how and experience to pull it off. I certainly know the restaurant business, and I have lots of contacts in the industry, thanks to working for my parents.

But I do feel torn. My dad says I should start my business as an offshoot of the family's. I don't see how. It's not a gourmet place. As an alternative, he's suggested that he and I become partners in *my* business. (He insists you need family to make a go of things.) I think that arrangement has the same problem as the first one.

I just don't know. On my own, with my family, partners—what *is* the best choice?

Opportunities for Business Ownership

You've decided that you want to own your own business. Now the question is, How you are going to go about accomplishing that? There are three main possibilities:

- Taking over a family business
- Buying a business
- Starting a business of your own

The choice that works for you will depend on the kind of business you want, your financial resources, and your particular needs.

Whichever route you choose, it is important that you do your homework. Answering all the crucial questions before you start up a business will minimize the number of problems you encounter. It will also enhance your chances of success.

Entering the Family Business

One way to become an entrepreneur, if you have the option, is to go into the family business. Such enterprises, often called "mom and pop" businesses, are an important part of the U.S. economy. It is estimated that family businesses contribute about 40 percent of GNP and over one-half of all jobs nationally.

Family businesses are not generally high-growth businesses. Some, however, like Mattel Toys, have become very large, successful companies. At the same time, only about one-third of family-run businesses survive to the second generation.

THE UPSIDE—AND THE DOWN. The reason for so many failures lies in the dynamics of the family itself. The very advantages that family businesses have can often destroy them. The origins of this apparent contradiction can be seen in Figure 8–1. Notice how easily advantages can be turned into disadvantages.

In general, the greatest disadvantage of a family enterprise is that its owners can never get away from the business. As a result, they may have difficulty viewing the venture and its problems objectively.

The greatest advantage of a family business is rooted in the trust and togetherness that family members feel when they are with each other. Because of this feeling of unity, a family working as a team can often achieve more than all of its individual members working apart. This phenomenon, called **synergy,** can be a real asset in running a business.

In order to prevent some of the problems associated with family businesses, you should do the following:

- Establish clear lines of responsibility.
- Try to be objective about family members' qualifications.

Dynamics of Family Businesses

Family Dynamic	Advantages	Disadvantages	Solution
Confusion between business and family roles	Because business members are family, they tend to be more loyal and can make decisions quickly.	Drawing family issues into business can result in an inability to make decisions objectively.	■ Assign specific roles and responsibilities to family members. ■ Make it a rule not to bring business matters home.
Family history	Knowing each other's strengths and weaknesses can allow the most capable people to be assigned where they are needed.	Knowing too much about each other can prevent family members from growing and developing. There may be a tendency to focus on each other's weaknesses.	■ Establish responsibilities on the basis of track record. ■ Encourage family members to learn new areas of the business. ■ Hold regular meetings to air grievances.
Family emotions	When emotions are positive and supportive, they can create a sense of loyalty and sharing.	Negative emotions can result in an unhealthy work environment.	■ Make an effort to argue issues, not emotions. ■ Stick to the facts and leave your feelings out of business discussions.
Family members' needs	Respecting the needs of individual family members can lead to greater satisfaction and loyalty.	Not considering family members' individual needs can result in rivalries and a dysfunctional work environment.	■ Hold family meetings to discuss individual needs and goals.

Figure 8–1   The way that family members relate to each other can have a profound impact on a family business. What term used in this table refers to such patterns of behavior?

- Keep decisions unemotional, if possible.
- Respect individual family members' needs.

These practices can go a long way toward minimizing family conflicts.

QUESTIONS TO ASK YOURSELF. To decide if a family business is the best choice for you, ask yourself the following questions:

- Do I have the ability to work for a member of my family?
- Do I get along well with the family members who will be involved in the business?
- Do we share the same goals for the business?
- Do we share the same general goals for our personal lives?
- Can I leave business problems at work when I go home each night?

If you answered no to any one of these questions, you have identified a potential area of conflict. You will have to weigh the advantages of being in the family business against this potential problem. If the benefits are substantial, it might be worth your while to try to resolve the conflict.

Buying a Business

Another way to acquire a business is to buy one. In some cases, buying a business is less risky than starting one from scratch. It may also be an attractive alternative if you do not have a great deal of business experience.

Buying a business was the route taken by Ray Kroc. He acquired a hamburger stand from the McDonald brothers and turned it into the venture that launched the fast-food industry.

KINDS OF BUSINESSES AVAILABLE. The example of Ray Kroc highlights the two purchase options available. You can buy either an existing business or the right to set up a new business patterned on an existing model.

An existing business, of course, is one that already has a location and a physical plant. It may even have experienced employees and regular customers. The last are especially important. Their continued business after you take over enormously increases your chances of success. Such loyalty, called **goodwill**, is an extremely valuable business asset.

Goodwill does not attach just to an existing business. It can also attach to a business concept. Millions of people, for example, eat regularly at McDonald's—*any* McDonald's. The name itself has come to stand for a certain type of food prepared quickly and served in a clean and pleasant environment.

McDonald's is an example of a franchise. A **franchise** is a legal agreement to begin a new business in the name of a recognized company. Burger King, Kentucky Fried Chicken, and Taco Bell are other examples of fast-food (or service) franchises. Oldsmobile, Chrysler, and Chevrolet dealerships are examples of automobile (or product distribution) franchises.

The buyer of a franchise is called the **franchisee**; the seller, the **franchisor**. The franchisee is buying a way of operating a business—and a product with name recognition. The franchisor is selling its planning and management expertise.

If, for example, you buy a McDonald's franchise, you will be trained in that company's methods of operation. You will learn how to prepare McDonald's products. You will be supplied through McDonald's own distribution channels. You will have the benefit of the company's national advertising. All of these things are enormously helpful to owners who have never run a business let alone set one up. And all of them reduce the risk of failure.

A GOOD DEAL OR A BAD? Acquiring an existing business, then, has many potential advantages. We've already mentioned location, goodwill, staff, and plant. There are many others, each with a particular contribution to make.

For example, an existing business may have established procedures in place. (It's easier to modify a system than create one from scratch.) There may be substantial inventory and established

For inexperienced entrepreneurs, the support system provided by a franchise can make the difference between success and failure. What elements of that system are shown here?

trade credit. (Relationships with suppliers take a long time to build.) There may even be an owner willing to offer his or her expertise during the transitional period. (An experienced guide to show you the way is helpful in any endeavor.) *Note:* If you are buying a franchise, these sorts of things will certainly be available. They are part of the package you are buying.

So, who could ask for a better deal? The problem is that this may not be the deal that you are offered. You need to be aware of some pitfalls.

Many times a business is put up for sale precisely because it is *not* successful. It may be losing money. It may not be highly regarded. Its inventory may be dated; its equipment and facilities, in need of major repairs. Its employees may lack the skills needed to keep the business competitive. With all of this, it may be overpriced. (Business owners often value their businesses higher than the market does.)

What can you do to protect yourself against purchasing a business burdened with such negatives? You can do some research. Investigate both the company and the industry very carefully. Don't rely just on what the seller tells you. For example, the value of a retail business can be determined by verifying the value of its inventory, accounts receivable, and assets. Check these figures for yourself, or get an expert like an accountant to advise you.

If you are contemplating the purchase of a franchise, you face a different set of negatives. The first is cost. You get a great deal with a franchise, but you pay for it. Purchase prices are often very high. You may also have to pay a fee for advertising and a percentage of your sales on an annual basis.

A second negative is lack of freedom. In the beginning, the prepackaged system may inspire confidence, but it can become confining. The franchisor may limit your choices as to how you can run the business.

WHERE TO FIND A BUSINESS. People find available businesses in many ways. The simplest is to look in the newspaper. Businesses that are for sale are listed in local papers as well as national business publications like the *Wall Street Journal*.

One very effective way to locate a business is to begin networking with people in the community. Accountants, attorneys, bankers, and local government administrators are particularly good sources. Let these people know what kind of business you are looking for. Then keep in touch with them.

One last source is a business broker. This is a person who lists businesses for sale and whose job it is to bring buyers and sellers together. You can find business brokers in the telephone book.

QUESTIONS TO ASK YOURSELF. Before considering the acquisition of any company, you should ask yourself the following questions:

- *Is the business interesting to me and to others?* If you do purchase the business, you will be devoting a tremendous amount of time and effort to making it grow and succeed. Therefore, you will want to make sure that you

really enjoy it. Also, since you may eventually want to sell the business, it is important that others be interested in it, too.

- *Why is the owner selling?* Owners sell for many reasons—retirement, lack of interest, illness, need for cash. What you really want to know is if the owner is selling because the business is not doing well or the industry is in decline. One way to find out is to check the firm's financial statements against information from suppliers and competitors.

- *What is the business's potential for growth?* Businesses and industries have a life cycle, just like human beings. They are born, grow, mature, and eventually decline. The length of each stage in the cycle depends on the industry. Try to determine where the business you are considering is in the cycle. Don't be discouraged if you find that it is in the maturity stage. That may just signal that the enterprise needs a "shot in the arm," some new ideas that will take it in a different direction. However, it is probably best to avoid a business or industry that is in decline. By yourself, you can turn around an enterprise. You probably can't reverse an economic trend.

Starting Your Own Business

Suppose your family doesn't own a business and you can't find or don't want to buy an existing business. You may choose to start your own.

This was the route chosen by Mo Siegel of Celestial Seasonings. In his geographic area (Colorado), there were no herbal tea companies or related businesses. So, he decided to start his own.

WHAT YOU GAIN, WHAT YOU LOSE. Starting a new business generally entails more time and effort than the other options we have discussed. Think of all you have to do before you can even open your doors. After you determine for yourself that your venture is sound, you will have to prepare a business plan to convince others. You will have to find outside advisors like accountants, lawyers, and public relations consultants. You will need to lease facilities, purchase equipment, and hire employees. You will have to initiate relationships with suppliers, set up distribution channels, and establish name recognition. And that is only a partial list of start-up tasks.

There are some compensations for all this extra effort, however. The principal one is knowing that you can do things your own way, unencumbered by others' mistakes. By starting your own business, you avoid inherited weaknesses like bad organization, poor marketing, and weak management. You are free to build your company with fresh ideas and a beginner's enthusiasm.

QUESTIONS TO ASK YOURSELF. If after considering the soundness of your idea you still want to start your own business, you might ask yourself these additional questions:

- Do I have the motivation and persistence to start from nothing?
- Do I have sufficient knowledge of basic operations to undertake the business I am interested in?
- Do I have enough financial resources to start from scratch?

Applying for a DBA is often the first official step that entrepreneurs take in setting up their enterprises. What is this document, who issues it, and why is it needed?

Legal Forms of Business Ownership

Before opening the doors on your new business, you will need to decide on the legal form that it will take. Your three choices are sole proprietorship, partnership, and corporation. Each of these has variations. For purposes of our discussion, however, the basic forms are sufficient.

Sole Proprietorship

The sole proprietorship is the easiest and most popular form of business to create. Nearly 76 percent of all businesses in the United States are sole proprietorships.

In such businesses, the owner is the **sole proprietor**. This means that he or she is the only person responsible for the activities of the business. He or she is also the only one who receives the profits and is responsible for any losses.

FIRST STEPS. To operate as a sole proprietorship, you first need to decide on a business name. Will you use your own name for the company or another, unrelated name? If you choose the latter, you will need to apply for a Certificate of Doing Business Under an Assumed Name. This is often called a DBA (for "doing business as"). You obtain a DBA from the government of the community in which your business will operate. In filing for the certificate, you ensure that you are the only business in the area using the name that you have chosen.

Risk Takers, Profit Makers

Richard Topps

Richard Topps never dreamed of owning a successful Chicago flower shop. He only became involved with the flower industry as a part-time bookkeeper during college. So when he was told by his employer that he "didn't have what it takes" to be her business partner, he listened—and went into business for himself!

Topps didn't quit his job on the spot when he found out that his boss had cut him out of their planned partnership. Instead, he switched to night hours and studied business and floral design during the day. He did extensive library research on the details of running a business. He carefully targeted his market. (He would specialize in doing floral arrangements for restaurants, benefits, and corporate parties.)

Despite Topps's extensive preparation and detailed business plan, neither banks nor the SBA would give him a loan. Topps was forced to start up his business relying entirely on his own money. He plowed $45,000 of personal savings into his new business. Nine months after his former boss gave him the bad news, Topps Floral Design opened its doors.

In the end, the personal financing approach proved to be a good one. Having no loans to pay off, Topps turned a profit in a mere six months. In five years, he had a staff of three and was grossing over $200,000 annually.

Topps credits his success to the work ethic he learned from his parents, who once owned a farm. He says it helped him overcome the racism he encountered while attending a prestigious school of business. It also helped him deal with repeated rejections from skeptical advisors and unwilling lenders. Hard work tempered by patience—that, Topps believes, is what leads to success.

To keep business healthy, Topps stresses the quality of his product. This means that he has a higher break-even point than many other florists. However, Topps finds that by offering the freshest possible flowers, he keeps his customers happy—and loyal. He also justifies the added expense another way. Customer satisfaction, he stresses, is more important to his business since he does less advertising than most florists and relies heavily on word-of-mouth.

Today, Topps's stature reaches well beyond the floral industry. As a successful black businessperson, Topps frequently lectures at local high schools. Engaging and articulate, he has also appeared on television as a floral expert and community spokesperson.

If you are going to have employees, you will also need to apply to the Internal Revenue Service for an Employer Identification Number (EIN). The number facilitates federal income tax withholding and the filing of federal income tax returns.

SOME PROS AND CONS. The sole proprietorship has several advantages over other forms of ownership. It is easy and inexpensive to create. It allows the owner to have complete authority over all of the business's activities and to receive all of the profits. It is the least regulated form of ownership, and its income is generally taxed at a lower rate.

While these advantages may be enticing, sole proprietorships have several disadvantages as well. The principal ones are financial. To start, the owner has unlimited liability for all debts and actions of the business. This means that debts incurred by the firm may have to be paid from the owner's personal assets. In other words, the owner's home, car, and bank account could all be at risk. In addition, it is more difficult to raise capital for sole proprietorships. This is because the owner by him- or herself may not have sufficient assets to qualify for a loan.

Other disadvantages center on the owner as a person. A sole proprietorship can be limited by its total reliance on the abilities and skills of the owner. These simply may not be sufficient to keep the enterprise going. Finally, the death of the owner automatically dissolves the business.

Partnership

In a **partnership** two or more people own a business and share in the assets, liabilities, and profits. Therefore, as a legal form the partnership compensates for some of the shortcomings of a sole proprietorship. Specifically, the business can draw on the skills, abilities, and financial resources of more than one person.

THE PARTNERSHIP AGREEMENT. The law does not require a partnership to be based on a written agreement. Nonetheless, it is a good idea to have one.

Partnership agreements are usually drawn up by attorneys based on the Uniform Partnership Act. Typically, agreements answer questions about profit sharing among partners, business responsibilities, and what happens if one of the partners dies or quits.

A well-written partnership agreement can help joint owners avoid problems that are likely to arise between them in the course of operating their business. How?

GENERAL VS. LIMITED PARTNERS. A partnership may be set up so that all of the partners are **general partners**. This would mean that they all have unlimited personal liability and take full responsibility for the management of the business. The law requires that every partnership have at least one general partner.

Partners do not have to share equally in the business, however. Sometimes a business seeks **limited partners**. Essentially, these are investors whose liability is limited to their initial investment. So, if a limited partner invests $10,000 in your business, the most that partner can lose if your business fails is $10,000. The important point to remember about limited partners is that they cannot be actively involved in the management of the business. If they are, they lose their limited liability status.

SOME SPECIAL DIFFICULTIES. The advantages of a partnership are similar to those of a sole proprietorship. The form is fairly inexpensive to create, and the general partners have complete control. But partnerships have other benefits as well. They include group synergy, the stimulation of shared ideas, and the availability of more investment capital.

Despite these advantages, the partnership is the least preferred form of ownership. Why? Because it is at best a fragile entity.

For example, it is very difficult to dissolve one partner's interest in the business without dissolving the entire partnership. In other words, if one of the partners wants to pull out or dies, that terminates the business. Only if provisions to the contrary have been placed in the partnership agreement is the business likely to survive.

The major threat that partnerships face, however, is the potential for devastating personality conflicts. This factor results in more partnership dissolutions than any other. Generally problems start as disagreements about personal power and authority. They arise because of a failure to specify in the partnership agreement who is responsible for what.

There are other, more technical disadvantages as well. Partners, for example, are bound by the laws of agency. This means that they can be held liable for each others' actions. Thus, if one partner signs a contract agreeing to buy all of the business's raw materials from one supplier, the other partner must honor this arrangement. Otherwise the business can be sued for breach of contract.

MAKING IT WORK. Partnerships start with the best of intentions. Just as in a marriage or a relationship with a best friend, however, disagreements are bound to occur. It is important, therefore, that partners consider each other's needs before committing the partnership to anything. It is even more important that they plan for the disagreements that will inevitably occur.

As an example of these techniques, consider a business partnership that works—Randy and Debbi Fields of Mrs. Fields Cookies. From the beginning, they found that they could work well together *because* they divided responsibilities based on their interests and past experiences. Randy took care of finance and computers, while Debbi was responsible for everything else. On major strategy, they shared the decision making—with the understanding, of course, that when they disagreed, Debbi's ideas would win out!

In general, your partnership has the greatest chance of surviving if you and your partner(s) do the following:

- Share business responsibilities.
- Put things in writing.
- Always be honest about how the business is doing.

Corporation

A **corporation** is very different from the other two forms of ownership. It is a business that is chartered, or registered, by a state and legally operates apart from its owner(s). In other words, a corporation can live on after the owners have sold their interests or died.

A COMPLICATED FORM. Corporations are more complex than sole proprietorships and partnerships, both in the way they are created and in the way they operate. Usually an attorney will guide you through the incorporation process. This includes the filing of a Certificate of Incorporation with the state in which the company will be operating. It also includes issuing **stock**—certificates indicating the amount of **equity,** or ownership, each investor has in the business. Corporations are also required to have a board of directors. This body meets periodically to make policy decisions. It also selects the chief executive officer and chief financial officer.

FINANCIAL CONSIDERATIONS. Financially, the corporation has some distinct advantages over the other two forms of ownership. First and foremost, it has a relatively easier time raising money. It does so by issuing shares of stock. It can continue increasing its stock offerings up to the amount authorized in its charter.

Another important financial advantage is the limited liability a corporation offers its owners, or shareholders. Like limited partners, they are

Legal Forms of Ownership—A Comparison

Legal Issues	Sole Proprietorship	Partnership	Corporation
Number of owners	One	No limit	No limit on number of shareholders
Start-up costs	Filing fees for DBA and business license	Attorney's fees for partnership agreement, filing fees for DBA	Attorney's fees for incorporation documents, filing fees, taxes, and state fees
Liability	Owner liable for all actions of business	All partners liable for actions of business, but limited partners liable only to amount invested	Shareholders liable only to amount invested; officers may be personally liable for full amounts owed
Continuity of business	Dissolves on death of owner	Dissolves on death of general partner, unless partnership agreement states otherwise; not so on death of limited partner	Not affected by death of shareholders
Control of business	Rests entirely with owner	Shared equally by general partners	Rests with shareholders who own majority of stock*
Distribution of profits	All to owner	Shared as specified in partnership agreement	Paid to shareholders according to amount invested
Transfer of interest	Owner can sell business at any time	General partner requires consent of other general partners to sell interest; limited partner's ability to sell depends on partnership agreement	Shareholders free to sell at any time unless restricted by agreement

*Day-to-day control rests with management hired by board of directors

Figure 8–2   The various legal forms of ownership differ in ways that can make one form more appropriate for a business than another. Suppose an engineer who has very little cash wishes to set up a manufacturing business that requires many employees and a great deal of expensive equipment. What legal form would be best?

liable only up to the amount of their individual investments. Note, however, that this rule may not apply fully to new companies. Many banks and creditors require them to have corporate officers who will personally guarantee any debt that the business takes on. In such a case, the officers lose the protection of the corporation.

For most entrepreneurs, however, the corporate form poses more basic financial problems. For one, it is expensive to set up. It takes a good deal of time and between $500 and $2,500 in attorneys' and other fees to create a corporation. For another, its income is more heavily taxed.

Specifically, corporate income is taxed twice. The corporation pays federal taxes (and sometimes state and local taxes as well) on its profits. From these profits, in turn, it pays its stockholders earnings, or **dividends**. The stockholders must then pay personal income taxes on their dividends.

It is possible, however, to avoid this double taxation by setting up a business as a Subchapter S corporation. This is a special kind of corporation reserved for small businesses. (For example, the corporation can have only 35 shareholders.) The beauty of a Subchapter S corporation is that it is taxed like a sole proprietorship or partnership. Profits pass through the corporation and are taxed only once, at the shareholder level and rate.

REGULATION AND CONTROL. Finally, corporations face some obstacles that other forms of business do not. Because of their limited liability and ease of capital formation, they are subject to increased governmental oversight. This means that they are required to file numerous reports with government agencies. Sole proprietorships and partnerships face substantially less regulation.

The founder of a corporation, the person who started the business, faces an additional risk with this form of ownership. He or she can lose control of the company. This can happen if enough shares of stock are bought by others. To prevent such a situation, some corporations offer no more than 49 percent of their stock to the public.

To determine which of the legal forms of ownership would be best for your enterprise will take careful thought. Be sure to consider the features, advantages, and disadvantages of each before you choose. Figure 8–2 can serve as a starting point. It provides a summary comparison of all three forms.

The Need for an Attorney

After reading this chapter, you should understand that owning a business is a serious undertaking. It has not only personal consequences but also serious financial and legal consequences as well. As such it should only be done with the advice of an attorney.

Hiring an experienced business attorney may be costly. In the end, however, it will probably save you money. It is, after all, an attorney's job to foresee difficulties that you may not. In Chapter 12 you will learn in more detail about the ways that attorneys can help you through the legal requirements associated with starting and owning a business.

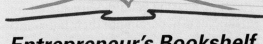

Entrepreneur's Bookshelf

To learn more about the subjects discussed in this chapter, consider reading these books and articles:

- *Winners: The Successful Strategies Entrepreneurs Use to Build New Businesses* by Carter Henderson (© 1985)

- *"So You Want to Be Your Own Boss!"* by William Olsten, *Management World* (November–December 1986)

- *Franchise Opportunities Handbook*, U.S. Department of Commerce Publication

Chapter 8 Review

Recapping the Chapter

- You can acquire a business by taking over a family concern, buying an existing business or franchise, or starting your own enterprise.
- The close personal ties that are a family business's principal advantage can also be its downfall.
- Buying an existing business is less risky for an entrepreneur, especially if that business has been successful.
- Starting a business from scratch demands more time and effort than other options but allows entrepreneurs to do things their own way, unencumbered by others' mistakes.
- The three basic legal forms of business ownership are sole proprietorship, partnership, and corporation.
- The sole proprietorship is the easiest form of business to create and gives the owner full responsibility for business activities, profits, and liabilities. In a partnership these responsibilities are shared by two or more owners, although not necessarily equally. In a corporation, profits and liabilities are shared by stockholders according to their initial investments in the company.
- By consulting an attorney before acquiring or starting up a business, you can avoid costly difficulties that you yourself may not have foreseen.

Reviewing Vocabulary

Assume that you are an attorney who is being consulted by a would-be entrepreneur. In a paragraph or two, explain the legal forms of ownership to your client. Use at least ten of the following vocabulary terms.

- synergy
- goodwill
- franchise
- franchisee
- franchisor
- trade credit
- sole proprietor
- partnership
- general partners
- limited partners
- corporation
- stock
- equity
- dividends

Checking the Facts

1. What are the sources of synergy in a family business? What is its effect?
2. What are two ways to buy a business?
3. Before buying a business, what three questions should you ask yourself?
4. What are the advantages and disadvantages of starting your own business?
5. Which is the most popular form of business ownership in the United States?
6. In what respects is a partnership superior to a sole proprietorship as a business form?
7. Name three disadvantages of the corporation as a form of business ownership.

Thinking Critically

1. Compare and contrast buying an existing business and buying a franchise.

Chapter 8 Review

2. Assume you have a successful business. Would you change its form from sole proprietorship to corporation? Why or why not?

Discussing Key Concepts

1. Do you believe that most entrepreneurs own businesses for financial gain? If not, what do you feel their reasons are?
2. What are some special considerations you might have about taking over a family business in addition to those mentioned in the chapter?
3. Working with a classmate on a project is similar in many ways to a partnership. What are some advantages and disadvantages that you recall from that experience?
4. Think of a business that you would like to have. Would you buy an existing operation or start from scratch? Explain your reasoning.

Using Basic Skills

Math

1. Suppose that in your community last year 650 new jobs were created by start-up ventures. During that same period, business failures resulted in the loss of 325 jobs. What was the net amount of new job creation last year?

Communication

2. Your father wants you to join the family business, Calvert Plastics Corporation. This is not your only opportunity, however. Your best friend has an idea for a new business and wants you to come in as a partner. Analyze the pros and cons of each method of becoming an owner. Incorporate this information in a letter explaining to your father or your friend why you have decided against the offer you ultimately reject.

Human Relations

3. You and your best friend form a business partnership. All runs smoothly until one day your partner commits the firm to leasing more space than you feel it can afford. What can you do about this situation?

Enriching Your Learning

1. Interview three entrepreneurs in your community. Ask the following questions:

   - How did you acquire your business?
   - What is your business's legal form?
   - Did you choose that legal form? If so, why?
   - Has your business changed forms during your ownership? If so, how and why?

   Make a brief oral report of your findings to the class. Emphasize any reasons provided by your interviewees for selecting or changing forms.
2. Gather information on two businesses that are for sale in your community. In a written report, compare the advantages and disadvantages of each. Conclude with a brief discussion of which, if either, you would purchase and why.
3. Research the procedures involved in purchasing a franchise and prepare a five-minute presentation for the class.

Chapter 9

The Business Plan—
An Overview

Objectives

After completing this chapter, you will be able to

- tell what a business plan is and describe its components,

- explain the process involved in researching a business plan,
- name several sources of business plan information, and
- identify the purposes of a business plan.

Terms to Know

business plan
organization chart
job descriptions
resumes
market analysis
marketing mix
pro forma
feasibility

Decisions, Decisions

I was really excited about being an entrepreneur—until today, when I found out about business plans. What a waste of time!

I looked at a sample our teacher, Mr. Miller, put on reserve at the library. The thing must have been 40 pages long. The forms alone were unbelievable. There must have been a dozen financial statements—just column after column of figures. And get this. They were all made up. They were projections! There was no guarantee that things would actually work out that way.

Unfortunately, I've already talked to a loan officer from my bank. She told me they like you to have a written plan for a business loan. You'd think a bank would put a premium on efficiency, but this business plan thing sounds like a lot of needless duplication. I mean, I won't know what I should put into a plan until after I've talked to all the people I'll need to talk to. But by then I won't need a plan because I'll have sat down and figured things out. I'll know everything I need to know, and I can just tell the people at the bank.

Amazing—I'll be ready to open my business, and they'll be ready for me to shuffle papers. Wouldn't it make more sense just to go for it?

What Is a Business Plan?

A **business plan** is a written proposal addressed to potential lenders or investors. Typically, it describes a new business and tells why it is deserving of financial support.

Doing a business plan involves a great deal of research. Because there is so much information to be drawn from so many different sources, you can easily feel overwhelmed. This chapter, by providing you with an overview, should help avoid that response.

The chapter describes in broad terms the major parts of a business plan and suggests a way to organize the information you find. It leaves the details for later. (They will be developed in Chapters 10–20.)

Parts of a Business Plan

There is no one correct format for a business plan. Plans are as varied as the businesses they describe. Some are very long, complex, and detailed. Others are relatively short and simple. Some have no more than six or seven major parts. Others have ten or more. Some include a particular type of information, while others do not.

Ultimately, the content and format of your business plan will depend on two main factors. The first is the type of business you wish to start. A plan for a manufacturing business, for example, would discuss at length the production process to be used. That would be central to the business. Such a discussion, however, would have no place in a plan for a wholesale business. It would devote more space to describing relationships with manufacturers and retailers.

The second factor influencing your business plan is the preferences of those who will be reading the document. Certain lenders or investors may require information that others do not. To appeal to these people, you may have to add documents or whole sections to your plan.

Given all of these variables, how *do* you know what to include in your plan? Even among the most diversely formatted business plans, there are some common features. Certain elements, in one form or another, are part of every plan.

STATEMENT OF PURPOSE. The "purpose" required here is the purpose of the plan, not the business. That purpose is to encourage others to lend you money. Therefore, the section should explain the reason for the loan. It should also specify the amount you are applying for, the type of loan, and the amount of time you will need for repayment.

Most lenders will also want to know how much money you will be investing in the business. They will want to know that you have enough confidence in your venture to risk your own money.

BUSINESS SUMMARY. The summary should include little more than the proposed name and location and a brief statement of the nature of the business. It should also specify the names of the owners and the legal form of ownership (sole proprietorship, partnership, etc.).

BUSINESS DESCRIPTION. Now, with the preliminaries out of the way, you can get down to specifics. This section allows you to present a picture of how your business will operate. Here you describe such things as physical layout, hours of operation, and the steps involved in getting your product to your customers.

You bolster this individual business information with research on the industry as a whole. From your findings you cite favorable trends or outlooks, appealing aspects of the business, and other factors that suggest probable success.

MANAGEMENT PLAN. This section has two parts. The first deals with and is based on three kinds of documents you are probably familiar with. You lay out management and employee responsibilities in visual form, through an **organization chart**. To detail the duties and responsibilities of company personnel, you use **job descriptions**. Finally, to indicate the skills and experience levels of individuals filling key positions, you provide short **resumes**.

The second part of the management plan discusses operations. It describes the business's policies on such day-to-day matters as credit, returns, deliveries, and customer service.

MARKETING PLAN. Before you can do a marketing plan, you have to do some **market analysis**. You have to research your potential customers, your proposed product or service, the competition, the market trends, and the available suppliers. You summarize this research and include the results as background before you present your actual marketing plan.

The plan itself should describe your marketing strategy. Specifically, it should present your decisions regarding the characteristics of your product, its price, the places where it will be sold, and its promotion. These four items, known as the four P's of marketing, comprise your **marketing mix**.

FINANCIAL PLAN. The financial section of a business plan is made up of a number of **pro forma**, or projected, financial statements. These can include profit and loss statements, cash flow projections, and balance sheets. They should be accompanied by an explanation of how the figures were arrived at and a statement of how any profits will be used.

APPENDIX. Any documentation that supports these business plan components is placed in an appendix. Here you might include proof of legal form of ownership, personal financial statements, personal income tax returns, and a personal resume. Any other documents that would round out the picture of your business for lenders could also go in this section. Possibilities include a cost-of-living budget; letters of reference and intent; promotional materials; and contracts, leases, and other legal documents.

Business Plan Research Process

Set Up Business Plan Notebook

Market Analysis

Marketing Mix

Legal Requirements

Equipment, Supplies, Inventory

Site Selection

Physical Layout

Protection of Business

Operations, Staffing

Promotion

Record Keeping

Draft Management Plan

Draft Financial Plan

Draft Marketing Plan

Finalize Business Plan

Figure 9–1   Three major plans comprise the final business plan. Which kinds of information contribute to the marketing plan? the financial plan?

How to Develop a Business Plan

Between learning what goes into a business plan and actually putting one together, there are many steps. Most of these correspond to areas that must be investigated. Figure 9–1, which lays out the whole research and writing process, shows these areas along its central axis.

If you compare those areas to the Table of Contents, however, you will see that they also correspond to the remaining chapters in this Unit. In other words, they track the steps in the entrepreneurial process. So, over the next 11 chapters, you will in fact be doing two things at once. You will be gathering information and making decisions about creating a new business. But since much of what you find out will work its way into your business plan, you will also be doing research for that document.

GATHERING INFORMATION.   As you work your way through the research process, you will quickly discover that doing a business plan is not a matter of "filling in the blanks." You cannot just go to the library one night to find out everything you need to know for your marketing section and then return the next night to do your management plan. The type of information you need does not lend itself to such a straight-line approach.

To start, data will not come to you in ideal form and sequence, according to the various business plan parts. For example, it will seldom fit neatly into one business plan category. Take site data. Some of it will go into the summary, some into the business description, and some into the marketing section.

Business plan research is also subject to more predictable complications. The information you find may be incomplete. It may need to be updated. It may require support or clarification. In all of these instances, you will have to consult multiple sources. You may even find yourself backtracking, consulting the *same* sources a second or possibly even third time.

ORGANIZING YOUR DATA.   Because you will be gathering a great deal of information from

Risk Takers, Profit Makers

Mona Garcia y Gold

It took a great deal of self-confidence—and a pronounced lack of squeamishness—for Mona Garcia y Gold to establish herself as a premiere New Mexico artist and entrepreneur. Personally, she persevered when no one else believed in her plan to fashion and sell "Bone Deco" artwork. Literally, though, her art required some strange raw materials—namely, leftover cows' heads from slaughter-houses.

But no one questions the Albuquerque artist's lofty goals or messy procedures any more. Today her Bone Deco cow skulls are prized by collectors worldwide.

Garcia y Gold stumbled upon her career in 1989 when she was a business student at the University of New Mexico. She wanted to decorate her house with cow skulls, so she picked some up from the local meat plant. When passersby noticed the cleaned and bleached skulls baking in her parents' yard, they stopped and asked about buying them. It was then that Garcia y Gold realized she could capitalize on the booming interest in Southwestern art. She invested $400 in bone preparation equipment and soon was in business.

However, Garcia y Gold wasn't content with just selling skulls. She wanted to leave her own artistic stamp on them. She wanted to embellish them with motifs that reflected the heritage of her family and of New Mexico. With no formal artistic training, she set about developing designs for the skulls. Then she took courses in entrepreneurship at the Albuquerque Technical-Vocational Institute. There, she received additional encouragement and became aware of her art's marketability. Finally, with the help of a vat designed by her father, she increased her production to 20 skulls a week.

Today Garcia y Gold is established in artistic circles. Her skulls, once impressed with her designs, retail for up to $425. They hang in galleries in North America, Asia, and Europe. She has won numerous artistic and entrepreneurship awards. She also lectures at schools and colleges, explaining the means and meaning of her work while encouraging students to make a living doing what they love.

Garcia y Gold herself is most pleased by her work because it explores and illustrates her heritage. Like her great-great-grandfather, Jake Gold who owned and operated Santa Fe's first trading post in 1816, she bridges cultures with her work. Each skull links past and present (the Southwest then and now) and art and science (O'Keeffe and anatomy). Through her art, Garcia y Gold breathes new life into empty skulls.

different sources, you should try to organize it as you go. If you keep the information you gather in reasonable order throughout the process, putting the pieces together at the end won't be too difficult.

One effective and uncomplicated technique you can use is to set up a business plan notebook (preferably loose-leaf). The notebook should have a separate section and at least one folder for each of the parts of your business plan. As you do your research, record your findings and conclusions in the appropriate section or sections. Then drop any literature, forms, or similar materials you have acquired into the related folders.

Only after you have done all your research will you be ready to put together a draft of your business plan. At that point, you sort out the data in your various notebook sections. You do your financial calculations. You make your key decisions. Then you write.

Once you have completed your first draft, you can evaluate all the parts of your plan together. If any obvious gaps or inconsistencies emerge, you may have to do a little more research. At the very least, you will have to make some adjustments. Once you have finalized your plan's components, you can assemble the finished document.

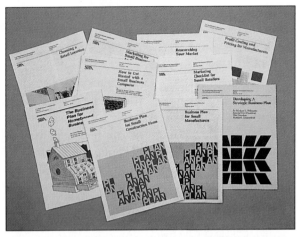

New entrepreneurs often begin their business plan research with SBA publications like these. What other source might provide similar publications for specific types of businesses?

Sources of Information

Where should you start gathering information for a business plan? With two categories of sources that provide general assistance to entrepreneurs. First are agencies whose primary purpose is to assist entrepreneurs. Second are agencies and firms with whom entrepreneurs do business.

SMALL BUSINESS ADMINISTRATION (SBA). The SBA is a federal agency. It provides many services to small businesses and several that are of special interest to new entrepreneurs. For a minimal charge the agency offers a number of publications on the start-up and growth of small businesses. It also provides special assistance programs for women, minorities, and the handicapped. Finally, it offers financial assistance, mainly in the form of loan guarantees. (In other words, the agency promises to pay if the borrower does not.)

The SBA has district offices in most major metropolitan areas. These offices serve as hubs for agency activities. They conduct seminars for entrepreneurs and prospective entrepreneurs. They also provide consulting services and information on local sources of business opportunities and financial assistance. Finally, the Service Corps of Retired Executives (SCORE) works out of SBA district offices. Its members provide free advisory assistance to entrepreneurs.

SMALL BUSINESS DEVELOPMENT CENTERS (SBDCS). These centers provide individual counseling and management assistance to existing and prospective entrepreneurs. They are generally located at community colleges and universities.

CHAMBERS OF COMMERCE. Local chamber offices serve as clearinghouses for information about the local economy, business trends, and business needs. In many cities, chambers of commerce have a small business development and assistance program as a part of their operation. In addition, they often serve as the contact point for SCORE representatives in cities not served by an SBA district office.

STATE AGENCIES. Every state has agencies or offices that concern themselves with new business development. Usually they operate out of the state's department of commerce and offer general assistance to entrepreneurs.

Some states have special offices that assist entrepreneurs in dealing with state agencies. Staff members attempt to resolve problems and assist minority and female entrepreneurs. These offices can be located by calling the information number for your state capital.

TRADE ASSOCIATIONS. These organizations offer both technical and general assistance to entrepreneurs in the profession or industry they represent. Trade associations can supply information such as average start-up and operating costs, trend analysis, research involving state-of-the-art technology, and supplier contacts. They can be identified by consulting trade association directories at your local library.

OTHER SOURCES. There are many other sources that can provide you with specific operational and cost information. They include competitors in other markets, attorneys, bankers, insurance agents, accountants, suppliers, telephone and utility companies, tax and licensing offices, realtors, and advertising media. These sources will be discussed in more detail in subsequent chapters.

Why Do a Business Plan?

It has often been said that business plans are for bankers, not entrepreneurs. This statement reflects the typical entrepreneur's preference for action over paperwork. Even if lenders did not require it, entrepreneurs would go out and get the information they needed. Then they would sit down, think a bit, and decide what to do. But they would not necessarily see the need for putting the whole process down in writing. Why, then, *do* entrepreneurs need business plans?

To Obtain Financing

The primary reason is, in fact, because bankers and other financing sources require it. If you need any sizeable amount of money to start up your business (and most entrepreneurs do), you are going to have to borrow or find investment capital. Prospective lenders and investors will need to know specifically what you plan to do, how you plan to do it, and what the potential is for repayment.

For example, they will want some proof that your business can make a profit. To this end, they will want to know all about your potential customers. Who are they? Where are they? Why will they prefer your product? Lenders will also want to know about your competition. Who are they, and how much of their business can you capture? Finally, lenders will want to know the prospects for growth in your field. All of this is the kind of information that goes into a marketing plan. Without this section—and all the others in a business plan—financial institutions and investors are not going to consider lending you money.

Writing a business plan takes a great deal of time and effort. Why wouldn't a large diagram or checklist suffice instead?

To Organize Information

A business plan can also help you organize and analyze critical data. It is possible to record your research findings in loose notes or even to carry them around in your head. A formal business plan, however, ensures that you consider all aspects of your business's operation, that you don't leave anything out. It also ensures that you don't make any undue assumptions. All of these things are possibilities with a less systematic approach.

To Serve As a Feasibility Check

Doing a business plan also helps you determine the **feasibility** of your business. You made a preliminary estimate of feasibility earlier, when you first considered what business to go into (see Chapter 7, page 90). At that time, however, your venture was little more than an idea based on personal attraction to a field. With limited first-hand knowledge, you could not really know whether it was practical or not.

The process of putting together a business plan, on the other hand, can give you a solid basis for such a conclusion. At each step, you gather information that can either confirm or deny the workability of your idea.

For example, when you do a market analysis, you determine who your potential customers are, where they are, and how many there are, among other things. Once you've completed this step, you know whether there is a sufficient customer base to support your enterprise. You can be a little more sure of the feasibility of your idea than when you first considered it.

By the time you reach the end of the process, if you have gathered similarly favorable data in other areas, you will be very sure. You will have analyzed all your data, made the key decisions about how you will run your company, and even projected your income and expenses. You will be ready to move ahead and make your business idea a reality.

Of course, all the information you gather and your conclusions based on it may not turn out to be favorable. But if at any point you determine that your idea won't work, then you can quit. That's one of the principal advantages of a business plan. Doing one allows you to test your idea—on paper and at very little risk.

To Provide a Start-up Blueprint

Sometimes things left to chance turn out well. Most people, however, leave few really important things in their lives to chance. For example, if you were going on a long-awaited vacation, would you just get on a plane and hope there was a room for you at your destination? Probably not. You would phone ahead and make a reservation. You would *plan*.

The same holds true for setting up a business. You could just jump right in and hope for the best. But if you value your time, effort, and money, you won't. To ensure your venture's success, you will plan. You will make yourself a blueprint and follow it as you get your venture under way.

That "blueprint" is your business plan. It contains the sum of all you learn by reading, interviewing, organizing, and thinking about your enterprise. As such, it is your best guide to making your business both a reality and a success.

Entrepreneur's Bookshelf

To learn more about the subjects discussed in this chapter, consider reading these books:

- *Ernst and Young Business Plan Guide* by David Carney, Brian Ford, Loren Schultz, and Eric Seigel (© 1987)
- *Business Plans that Win $$* by D. Gumpert and Stanley Rich (© 1987)
- *The Start-up Business Plan* by William Luther (© 1991)

Chapter 9 Review

Recapping the Chapter

- A business plan is a formal document that describes a new business and tells why it is deserving of financial support.
- While business plans differ in their specifics, most contain the following parts: statement of purpose, business summary, business description, management plan, marketing plan, financial plan, and appendix.
- In developing their business plans, entrepreneurs can obtain information from sources like the SBA, chambers of commerce, small business development centers, and trade associations.
- When doing a business plan, you should gather all your data first (organizing it as you go), make your key decisions, and do your financial projections. Only then should you write—a first draft which you can refine into your final plan.
- The main reason entrepreneurs must do business plans is because lenders require them.
- Business plans are also useful in organizing information, determining a venture's feasibility, and providing a blueprint for the start-up process.

Reviewing Vocabulary

All of the vocabulary terms below describe something. In each case, briefly explain what.

- business plan
- organization chart
- job descriptions
- resumes
- market analysis
- marketing mix
- *pro forma* financial statements
- *feasibility* check

Checking the Facts

1. What two factors determine the content and format of a business plan?
2. Describe with a brief phrase or two the contents of each business plan part.
3. Describe one way to organize all the data you collect while doing research for a business plan.
4. What do the following abbreviations stand for? What do the organizations themselves do for prospective entrepreneurs?

   - SBA
   - SCORE
   - SBDC

5. Why is the business plan format often considered more acceptable to bankers than entrepreneurs?
6. How exactly can a business plan help an entrepreneur determine if his or her venture is feasible or not?

Thinking Critically

1. Review the components of a typical business plan. Is there any section you could do without? Explain your reasoning.
2. If you plan your contacts carefully and ask the right questions, shouldn't you be able to complete each section of your business plan as you gather the information? Explain why or why not.
3. With all of the agencies available to assist entrepreneurs, why would you have to go to any other source in putting together your business plan?
4. In what way is doing a business plan different from doing a report based on an encyclopedia article?

Chapter 9 Review

Discussing Key Concepts

1. How would you plan your business if there were no such thing as a business plan?
2. Consider two business plans—one for a retail operation and another for a manufacturing company. Other than in their operations sections, how would the two documents differ from each other?
3. Which of the agencies that exist to assist entrepreneurs do you think would be most useful? Why?
4. If you already had all the money you needed to start your business, would you prepare a business plan? Why or why not?

Using Basic Skills

Math

1. In the course of researching your marketing plan, you contact 14 different sources a total of 37 times. What was the average number of contacts per source?

Communication

2. Phone the nearest Small Business Administration district office to obtain a brochure and price list of SBA publications. Identify publications that would be useful to you in planning your business. Then write a letter ordering those materials.

Human Relations

3. You have scheduled a meeting with a SCORE representative who works out of your local chamber of commerce. The purpose of the meeting is to get ideas about local contacts for you to make in putting together your business plan. You understood from your conversation with the chamber secretary that the name of the person with whom you'd be meeting was Mr. Grady. Throughout your discussion, you refer to him by that name. As you are leaving, however, he hands you a business card. It shows that his last name is *Greevey*. How should you handle the situation? What should you do to avoid its repetition in the future? Why?

Enriching Your Learning

1. Contact a small business development center or other agency that assists entrepreneurs in preparing their business plans. Request a copy of an actual plan. Review the document to determine the following:

   - Does the plan have all the basic components identified in this chapter? (*Note:* Alternate titles may be used.)
   - How did the author handle the contents of each section of the plan?
   - Write an evaluation of the business plan in terms of its completeness.

2. Interview an entrepreneur who has recently gone into business. Ask these questions:

   - How important was your business plan in setting up your enterprise? Explain.
   - Which agencies were most helpful to you in putting together your business plan? Again, explain.

   Write a short report summarizing what you learned.

3. Visit your local chamber of commerce and inquire about the specific forms of assistance the organization makes available to entrepreneurs. Report your findings to the class.

Chapter 10
Market Analysis

Objectives

After completing this chapter, you will be able to

- recognize areas in which market analysis should be done,

- list the steps involved in conducting market research, and
- understand how to organize and use the results of market analysis.

Terms to Know

marketing
  concept
market
demographics
psychographics
target market
sales potential
market share
market research
research designs
exploratory
  research
focus group
  interviews
descriptive
  research
historical research
primary data
secondary data

Decisions, Decisions

I've gotten to know my Uncle Ken a lot better since I've been talking about going into business for myself. He had his own business once. It was a construction company. It didn't do very well, and he had to sell it to keep from losing it. He still likes to talk about it, though. Mostly it's stuff like "If this had happened, I'd own the biggest construction company in town today" or "If I would've done that, I'd have it made by now."

Since he's been so willing to share his experiences, I thought he might be able to give me some pointers on getting started. So, the other day I asked what kinds of things I should check out before I start to put my business together. He must have thought it was funny because all he did was grin and say, "I never worried about that kind of thing. I used to just find a vacant lot, build a house, and hope someone would buy it."

I like my uncle, but I didn't think that was funny. I thought it was scary. I mean, you really should know who's going to buy what you make and who your competition is and stuff like that, shouldn't you? I guess I know why my uncle didn't make a go of it.

Anyway, I don't want to make the same mistake. I know I need information, and Uncle Ken isn't going to be much help. So, how do I find out what I need to know? Who do I ask? And how do I keep from missing things that are really important?

Defining Areas of Analysis

If a business is to succeed and make a profit, it must focus all of its efforts on satisfying its customers. Every business starts with this basic **marketing concept**. However, you cannot satisfy your customers (or potential customers) if you don't know who they are and what they want. To find out, you do a market analysis.

A thorough market analysis requires that you examine your market from two entirely different perspectives. On one hand, you will need to identify your prospective customers and determine their buying habits. On the other hand, you will need to analyze your field, or industry, and rate your prospects for success within it.

Identifying Your Market

A **market** is a group of people or companies who have a demand for some product and are willing and able to buy it. The group you are interested in, of course, is the one that has a demand for your particular product. Since they will be the focus of all your company's efforts, you will want to know everything about them—and in as much detail as possible.

MARKET SEGMENTATION. Getting the detail you need usually involves dividing, or segmenting, the total market into smaller groups of buyers with similar needs and interests. For example, consumer markets (customers who buy for personal use) are usually segmented on the following bases:

- *Geographics*—region, state, country, city, and/or area
- *Demographics*—age, gender, family size, family life cycle, income, occupation, education, religion, race, nationality, and/or social class
- *Psychographics*—personality, opinions, and life-style elements like activities and interests
- *Buying characteristics*—knowledge of actual goods or services, personal experience with them, and/or responses to them

Industrial markets (customers who buy for business use) are segmented in a somewhat different way. Variables there would include things like type of business, size, goods or services sold, geographic location, products needed, buyer situation, and preferred contractual arrangements.

Subdivision of the total market in this manner allows you to create detailed profiles of the market segments you are considering. Figure 10-1 provides two examples. Notice that only those variables relevant to the business are included in each profile.

TARGET MARKETING. After all the segments within your range of consideration have been identified, you are ready to select your **target market**. This is the specific market segment on which you are going to concentrate your efforts. Here are some guidelines to use in making your choice:

- *The market segment should be measurable.* If you have no idea how many potential buyers there are in the market, you cannot know if it is worth pursuing.
- *The segment should be large enough to be potentially profitable.* You will have to spend money to market your product. The segment you select must be big enough to enable you to recover your costs and make a profit.
- *The segment should be reachable. Reach* has two meanings in this instance. First, you must be able to reach potential customers with words. You must be able to get information about your product and its availability to

Market Segment Profiles

Situation: **Sporting goods operation** specializing in letter jackets and uniforms, located in a large metropolitan area with several high schools and colleges.

Profile of one market segment: High school students 15-18 years old, male and female. Reside within city and in nearby suburbs. Part-time annual income of $1200-$2000, rarely buy big-ticket sports items, dependent on parents for large purchases. Active in sports, gain feeling of importance from athletic recognition. Aware of what is "in," attitude toward where to buy influenced by peers.

Situation: **Business forms company** specializing in forms for institutions and large offices.

Profile of one market segment: Medical offices and clinics with three or more physicians. In business for over one year, provide a wide range of medical services. Office manager typically does buying with input from medical personnel. Need registration, billing, medical record, and patient instruction forms. Located in southern half of the state. Will remain with the same business form company as long as service is timely, pay on first billing.

Figure 10–1 Study the two market segment profiles presented here. Which business is targeting an industrial market? Which is targeting a consumer market? How do you know?

interested buyers in the segment. Second, you must be able to reach potential customers physically. You must be able to deliver your product to their homes or businesses or to the places where they shop.

- *The market segment should be responsive.* You should have some indication from your research that people in the segment would, in fact, be interested in your product and willing to buy it.

It is possible for a business to select and serve multiple market segments. If you have identified more than one target market, you will need to take your analysis a step further. You will need to determine if you have the capacity to serve all of your target markets. If not, you will have to choose the ones you will pursue initially and those you will leave for later, when you are ready to expand.

Analyzing Your Potential for Market Success

Once you have identified your market, you will be ready to evaluate your prospects for success in dealing with it. Those prospects will depend in large measure on two factors—the sales potential of your product and your competition.

SALES POTENTIAL.   How much of your product can you realistically expect to sell? The answer to that question—a projected, or estimated, figure—is called **sales potential**. It can be arrived at by considering three variables.

The first is the nature of your product. Obviously, what you plan to sell influences how much you can sell. You should assess your product by asking yourself the following questions:

- How well does the good or service I am offering match up with my target market?
- Where is my product in its life cycle? (Is it a new product whose sales have just begun to take off? Is it an established product whose sales are leveling off? Is it a mature product whose sales are on the decline?)
- How have products of this type been affected by changes in the economy? by seasonal factors?

Clearly, products that are well matched to their markets have a high potential for success. Products that are relatively new and resistant to the ups and downs of the economy may also have an edge. But rejuvenated old products or products that catch an economic wave can be winners, too.

Market trends can also help you predict your product's sales potential. In the course of your research, you should look for future sales figures for your industry. Even past and current sales levels, if graphed or charted, can help. They can be visually or mathematically extended to provide a basis for prediction. Try to project current trends 3–5 years into the future.

Finally, your sources of supply will have an impact on your sales. You must have access to affordable sources of inventory, raw materials, or needed goods and services. Otherwise you will not be able to offer your product at the kinds of prices that will generate interest and sales. You should also consider where your suppliers are located, the trade discounts they offer, and the availability of alternate sources. These, too, can affect your costs, your pricing, and ultimately your sales.

COMPETITION.   Outstanding sales potential for your product is no guarantee of success. This is because products are seldom offered to consumers in a vacuum. Usually there are other,

Market trends can affect the sales potential of your business. In what forms are you most likely to find such information?

competing products already established in the market. To succeed, you must therefore be able to capture market share from other companies in the field. **Market share** is simply a portion of the total sales generated by all the competing companies in a given market.

To determine if you can capture enough market share to succeed, you must do a thorough analysis of your competition. Here are some areas you should research:

- *Identity of competitors.* Determine their names and locations. Estimate or obtain data regarding their percentage of market share and sales volume. Also, estimate the sales volume they would lose if you came into the market.
- *Strengths and weaknesses of competitors.* Obtain information on your competitors' products, prices, quality, selection, advertising, personnel, customer service, and distribution methods. Evaluate each of the companies on the basis of their strengths and weaknesses in these areas. If possible, try to determine their responsiveness to changing market conditions.

Make note of any similar companies that have recently gone out of business, and try to determine why.

- *Your advantages over competitors.* Identify those things about your proposed business that are clearly unique and would enable you to take business away from your competitors.
- *Your projected market share.* Gather business or industry information from which you can project total market sales for the next three years. Project your own total sales, and estimate your market share for the same years.

Conducting Market Research

You now know the areas you need to investigate as part of a market analysis. This section will give you a process that you can use to do your investigating. That process is called **market research**. The steps involved in the process are the same whether you are doing research for an existing business or a new venture.

The best way to evaluate your potential competition is in person. What sort of information could you gather on such a trip?

Risk Takers, Profit Makers

Pat and Andrew Brazington

Aren't most people happy to receive a gift no matter what it's wrapped in? Pat and Andrew Brazington don't think so. A few years ago while they were shopping for a niece's christening present, they were dismayed by the prevalence of blond, blue-eyed babies on most wrapping papers. Recognizing an unfilled niche, the Brazingtons established Ethnic Reams, Rolls, and Bags Plus (ERRB, for short) to provide customers with culturally diverse wrapping paper and gift bags.

Although the Brazingtons began planning their venture in 1990, ERRB didn't open for business until June 1991. Most banks balked at investing money in a company entering the already competitive gift wrap market. Regardless, Pat Brazington, a model and business owner, and Andrew Brazington, a Drexel University graduate with a business degree, remained determined. Undaunted, they risked their own money to start the business.

The Brazingtons first promoted their products at Black Expos and conventions in various cities. There, retailers quickly recognized ERRB's importance and appeal. After only one year of business, the Brazingtons didn't sell their products just through direct mail catalogs and Afrocentric shops. They also did business with chain retailers like Hallmark and Sears. ERRB products, the chains conceded, met community needs their own products did not.

ERRB's first line of products reflects the Brazingtons' aesthetic and social sensibilities. The Garvey design (named after 1920s African activist Marcus Garvey) consists of red, black, and green stripes—colors associated with African pride. Another pattern resembles colorful Kente cloth from Ghana. While both motifs are festive additions to any occasion, they also serve as reminders of African-American culture and history.

So positive has the feedback been that the Brazingtons are busy developing their next lines of products. They've already commissioned African-American artists to design future prints and are developing paper goods such as stationery and party favors. They also look forward to introducing lines featuring Hispanic, Native American, and other distinctive cultural designs.

Despite their auspicious start, the Brazingtons admit that they may not see profits until 1993. That's when they expect to have paid off their start-up costs. Still, they find satisfaction in each 16-hour work day. For Pat and Andrew Brazington, success means promoting cultural awareness and pride with their gift wrap—even if most people just want to tear it apart.

Define the Problem

This first step is extremely important because it helps you isolate the problem you need to deal with. This, in turn, allows you to focus your research on gathering critical information. It also reduces the chances that you will spend time gathering information you won't use.

Problem definition should be your starting point when analyzing each of the areas identified in the previous section. You can frame your problem as either a question (Who are my competitors?) or a statement (I need to identify my competition).

Select a Research Approach

Once you have defined your problem, you can select a research approach. There are several basic ways to structure research studies. These are called **research designs**. The kind and amount of information you need will determine which design you use.

EXPLORATORY RESEARCH. Exploratory research is used to expand your knowledge when you know little about a problem. While conducting such research, you might examine government or industry publications. You might talk to people who are knowledgeable about your field in order to gain insights. You might even organize or observe **focus group interviews**. These are interviews with small groups of potential customers or businesspeople involved in your field.

DESCRIPTIVE RESEARCH. Descriptive research is done when the problem involves determining the current status of something. This is the type of research you would do if, for example, you wanted to get information about the age, gender, occupation, income, or buying habits of potential customers. Descriptive information is usually collected through questionnaires, interviews, or observation.

HISTORICAL RESEARCH. Historical research is carried out to explore past occurrences, including their causes and effects. The rationale behind this approach is that the past may help to explain present circumstances or predict future trends.

Useful historical data may be available through trade associations or trade publications. Owners of similar businesses operating in different markets can also be helpful.

Gather Information

With your problem defined and your research approach selected, you can now begin to collect your data. Market research data is usually described as either primary or secondary. **Primary data** is information that is collected for the first time and is specific to the problem being studied. **Secondary data** is data that has been collected for some other purpose.

SECONDARY DATA. Secondary data is the logical starting point for prospective entrepreneurs. This is because it can be easily obtained and is relatively inexpensive.

Sources of secondary data related to economic conditions include the government and community organizations described in Chapter 9 (the SBA, chamber of commerce, etc.). Secondary data specific to your market and industry can be obtained through trade associations, trade publications, and, in some instances, commercial research agencies.

PRIMARY DATA. Most entrepreneurs will resort to primary data only if they must. Most often this happens when secondary data is unavailable, outdated, or not sufficiently relevant.

The most commonly used methods of gathering such data about consumers are observation and surveys. The observation method involves watching and recording the actions of potential customers. The survey method has individuals answer questions in person, by telephone, or through the mail. Focus groups, described earlier, can also be used.

Primary data about a type of business or an industry is most often gathered by interviewing individuals who work in the field. However, focus groups can be used here as well.

Primary data has some distinct advantages over secondary data. It is up-to-date and deals directly with the problem under study. But it has major drawbacks as well. As you can probably tell from the techniques involved, it is expensive and time-consuming to collect. In addition, the amount of data gathered can be difficult to handle. For example, one 10-question survey answered by 100 people would generate 1,000 answers for analysis. Before such data can be effectively analyzed, it must be organized and consolidated. This could mean even more time and expense.

Analyze and Interpret the Information

When all of your data has been gathered and sorted out, you will need to determine what it means in relation to your research problem. Suppose you want to enter a particular market. If the trend data you have collected shows that that market is shrinking, you might reconsider.

Organizing and Using Your Data

As the data you gather is organized for the final step in the market research process, it should be set up in charts and recorded in report form. These charts and reports will reflect more than just the information you gathered. They will also contain your interpretations and projections.

The results of your market analysis will provide yet another chance for you to assess the feasibility of your venture. In fact, you may find it useful to write up your views on the subject in a formal statement. Even if it is not included in your final business plan, such a statement has value. It can inspire confidence—your own and others. Its content and tone will likely work their way into your presentations to lenders or potential investors.

If possible, summarize any statistical data you gather in chart or table form. Why do you think this is the preferred approach?

Assuming that your decision is to move forward with your venture, you should place your market analysis materials in the marketing section of your business plan notebook. You should understand, however, that they are not complete. As you continue through the entrepreneurial process, you will gather additional information. That data will supplement your findings and enable you to refine your market analysis. It is these combined materials that will eventually serve as the basis for your marketing plan.

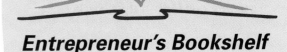

Entrepreneur's Bookshelf

To learn more about the subjects discussed in this chapter, consider reading these books:

- *Cheap But Good Marketing Research* by Alan R. Andreason (© 1988)
- *Do-It-Yourself Marketing Research* by George Breen (© 1989)
- *How to Check Out Your Competition: A Complete Plan for Investigating Your Market* by John M. Kelly (© 1987)

Chapter 10 Review

Recapping the Chapter

- A market analysis identifies a business's target market, estimates its sales potential, and sizes up its competition.
- Market research is the process used to collect and evaluate market data. It involves (1) defining the problem, (2) selecting a research approach, (3) gathering information, and (4) analyzing and interpreting that information.
- Market analysis data provides the basis for development of a marketing plan.

Reviewing Vocabulary

Study each pair of terms. Then in your own words describe how they are related to each other. (*Hint:* Are they the same? Are they opposites? Are they both? Is one part of the other? Is one the result of the other?)

- primary data—secondary data
- demographics—descriptive research
- psychographics—focus group interviews
- market research—research designs
- sales potential—market share
- exploratory research—historical research
- marketing concept—target market

Checking the Facts

1. Name four kinds of variables that might be used to describe consumer markets. Name four kinds of variables that might be used to describe industrial markets.
2. What guidelines would you use to select a target market from among all the market segments you have identified?
3. Name three kinds of sales figures you should look for when researching market trends.
4. Why is it important to analyze your potential competition?
5. When would you use primary rather than secondary data in doing market research?
6. When and where will you use the results of your market analysis?

Thinking Critically

1. Review the sample profiles in Figure 10-1. Then for each business situation, describe another market segment.
2. Review the four types of variables used as a basis for segmenting consumer markets. Is any one type more important than the others? Explain.
3. Can target market selection be done *before* market segmentation? Should it be done at that point? Why or why not?
4. Is source of supply as important in determining a business's sales potential as market trends or the nature of the product being sold? Why or why not?
5. How useful a figure is projected market share to an entrepreneur evaluating his business's prospects for success? to an entrepreneur seeking a loan? Explain.
6. For each area of market analysis, which research design—exploratory, descriptive, or historical—do you think would be most appropriate? Why?

Discussing Key Concepts

1. Under what circumstances could you do a market analysis earlier (or later) in the

Chapter 10 Review

process of creating a business? Why would (or wouldn't) this be a good idea?

2. Are there any other areas you might research as part of a market analysis besides the ones listed in this chapter? What are they, and why would you consider them?

3. Do you think that market analysis really requires a formal market research process? Why or why not?

4. Does a favorable market analysis (one that indicates you should go forward with your venture) guarantee success in business? Why or why not?

Using Basic Skills

Math

1. According to projections you have obtained, total market sales for your industry should be $4 million your first year of operation, $6 million your second, and $9 million your third. You have estimated your company's total sales to be $200,000 in your first year, $450,000 in your second, and $900,000 in your third. What would be your market share percentage in each of the three years?

Communication

2. Determine whether or not secondary data is available that would be useful to you in doing a market analysis of your business. Speak to someone at the reference desk of your local library. Also, telephone your local chamber of commerce.

3. Write a trade association in your field to find out what market information they have available. Specifically, inquire about materials on market segmentation and target marketing, market trends, and suppliers.

Human Relations

4. After making several inquiries to obtain information for your market analysis, you receive a telephone call from a local businessperson active in your field. He has heard that you are planning to start up a new business and feels it is not a good idea. He tells you that the local market will not support another operation like the one you are planning and that everybody would be better off if you just dropped the idea. What are your options? What would be the best way to handle the situation?

Enriching Your Learning

1. Survey and identify those businesses that would be your competitors when you start up your enterprise. Specifically, do the following:

   - List the companies by name and location.
   - Determine as nearly as possible the market share percentage for each company and estimate its sales.
   - Estimate how much each company would lose in sales if you entered the market.

   Draw up a chart that summarizes the information you have gathered and your estimates.

2. Do a market analysis for your selected business.

Chapter 11
The Marketing Mix

Objectives

After completing this chapter, you will be able to

- identify and describe the four strategies that make up the marketing mix,

- list some areas you should consider in developing long-range marketing goals, and
- explain the process involved in organizing and developing a marketing plan.

Terms to Know

brand
package
label
product
  positioning
product mix
psychological
  pricing
prestige pricing
odd/even pricing
channel of
  distribution
intermediaries
intensive
  distribution
selective
  distribution
exclusive
  distribution
promotional mix

Decisions, Decisions

Yesterday I talked with a counselor at the small business development center. I told him the target market for my denim wear shop would be males and females, 16–24 years old, living within our county. He agreed the area had enough population to support a business like mine, but he wasn't exactly enthusiastic about my marketing plan. I'm not sure why.

Mainly, I want to carry jeans and other casual clothes in denim. I also thought bib overalls and denim jackets for little kids would be good additions.

I plan to set my prices just above cost. I figure once customers find out what bargains I'm offering, they'll keep coming back for more.

At least in the beginning, I thought I'd lease space in a building a few miles outside of town. There aren't any other retailers there, and there's not much traffic. But there is plenty of parking, and the rent is low. (There's nothing wrong with trying to save a few bucks when you're getting started, right?)

I'm sure I won't have any problem getting customers to come out to my store if I use the right kind of advertising. I can get pretty good rates for early morning TV spots. I know 5–7 A.M.'s a little early, but everyone watches TV, right? I also thought I might go with some billboards on the road to the store. The commercials would get people's attention, and the outdoor ads would lead them in.

All these seemed like good ideas to me, but the counselor didn't think so. What's he mean "not keeping my eye on my target market"? I was really careful about choosing my market, and I covered all the four P's. Where did I go wrong?

Working with the Four P's

Once you have completed your market analysis, you are ready to do a marketing plan. Recall that this plan describes the particular marketing mix you will use. It describes your strategies for product, price, place, and promotion—the four P's. If you are to be successful, you must direct all of these strategies toward your target market. Your marketing plan tells how you will do this.

Recall another important point from Chapter 9. Doing a business plan is not a simple, quick, or orderly affair. It is an ongoing process in which information comes to you in pieces, from different sources, and over time rather than all at once. This chapter reflects that fact. Here we will complete our discussion of product and price. Place and promotion, however, are larger topics with chapters of their own. You will learn much more about them later.

It might, therefore, be more accurate to say that what you will be developing here is a *preliminary* marketing plan. You will expand and refine that plan as you continue through the steps of the entrepreneurial process.

Product

The product strategy deals with the goods or services your business will provide. Product decisions are crucial to the success of your business. Products that don't match up with customer needs or expectations of quality will not sell. Such shortcomings are insurmountable. You cannot overcome them with attractive prices, easy availability, or extensive advertising.

You have probably already gathered some product information and even made some product decisions as part of your market analysis. Now, however, you must address such considerations more thoroughly and systematically.

PRODUCT FEATURES. A product is made up of all the benefits it offers to consumers. So, when you think about your product, you must think of it as a package of features and examine each feature carefully.

Features of goods (like cars or appliances) include physical things such as style, distinctive characteristics, color, quality, and options. They may also include intangibles like warranties, service contracts, delivery, installation, and instructions.

A physical product, or good, is more than just a thing. It is a package of features (or benefits) that can satisfy consumer wants. What are the features of the consumer product (sofa) shown here?

In the case of service businesses (like dry cleaners or financial institutions), there may be little in the way of physical features. What they offer is a package of intangible benefits that improve the quality of consumers' lives. These may include convenience, saved time, improved health, or a sense of well-being.

BRANDING, PACKAGING, AND LABELING. How will you identify your product and make it stand out from the competition? A part of the answer may lie in branding, packaging, and labeling. A **brand** is the name, symbol, or design used to identify a product. A **package** is the physical container or wrapper that holds it. The **label** is that part of the package used to present information. All three contribute something to the product and in the process become part of it.

PRODUCT SELECTION. Which products will you choose to sell through your business? That will depend on whether you are going to manufacture them or sell them.

Developing and manufacturing new products to sell involves several steps. First you generate product ideas and sort out the good ones from the bad. Then you study the product's potential costs and revenues. You develop the product and test-market it. Finally, if everything looks promising, you introduce it.

Choosing products for resale, on the other hand, is largely a matter of gathering information. You study consumer demands and product availability and then make decisions to bring the two together. A second, related concern is how well your product would fit in with any other items you produce.

PRODUCT POSITIONING. **Product positioning** refers to how consumers see your product compared to the competition's. Do you want your product to be seen as more prestigious? as a better bargain? as equal in quality? How you position your product relative to your competition will depend on your marketing goals.

Positioning can be achieved through differences in quality, availability, pricing, and uses. Branding, packaging, and labeling can also have a bearing on your product's image and, thus, on its positioning.

PRODUCT MIX.   Finally, you will need to consider your **product mix**. This term refers to all the products a company makes or sells.

If you are going to offer multiple products, you should think about how they relate to each other. The answer will depend on the image you want to project and the market you are targeting. If you want to reach a single market, you may decide to include only products that complement each other. If you are trying to reach multiple markets, you may decide on a more diversified mix.

PRODUCT DECISIONS.   As you consider the product strategy for your marketing plan, ask yourself the following questions. Keep your target market in mind as you decide on your answers.

- What products should I manufacture or sell?
- At what quality level should my goods or services be produced and/or sold?
- How much inventory should I maintain?
- How will my products be different from or better than my competitors'?
- How will I position my products?
- What will my customer service policy be?

Price

When you did your market analysis, you probably learned something about the range of prices in your field. Price strategy, however, involves more than just the dollar value assigned to products. It must also take into account such things as quantity purchases, promotional assistance, the availability of credit terms, and discounts.

FACTORS AFFECTING PRICE.   Of the factors that directly affect price, two are economic. You should recognize them. Is demand for your product high and supply relatively low? The laws of supply and demand suggest that your product can command a high price. Is demand so high that people will pay almost any amount for it? If

Competition is a major factor that affects the prices you can charge. If you were starting up a similar business just down the street from this one, where would you set your prices and why?

so, inelastic demand may mean that you have a free hand in setting the price for your product.

Another factor that affects price is the series of businesses involved in selling or distributing your product. How much profit does each require to make handling your product worthwhile? Their profit margins added together will raise your price.

Competition is another factor that can affect price. When buyers are price conscious, how the competition is pricing their products may determine how you will price yours.

Finally, your costs and expenses will affect how you price your product. To make a profit, your prices must be set so that they exceed your costs and expenses. This is the only way you can stay in business.

Risk Takers, Profit Makers

Bill Sanderson

When Bill Sanderson discovered the cost of running a restaurant, he gave up his dream of serving healthy gourmet meals. Instead, he decided to offer healthy snacks and candies from boutiques.

The outcome for Sanderson has been sweet. Today his Popcorn Palace and Candy Emporiums are a $10 million international business.

Sanderson opened his first Popcorn Palace in an Irvine, California, strip mall in 1982. Because his business debut was not very well calculated, he experienced his share of trials. (In fact, neighboring retailers had a pool on how long the store would last.) The Irvine shop is still in operation today, although it benefited Sanderson more in practice than in sales during its first year.

Based on his experience in Irvine, Sanderson refined his marketing strategy. He paid more attention to the seasonality of popcorn sales. (Popcorn sold phenomenally during the holidays, but he made as little as $29 a day at other times of the year.) He also determined what made his shop successful—motivated workers, quality products, and a location that facilitated impulse buying. Then he played on those strengths.

After opening a second Popcorn Palace in the Glendale Galleria, a high-profile Southern California shopping mall, Sanderson assembled a management team to help guide his business. By 1991, he had established ten more Popcorn Palace and Candy Emporiums. Although sizes and requirements differed, he applied the same principles to each location. They all turned a profit.

Sanderson's expansion experiences have reinforced his belief in focusing completely on a well-defined target market. He once considered wholesaling and even selling popcorn as packing material. To Sanderson, they seemed like sure

things, but they stretched the company's resources too far and were abandoned.

In contrast, ventures that fit the food boutique philosophy have thrived. Erecting temporary mall kiosks during holiday periods and buying a chain of restaurants have been especially profitable.

Sanderson's boldest move—establishing a shop in Osaka, Japan, in 1990—has also proved his most rewarding. However, when a Japanese traveler first proposed the venture, Sanderson stalled. He wasn't familiar with Japanese tastes or with the Japanese market. After an experienced (and wealthy) Japanese partner surfaced, though, he readily agreed. In its first year, the Osaka Popcorn Palace earned seven times the average of what American stores earned per square foot. Continued success in Japan and America add up to a savory future for Sanderson and his Popcorn Palaces.

PRICING GOALS. Once you have considered the factors that affect your prices, you will need to consider your own pricing goals. How can pricing help you achieve your business objectives? Would lower prices help you beat the competition and obtain market share? Would higher prices give you a better return on your investment?

PRICING STRATEGIES. There are three basic strategies you can use to price your product. Here is what they involve.

- *Cost-based pricing.* First, figure your cost to make or buy your product. Then figure the related cost of doing business, and add the two together. Finally, add your projected profit margin to arrive at your price.
- *Demand-based pricing.* Find out what customers are willing to pay for your product, and set the price accordingly.
- *Competition-based pricing.* Determine what your competitors are charging. Then decide if it is to your advantage to price below the competition, in line with the competition, or above the competition.

It is quite possible that you may use a combination of these strategies. If you have a range of products, you may even use all three strategies separately. In any event, whatever strategy (or strategies) you choose must be compatible with your target market and consistent with your pricing goals.

PRICING POLICIES AND TECHNIQUES. To attract customers, you may also want to consider certain pricing policies and techniques. For example, will you allow bargaining? With a one-price policy, all customers pay the same. With a flexible-price policy, customers can negotiate for the best deal they can get.

There are two principal kinds of pricing techniques—**psychological pricing** and discount pricing. The former uses price to affect customers' perceptions of a product or company. For example, **prestige pricing** employs higher-than-average prices to suggest exclusiveness,

status, and prestige. **Odd/even pricing** uses a different means to achieve a similar end. It employs odd prices ($19.99) to suggest bargains and even prices ($20) to suggest higher quality. Discount pricing techniques include giving discounts for paying cash or for buying in large quantities.

PRICING DECISIONS. When you consider your pricing strategy, ask yourself the following questions. Once again, keep your specific target market in mind as you make your decisions.

- What motivates the customers who will buy my product? Are they price sensitive? Are they status conscious?
- How much will my customers be willing and able to buy at what prices?
- What will my primary pricing strategy be? my secondary pricing strategy (if any)?
- Will I offer discounts to my customers?
- Will I offer credit terms? If so, what will they be? Will I handle the financing myself?
- What will my pricing policy be?

Place

Place strategy involves how you will deliver your goods and services to your customers. *Where* will they go to buy? *When* will they buy? Will your product actually be there, ready and *available* for sale? Notice that movement of your product (both to your location and to your customers) is at the core of all these questions. For this reason, this part of the marketing mix is also known as the distribution strategy.

You have probably already begun to formulate some portions of this strategy for yourself. As you did your market analysis, you no doubt learned how your competitors operate. Do you want to copy them or go your own way? You will not know for sure until you have investigated things like sources of supply and site selection. But you can make a start by considering the following areas.

CHANNELS OF DISTRIBUTION. In order to make place decisions, you will need to know how a channel of distribution works. A

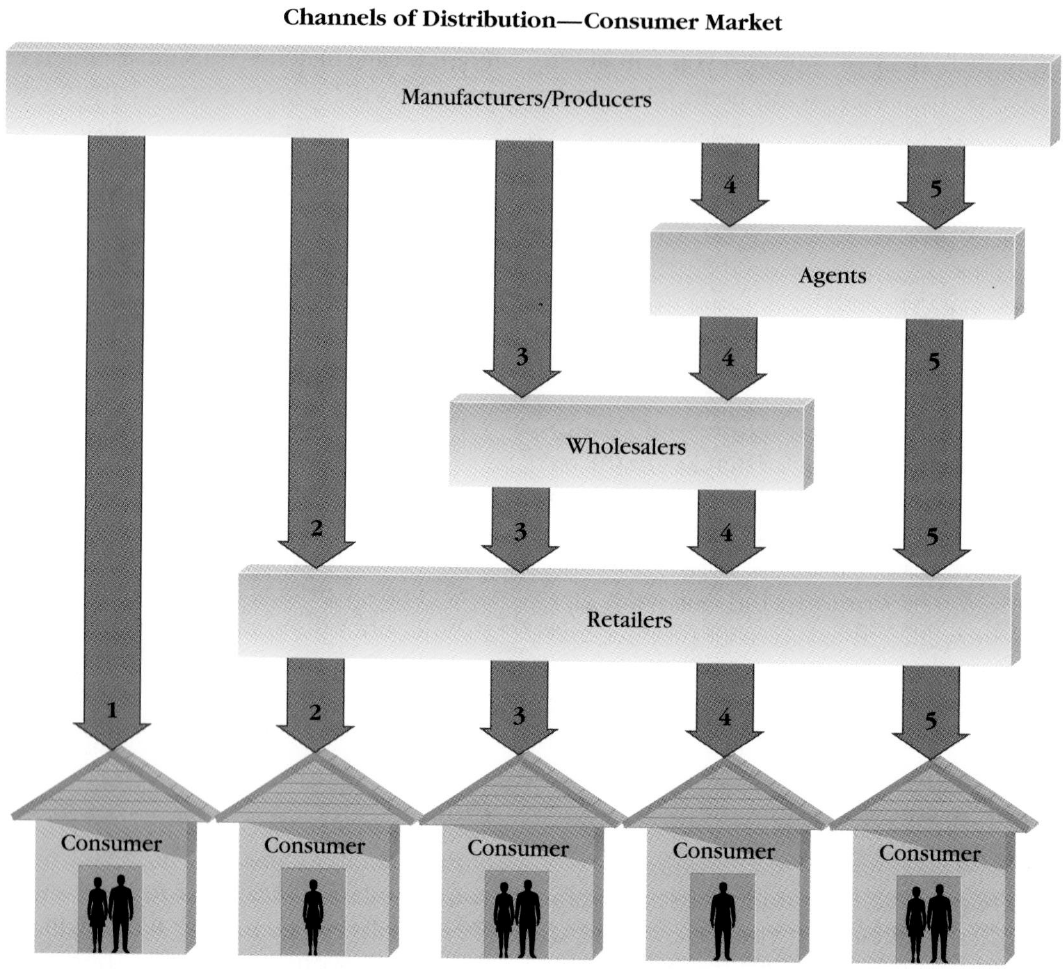

Channels of Distribution—Consumer Market

Figure 11–1   *The path your product takes to reach the person who finally buys it can be either direct or indirect. How many of the channels of distribution shown here are indirect? How do you know?*

channel of distribution is the path a product takes from producer (or manufacturer) to final user (or customer).

As you can see from Figures 11-1 and 11-2, channel members are different for consumer and industrial markets. Despite the differences, however, both figures contain only two basic types of channels—direct and indirect.

A direct channel moves a product from producer to customer with no one in between. Service businesses are typical examples. You give your financial records to your tax preparer, and a few days later he or she gives you your finished tax return. No one else is involved.

An indirect channel, on the other hand, employs **intermediaries**. These are people or businesses that move products between producers and final users. They include wholesalers and retailers (who sell in the consumer market), distributors (who sell in the industrial market), and agents (who simply arrange sales). A clothing designer, for example, might use an agent to reach wholesalers and retailers. In this way, the designer reaches a large market but avoids having to maintain either a sales staff or stores. The indirect channel simplifies the business and allows the designer to concentrate on what he or she does best—designing.

Channels of Distribution—Industrial Market

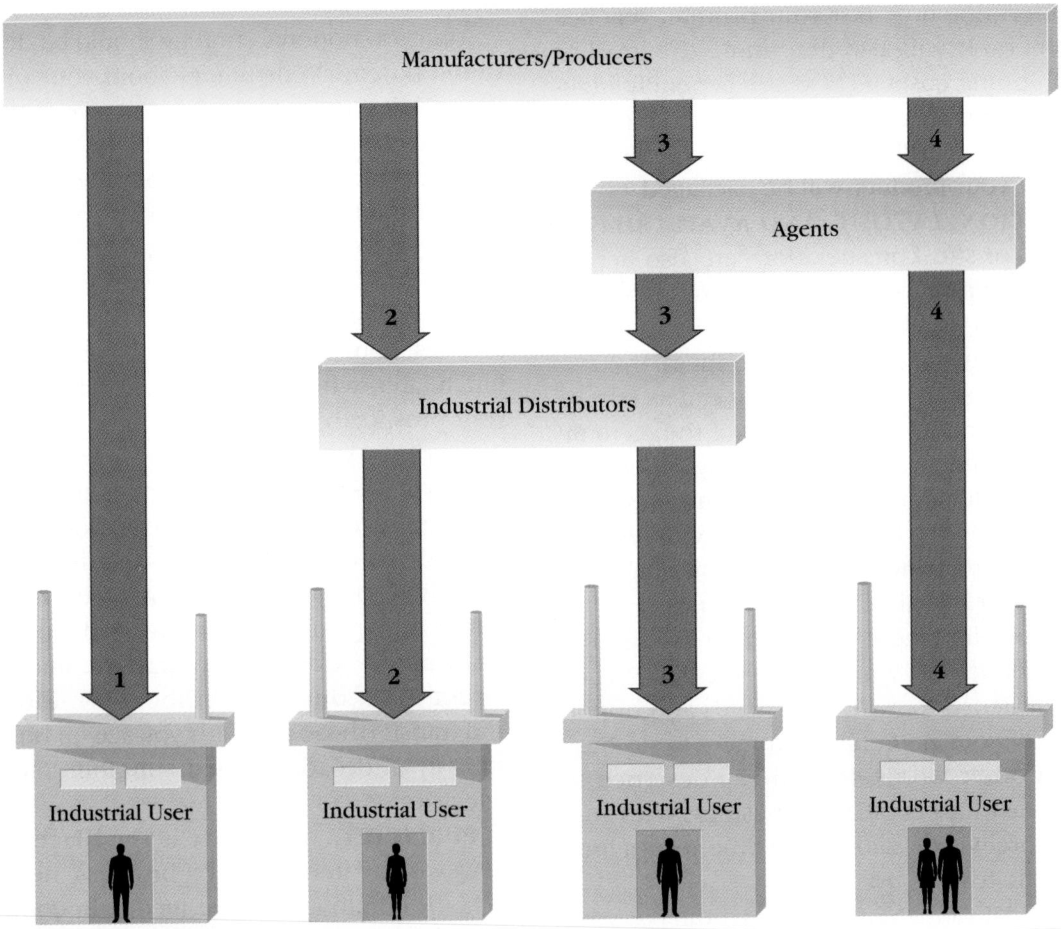

Figure 11–2   Channels of distribution for industrial products differ from those for consumer products. How?

The type of business you have will determine where you fit in your channel of distribution. If you are a producer, you will be concerned with sending products through a channel. If you are a retailer, you will be concerned with receiving them. If you are a wholesaler, you will be concerned with both. You may also use or be involved in more than one channel.

The channel of distribution you choose can affect your product in many ways. It can raise or lower your product's cost. It can affect the potential for loss or damage to your product in transit. Most important, it can determine how quickly your product reaches your customers. If you can find a channel that is more efficient than the ones similar businesses are using, you can gain a competitive edge.

INTENSITY OF DISTRIBUTION.   How broadly will you distribute your product? You have three choices. **Intensive distribution** involves placement of a product in all suitable sales outlets. **Selective distribution** limits the number of sales outlets in an area. **Exclusive distribution** limits the number of outlets to one per area.

TRANSPORTATION.   The physical movement of goods will also enter into your place decisions. How will your product be shipped? Your choices include by truck, train, airplane, ship, or pipeline.

Which method of transportation you choose will determine how fast your product reaches consumers. It will also determine the level of your shipping costs. (These are generally highest for air transportation and lowest for shipment by waterway.) Finally, it will dictate in some measure how your product will be packaged.

LOCATION, LAYOUT, AND AVAILABILITY. Location, or site, considerations are also important to your place strategy. They are especially important to retail and service businesses that depend on customers to come to them.

If yours is such a business, you can as part of your place strategy do a number of things to increase customer access and encourage sales. You may select a location near transportation routes. You may decide to lay out your site with entries from both street and parking lot. You may favor evening over morning hours of operation.

What do all of these options have in common besides connection with your business site? They are all designed to match the needs and opportunities of your potential customers to do business. In other words, they are all designed to make it easy for people to do business with you. Much more will be said about these areas a little later in the text.

PLACE DECISIONS. When you make your place decisions, ask yourself the following questions. Again, as you think about your answers, keep your target market in mind.

- How will my product be sold and distributed?
- Will my product go directly from producer to user, or will it go through an intermediary?
- Are there opportunities to use more efficient channels of distribution?
- Who are the channel members I will use to obtain my products? to distribute my products?
- How intensively will I distribute my products?
- Is my location appropriate for my target market (or markets)?
- What is the physical layout (floor plan) of my business? Will it encourage or discourage sales?
- Do my hours of operation match the times that my target market prefers to do business?

Promotion

Your promotional strategy should be designed to tell potential customers about your product. Specifically, it should discuss your product's characteristics, benefits, and availability. It should also explain where and how to purchase the item. Your promotional strategy can also be used to enhance your company's image.

You have already probably observed promotional strategies in action as you did your market analysis. Your own strategy will likely take shape much later, when you have learned more about your prospective business. For now, just consider the various types of promotion you can use.

ADVERTISING. Advertising is the paid nonpersonal presentation of ideas, goods, or services directed toward a mass audience by an identified sponsor. Advertising media can be divided into print and broadcast. Examples of print media include newspapers, magazines, direct mail, outdoor (billboards), directory, and transit (those print ads you see on buses and subways). Broadcast media include radio and television.

PUBLICITY. Publicity is the placement of newsworthy items about a business, new products, or employees in the media. In contrast to advertising, publicity is not paid for by the business. Good public relations with the community, the press, and customers increases opportunities for publicity.

SALES PROMOTION. Sales promotion is the use of incentives or interest-building marketing activities to stimulate traffic and/or sales. It does not include advertising, publicity, or personal selling activities. Examples of sales promotion are displays, premiums, sweepstakes, contests, rebates, and free samples.

PERSONAL SELLING. Personal selling consists of oral presentations to one or more potential buyers with the intent of making a sale. Personal selling is most often designed to bring the sale to a close after the customer has been attracted by advertising, publicity, and/or sales promotion.

Promotions of various kinds can tell people about your product or enhance your company's image. What kind of promotion is being used here? Which is being stressed—product or image?

PROMOTIONAL MIX. Promotional mix refers to a combination of these different types of promotion. The promotional activities a business uses should be coordinated and designed to complement each other.

PROMOTIONAL DECISIONS. As you make your decisions about promotion, ask yourself the following questions. As with the other three strategies, keep your target market in mind.

- What kind of advertising media should I use? What will be my message or theme? Should I have a coordinated campaign?
- What public relations efforts should I plan? what publicity activities?
- What sales promotion devices and activities would be appropriate for my business?
- Will I use personal selling? How? Who in my organization will do such selling?
- How will my promotional activities be coordinated with each other?

Developing Long-Range Marketing Goals

In addition to drafting a marketing plan for the initial phase of your operation, you will need to formulate long-range marketing goals. These will reflect what you hope to achieve in 3–5 years. They will provide direction for the growth of your business.

Organizing and Using Your Marketing Plan

After reading this chapter, you should be able to rough out a marketing plan that is based on your market analysis. This preliminary plan will serve as a guide for many of your decisions as you carry out the entrepreneurial process. In addition, it will ensure that all of your efforts focus on meeting the needs of your target market.

After you complete your preliminary marketing plan, place it in your business plan notebook. Review it periodically as you continue to explore the prospects for your business. Incorporate new information that you gather, and use it to refine your plan. By making changes in this fashion, as you go, you will simplify the task of writing your final marketing plan. You will also speed the assembly of your final business plan.

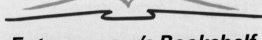

Entrepreneur's Bookshelf

To learn more about the subjects discussed in this chapter, consider reading these books:

- *Develop a Winning Marketing Plan* by William A. Cohen (© 1987)
- *Total Marketing: Capturing Customers with Marketing Plans that Work* by Don Debelak (© 1989)
- *Guerrilla Marketing Attack: New Strategies, Tactics and Weapons for Winning Big Profits from Your Small Business* by Jay Conrad Levinson (© 1989)

Chapter 11 Review

Recapping the Chapter

- A marketing plan, or marketing mix, is made up of coordinated strategies for product, price, place, and promotion.
- The product strategy deals with decisions about the goods or services provided to meet customer demand.
- The price strategy is concerned with all of the variables that go into establishing prices customers will be willing and able to pay.
- The place strategy involves how to deliver goods or services to customers where and when they want them.
- The promotion strategy involves decisions regarding the best ways to reach customers with messages about goods or services.
- Long-range marketing goals reflect what you hope your business will achieve in 3–5 years.
- Based on your market analysis, you prepare a preliminary marketing plan that you expand and refine as you go through the steps in the entrepreneurial process.

Reviewing Vocabulary

Illustrate the terms below with examples (products, stores, or ads) that you are familiar with.

- brand
- package
- label
- product positioning
- product mix
- psychological pricing
- prestige pricing
- odd/even pricing
- channel of distribution
- intermediaries
- intensive distribution
- selective distribution
- exclusive distribution
- promotional mix

Checking the Facts

1. What are the features of a service business?
2. Name the steps in the process of developing and manufacturing a new product.
3. What are the three basic strategies used to determine price?
4. What two basic options do you have in selecting a pricing policy?
5. Who are the possible members of distribution channels for consumer products?
6. Who are the possible members of distribution channels for industrial products?
7. What are the main forms of advertising media?
8. When is personal selling typically used in relation to other types of promotion?

Thinking Critically

1. Could you prepare a marketing plan before choosing your target market? Why or why not?
2. Do the strategies in the marketing plan really apply to service businesses? If so, explain how they apply. If not, explain how they should be different.
3. When could your selected business be involved in channels of distribution for both consumer and industrial products? Explain.
4. Could you have an effective marketing plan without a promotional strategy? Why or why not?
5. Would a statement of your long-range marketing goals be a useful supplement to your marketing plan? Explain why or why not.

Chapter 11 Review

Discussing Key Concepts

1. If the product strategy is the most critical strategy to the success of your enterprise, which is the next-most important? Why?
2. Product mix is a consideration within the product strategy; promotional mix, within the promotional strategy.

   - Should consideration be given to a price mix? Why or why not? What would it consist of?
   - Should consideration be given to a place mix? Why or why not? What would it consist of?

3. Which is the best pricing strategy? Why?
4. What might be a channel of distribution that would give your selected business an edge over the competition? Explain why you believe the channel would work.
5. What is the most effective type of promotion? Defend your answer.

Using Basic Skills

Math

1. You are calculating the price of a product you are planning to manufacture. Your cost to produce each unit will be $60. Your related overhead and projected profit are $20 (33 1/3 percent of cost). If the wholesaler's markup is 50 percent of its cost and the retailer's markup is 100 percent of its cost, what would be

   - the manufacturer's price to the wholesaler?
   - the wholesaler's price to the retailer?
   - the retailer's price to the consumer?

Communication

2. Obtain a marketing textbook and read its sections on marketing mix. Determine how that presentation is different from the presentation in this textbook, which focuses on starting a business. Report your findings and conclusions to the class.

Human Relations

3. You did a market analysis for your planned business and have clearly identified your target market. The potential partner you have recruited has the money to help you get the business underway but has not been involved in the market research. She believes you ought to focus your marketing plan on reaching everybody, not just one targeted group. What can you do to change her mind without losing her participation in the project and without spoiling your business relationship?

Enriching Your Learning

1. Develop a marketing plan for your selected business.
2. If you are employed, choose a product sold by your company and determine the following:

   - The complete channel of distribution for the product. (In addition to names and locations of channel members, record the type of transportation between each point.)
   - The pricing structure at each point in the channel.
   - The strategies used by each of the members to promote the product. (Identify the target market they are trying to reach with their promotional efforts.)

   Note: If you are not employed, interview a local businessperson to obtain the same kind of information for a selected product.

Chapter 12
Legal Requirements

Objectives

After completing this chapter, you will be able to

- suggest ways to get legal protection for the business products you create,
- describe some of the legal restrictions on selecting a business site,
- list the basic elements of a legal and binding contract,
- discuss some of the ways government regulates businesses in their dealings with both customers and employees, and
- identify some of the taxes businesses are obligated to pay.

Terms to Know

patent
claims
copyright
trademark
service mark
contract
counteroffer
consideration
capacity
zoning laws
lease
escrow period
warranty of
 merchantability
product liability

? Decisions, Decisions

I've come up with what I think is a great idea for a new product. I'm calling it the Solarchair. Imagine this: You're on the beach or out by the pool. The sun's moved, but you haven't. You're getting fried on the right side, so you have to stand up and drag that heavy lounge chair into a new position. Well, no more. The Solarchair not only swivels, but it does it on its own!

"How?" you ask. That is a secret between me and Phil, a friend of mine who's building the prototype. I worry sometimes, though, that someone will see the thing in his garage and steal the idea. Phil just says, "If you're so worried, why don't you take out a patent?" Just what I need—more dealings with government.

Do you have any idea how many legal requirements even a small business has to meet? Take location. I've been looking for a small building to use as a factory. You'd think I wanted to put in a foundry or something. You can't put it here—that's zoned residential. You can't put it there—that's zoned commercial. I still haven't found a place nearby where I can put it.

And the paperwork, the forms—it's mind-boggling. I thought you just needed a business permit. But if you're going to sell things to people, then you have to collect sales tax. That's a set of forms every couple of months. If you're going to have employees, then you have to withhold payroll taxes. That's multiple sets of forms multiple times each year to multiple levels of government. And it's the same thing for unemployment contributions and business taxes.

Now Phil wants me to take out a patent? I can just imagine what those forms are like. Does this ever end? When do I get a chance just to do business?

Coping with Government Regulation

Businesses, both large and small, are affected on a daily basis by the laws of federal, state, and local governments. To enforce these laws, governments use a variety of agencies. These agencies write the actual regulations, or requirements and restrictions, by which businesses are bound.

Most businesspeople recognize the need for some regulation. Businesses, employees, customers, and the general public must be protected in some circumstances. However, owners of small businesses also recognize the costs imposed by such regulation.

They find the time and expense of doing all the required paperwork especially burdensome. (Each year businesses spend an estimated 2 billion hours filling out government forms!) Small businesspeople often complain that this burden far exceeds any benefits that might be derived from the regulations.

While it is impossible to discuss all of the laws that affect business, this chapter will touch on some of the major ones. It will give you a better sense of what you need to know before starting your own enterprise. Figure 12-1 provides an overview of the areas that will be covered.

Laws Affecting a New Business

Product Idea
- Patents
- Copyrights
- Trademarks

Start-up
- Permits
- Licenses
- Contracts

Trade Issues
- Price discrimination
- Consumer protection
- Uniform Commerical Code

NEW BUSINESS

Location
- Zoning laws
- Building codes
- Leases
- Contracts for purchase of real estate

Employees
- Equal employment opportunity
- Hours and compensation
- Health and safety

Taxes
- Sales tax
- Payroll taxes
- Federal unemployment tax
- Business income taxes

Figure 12–1   From the very start, a new business is affected by a large number of government regulations and requirements. Speculate about what each of the bulleted items in the diagram requires businesses to do. Do you think any of the provisions are designed for the benefit or protection of businesses? If so, which? Explain your reasoning.

Protecting Your Ideas

Suppose you have an idea for a good or service that you want to market. To move on the idea, you know you will need help. But you don't want to ask for that help because you're afraid someone will steal your idea. What can you do? Depending on your product, you have several options.

Patents

A **patent** is a grant to an inventor that gives him or her the exclusive right to produce and sell an invention for a period of 17 years. To receive a patent, you must file an application with the federal Patent and Trademark Office (PTO). In the application, you confirm that you are the inventor of your product and describe in detail all of its components. The definitions of these components are called **claims**.

Prior to submitting your application, you, your attorney, or a hired patent practitioner must do a patent search. This involves going through the records of all existing patents to verify that you are, in fact, the inventor of a unique product.

It takes the PTO about two years to conduct its own search of the patent records. During that time, you are protected by a special status assigned to your invention. You may make and market your product provided you clearly label it "patent pending."

If the PTO decides your claims are valid, it will issue you a patent. It may, however, decide that some or all of your claims are not valid. In that case, you may revise them and resubmit your application.

Copyrights

A **copyright** is similar to a patent, except that it protects original works of authorship. These include such things as books, movies, musical compositions, and computer software.

If you plan to publish (or make public) your work, copyright law requires that you do two things. First, you must place a notice of copyright in a prominent location on the work. This notice must include either the symbol © or the word *Copyright,* the year of first publication, and the name of the copyright holder. The second thing you must do is deposit two copies of the work with the Copyright Office. The office is a branch of the Library of Congress.

It is important to understand that a copyright protects only the form in which the idea is presented. It does not protect the idea itself. For example, if you write a database software program, the program that produces the database is protected, but the idea of a database is not. Thus, there are several different companies producing their own versions of database software.

A copyright lasts for the life of the author plus 50 years. After that, the work goes into the public domain and can be used by anyone free of charge.

Trademarks

A **trademark** is a word, symbol, design, or combination of these that a business uses to identify itself or something it sells. When used, it is followed by the registered trademark symbol ®. For example, a rainbow-colored apple with a bite taken out of it is a symbol recognized by consumers worldwide. It is the trademark of Apple Computer. When a design or symbol describes a service business, it is called a **service mark**.

Like a patent and a copyright, a trademark provides legal protection. If a business registers its trademark with the PTO, that trademark cannot be used by a competitor. However, a trademark cannot be registered with the PTO until it is actually going to be used. Like a patent applicant, a business seeking trademark status for its symbol must prove that the design is original and distinctive.

Unlike a patent, a trademark can be held indefinitely—unless it becomes common usage in the English language. Words like *aspirin, yo-yo,* and *thermos* were once registered trademarks. Today they can no longer be used exclusively by the businesses that created them because they have become generic terms.

An attractive trademark can give a business visibility and name recognition within the community. What is this company's trademark? Is it registered? How do you know?

Risk Takers, Profit Makers

Barbara Nyden Rodstein

Barbara Nyden Rodstein started her plumbing fixtures business for two reasons. First, while shopping for a faucet, she found herself unimpressed by the quality and selection of what was available. More importantly, her and her husband's pneumatic tools venture was being devastated by imports. Thus, it was with an ailing business at hand and an unsatisfied market in mind that Rodstein launched Harden Industries in 1982.

Despite her previous involvement in manufacturing, the Los Angeles entrepreneur had little to found her business on. The pneumatic tool and fixtures manufacturing businesses were very different in production and marketing. They were alike only in being dominated by established and insulated companies run by males. These conditions, plus her husband's declining health and eventual death, left Rodstein with a daunting task—learning a new trade with little preparation or help.

Rodstein compensated for her technical deficiencies with pragmatism. She offered high commissions to salespeople and improved on quality and distribution. She also stressed innovation. By introducing interchangeable parts to a mostly stagnant industry, Harden allowed customers to adapt fixture pieces to their own needs. Indeed, Rodstein credits always heeding the opinions of customers, retailers, and workers with the growth and profits Harden has experienced.

Because she owns and runs the company herself (unlike her larger competitors), Rodstein effects change easily. While Harden Industries can't always muster the capital or influence of larger corporations, it can adapt to trends and demand more quickly.

Rodstein feels that her biggest nemesis as a business owner has not been the competition, however. It's been government regulation. Too big to be treated as a small business and too small to cope effectively with regulatory demands, Harden maintains a staff of attorneys for guidance on legal matters. Legal difficulties, compounded with a national economy that she finds unyielding and inefficient, prompt Rodstein to recommend an overhaul in American business practices.

Rodstein asks entrepreneurs to look out for business in general as well as their own businesses. That entails participating in chambers of commerce and joining lobbying groups. For Rodstein it also means assisting young entrepreneurs through collegiate programs. Conditions may never be perfect, but Rodstein perseveres to pay the bills—and to pave the way for future business owners.

Starting Up Your Business

Certain legal requirements and procedures are fundamental to your ability to do business. If you cannot meet the requirements, you cannot even start up your enterprise. If you cannot master the procedures, you will continue in business only with the greatest difficulty. We shall discuss two such areas in this section.

Permits and Licenses

You were introduced to some of the legal procedures for starting up a business back in Chapter 8. There you learned about legal forms of business ownership and applying for a DBA certificate. Both represented decisions you would make relatively early in the entrepreneurial process.

Before you can officially open your doors, however, you will need some additional documentation. At the very least, you will need to get a business permit from your local government. This permit will allow you to do business in your community and will most likely have to be renewed annually. This means that you will be required to pay periodic license fees throughout the life of your enterprise.

Depending on the business you have chosen, you may also have to meet licensing requirements. Usually this involves taking and passing an examination to show that you have the necessary education and training to do the job. For example, doctors, nurses, barbers, accountants, and counselors all need special licenses. Licensing is designed to protect consumers from unskilled or unqualified business operators. Licensing requirements vary from one state or locality to another.

Be sure you have the necessary licenses before you start your business. You can check with your local government and your state department of licensing and regulation for information.

Contracts

As an entrepreneur, you will be involved in numerous contracts. Some will be with vendors or landlords, others with clients, and still others with government agencies.

Understanding some of the basic legal issues in contract law is therefore vital to your business. You will not always be able to check contract terms with an attorney. For the simplest contracts, you will probably not be able to afford the time or the expense. The price of misunderstanding, however, can be high.

Most contracts are complied with in full. However, when one of the parties fails to meet his or her obligations, the other party may be entitled to monetary damages. The right to such compensation is usually determined in court. This is why it is so important to draw up a legally binding contract that clearly states the intentions of all the parties.

A **contract** is a binding agreement or promise to do something. To be a valid, legal contract, a document must contain four elements.

AGREEMENT.   Agreement occurs when one party to a contract makes an offer or promises to do something and the other party accepts. For example, suppose a vendor offers to sell your business a fax machine. There is no agreement until you have either sent the vendor a purchase order or a check signifying that you accept the offer. Note, however, that if you change any of the terms of the vendor's offer, you have created a **counteroffer**. This is a new offer that now requires the acceptance of the vendor to form a contract.

CONSIDERATION.   The second required contract element is consideration. **Consideration** is what is exchanged for the promise. The money you pay to the vendor for the fax machine is valuable consideration and causes the contract to be binding. Note, however, that while you may think of consideration as payment for the promise, it need not be in the form of money.

CAPACITY.   Capacity is the third contract requirement. **Capacity** means that you are legally able to enter into a contractual agreement. By law, minors, intoxicated persons, and insane persons cannot enter into valid contracts. If they do make themselves parties to contracts, the agreements can be considered void.

LEGALITY. The final contract element is legality. For a contract to be valid, it must be legal. In other words, it cannot have any provisions that are illegal or result in illegal activities.

Choosing a Location

Commercial buildings are inspected at various stages throughout their construction. Why?

Place is one of those topics you have already touched upon in your preliminary marketing plan. Now, however, you can add a new dimension to the information you have already gathered. Now you can consider how legal requirements influence your choice of a business location.

Zoning Laws and Building Codes

Whether you are constructing a new facility or locating your business in an existing building, you will need to conform to local **zoning laws**. You should first check with your local government to see if your type of business is allowed in the neighborhood you have selected. Cities typically designate particular areas, or zones, for certain uses. Zones are usually designated as residential, commercial, industrial, or public. You cannot, for example, locate a manufacturing plant in the middle of a residential neighborhood.

Zoning laws also address environmental issues. They may restrict such things as disposal of toxic waste, noise and air pollution, and incompatible building styles. For example, a residential neighborhood might permit office buildings—but only those that are low-rise and fit in with the predominant residential architecture. Zoning laws may also define the type and style of signs that

businesses can use and the appearance of their facades.

In addition to restrictions on use and appearance, you need to check on laws that relate to the actual construction of your facility. These are called building codes. Building codes set standards for construction and/or modification of facilities. These standards include such things as the strength of concrete, the amount of insulation, and other structural requirements.

Local governments employ inspectors to verify that building code requirements are met at each stage of construction. What can you do to be sure their requirements are met? Licensed building contractors or architects are usually familiar with local building codes. You can assure that your facility is built to code by hiring such a person to supervise your project.

Leasing

Most entrepreneurs start with few resources and little money. Therefore, prudent entrepreneurs will usually lease buildings and equipment rather than buy them. A **lease** is a contract to use a facility or equipment for a specified period of time. The lessee (the person who is leasing the building or equipment) has no ownership rights.

Leasing usually does not require spending a large amount of money up front. The money saved can be used for purchasing inventory and supplies and hiring employees. This can be a definite advantage for a new business. Another advantage is that some lease expenses are tax deductible. This can reduce the tax liability of the company.

Nevertheless, leasing has some drawbacks. A lease is a very complex document. It states the terms—the length of the lease, the monthly rent, the penalty for failing to pay, and the procedure for termination. Because a lease is a long-term contract, an entrepreneur should consult with an attorney before signing one.

Buying

You may have the desire and means to purchase an existing building rather than lease one. Or you may not be able to find an existing building that suits your needs. In either case, you will have to deal with a contract for the purchase of real estate. These, by law, must be in writing.

Real estate contracts spell out the terms of the sale for the parties involved. These include the price, down payment, and **escrow period** (the length of time for the transaction to go through). Again, because a long-term contract is involved, you should consider consulting an attorney before signing. He or she will help you decide whether the agreement's terms are in your best interest.

Hiring Employees

If you start a business, at some point you will probably hire employees. You should be aware that many laws exist that affect the hiring, firing, and compensating of employees.

Equal Employment Opportunity Commission

The Equal Employment Opportunity Commission (EEOC) is charged with protecting the rights of employees. It ensures that employers do not discriminate against employees because of

- age;
- race, color, or national origin;
- religion;
- gender; or
- physical challenge.

For example, as an employer you may not refuse to promote or give pay increases to an employee based on any of the characteristics listed above. This is where the expression *Equal pay for equal work* comes from.

Nor can you refuse to hire someone based on the listed characteristics if he or she is otherwise qualified. If you give any tests or use any screening devices, the U.S. Department of Labor says that they must be related directly to the type of performance expected on the job. You cannot, for example, test someone's physical stamina when he or she is applying for a desk job.

Fair Labor Standards Act

The Fair Labor Standards Act was passed in 1938. This law established a minimum wage and maximum working hours. It also ensured that children under the age of 16 could not be employed full time except by their parents.

Occupational Safety and Health Act

The Occupational Safety and Health Act of 1970 was passed to ensure that employees had safe and healthy working conditions. You have probably heard of the agency that was created by this Act—OSHA, the Occupational Safety and Health Administration.

OSHA frequently comes under fire from businesspeople for the stiff rules and regulations it enforces. The agency also requires that a large amount of paperwork be done and levies heavy fines for noncompliance.

In general, OSHA requires that employers look for areas of hazard in their workplace. Employers must also maintain health and safety records, provide safety training, keep up-to-date on new OSHA standards, and remedy violations promptly.

OSHA's team of inspectors examines the working environment of a business when its name appears on a targeted list. A business gets on the list because of a particular hazard, such as asbestos exposure or a recently reported violation. OSHA offers consultation and assistance to inspected firms, as well as a list of violations that must be remedied.

Dealing with Trade Issues

Our country has placed great value on the ability of businesses to compete freely in the marketplace. In general, government does not interfere. However, since the 1800s, business has accepted the imposition of certain laws designed to preserve competition.

It could be said of the firm doing this site cleanup that government regulation is its business. In what sense?

One of the first of these laws was the Sherman Antitrust Act of 1890. Simply put, it prohibited any restraint of free trade. Other laws, which you should become familiar with, have come about as a result of the Sherman Act.

Price Discrimination

The Clayton Act of 1914 and the even stricter Robinson-Patman Act of 1936 proclaimed that a business cannot sell the same product to different people at different prices. Businesses must justify their giving one customer a lower price than another. They must show that the favored customer bought more, bought lower-quality goods, or benefited from cost savings on the seller's part.

What does this mean to you as a potential entrepreneur? It means that you must take care to be fair to all of your customers when setting your prices. The Federal Trade Commission (FTC) is empowered to enforce laws against price discrimination.

Consumer Protection

Perhaps the greatest number of laws in the area of trade come under the heading of consumer protection. Basically, these laws protect against the following:

- Unscrupulous sellers
- Unreasonable credit terms
- Unsafe products
- Mislabeling of products

One of the largest federal agencies monitoring product safety is the Food and Drug Administration (FDA). It is responsible for researching and testing new products and inspecting the operations of food and drug manufacturers. If your new product idea is a cosmetic, drug, food item, or even suntan lotion, you will need to have approval of the FDA to market it.

If your business involves producing packaged food products, you will almost certainly have to label them to meet government standards. Based on your own experience with such products, what sort of information will you have to provide?

The Consumer Product Safety Commission (CPSC) serves as the watchdog for consumers over products that may be considered hazardous. It also creates safety standards for certain products, like toys for children under the age of five.

The Fair Packaging and Labeling Act helps consumers shop more wisely. The act requires that manufacturer labels truthfully list all raw materials used in the production of products. The act also requires that the size and weight of the product be on the label.

If you are manufacturing products for public consumption, you will need to become familiar with consumer protection laws. That way, you can avoid both the possible recall of your product and potential lawsuits.

The Uniform Commercial Code

The Uniform Commercial Code (UCC) is a group of laws that covers everything from sales to bank deposits and investment securities. The UCC has been adopted by all states. Since it applies to sales transactions between merchants, its provisions are likely to affect you as an entrepreneur.

FORMATION OF CONTRACTS.   When you enter into an agreement to sell a product, you create a valid contract. This means that you must abide by the laws of contract. However, as a merchant, you must also abide by the requirements of the UCC. In some cases, the two are not the same.

For example, in a valid contract, all the terms of price, place, delivery date, and quantity should be present. Suppose you are a manufacturer who has ordered some parts from a supplier, but you have not asked the price. When the parts arrive, you find they cost more than you expected. Do you have a contract despite the confusion about price?

The UCC says yes but assigns a price that is reasonable at the time of delivery. The code assumes the parties intended to form a contract and knew the consequences of any ambiguity. Why? Because both are merchants, professionals who understand the business. Different rules—UCC rules—apply to them than would apply to nonmerchants.

For similar reasons, any changes to a valid contract between merchants do not automatically become a counteroffer. Rather, they become binding just as if they were part of the original contract.

WARRANTIES AND PRODUCT LIABILITY. Have you ever heard the term *caveat emptor*—let the buyer beware? That used to be a basic principle of the U.S. marketplace. Today, however, many believe the emphasis has shifted to the point where it is the *seller* who must beware. This is in part an outgrowth of laws regarding sales warranties. It is also a product of court decisions favoring the safety and economic interests of buyers. Many of these laws and legal principles have been made part of the UCC.

Whenever a merchant sells goods, he or she gives a **warranty of merchantability**. The merchant has no choice about this. The warranty is implied by law. Even if the merchant does not express it in words, it can be assumed by the customer. The warranty assures the buyer that the product he or she is purchasing is of at least average quality and fit for the purpose for which it was intended.

You have probably seen or heard news stories about **product liability**. This is the legal theory that manufacturers are responsible for injuries caused by their products. For example, automobiles are recalled because of defects. Manufacturers are sued because their products have caused injuries. Actions like these have serious consequences for businesspeople. They have sent insurance costs for manufacturers way up. Consider just one example: about 25 percent of the cost of a football helmet goes for insurance.

If you are going to make a product for sale to consumers, you must be very careful. Be sure to include clear instructions for the product's use. Also, give clear warnings of any potential dangers involved.

Truth in Lending

The Consumer Credit Protection Act, more commonly known as the Truth-in-Lending Act, is an important source of legal requirements for retail businesses. The act requires that those who extend credit must disclose fully all the terms and conditions of their credit agreement. Like price discrimination legislation, it is enforced by the Federal Trade Commission.

The Truth-in-Lending Act applies to anything purchased over a period of time greater than four months. For example, suppose your new business is selling reconditioned classic cars. Your first customer wants to finance his purchase over a two-year period. As the seller (and the person providing the credit), you must disclose the following things, among others:

- Price
- Down payment
- Dollar amount of finance and any other charges
- Total amount to be financed
- Annual percentage rate of interest

- Unpaid balance
- Deferred payment price

The deferred payment price is the amount actually paid at the end of two years, including interest and any other charges. You should also be aware that a credit grantor cannot discriminate on the basis of race, religion, national origin, gender, or marital status.

Truth in Advertising

The Federal Trade Commission is also concerned about protecting customers from false and misleading advertising. The laws established to address this trade issue are sometimes referred to collectively as truth-in-advertising laws. Regardless of your business, when you advertise, you should be aware of the following restrictions:

- *Misleading ads.* Your advertising should not mislead customers about what your product can do. Neither should it claim that the product can do something that it cannot.
- *Sale prices.* You cannot offer a reduced price on your product unless it has been offered to the public at the regular price for a period of time.

When you see a bargain price offered on an item, you are entitled to make a key assumption about it. What is that assumption?

- *Price comparisons.* You cannot use list price as your comparison selling price unless your product has actually been sold for that amount. (List price is the manufacturer's suggested retail price.) Also, you must have proof that your prices are lower than your competitors' if you intend to use that fact in your advertising.
- *Bait-and-switch.* You cannot use bait-and-switch advertising. This illegal technique uses a bargain-priced item to lure potential customers into a store. Then a salesperson tries to switch them to higher-priced merchandise.

Dealing with Taxes

One of your legal responsibilities as a business owner is to pay certain taxes. These may include sales tax, payroll taxes, unemployment tax, and income tax.

Sales Tax

In Chapter 5, you learned how to do the calculations for sales tax. Recall that the tax is a percentage of purchase price.

Retailers collect sales tax from their customers and send it to the appropriate government agency. Usually this is the state board of equalization. Retailers make payments about every three months.

Payroll Taxes

As you may also recall from Chapter 5, if you hire employees, you will need to deduct certain payroll taxes from their earnings. You must also obtain state and federal employer identification numbers (EINs). These facilitate the filing of tax returns.

One of the payroll taxes you will deduct from employee earnings is the FICA, or social security, tax. (FICA stands for Federal Insurance Contribution Act.) The tax is figured as a percentage of an employee's income. As of 1992 that percentage was 7.65 (6.20 percent for social security and 1.45 percent for Medicare). So, if an employee makes $265 in a week, he or she would pay a FICA tax of $20.27 ($265 x .0765).

As an employer, you are also required by law to contribute an amount equal to that deducted from each employee's paycheck. So, if you deducted $20.27 from an employee's paycheck for FICA, you, the employer, would have to match that amount. You would send a total of $40.54 to the Internal Revenue Service.

There is a ceiling on the amount of wages subject to the FICA tax. When that ceiling is reached, no more tax is paid. As of 1992, the ceiling was $55,500 for social security and $130,200 for Medicare. Suppose one of your employees made $65,000 in one year. He or she would pay the full FICA tax (7.65 percent) on $55,500. He or she would pay only the Medicare portion of the tax (1.45 percent) on the remaining $9,500.

You can see that withholding for these taxes can be complex. As an employer you must be aware of any changes in the FICA tax rate or in the amount of wages subject to it. The Social Security Administration can update you on this information.

You are also required to withhold certain income taxes from an employee's paycheck. These include federal and, in most cases, a state income tax. These taxes are based on a percentage of gross pay. You will need to contact your local and state governments and the IRS for information about these deductions.

Federal Unemployment Tax

As an employer, you are required to make contributions under the Federal Unemployment Tax Act (FUTA). The act was designed to provide compensation to workers who are temporarily unemployed. You may also be responsible for state unemployment taxes. However, they are usually credited against the federal taxes paid.

Major Federal Regulators

Agency	Function
Consumer Product Safety Commission	Establishes product safety standards and recalls products
Environmental Protection Agency	Creates and enforces standards for the environment, regulating air, water, and noise pollution as well as toxic waste
Equal Employment Opportunity Commission	Establishes the rules relating to discrimination in the workplace
Federal Communications Commission	Licenses the operation of television, radio, telephone, and telegraph operations
Federal Trade Commission	Enforces the antitrust, truth-in-lending, and labeling laws
Food and Drug Administration	Creates the standards for foods and drugs and approves any new drugs
Internal Revenue Service	Enforces the tax statutes and resolves disputes
Interstate Commerce Commission	Determines the trade practices, rates, and routes for interstate railroads, bus companies, and pipelines
Justice Department	Enforces the laws to maintain free trade
National Labor Relations Board	Monitors and governs the relationship between employers and unions
Occupational Safety and Health Administration	Establishes and regulates safety and health standards for employees
Patent and Trademark Office	Issues patents and trademarks for new products

Figure 12–2   Many of the agencies that have the greatest impact on small businesses are part of the federal government. Here is short list. Which ones will directly affect you when you start your own business?

The FUTA tax is 6.2 percent of the first $7,000 of wages paid to an employee. So, if an employee makes $15,000, you pay $434 ($7,000 x .062).

Business Income Taxes

Your business is also legally responsible for paying federal and possibly state and local taxes on the income it earns. If you are a sole proprietor or a partner in a partnership, the income your business earns is, in fact, your personal income. Therefore, the business income is taxed at your personal tax rate.

Let's say you are the sole owner of a catering business. Based on your income statement, your business's net income before taxes is $32,500. You would use that amount as your personal income when paying taxes to your state and the IRS.

You also need to know that as a self-employed business owner, you, too, pay a FICA tax. However, the rate, as of 1992, for a self-employed person is 15.3 percent. That is exactly double what an employee pays—because you are considered *both* employer and employee. The ceiling on the amount taxed is the same.

If, however, you have a corporation, your income tax situation is much different. The business will pay a corporate income tax. You will pay personal income tax based on the salary you earn and any other income derived from the business. In addition, the shareholders will pay personal income tax on salaries drawn or dividends.

There are severe penalties for failure to file and pay income taxes. Therefore, it is advisable to consult an accountant to help you learn how to plan for taxes.

Getting Legal Advice

As we have mentioned before, at any and every stage of developing a new business, you will probably need to seek some kind of legal advice. You can, however, research a great deal of information on your own.

There are a number of sources that you can use either to help you find an attorney or to give you up-to-date information on your legal obligations as a business owner. They include the American Bar Association, the National Resource Center for Consumers of Legal Services, and the Commissioner of Patents and Trademarks.

The IRS can be of special help in tax matters. It periodically holds workshops and seminars to make business owners aware of their tax obligations.

If your business is heavily involved with areas regulated by government, you might want to consult the appropriate governmental agencies. Some possibilities are listed in Figure 12-2. You should be able to find their addresses and telephone numbers in your local library. You could also consult an attorney who specializes in regulatory matters.

Recording Your Data

This chapter is the first of several that will affect multiple sections of your business plan. As you can now readily appreciate, having finished the chapter, legal requirements impact new businesses in virtually every area. Product, pricing, location, finances, dealing with employees, dealing with the public—you will have legal requirements to meet in all of these areas.

You should recognize, however, that not all of the legal data you gather will be prominently featured in your final business plan. Much of it may appear only in the form of passing references. This might be the case, for example, with information about patents or licenses. Both might be just mentioned in the business description or in the marketing plan's discussion of product.

The two places where legal data will have a substantial impact are in the management and financial plans. Labor laws will influence whom you hire and how much you pay them. Trade laws will shape your approach to pricing, product labeling, and warranties. Both sets of decisions should be recorded in the management section of your business plan notebook. Taxes and fees (for licenses, zoning permits, etc.) will affect your financial statements. So also will your ongoing expenses for salaries, rent or mortgage payments, and health and safety provisions. All of these costs should be entered in the financial plan section of your notebook.

Entrepreneur's Bookshelf

To learn more about the subjects discussed in this chapter, consider reading these books and articles:

- *The Entrepreneur's Guide to Doing Business with the Federal Government: A Handbook for Small and Growing Business* by Charles R. Bevers, Linda G. Christie, and Lynn R. Price (© 1989)
- *How to Get the Best Legal Help for Your Business (At the Lowest Possible Cost)* by Mead Hedglon (© 1992)
- *Tax Guide for Small Business,* IRS Pub. No. 334

Chapter 12 Review

Recapping the Chapter

- To protect your business products, you can use patents, copyrights, and trademarks.
- The building in which you locate your business must meet zoning and building code requirements.
- To be binding, a contract must contain four elements—parties who have the legal *capacity* to enter a contract, *agreement* among those parties, *consideration*, and *legality* of purpose and provisions.
- In hiring and compensating employees, a business may not discriminate on the basis of age, race, religion, gender, or physical challenge.
- Federal laws protect consumers against price discrimination, unscrupulous sellers, unreasonable credit terms, unsafe products, and mislabeling.
- Businesses are responsible for collecting and paying sales taxes; payroll taxes; unemployment taxes; and federal, state, and local income taxes.

Reviewing Vocabulary

The chapter vocabulary words have been grouped into four categories below. Describe four different business situations—one using each group of words.

Group 1	Group 2
patent	zoning laws
claims	lease
copyright	escrow period
trademark	
service mark	

Group 3	Group 4
warranty of merchantability	contract
product liability	counteroffer
	consideration
	capacity

Checking the Facts

1. How long does a copyright last? a patent?
2. A vendor offers to sell you a copy machine. To form a contract, how would you accept? Name two ways.
3. What is the purpose of zoning laws?
4. What are the two ways you can acquire a building for your business?
5. What is the purpose of the Equal Employment Opportunity Commission?
6. Why was OSHA established?
7. What does the Truth-in-Lending Act require retail businesses to do?
8. What is the difference between FICA and FUTA?
9. Who would you contact if you had questions about the following?

   - Patents
   - Federal income taxes
   - A new kind of pizza you wanted to market

Thinking Critically

1. Suppose you have an idea for a new kind of applicator that takes the mess out of applying suntan lotion. How would you go about protecting your invention?
2. Compare and contrast a lease with a contract to buy a building.

Chapter 12 Review

3. Let's say your new business is manufacturing low-cost camping equipment. How would the implied warranty of merchantability affect the way you make these goods?
4. Is it necessary to employ an attorney to meet all of the legal requirements of your new business? Why or why not?

Discussing Key Concepts

1. How would you defend the use of zoning laws in cities?
2. Why is it important to have consumer protection laws?

Using Basic Skills

Math
1. Suppose that one of your employees earns $1,500 this month. How much in FICA contributions will you deposit with the IRS in the employee's name?

Communication

2. From Figure 12-2, choose one of the agencies that may regulate some area of your new business. Write a letter requesting information about the regulations they oversee, ways of complying with those regulations, and fines or fees for noncompliance.

Human Relations

3. Your new business is writing articles about historic places and events in your state. You sell your articles to a variety of publications, such as local newspapers, regional magazines, and travel guides. However, you retain the copyrights. While reading one of the local newspapers, you discover that they have reprinted an article you sold to a magazine. When you call the newspaper's editor, he admits that the article probably was picked up without the proper permission. He says, however, that the paper cannot afford to pay for articles. How would you handle this situation? What would you tell the editor?

Enrichment Activities

1. Use your local telephone directory to compile a list of city/county government offices that could provide you with information on obtaining DBA certificates, business permits, and business licenses.
2. Interview the owner of a small manufacturing business, a small retail store, or a small restaurant in your community. Ask the following questions:

   - How do government regulations affect your business?
   - In general, how much does it cost your business to comply with regulations?
   - What, if any, regulatory changes would be helpful to your business?

   Prepare a brief oral presentation for the class summarizing what you learned.
3. Interview a local entrepreneur to find out about his or her hiring practices. Ask how the entrepreneur meets the requirements of the EEOC.
4. Contact the National Resource Center for Consumers of Legal Services. Find out what kind of legal assistance is available in your area for your type of new business. Also, inquire about cost.

Chapter 13

Equipment, Supplies, and Inventory

Objectives

After completing this chapter, you will be able to

- identify the basic operational needs of all businesses and the specific needs of your own business;

- describe how to locate and contact suppliers;
- discuss the factors that influence equipment, supply, and inventory decisions; and
- explain how to begin recording and organizing cost data for future use.

Terms to Know

equipment
fixtures
supplies
start-up costs
vendors

? Decisions, Decisions

It seemed so simple. The novelty gift mail order business was a natural for me. I'd bought lots of gift items that way myself.

My starter product was a wooden plaque with a family coat-of-arms on it. I found the idea in an ad. The supplier furnished everything you needed—and I mean *everything*. I got a coat-of-arms master book, a sealer machine for fixing the coat-of-arms decals to the wooden plaques, the solution needed to make the process work, a supply of common-name coat-of-arms decals, blank plaques. They even sent me masters for ad layouts and a guide for finding periodicals to match my target market. Additional decals, plaques, solution, and other items could be ordered from the supplier as needed.

The initial package cost me $6,500. Outside of that, all I had to pay for was magazine ads and supplies as I ran out. And that was pretty quick. Business just took off. I got my first ads in place in November, and the Christmas business was great. I thought it would level off after that, but people apparently want these plaques for all kinds of gift occasions.

Then I got this letter. It said, "This is to inform you that Heraldic Enterprises is going out of business. We will no longer be able to furnish you with solution, decals, plaque stock, or replacement parts for your sealer machine. We wish you luck in finding an alternate source of supply."

It didn't take me long to find out that there *were* no alternate sources for some of the stuff, like machine parts and decals. If I'm going to stay in business, I'll have to have them made. Other things, like the solution, take a long time to get. Boy, I really feel cheated. I mean, what could I have done differently? Who could have predicted this?

Getting Down to Specifics

Till now your entrepreneurial efforts have involved thinking in rather general terms. You have been making major decisions and mapping out broad plans. Doing these things at the beginning of the entrepreneurial process is essential.

Now, however, you must begin to think about specifics. You cannot make your business a reality without planning its organization in detail. To start, you should ask yourself three key questions:

- What am I going to need to operate my business?

- Where am I going to get what I need?
- How do I decide which suppliers to use?

This chapter can help you find the answers to these questions.

What Does Your Business Need?

Every business needs equipment, supplies, and/or inventory in order to function. **Equipment** refers to implements used in a business's operation. Typically, it includes machinery and tools needed to carry out the main physical labor of a business. Forklifts, mechanic's tools, and computers are all equipment in this sense. However, equipment also includes things used in managing the business or selling its products. This means that furniture and appliances (like telephones and electric pencil sharpeners) are equipment. So also are **fixtures**, or things attached to the building or thought of as part of it (like ceiling lights and display cases).

Supplies are items that are used up in the operation of the business. They may be necessary to the main purpose of the company (like lubricants for production-line machinery). They may also support the administrative side of the operation. (Things like computer paper, pens, or paper clips readily come to mind here.)

Inventory, as noted earlier in the book, consists of goods a business has stored for eventual resale. It can take a number of forms. First, there are raw materials kept on hand for conversion into saleable products. Next, there are goods in the process of being manufactured. Finally, there are goods available for immediate resale.

Identifying General Needs

The three categories of needs—equipment, supplies, and inventory—are the same for all businesses. However, within these categories each type of business has its own particular needs. Figure 13-1 illustrates this point. The figure lists some of the different kinds of equipment, supplies, and inventory commonly used by five different kinds of businesses.

In addition to the distinctive needs that Figure 13-1 emphasizes, there are some items that almost all businesses use. Indeed, it would be difficult to operate without them. These "essentials" fall mostly within the equipment and supply categories. They include the following:

- *Furniture.* Desks, chairs, file cabinets.
- *Fixtures and appliances.* Lights and telephones.

- *Office supplies.* Stationery, envelopes, paper clips, bookkeeping materials.
- *Maintenance supplies and equipment.* Cleaning products and equipment, tools for minor repairs.

Many entrepreneurs would include other items in this list—computers, adding machines, security systems, business forms, dollies. These items, however, only *seem* essential. If you had to, you could do without them—especially in the early stages of a business.

Identifying Your Needs

Now that you know what the operational needs of a business are in a general sense, you can focus on the needs of your own enterprise. Figuring out your business's specific needs is a two-step process.

REVIEW YOUR OPERATION. The first step is sitting down and mentally reviewing your proposed operation and what it will take to carry it out. As you go through each aspect of your operation, list the specific equipment, supplies, and inventory you think you will need.

After listing the items in each category, go back and estimate the quantities you will need to start up your enterprise. Also, make rough estimates of what you will use up or sell over a month's operation. This will give you an idea of how much in the way of supplies and inventory you will have to replace, or purchase.

CONFIRM YOUR PROJECTIONS. The second step in determining your needs is finding out how realistic your projections are. This requires getting input from others who have experience in the business. Some sources we discussed earlier can be helpful here.

Entrepreneurs who are in your field (but not direct competitors) are an example. They can quickly point out things you have overlooked in your lists and estimates. In addition, they can tell you which are the high-volume and low-volume months in your business. This information is

Different Businesses—Different Needs

Type of Business	Equipment	Supplies	Inventory
Manufacturing	■ Heavy machinery ■ Robots ■ Tools ■ Design equipment (computers, drafting boards, etc.) ■ Communication equipment ■ Forklifts ■ Trucks	■ Lubricants for machinery ■ First aid supplies ■ Safety accessories (goggles, gloves, etc.) ■ Replacement parts for equipment ■ Maintenance supplies (paint, solvents, etc.)	■ Raw materials ■ Component parts (motors, computer chips, etc.) ■ Products in process ■ Finished products
Wholesaling	■ Shelving ■ Conveyor belts ■ Refrigeration cases ■ Forklifts ■ Trucks ■ Scanners ■ Pricing equipment	■ Price tags ■ Boxes and bags ■ Packing materials	■ Packaged products for resale ■ Bulk products for resale
Retailing	■ Counters (display and storage) ■ Display items (stands, mannequins, shadow boxes, etc.) ■ Mirrors ■ Security system ■ Cash registers ■ Pricing guns	■ Price tags ■ Wrapping paper (regular and gift) ■ Bags and boxes	■ Merchandise for resale
Service	■ Service-related equipment (hoist for a car repair business, hairdryers for a beauty salon, exercise equipment for a health club, etc.) ■ Service-related tools (wrenches in a car repair business, scissors in a beauty salon, etc.) ■ Truck, van, or car	■ Supplies consumed in service (grease in a car repair business, shampoo in a beauty salon, etc.) ■ Cleaning materials	■ Products complimentary to service (auto accessories in a car repair business, hair-care products in a beauty salon, health food snacks and beverages in a health club)
Extraction	■ Machinery (tractor for a farm, jackhammer for a mine, winch for a fishing boat, etc.) ■ Tools ■ Communication equipment (telephones on a farm, walkie-talkies in a mine, shortwave radio on a fishing boat, etc.)	■ Materials used in the extraction process (fertilizer on a farm, explosives in a mine, bait on a fishing boat, etc.) ■ Safety accessories (goggles, gloves, etc.) ■ Maintenance items for equipment	■ Extracted materials (ore, crops, fish, etc.) ■ Semi-processed materials

Figure 13–1   Equipment, supply, and inventory needs vary with the business. In this table, where would an auto detailing company fall? What would its needs be?

essential if you are to project your operating costs accurately.

Trade associations are another possible source you might wish to contact. They often have prepared informational packages that include both needs and cost data for their fields. Typically the packages give industry averages for operating and **start-up costs**. (The latter are the expenses you incur before you open your business.)

How Can You Meet Your Business Needs?

Once you have contacted businesspeople in your field to confirm your needs lists, you may still find it helpful to consult a telephone directory. For what purposes?

Once you have decided what you need to operate your business, you must determine where and how to get it. First, you must locate and contact several different suppliers and vendors. (**Vendors** are businesses that can provide you with inventory as opposed to things you will use in your operation.) Then you must get detailed information from them.

Your sources may include manufacturers and distributors of machinery, tools, furniture, appliances, and office fixtures and supplies. If yours is a manufacturing business, you will also need to contact businesses that can provide you with raw materials, components, or materials consumed in the production process. If you are planning a wholesale or retail operation, you will need to contact firms that can provide you with appropriate inventory.

Contacting Suppliers and Vendors

Locating suppliers and vendors is not difficult. Businesspeople and trade associations in your field can help you identify some. Others can be found by looking in local (or nearby metropolitan) telephone directories.

Once you start contacting individual suppliers, you will find that the process takes on a life of its own. For example, if a particular supplier

can meet some of your needs but not others, that supplier will likely put you in touch with other firms that carry what they do not. It is also likely that once you begin an active search for information, additional suppliers and vendors will hear and find you.

For some items, catalogs or price lists may be all you need to make your decisions. In those instances, the necessary materials can usually be requested by mail or telephone. (Many suppliers even have 800 numbers.)

Situations in which you are seeking expensive inventory items or equipment that requires demonstration or examination are different, however. You would either have to visit the supplier in person or request that a sales representative call on you.

Getting the Information You Need

In your contacts with potential sources, you should concentrate on getting answers to the following questions:

* What does this source have that will meet my needs?
* How much will it cost me?

You can then add questions based on your specific operational needs.

How many suppliers should you contact? As many as you need to get enough information for sound decision making. Exactly how many that is will vary with each item. For example, you will probably want to interview more potential sources for things that are important to your operation. The size of the purchase and the nature of the item might also dictate more contacts.

EQUIPMENT. Equipment decisions will ordinarily require that you ask many questions to find out if the items offered meet your needs. Here are some possibilities:

- Will the item do the job I want it to do?
- Will there be enough space for it in my facility?
- Will it be compatible with all of my other equipment?
- Is it too expensive for the job at hand? (In other words, could I compromise on quality, given how I'll use the item?)
- How will it hold up over time? Will it require a great deal of maintenance?
- If repairs are necessary, how fast can they be made? Are replacement parts readily available?

SUPPLIES. Supply decisions can be relatively simple or complex, depending on how important they are to your business. For supplies that are incidental to your operation (like paper clips, paper towels, and so on), a minimal survey of sources will ordinarily suffice. For supplies critical to your operation, however, you will probably want to contact more suppliers and question them more thoroughly.

INVENTORY. As a general rule, inventories you purchase must be thoroughly researched and planned. This is true whether they are inventories of merchandise for resale or of raw materials that go into finished goods. The reason is simple. In both cases, they are critical to the ultimate success of your business.

If your enterprise is a retail or wholesale business, your inventory will consist of the items in the product strategy of your preliminary marketing plan. Therefore, before questioning any suppliers, you might want to do some reviewing. Check your notebook entries in that area. Go back over the product considerations and decisions presented in Chapter 11. Finally, give some attention to any related marketing strategy factors. (For example, you might consider the ease or difficulty of obtaining items and the possibility of receiving promotional assistance in marketing them.) All of these things will help you identify the additional information you will need for choosing inventory vendors.

If your business is a manufacturing operation, you will have to maintain an inventory of raw materials. It is especially important that you consider these carefully because they determine so much about your business. They have a major effect on the quality and price of your product. They must be compatible with your equipment. They may produce waste and hence disposal problems that you have to cope with. For these reasons, you should try to obtain detailed information about any raw materials you will need. Inquire about their quality, their composition, and the effects of using them.

How Do You Make Your Choices?

Assume you've gathered all the information you need on each of your equipment, supply, and inventory items. Now you are ready to choose from among competing products (and suppliers). Your decisions will be guided by two factors.

One is your beliefs about the best approach to starting a business. You no doubt have an ideal vision of what you want your business to look like. However, when you get down to specifics, you must face reality. In the area of equipment, for example, that reality is reflected in two key questions:

Risk Takers, Profit Makers

Rick Salsman

When Rick Salsman attended high school in 1986, he printed T-shirts for fun. Today, his fingers are still inky, but he's no longer satisfied with just making shirts. His high school hobby is now a prosperous Berkeley business. At 23, Salsman owns and operates Inky Fingers, a full-fledged advertising specialties venture printing designs and logos on shirts, mugs, decals, and other promotional media.

Inky Fingers was born while Salsman was studying Spanish linguistics at the University of California, Davis. He was living in Berkeley and printed T-shirts in his basement to raise money for the day camp where he worked. Later he printed shirts for other counselors to use in their businesses. Though overhead was low and profits were high, Salsman hardly planned to hawk T-shirts for a living. It wasn't until he graduated—and couldn't find a more attractive job—that he chose advertising specialties as a career.

First, though, Salsman resolved to increase his knowledge of selling and business procedures. From friends, former customers, and helpful city hall clerks, he learned about legal requirements and fiscal strategies. He became familiar with business jargon and joined an ad specialties guild. Then, more confident in himself than banks were, he borrowed to the limits of his 11 credit cards and leased space near the Berkeley campus. He also began advertising.

From the start, advertising played a key role in the success of Inky Fingers, which opened in 1990 in the midst of a recession. While other businesses cut costs by advertising less, Inky Fingers campaigned aggressively to attract clients. This strategy worked. It brought new customers in, which was all that Salsman needed. Once people tried Inky Fingers, they tended to return.

Today Salsman does business in a strategically located and well-equipped shop. He tries, however, to respond to customers just as he did when he was operating out of a basement. This means giving customers exactly what they want. For example, unlike most large operations, Inky Fingers accepts orders as small as one unit. The shop also takes rush orders. Why? Salsman has found that from small jobs come large ones.

Salsman's commonsense approach has also been apparent in his growth strategy. He has only purchased new equipment when a job paid for it. (In other words, he didn't purchase a color printer until he received a color printing job that covered its cost.) As a result, Salsman has been able to erase his start-up costs (all those credit card bills) in less than a year and a half. Because Salsman's ego and outlook rest comfortably in the basement, Inky Fingers' gross receipts—now $250,000 a year—continue to reach skyward.

Cost control is often critical to the success of new businesses. What potential solution is this entrepreneur exploring?

- Does all the equipment have to be in place from the beginning, or can some things be phased in?
- Does all the equipment have to be the newest, the biggest, and the best available?

It is natural to want to have everything perfect when you open the doors of your business. However, you also have to consider that overspending often leads to the downfall of new ventures. Given that fact, a strong case can be made for starting a business with the absolute minimum in equipment, supplies, and inventory.

The second factor that will guide your decisions is the range of options you have available. You will make choices among products and suppliers based on price, quality, service, and so on. You may also have to consider supplier stability and the availability of alternate sources. (This is especially true if your business will be dealing with unique items.)

Bear in mind that later decisions (like site selection, layout, and insurance needs) will be influenced by what you decide here. You should therefore make every effort to determine your actual needs at this point. Even so, these, like other initial decisions, may change as you go through the process of molding your business.

Organizing and Using Your Data

Decisions you make at this stage of the entrepreneurial process are different in nature from most of those you made earlier. These decisions all involve projected expenditures and will form the basis of your financial plan.

The information you gather here (mostly quantities and prices) will be easy to lose track of. Therefore, you must keep well-organized records of your cost decisions. To do this, you should set up two separate lists in the financial section of your business plan notebook:

- *Start-up costs.* This list will include items you must buy before you open.
- *Operating costs.* Here you will list your expected monthly expenses once you are open.

You will add to these lists as you complete the next several steps of the entrepreneurial process.

Any price lists, catalogs, and similar documentation you acquire should be placed in your financial plan folder. However, in some instances you may want to prepare separate folders for equipment, supply, and inventory data. This would be the case if the material were voluminous (as it might be for, say, a retail business).

Entrepreneur's Bookshelf

To learn more about the subjects discussed in this chapter, consider reading these books:

- *Avoiding the Pitfalls of Starting Your Own Business* by Jeffrey Davidson (© 1988)
- *The McGraw-Hill Guide to Starting Your Own Business: A Step-by-Step Blueprint for the First-Time Entrepreneur* by Stephen C. Harper (© 1991)

Chapter 13 Review

Recapping the Chapter

- All businesses need equipment, supplies, and/or inventory to carry out operations.
- To determine your business's specific needs involves (1) mentally reviewing your operation and listing what you need and (2) confirming and refining your ideas by talking to others in the field.
- You can locate and contact suppliers through businesspeople, trade associations, telephone directory listings, trade publications, and other suppliers.
- You should gather information about each equipment, supply, and inventory item from as many sources as you need for sound decision making.
- Both your beliefs about the best approach to starting a business and your available options will influence your final equipment, supply, and inventory decisions.
- You should break your cost data into start-up costs and monthly operating costs.

Reviewing Vocabulary

Write a sentence for each pair of terms below. In each sentence, use the terms in a way that shows that you understand the difference between them.

- equipment—supplies
- fixtures—inventory
- start-up costs—operating costs
- vendors—suppliers

Checking the Facts

1. What are the key questions that move you from broad planning to the specifics of creating a business?

2. Under what circumstances would a business need an inventory of raw materials?
3. What types of equipment does a manufacturing business need?
4. What kind of inventory might a service business need? Give an example.
5. Name two sources that can help a prospective entrepreneur confirm projected equipment, supply, and inventory needs.
6. Other than suggestions from outside sources, what is the simplest way to locate suppliers and vendors?
7. What two questions (at a minimum) must you ask suppliers and vendors to get the information you need?
8. How are the decisions you make about equipment, supplies, and inventory different from all the others you have made thus far in the entrepreneurial process?

Thinking Critically

1. Review the paragraph that describes equipment and supply needs common to almost all businesses (page 158). Then answer these questions:

   - Are there common items that should appear but do not?
   - Are there items that do appear but should not?
   - Why are inventory items not discussed?

2. Other than the two-step procedure given in this chapter on pages 158 and 160, is there any other way to identify completely and accurately the specific needs of your own business? Explain.

3. Would it be a good idea to order all of your equipment, supplies, and inventory from supplier catalogs? Why or why not?

Chapter 13 Review

Discussing Key Concepts

1. Are there any exceptions to the statement that every business needs equipment, supplies, and/or inventory? What are they?
2. Which would be the best source for assisting you in refining your needs list—a trade association, a business owner in your field, or some other source? Why?
3. Which type of supplier—equipment, supply, or inventory—should you contact first? Why?
4. Which do you believe is the right start-up approach for your business—starting with the minimum or starting with the best of everything? Explain your choice.
5. When making your final equipment, supply, and inventory choices, what kinds of decisions would be the easiest? What kinds would be the most difficult? Why?

Using Basic Skills

Math

1. In your search for a cash register, you have narrowed your options to three. All are comparable in quality and will meet your business needs. Price, therefore, will be the determining factor. Calculate the various purchase prices from the information given below, and make your decision.

   - *Register 1* sells for $639, but the supplier offers a 5 percent discount for first-time orders.
   - *Register 2*, a used machine, can be bought for $365, but reprogramming and cleaning will cost $195.
   - *Register 3* is priced at $715, but the supplier will include a year's supply of journal tape worth $38 and an extra cash drawer worth $73.

Communication

2. Identify those suppliers and vendors who would be important sources for your selected business but are not in your immediate area. Write a letter to each requesting catalogs and price lists.
3. Write or telephone trade associations in your selected field for lists of recommended start-up equipment, inventory, and supplies. Also, request supplier lists.

Human Relations

4. You have made an appointment with a business owner who is in your selected field but in a different market area. Your goal is to get input on your own equipment, supply, and inventory lists. The owner is very cordial at the beginning of your interview. However, it quickly becomes apparent that he is reluctant to share cost-related details with you. Because your business is unique, there is no one else you could realistically ask for this kind of help. What should you do?

Enriching Your Learning

Determine the equipment, supply, and inventory needs for your own business:

- Mentally review your projected operation, and develop your own needs list.
- Search the Yellow Pages for suppliers of equipment, supplies, and inventory you would need in your selected business. Record the names, addresses, and telephone numbers of the suppliers you locate.
- Interview a business owner in your field to confirm your list and get assistance in refining it. At the end of your interview, request suggestions regarding suppliers and vendors you might contact for detailed information.

Chapter 14
Site Selection

Objectives

After completing this chapter, you will be able to
- describe how to select a community in which to start your business,
- explain the criteria that owners of different kinds of businesses apply when considering a business site,
- list the factors that enter into selecting a building, and
- discuss the advantages of starting a business at home.

Terms to Know

economic base
incentives
enterprise zones
Standard
  Metropolitan
  Statistical Areas
  (SMSAs)
census tracts
trade area
industrial parks
gross lease
net lease
percentage lease

Decisions, Decisions

My partner and I want to start a custom printing business. We've done our market research, figured out what equipment we'll need, contacted suppliers. We've even sat down with an attorney to map out a partnership agreement. We did all that without a problem. Now, for the first time, we're at odds over (of all things) where to put the place.

My partner's big on impressions. He wants a place that looks like an office, that's even located right in there with other offices. He says we can put all the printing equipment in the back. Of course, given the equipment we'll start with and everything we eventually want to add, the "back" is going to have to be pretty big. In an office building, that's going to cost a fortune.

Now, I think good-quality work, not a fancy front office, makes the best impression. I even think lots of equipment makes a good impression. It shows you're willing to invest to serve your customers better. And I think our kind of customers will recognize that.

The people we want to focus on are small businesses. We'll print whatever they want—business cards, stationery, forms, brochures. We'll even help them design the stuff. Well, those kinds of customers don't care what your place looks like. We could locate in the industrial park at the edge of town, and they wouldn't care.

Needless to say, that's an idea that makes my partner cringe. "Sure we'd save money," he says, "but we wouldn't have any customers. No one would come out that far just for a printing job."

So, who's right? Which is the better site for a business like ours? How can you tell?

Choosing a Location for Your Business

For you as an entrepreneur, the decision of where to put your new business is a major one. For one thing, a location can make or break certain kinds of enterprises. It can determine who sees your business, how easily they can get to it, and whether or not they give it a try. For another thing, your choice of location can for all practical purposes be a permanent decision. Once you have invested in land, a building, fixtures, or heavy equipment, it may be difficult if not impossible to move.

In this chapter you will learn what criteria to consider when choosing a location for your new business. You will start at the broadest level of consideration—how to choose a community—and work your way down to the actual building.

How Do You Select a Community?

Unfortunately, the community that you live in is not always the best place to start your business. Just because you are familiar with an area does not make it suitable for your enterprise. To judge your community fairly, you will need to step back and look objectively at what it has to offer.

Examine the Economic Base

When evaluating a community, you should consider its **economic base**. This is simply the major source of income for the community. Usually a community's economic base is characterized as "primarily industrial" or "primarily service oriented" or something similar. What you want to know, however, is whether that economic base is growing or shrinking. Fortunately, the local government wants to know that, too. One of its agencies probably does an economic base analysis regularly. You should be able to obtain a copy.

What constitutes a growing economic base? One in which there is more money coming into a community than there is leaving it. Suppose a community's major economic activity is farming. It sells agricultural products to other communities, which brings money in. Because the only major mall in the area is in the next town, however, residents do much of their shopping elsewhere. This sends money out of the community. If the revenues from farming exceed the expenditures for shopping, then the community's economic base is growing. However, if the residents are spending more at the mall, then the community's economic base is shrinking.

Thus, the most favorable type of community for your new business is one in which "exports" exceed "imports." Because it is always receiving new money from outside, such a community doesn't have to rely on just what is available locally. This makes more growth possible. Additional money creates additional demand, which translates into new business opportunities. Additional money also provides the investment capital that entrepreneurs can use to exploit those opportunities. In this way, a community with a growing economic base provides a favorable environment for new businesses.

Look for Financial Incentives

Many communities actively try to attract new businesses. Some are looking to continue the expansion of their economic bases. Others are seeking to revitalize faltering economies. Communities in both situations frequently offer special **incentives** to attract new enterprises. These incentives include such things as lower taxes, cheaper land for building facilities, and employee training programs.

You should check to see if such incentives are available in the community you are considering. Often they will be offered to locate new businesses in a particular area. For example, some states establish **enterprise zones** in communities that request them. Businesses that locate in these zones receive favorable tax treatment from the state based on the number of new jobs they create. Your local economic development department can tell you if any such programs are available to help your new business.

Incentives say a great deal about a community's attitude toward business. Their presence indicates that the community welcomes new enterprises and recognizes the benefits they bring. Their absence can indicate just the opposite. Faced with the latter situation, you should carefully check local tax laws and business regulations. If your community of choice makes it difficult for businesses to operate, you might want to look elsewhere.

Analyze Population Data

If you find a community's economic base and its attitude toward new businesses are favorable, you should next look at its population. Is it growing or declining? Is it aging as young people move away or getting younger as more families with children settle in the area? Such trends can suggest all sorts of things significant to your business. These include who will spend, how much, and on what types of products.

Most communities have agencies that keep statistics on local population trends. Your local economic development department or chamber of commerce are good possibilities.

DEMOGRAPHICS. Demographics comprise some of the most useful population information you can gather. Recall that demographics are statistics that deal with the personal characteristics of a population. These characteristics include age, education, gender, race, religion, and income level.

Why is it important to know such characteristics? Suppose you were going to open a restaurant catering to young, upscale professionals. Wouldn't you want to know if your community had a sufficient number of such individuals to patronize the business? Demographic data could tell you if this were the case. In other words, it could tell you if the demographics of your location and the demographics of your target market matched.

Where do you find demographic data? Your public library or local college library are good places to start. Both should have the *1990 Census Basics,* published by the U.S. Bureau of the Census.

Each decade the Census Bureau surveys every citizen of the United States in order to track changes in population size and characteristics. The bureau divides the United States into **Standard Metropolitan Statistical Areas (SMSAs)**. These are generally geographic areas that include a major metropolitan area, such as Boston or Los Angeles. The SMSAs are further divided into **census tracts**, each containing approximately 4,000–5,000 people, and additionally into blocks.

So, for any urban area that you may be considering, you can obtain all sorts of valuable information on the residents, courtesy of the Census Bureau. For example, suppose you wanted to start a housing-related business. To understand the market you wished to serve, you could consult the federal government's *Census of Housing* and *Annual Housing Survey,* both available in your library.

LABOR SUPPLY. Population data can also reveal the number of people available for work. When considering a community as a potential business location, you must seriously consider

Demographic Data for Census Tract 6204*

Population by Age		Household Income (1989)	
13 and under	663	Less than $9,999	47
14–24	518	$10,000–$19,999	49
25–39	1,430	$20,000–$34,999	267
40–54	1,073	$35,000–$49,999	205
55–69	701	$50,000–$74,999	430
70 and over	241	$75,000 or more	915
Educational Attainment (Persons 25 and Over)		**Workers per Household (1989)**	
Less than 9th grade	37	None	106
High school graduate	579	1	361
Associate's degree	287	2	668
Bachelor's degree	1,207	3 or more	177
Graduate/professional degree	599		

*California, Los Angeles County
Source: U.S. Bureau of the Census, 1990 Census of Population and Housing

Figure 14–1 Here is a sample of the kind of data the Census Bureau makes available for every census tract in the nation. If you were planning to open an art gallery, would this area be a promising location? Why or why not?

your employment needs and how well the local labor supply can meet them. Ask yourself the following questions:

- How many employees will I need?
- Is there a sufficient pool of labor in the community to meet my needs?
- Does the available labor pool have the appropriate skills to help my business?

Do not be tempted to rely on high unemployment figures as an indicator that a sufficient labor force is available. Often the unemployed lack the skills and training employers need. Rather than relying on federal unemployment statistics, look to local sources for work force information. The community's employment development department, economic development department, or chamber of commerce would probably have more relevant and specific information.

How Do You Select a Business Site?

Once you have determined which community is suitable for your business, you can begin to look for a site within that community. The criteria used to judge sites vary with the type of business.

Retail Business Considerations

If you have chosen to start a retail business, you have chosen to sell directly to the consumer. Therefore, you will need to go where the consumers are. You will need to find fairly large concentrations of consumers who fall within your target market.

One of the first things you will need to decide is your **trade area.** This is the region or section of the community from which you can expect to draw your customers.

The type and size of your business will determine the size of your trade area. For example, if you offer a specialized line of merchandise, you may draw customers from a great distance—perhaps from as much as 15–20 miles distant. On the other hand, if you offer general merchandise solely for the convenience of customers, you will draw from a much smaller area—perhaps a radius of a mile.

Once you have pinpointed the area of the community you wish to serve, you can begin to locate potential sites within it. At this point, a map is an especially helpful tool. If you mark critical data on it as you investigate each site, it can serve as a visual summary of your choices. In this way, it can simplify making your ultimate decision.

You should begin by drawing a circle delineating the trade area around each site you are considering. Then, within each trade area, you will need to examine and note four additional features. None is within your control, but all are critical.

NUMBER AND SIZE OF COMPETING BUSINESSES. You should first mark all potential competitors. Calculating the number, size, and location of stores that will compete either directly or indirectly with your business will give you a sense of where customers go to shop. It will also tell you how large, in reality, your trade area is. (It may, in fact, be larger or smaller than the circle you have drawn.)

Look for clusters of stores and low vacancy rates. A low vacancy rate may indicate that customers are strongly drawn to the site. This is something that a new business owner might be able to take advantage of.

One way to determine the vacancy level in a retail center is simply to walk through and estimate (or count) the number of vacant stores compared to leased stores. You could also talk to the management company for the center to find out the amount of leased versus vacant store space. Then you could calculate the vacancy rate for yourself. Here is the formula you would use:

A map can serve as a visual summary of a potential location's most important features. What do you think the circles on this entrepreneur's map indicate?

$$\frac{\text{Amount of vacant space}}{\text{Total space available}} = \text{vacancy rate}$$

Consider an example. Suppose a 100,000-square-foot shopping center has 5,000 square feet of vacant space. Its vacancy rate would be calculated as follows:

$$\frac{5,000}{100,000} = .05 \text{ or } 5\%$$

NATURE OF THE COMPETITION. Now that you know where your competition is located, you should try to figure out the way they do business. Specifically, you should consider whether your business will be compatible and what the implications are of this information.

For example, if your business is similar in size and merchandise to its competitors, you may want to locate near them to encourage comparison shopping. On the other hand, if your operation will be significantly larger and you will be able to offer a greater variety of products, you may want to take a different approach. You may be able to generate your own drawing power and on that basis locate away from your competitors.

CHARACTER OF THE AREA. Look carefully at the character of the area. Is it attractive and inviting? Does it have the appearance of success? In general, consumers like to shop in attractive, safe, thriving environments. Individual businesses or blocks that counter this impression are potential problems. You should mark them on your map.

ACCESSIBILITY AND TRAFFIC. You should also mark your map with the routes your potential customers could use to reach your business. Identify the highways, streets, and public transportation routes that lead to the site. If you find that there is no convenient route to your business or if the site is difficult to locate, you can bet that customers are not going to put out the effort to get to you.

You should also look for physical barriers that might impede customer access. A park, for example, can be such a barrier. So can a nearby high-crime area if people must pass through or go around it to get to your site.

Both foot and car traffic are important to a retail business. Entrepreneurs often stand at a potential site and count the number of cars and pedestrians passing by. If you decide to use this technique, you should recognize one key limitation. The traffic count will most likely vary with the time of day and the day of the week. You may therefore want to do more than one count. Once you've gathered such data, however, you can compare results from different sites to help you make a more informed choice.

Finally, make sure that your chosen site has adequate parking. Customers appreciate easy, safe, and free parking.

Service/Wholesale Business Considerations

In many ways service and wholesale businesses are similar in their needs to retail businesses. This is especially true if they have customers who come to their places of business. Barber shops or wholesale outlets that sell to the public are both good examples. If your service or wholesale business is of this sort, then all of the factors relevant to a retail site will apply to your business as well.

However, many service and wholesale businesses do not have customers or clients coming to their business sites. For example, exterminators and plumbers go to their customers' homes.

Sometimes the only way to get a feel for how much traffic passes a particular location is to do an actual count. What limitations does this technique have in terms of yielding accurate and useful information?

Rarely does a customer need to see their places of business. Distributors are in a similar position. Their clients are manufacturers and retailers who do business primarily through sales representatives and purchase orders.

One of the advantages of these kinds of businesses is that they do not need expensive, high-profile locations. They can choose less expensive areas of a community. They should, however, be located relatively near the customers they serve to save time and transportation costs.

Manufacturing/Extraction Business Considerations

If you decide to start a manufacturing or extraction concern, your location will be largely predetermined by the nature of your business. An extraction company, for example, must be near whatever it is extracting—ore, fish, trees.

A manufacturing firm, on the other hand, can locate only where local zoning laws allow. In an effort to keep noisy, odor-producing businesses away from homes, stores, and offices, most communities have set aside certain areas for industrial uses. Sometimes these areas are called **industrial parks**. Being restricted in this fashion is not necessarily a disadvantage. This is because industrial parks are usually equipped with electrical power and sewage plants appropriate to manufacturing.

The location decisions that manufacturers and extractors do face are very different from those confronting other entrepreneurs. For example, manufacturers and extractors do not concern themselves with pedestrian access. The access they are concerned with is their own—to sources of supply and major transportation routes.

ACCESS TO SUPPLIERS.   Manufacturers try to locate their plants close to their sources of supply. These may be extractors who provide raw materials or other manufacturers who provide parts. Suppose, for example, you are producing tomato products. It would be important to have your processing plant fairly close to the truck farms that produce that crop. Otherwise, your tomatoes would spoil before they reached your doors. Locating close to major suppliers can also cut transportation costs and shipping times.

ACCESS TO TRANSPORTATION.   Both manufacturers and extractors prefer to locate near major transportation networks. For example, a company that uses railroads to transport the goods it produces might choose a location on a railroad spur. Other possibilities for businesses with different transportation needs would include locations near interstate highways, docks, or airports.

Why is such planning important? It's a matter of simple economics. The farther you have to ship your products to *reach* a major transportation network, the more it costs you. Also, the more different transportation methods you use, the more people who handle your product and the more it costs you. In the end, higher shipping costs mean a smaller profit margin for you or higher prices for your customers. Either way, you are risking your business's ultimate success.

How Do You Select a Building?

Once you have chosen a site, you must consider what the existing building has to offer. You should look at three areas.

Determine Suitability for Your Purposes

A significant portion of the cost of starting most businesses is in the building. If you are able to find one that has all of the necessary amenities, you will be saving a great deal of money.

The building available on your site must meet your needs in several respects. It must be of sufficient size both to take care of present needs and to allow for future expansion. No matter what type of business you have, you will need room for customers, storage, inventory, an office, and rest rooms. Remember, it is far less costly to pay for a little more room at the outset than to pay later for a move. Moving is expensive in more than just monetary terms. It can also mean lost sales and time away from essential work.

EXTERIOR. You should begin your evaluation of the building by considering its construction. It may be worthwhile to hire a professional—perhaps a contractor, inspector, or appraiser—to examine the building for structural soundness.

You yourself should be able to judge the building from an aesthetic viewpoint. How does it look from the street? Is it attractive? Is it compatible with its surroundings? Does it say what you want it to say? Does it have the right size windows for your purposes and an inviting entrance? Remember, customers will get their first impression of your business from the front of your building.

Also, check any signage on the building. Most communities have regulations limiting the number, type, and size of signs you may have on or in front of your building. Make sure your signs are easy to read, attractive, and correct.

The exterior of a commercial building makes an important statement about the business within. What is this one saying?

Finally, don't forget parking for your customers, your staff, or both. Your community will probably have building code requirements demanding a specific number of parking spaces, depending on the type of business using the site.

INTERIOR. Next you should check the building's interior. Look at the walls, floors, and ceilings in terms of how they meet the requirements of your business. Are they functional, attractive, and easy to care for? Are there sufficient lighting fixtures and outlets for your needs? Do you have enough power to run your equipment? How efficient are the heating and cooling units?

Consider All the Costs

At this point you will have to consider seriously whether you wish to lease, buy, or build. The disadvantages of the last two options were discussed in Chapter 12. (Recall that both are more expensive than leasing. Building also involves you in the complications of building codes.) Here, therefore, we'll assume that you will be leasing an existing facility.

In many respects, the cost of leasing a building is a function of demand. Is the location so desirable that many potential tenants want to lease the site? That will drive up the rent. Is the type of building (retail, office, etc.) in short supply, or are there many similar vacancies? A shortage situation will also drive up the rent. Is the building new with modern amenities, or is it an older structure with relatively few up-to-date features? A newer facility will cost you more. Finally, how much space will you be leasing? The larger the square footage, the more you will have to pay.

In general, sites for retail and service businesses are more costly than sites for industrial operations. This is because retail and service sites are found in commercial areas. When such sites are located in malls, they are more expensive still. Thus, a retail or service site in a mall will be very expensive. One in a strip shopping center or office building will be less expensive. Such a site in an industrial area will be least expensive.

Risk Takers, Profit Makers

Michael Thomas

Some cities boast tourist attractions. Boston *is* a tourist attraction. On every block, current businesses and museums sit side by side with historic sites and buildings. Often, they are one and the same. It follows that millions of tourists flock to the city every year.

Shortly after historic old Quincy Market reopened in 1979, Michael Thomas, Sr., decided to capitalize on Boston's unique character. Along with his wife, Nan, he established the city's first trolley tour company.

When they began, the Thomases had no experience in tourism, transit, or trolleys. With only a good idea and their personal savings, they bought a renovated 1927 cable car affixed to a motorized chassis. With this nostalgic symbol of turn-of-the-century Boston, they offered tourists premium transportation, entertainment, and service. Tourists and trolleys proved to be a perfect match. To customers, the trolleys were an informative and structured—yet flexible—way to tour Boston. People who took them to the city's key sites could leave and reboard at strategic points. Meanwhile, guides provided a spiel that was usually educational, often insightful, and always entertaining.

There were pluses for the city, too. The trolleys reduced traffic and pollution. Their efficiency impressed city bureaucrats almost as much as it did tourists.

For the Thomases, however, their trolley business also had its shortcomings. As the business grew, they found themselves stifled by its size and structure. To remedy their dissatisfaction, they left the original company and launched the "Blue Trolleys" under the name of Boston Trolley Tours.

Starting over has entailed improving on an already successful formula to distinguish Boston

Trolley Tours from other companies. With the longest hours and most stops, the Blue Trolleys allow customers more freedom than other tours. Also, the Blue Trolleys are driven by the best-trained and most dedicated guides and offer the only tours accessible to the handicapped and disabled.

Today, the fleet of Blue Trolleys continues to grow in the face of stiff competition. With 20 trolleys running through historic Boston, the Thomases (with son Michael, Jr., and son-in-law Bob Worth) attribute their prosperity to their reverent treatment of customers. They believe that giving good tours requires caring as much about tourists as attractions. To the Thomases, it's learning about and pleasing people that makes their business personally rewarding. Judging from their popularity, the Blue Trolleys are on the right track.

One caution is in order about manufacturing sites, however. While they are generally the least expensive in terms of the building, they may be more expensive in other respects. For example, manufacturing operations generally pay higher utility, water, and sewage bills.

Thus, when investigating a particular building, you must be sure to consider *all* the costs associated with it. Forgetting a major expense—such as utilities—can be disastrous to your cash flow down the road.

Look at Your Lease Options

Once you have some idea of the building you would like to rent, you should inquire about lease terms. (Some of these, no doubt, will already have been mentioned in the course of your contacts with the owner or rental agent.)

It is important that you carefully study the lease that you will have to sign. Remember, leases are negotiable. You can discuss and agree upon the terms with the lessor.

There are three basic types of leases:

- *Gross lease.* A gross lease allows the tenant to rent the facilities from the landlord for a fixed rate, usually paid monthly. The landlord pays the taxes, insurance, and general operating expenses of the facility. (The last category includes such things as outdoor lighting, water, and landscaping maintenance.)
- *Net lease.* With this type of lease, the tenant pays the taxes and all expenses of operating the facility. This is in addition to a fixed monthly rental payment. The landlord, as the owner, pays the insurance on the building. Net leases are usually long-term leases and are probably the most popular business lease.
- *Percentage lease.* This is the most complicated type of lease. It can be based on a percentage of the net income of the tenant or on a flat rate plus a percentage of gross revenues. Consider the second type as an example. Each month a business tenant would pay a flat fee.

(Usually this would be based on the number of square feet occupied.) In addition, the tenant would pay a percentage of the gross revenues or sales the business brings in annually.

Why Not Start Your Business at Home?

Why not, indeed! It worked for Debbie Fields of Mrs. Fields Cookies and for Steven Jobs and Steve Wozniak of Apple Computers. It could work for you.

Today, more than ever before, people are discovering the benefits of starting a business from home. The main benefit is financial. One young entrepreneur, for example, has started a customized gift basket boutique from her grandmother's garage. She is looking forward to the day when she can lease a storefront location. Meanwhile, though, she is saving a great deal of money by not having to pay rent.

This kind of arrangement can work for many kinds of businesses. Mail order firms and other enterprises involving little personal contact with customers are possibilities. So are businesses in which work is picked up from customers and

Many entrepreneurial enterprises, particularly one-person operations, can be started and run from home. In the instance shown here, what is it about the nature of the business that makes this possible?

dropped off again when complete. In areas like these, newcomers can compete on an even footing with established firms. Indeed, with message machines, fax machines, and computers, the newcomers can look just as professional and successful.

Whether or not you decide to start your business at home will depend on a number of factors:

- Type of business you want to start
- Space and equipment available at home
- Effect on others living in your home

You might also want to consult an accountant before you make your decision. It is possible that you can save on your taxes by using your home as your office.

There is also one potential stumbling block to consider. Most communities have laws governing where you can locate a business. (These are the zoning laws discussed in Chapter 12.) Make certain that the business you want to run from home is permitted in a residential area. Generally, if your enterprise does not create any traffic, noise, or pollution, it won't be a problem. However, you may not be able to place any signs on your house identifying your business for passersby.

Organizing and Using Your Data

The decision of where to locate your business is one of the most important you will make. As such, it will affect multiple parts of your business plan.

The bulk of the information you gather will end up in the marketing section of your notebook. The demographic data on your trade area will find its way into your market analysis. There it will help you in your continuing effort to refine the description of your target market. Much

of the remaining information will feed into the place strategy of your marketing plan.

Smaller portions of the material will find their way into other sections of your notebook. The address, for example, would be a necessary element of the business summary. The business description might contain passing references to site-related considerations. Rent or mortgage payments, move-in costs, and estimates of any real estate taxes or operating expenses would be recorded in your financial plan section.

You may find yourself tempted to enter some information in more than one place. When in doubt, do. Far better to repeat information while you try to place it than risk leaving it out entirely. Gradually, as you alter and refine the various parts of your business plan, each piece of data will fall into its proper place. Should any repetitions remain, they will jump out at you in the draft stage. At that point you will be able to remedy them easily.

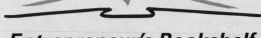

Entrepreneur's Bookshelf

To learn more about the subjects discussed in this chapter, consider reading these publications:

- *The Survey of Buying Power* from *Sales and Marketing Management* Magazine (Annual)
- *Choosing a Retail Location,* SBA Pub. No. MP10
- *Locating or Relocating Your Business,* SBA Pub. No. MP2
- *Practical Business Use of Government Statistics,* SBA Small Business Management Series, Stock No. 045-000-00131-8
- *Using Census Data to Select a Store Site,* SBA Pub. No. MA2.023

Chapter 14 Review

Recapping the Chapter

- To select a community in which to start your business, you need to examine the community's economic base, look for financial incentives, and analyze relevant population data.
- When choosing a site, retail businesses consider the character of the area, its accessibility to customers, and the nature and location of competitors. Wholesale and service firms base their site decisions on whether or not customers will be coming to their places of business. Manufacturing and extraction businesses look for sites with easy access to transportation and to suppliers or raw materials.
- A building should be chosen based on its suitability for the intended use, the costs involved, and the lease terms.
- Starting your new business at home can save you a great deal of money in overhead expenses.

Reviewing Vocabulary

Use eight of the words below in a description of an ideal location for a business of your choice. Devote separate paragraphs to community, site, and building.

- economic base
- incentives
- enterprise zones
- Standard Metropolitan Statistical Areas (SMSAs)
- census tracts
- trade area
- industrial parks
- gross lease
- net lease
- percentage lease

Checking the Facts

1. Describe in terms of its economic base the ideal community in which to start up a business.
2. Name two financial incentives a community might offer a new business.
3. What agencies can you contact to find out about makeup and availability of the local labor pool?
4. What determines the size of a business's trade area?
5. Why might a service business have different locational needs from a retail business?
6. Why is it important for a manufacturing business to locate near major transportation networks?
7. What exterior features determine a building's suitability for a particular enterprise? what interior features?
8. In general, which is the most expensive type of business site? the least expensive?
9. What restrictions do local governments usually place on home-based businesses?

Thinking Critically

1. Why is it important to know about the demographics of the community in which you are locating your business?
2. If you were starting up a business to manufacture a unique type of fat-free ice cream, what site considerations would you give a high priority. Why?
3. Describe how each of the following entrepreneurs might go about choosing a location for his or her business. Include community, site, and building considerations.

   - Owner of an exclusive clothing boutique
   - Caterer
   - Manufacturer of security systems

Chapter 14 Review

4. Compare and contrast the three types of leases described in the chapter. From the viewpoint of the tenant, what are the advantages and disadvantages of each?

Discussing Key Concepts

1. What kinds of population trends will *you* look for when considering a community?

2. Could you locate your new business at home? Why or why not?

Using Basic Skills

Math

1. Suppose you are opening a 1,000-square-foot baseball card store in a shopping center. You have signed a percentage lease that calls for you to pay a flat monthly rent of $1.75 per square foot, plus 5 percent of your gross annual sales. What is the total amount of rent you will pay in one year if you have sales of $85,000?

Communication

2. Find the name of a realtor who specializes in business sites. Write a letter to him or her and describe the kind of business site you are looking for.

Human Relations

3. You are out interviewing a successful entrepreneur in your community about how she chose her business site. She tells you that it happened by chance, that she did no research and thinks that it's a waste of time. How would you respond?

Enriching Your Learning

1. Choose a site for your own business. As part of your decision-making process, do the following:

- Using population, demographic, and zoning data, select one or more potential sites.
- Visit each of your potential sites. Note potential competitors in the area and available buildings that might be suitable for your business. (You might also check commercial realtors and newspaper classified ads for possibilities you may have overlooked.)
- On a map mark the trade areas, potential competitors, and transportation routes providing access for each of your potential sites.
- Compare your site possibilities. (You may want to review the weighing-your-options material in Chapter 6, page 76, at this point.) Summarize your findings in written or table form and make a final choice.

2. Interview two entrepreneurs to find out how they selected their sites. If possible, have them reconstruct their reasoning at the time about the pros and cons of the various sites they considered. Make an oral report to the class on what you learned.

Physical Layout

Objectives

After completing this chapter, you will be able to

- list the basic steps in planning the layout of a business,
- describe layout considerations and typical layout plans for different types of businesses,
- determine the interior and exterior details needed to finish a layout plan, and
- design the layout for your own business.

Terms to Know

layout
interrelationships
workstation
appointments
facade
drawn to scale

Decisions, Decisions

I really feel sorry for my next-door neighbor, Mr. Vanetti. He used to make these great loaves of bread and give them to all the neighbors. Everybody thought they were so good. They told him he should open his own bakery.

Well, last year when he retired from his regular job, Mr. Vanetti did just that. He took his pension in a lump sum and bought some baking equipment and display cases. Then he leased a little storefront over at the corner of First and Main.

At first he had a lot of business. Now, though, people don't go there much. His bread and rolls still taste great, but—how can I put it? The store just isn't a pleasant place to be. It's hot—stifling now that we're having warm weather. It's unbelievably crowded. With all the baking equipment and cases stacked everywhere, there's hardly any room for customers. And it's cluttered. There are boxes and papers and stacks of dirty pans everywhere. It makes you wonder if you really should be eating anything from the place.

I'd really like to say something to Mr. Vanetti about it, but what would I tell him? Clean up? But where's he going to put everything? I mean, the place is tiny! Besides, I'm not sure that even if it were twice as big, it would look much better. Mr. Vanetti's just not very organized. But then, what's "organized" for a bakery?

Layout Planning

At this point in the entrepreneurial process, you should know the equipment, supplies, and inventory you will need. You should also have a site in mind for your enterprise. Now, it's time to try to put the two together and plan the layout of your business.

A **layout** is basically a floor plan, or map. It shows how you intend to use the space your site provides to conduct your business. Layouts can show the design and organization of both interior and exterior spaces. An interior layout would show things like display cases, lighting fixtures, and the traffic pattern for customers and/or production processes. An exterior layout would show landscaping, parking spaces, and the traffic pattern for both pedestrians and vehicles.

Planning the layout of your business operation is important. A well-planned layout can mean a more efficient operation, a more appealing sales floor, or greater convenience for customers. A poorly planned layout, on the other hand, can mean just the opposite.

The basic steps in layout planning are the same for all types of businesses. There are six of them:

- Define the objectives of the facility.
- Identify the primary and supporting activities that will take place in the facility.
- Determine the **interrelationships**—access, arrangement, and flow—among all the activities.

- Determine the space requirements for all activities.
- Design alternative layouts for the facility.
- Evaluate the various layouts and choose one.

Layout Needs and Possibilities

While the steps in layout planning may be the same for all businesses, the layout options and considerations that enter into them are not. This is because different types of businesses have different operational needs. In other words, a manufacturing business by its very nature would have to be laid out differently from a service business.

This section is organized to help you focus on those factors and plans that are appropriate to your particular enterprise. It contains separate discussions of manufacturing, wholesale, retail, service, and extraction businesses. You should read all of the sections. However, as you go through the steps involved in layout planning, you will explore in depth only those considerations and layout options relevant to your type of business.

You should also supplement your reading and planning with observations in the field. Visit operations similar to your own, and see how they are laid out. People you have met through business and trade associations may also offer layout planning information.

Manufacturing Businesses

If your proposed business involves manufacturing goods, your key layout concern will be the placement of machinery. You will want an arrangement that maximizes the efficiency of your operation.

WHAT TO CONSIDER. The following groups of questions will help you formulate your specific layout needs:

- *Production processes.* What kind of manufacturing processes will you be involved in? Will you be breaking raw materials down into products? Will you be assembling products from parts? Will you be converting raw materials into products?
- *Production sequence.* Does your operation call for mass-producing standardized goods in assembly-line sequence? Or will you manufacture your products one at a time or in batches for individual customer orders? Will you use a combination of these two approaches?
- *Materials flow.* What is the most efficient flow of materials for your operation? Figure 15–1 shows your options. Will materials come in one end of your building and finished goods leave the other? (That's an *I* flow.) Will materials enter and finished products leave from the same end? (That's a *U* flow.) What do you do when space is extremely limited? (That's when you use an *S* flow.)
- *Control.* What is the best physical arrangement for management of your operation? What is the best arrangement for inventory control?

Flow Patterns for Production Materials

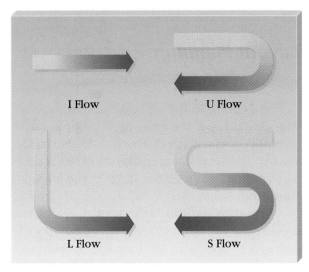

I Flow

U Flow

L Flow

S Flow

Figure 15–1   In most business operations, the flow of production materials is determined by the placement of entrances and exits and the total amount of space available. By this standard, when would you use an L *flow?*

- *Environmental needs.* What environmental considerations will you have in your operation? Are there chemical, water treatment, or other special processes that must be provided for? Are temperatures, noise, or fumes likely to be problems?
- *Space requirements.* How much space will you need for the placement and travel of equipment? What are your specific needs for machine maintenance, plant service, and storage? What is your anticipated production capacity?

TYPES OF LAYOUTS. The layout you use for a manufacturing business will be heavily influenced by your production process and sequence. There are three general types:

- *Product layout.* In this layout, all of the machines and supporting activities are arranged along a product flow line. As the products come down the line, something is done to them at each **workstation**. The product layout is often used in the assembly-line sequence. It is very useful for producing large quantities of a product.
- *Fixed product layout.* This layout is used when the product is too heavy or bulky to be moved around the plant. (An airplane would be a good example.) In fixed product arrangements, parts are brought to the job and workers come to the product.
- *Process layout.* This type of layout involves the grouping of machines and equipment by function. For example, those that perform welding functions might be placed in one area. Those that do sanding might be placed in another area, and so on. Products are then moved from one area to another, with a specific function being performed on them at each location. This setup is particularly efficient for producing small quantities of goods.

Of course, any of these three basic layouts can be modified to suit the needs of a particular operation. They can also be used in combination.

There are other, secondary areas that you should map out as well. Inside, these include areas for shipping and receiving, storage and warehousing, maintenance services, and office space. Outside, they include storage yards for materials, truck storage and repair areas, loading docks, and parking.

Wholesale Businesses

Wholesale operations can take a variety of forms. Here, however, we will focus on warehousing facilities used by wholesalers who take possession of goods.

There are two primary goals involved in planning warehouse layouts. The first is to provide cost-effective storage. The second is to allow efficient movement of products in and out of the facility.

WHAT TO CONSIDER. When planning the layout of a wholesale business, your foremost considerations should be storage and space utilization. When planning for storage, you should follow these guidelines:

- Store popular items near shipping points to minimize in-house travel distances.
- Store together those items that were received together and will be shipped together.
- Provide for a variety of storage space sizes.
- Assign storage space on the basis of ease of handling and popularity of item.

There will, of course, be exceptions to these guidelines. For example, you will almost certainly have to make special provisions for perishables, hazardous materials, or extremely valuable items. You will also have to consider which items can and cannot be stored together.

When planning how to use space, you should keep these guidelines in mind:

- Conserve space wherever possible.
- Observe limitations on space, such as ceilings, sprinklers, and safe stacking heights.
- Use adjustable racks and shelves where possible to accommodate changing needs.

- Plan entrances, exits, and aisles so that products can be easily reached.

TYPES OF LAYOUTS. Most modern wholesale operations are housed in single-story buildings. This makes controlling and moving stock easier.

You will want to arrange receiving, storage, order assembly, and shipping areas so that goods can be moved through them quickly and easily. This will mean working with or around certain key features. These include exterior access points (such as rail or truck sidings) and fixed interior obstacles (such as columns).

Your interior layout plans should include office space and, perhaps, showroom areas. Exterior plans might be done to show loading docks and facilities for vehicle storage.

Retail Businesses

The arrangement of a retail layout has a critical impact on sales and, hence, profits. The most important design consideration is the flow of customers through the operation. Merchandise and aisles should be laid out to "pull" customers through the store.

WHAT TO CONSIDER. For this reason, most of the options you will find yourself considering will center on merchandise placement. They include the following:

- *Products to be sold.* Does the merchandise require special care, like refrigeration or extra security? Can it be shelved, or must it have standing space? Does it require space for trying out or trying on?
- *Projected clientele.* Will customers be concerned with atmosphere (including space and comfort)? Or will they be concerned with getting in and out quickly?
- *Sales per square foot of selling space.* Is the store arranged to get the most sales out of each square foot of space? Is the opportunity for self-service maximized? Is the space for individual items of on-floor stock minimized?

- *Sales value of area within store.* Are the most saleable goods placed in the area with the highest potential for sales (the middle and right)? Are staples in the low-sales-value area (the rear)? Are impulse and convenience items spread throughout?
- *Product coordination.* Is related merchandise placed in the same area to facilitate customer shopping? Are complementary groups (like shorts and tops) placed together to encourage multiple sales?
- *Aisle exposure.* Does merchandise get maximum exposure? Do customers have ample time and space to examine it? Are there barriers to customer movement?

TYPES OF LAYOUTS. Retail layouts generally contain three types of floor space—selling space, storage space, and customer space. (The latter would include areas provided for the comfort and convenience of customers, like waiting areas and rest rooms.) What distinguishes one plan from another is the way these three kinds of space are configured. Different arrangements can produce different selling effects.

Most store layouts fall into one of four categories:

- *Right-angle grid.* This rectangular pattern of crossing aisles (shown in Figure 15–2A) provides a highly structured system for facilitating the flow of traffic. Main aisles move customers from entrance to exit. Secondary aisles draw customers from the main aisles and lead them past merchandise displays to sales stations. This layout provides an efficient use of space and reduces security concerns. It also lends itself to self-service operations, such as convenience and variety stores. An inherent drawback to the grid is its limitations in putting together a creative shopping environment.
- *Open.* Open layouts consist of completely open sales space bounded by outside walls. This type of layout (shown in Figure 15–2B) enhances visibility of merchandise, sales

coverage, and security. This is because there are no tall fixtures within the central store area. However, the arrangement also reduces the opportunity to separate merchandise and can thus lead to customer confusion.

- *Enclosed.* This layout involves the organization of types of merchandise into separate operations within the store. By placing walls between these units (as shown in Figure 15–3A), a retailer can create unique shopping environments for several different departments. This layout is used most often in full-line department stores that sell higher-priced merchandise. It tends to cost more because it requires increased security and staffing.

- *Landscaped.* The landscaped layout (Figure 15–3B) combines elements of the open and enclosed layouts. It places related merchandise in areas separated from each other by partitions and other fixtures. The arrangement has no main aisles. Rather, it establishes a traffic pattern through other means, such as carpeting design. Landscaped layouts improve customer and sales staff interaction and allow for the maximum exercise of creativity in planning the shopping environment. They also reduce the expense of remodeling. Major disadvantages are that space utilization is not efficient and the potential for shoplifting is increased.

Right-Angle Grid and Open Layouts

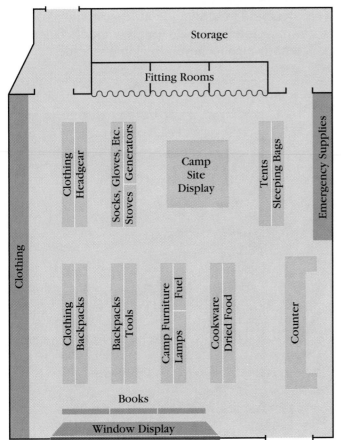

A. Grid Layout

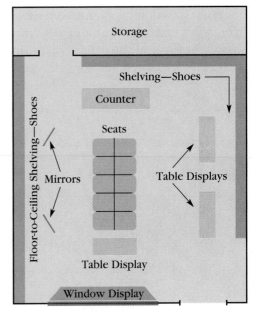

B. Open Layout

Figure 15–2 The retail layouts shown here take two very different approaches to arranging merchandise. The camping store on the left follows a grid plan; the shoe store on the right, an open arrangement. Could the two businesses successfully swap layouts? Why or why not?

Service Businesses

The physical layout of a service business depends largely on the specific service it provides. Consequently, there is no prescribed set of guidelines or layout patterns that can be applied to all such enterprises. It is possible, however, to break service businesses into some very general types. These are identified in Figure 15–4. Find the category in which your business would fit. Then study the examples and layout considerations listed with it. The considerations you will have to address will be similar.

Extraction Businesses

Like service businesses, extraction firms have unique layouts. This is because they must adapt to the particular environment in which their extraction operation takes place. There are, however, a few features that all extraction layouts share. They include an office area, storage areas for both equipment and supplies, and the extraction site itself.

The exterior physical operation of an extraction business may be spread out over a wide area. (As an example, consider a farm.) It can also be geographically separated from the business operation. (Some mining ventures are headquartered in large cities far removed from any actual mine site.) Finally, the business and extraction operations can be combined (as in a small fishing operation). All of these variations demand a different combination of layout plans.

Finishing Touches

Once you have settled on a particular layout for your business, you can begin filling in the final details. These include at least minimal office space, interior design features, and alterations or improvements in your building's facade.

Enclosed and Landscaped Layouts

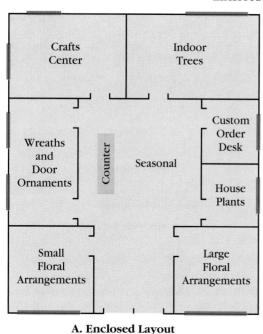

A. Enclosed Layout

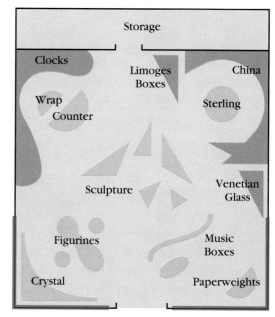

B. Landscaped Layout

Figure 15–3   Both of the retail layouts shown here are used in department stores. In fact, they are sometimes used together. Explain how this might work.

Layout Considerations for Different Types of Service Businesses

Business Type	Examples	Things to Consider
▪ Customers come to facility to use equipment	▪ Driving range ▪ Amusement park ▪ Laundromat	▪ Customer appeal ▪ Equipment to engage in service ▪ Space to engage in service ▪ Pay station ▪ Safety
▪ Customers come to facility for assistance	▪ Copy service ▪ Car repair ▪ Dry cleaner	▪ Customer appeal ▪ Ease of access ▪ Waiting area ▪ Customer contact station ▪ Equipment and/or service area ▪ Supply storage
▪ Customers come to facility for care	▪ Day care center ▪ Doctor's office ▪ Beauty salon	▪ Customer appeal ▪ Ease of access (drop-off and pickup) ▪ Waiting area ▪ Ease of contact with service provider ▪ Rest rooms ▪ Areas for performing service ▪ Office space ▪ Supply and equipment storage
▪ Business operator goes to customer to provide service	▪ Exterminator ▪ Painting contractor ▪ Interior designer ▪ Taxicab service	▪ Office space with telephone ▪ Storage areas for equipment, supplies, and vehicles
▪ Business operator brings customer and equipment together	▪ Car rental ▪ Video rental	▪ Customer appeal ▪ Display area ▪ Storage area ▪ Pay and return stations
▪ Business operator brings customer and service together	▪ Employment agency ▪ Real estate agency ▪ Tax preparation	▪ Customer appeal ▪ Office space (private and general use) ▪ Conference room ▪ Waiting area

Figure 15–4   The service businesses listed here differ in two principal respects: Those in the top half of the table have customers that come to them. Those in the bottom half either go to their customers or send a product with them. What effect does this have on the considerations listed in the last column? Why do you think this is so?

Planning for Office Space

Every business owner needs someplace to take care of the paperwork and other administrative aspects of his or her enterprise. In some cases, desk space in a back room is sufficient for this purpose. In other cases (where the office is the hub of the enterprise), virtually all of the work space is devoted to this function.

Basically, you have two options when planning office space—an open plan or a closed one. If cost, limited space, employee supervision, or access to files and equipment are important to you, an open-office layout is probably best. Such arrangements often use partitions to divide work space into cubicles, or workstations. If privacy and noise reduction are your main concerns,

Risk Takers, Profit Makers

Eric Bonecutter

For four generations, Eric Bonecutter's family has run businesses in New Mexico. They have owned and operated trading posts, art galleries, and jewelry manufacturers. So today, Bonecutter isn't just paying the bills when he makes and sells Navajo jewelry in Albuquerque. He's carrying on a tradition.

Bonecutter familiarized himself with the arts at an early age while working in his mother's gallery. There, he was exposed to the variety of Southwestern art and became acquainted with the business end of the field. After that, he worked with his grandfather and uncle. They taught him the traditional and commercial aspects of jewelry making. Two years later, Bonecutter used $4,000 of his savings to launch his own business.

Combining the artistic standards he learned from his mother and the traditional methods of his uncle and grandfather, Bonecutter started making his own jewelry. He began in his garage, developing his own designs and working with a skilled silversmith. He made his first sales to a sales representative from his mother's gallery and put the proceeds right back into expanding production. Soon he was making more jewelry than one sales representative could handle. So, he found another. Before long, a host of agents were marketing his wares nationwide.

Bonecutter attributes his success to the quality of his work. Southwestern art can be cheap, touristy, and trite. Bonecutter's work is genuine—and his prices reflect it. However, his customers don't mind paying extra. Every piece is personally designed by Bonecutter, stamped by a skilled silversmith, and finished by expert hands.

Keeping his designs fresh has been an ongoing challenge for Bonecutter. (It's always a challenge when working with a traditional art form such as Native American jewelry.) But by tastefully incorporating coral, shells, lapis, and elements other than the traditional turquoise and silver, Bonecutter keeps the customers' (and the competition's) attention. As a result of his inventiveness, his jewelry is worn in Europe, Asia, and all across America.

Today, Bonecutter's efforts have shifted from making jewelry to marketing it. He also maintains inventory, controls quality, and keeps 15 silversmiths happy. But regardless of his role as a modern businessperson, Bonecutter still considers his venture to be traditional. After all, what's new about selling products that have been made for over a hundred years?

however, then you will want to plan for closed offices. If your operation involves multiple offices, they may be arranged in two ways. One option connects offices (open, closed, or a combination of both) with corridors or aisles. The other arranges open work stations randomly and defines the traffic pattern between them with planters, fish tanks, and similar **appointments**. The first arrangement is more traditional and formal. The second makes for a more relaxed and informal atmosphere.

Detailing Interior and Exterior

Planning your operation's layout involves more than just organizing the floor space. You will want to keep in mind certain interior and exterior design details.

Interior design details can help you create an atmosphere in ways that a floor plan alone cannot. Such details include lighting, wall and floor coverings, furnishings, and decorative accessories. (*Note:* You may already have selected some of these items back in Chapter 13, when you initially considered your equipment needs.)

How these items fit into your plans will be determined by the type of business you have and the area you are laying out. A manufacturer's production area, for example, would call for detailing that focuses on pleasant and safe working conditions. The design details of a retailer's selling area, on the other hand, would be determined by store image and customer appeal.

Exterior design details include the **facade** (or face) of your building, signage, and entryways to your location. Outside design can range in importance from minimal (for a home-based business) to critical (for most retail operations).

Getting Your Layout on Paper

Earlier in this chapter, you were given a set of steps to follow in planning your layout. When you reach the step in which you actually design layouts, you will need to draw your plans. Only in this way can you visually communicate your ultimate layout choices to contractors, lenders, and others.

Specifically, your floor plans should be put in the form of two-dimensional maps. These should be **drawn to scale**. For example, ⅛ inch in your floor plan might stand for 1 foot at the actual site. Fixed features (walls, entrances, windows, and so forth) should be clearly depicted. So should the planned placement of furniture and equipment.

When all of your drawings are complete, place them in the appendix section of your business plan notebook. That way, when you describe your business in your final plan, you can cross-reference the drawings as supporting documentation.

Recording Your Costs

Much of what goes into your physical layout plan will not entail new costs. You have already gathered information regarding equipment and fixture costs in Chapter 13 and building costs in Chapter 14. At this point, however, you may need to refine some of those figures.

Nonetheless, you will have some new cost information. Most of it will relate to interior remodeling and exterior decorating (new signage or painting, for example). These costs should be recorded with your other start-up costs in the financial section of your business plan notebook.

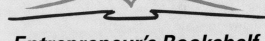

Entrepreneur's Bookshelf

To learn more about the subjects discussed in this chapter, consider reading these books:

- *The Entrepreneur's Guide to Starting a Successful Business* by James Halloran (© 1992)
- *Your Own Shop: How to Open and Operate a Successful Retail Business* by Ruth Jacobson (© 1991)

Chapter 15 Review

Recapping the Chapter

- In general terms, layout planning involves organizing, designing, and detailing the interior (and often exterior) of a business site.
- The specific steps in layout planning are (1) define facility objectives, (2) define primary and supporting activities, (3) determine activity interrelationships, (4) determine space requirements, (5) design alternative layouts, and (6) select the final layout.
- Layout considerations and plans are different for each type of business (manufacturing, wholesale, retail, service, and extraction).
- To finalize a layout, you should add design details and draw a floor plan to scale.

Reviewing Vocabulary

Most of the terms below are defined by example in the chapter. Using those examples, text content, and your own experience, try to formulate broader definitions. When you are through, check your work against a dictionary.

- layout
- interrelationships
- workstation
- appointments
- facade
- drawn to scale

Checking the Facts

1. Name one major layout consideration for your type of business.

2. In a manufacturing business, how does a product layout differ from a fixed product layout?
3. In a retail business, how does an open layout differ from a right-angle grid layout?
4. What are some interior design details? some exterior design details?
5. If privacy is a major consideration, what type of office space would you plan into your layout?
6. What sorts of things should you show in your layout drawings?
7. What kinds of *new* start-up costs would be identified through physical layout planning?

Thinking Critically

1. Review the basic steps in layout planning. Can these steps really be useful for all types of businesses? Will they work for your selected business? Explain why or why not.
2. Analyze the layout considerations listed for your type of business. Is any one consideration more important than the others? Explain.
3. Reexamine the illustrations and/or examples of layouts given for your type of business. Which, if any, would be most appropriate for your selected business? Give your rationale.
4. Which type of office space—open or closed—would work best in your selected business? Why?
5. Which, if any, of the decisions you made in selecting equipment back in Chapter 13 will affect your layout? Explain how.

Chapter 15 Review

Discussing Key Concepts

1. What kinds of problems could result from not planning the physical layout of your business?
2. What is the best way to get additional ideas for planning your physical layout? Why do you think that is the most useful approach?
3. Would the layout considerations listed for your type of business apply to all businesses in your field? What considerations should be added to make the list all-inclusive?
4. What is the most ideal type of layout for businesses in your field? Why?
5. What is the ideal amount of office space for a business in your field? Explain.

Using Basic Skills

Math

1. You are drawing layouts for your proposed business. What would be the dimensions of your floorplans in the following situations?

   - Your building is 40 feet wide by 60 feet long. Your scale is ½ inch = 5 feet.
   - Your building is 80 feet wide by 110 feet long. Your scale is ¼ inch = 2 feet.

Communication

2. Telephone trade associations in your field to request information on planning physical layouts. If none is available, ask for a referral to another organization or person who might be able to help you.

Human Relations

3. You and your best friend are gathering information by telephone for the business you plan to set up together. In a call to one trade association, your friend is extremely rude and demanding. When she gets off the phone, she says they were not very cooperative. What would you say to her?

Enriching Your Learning

1. Visit several operations similar to your selected business. Observe their interior and exterior layouts, and record your observations. Would their layouts work for your business? Why or why not? Do an analysis, and be prepared to explain your conclusions.
2. Interview a business owner in your selected field to determine layout options and the rationale for each. *Note:* If you are currently working in your selected field, carry out the interview with your employer.
3. Develop layout drawings for your selected business:

   - Draw a floor plan to scale. Include all projected equipment, furnishings, and special features.
   - Develop additional two- or three-dimensional drawings that show (a) a frontal view of your building or storefront and (b) important interior design features.

Chapter 16
Protecting Your Business

Objectives

After completing this chapter, you will be able to

- describe the risks facing a new business,
- define the four basic strategies that make up risk management,

- identify the major types of insurance that a new business owner should consider buying, and
- name the two types of insurance agents.

Terms to Know

burglary
robbery
electronic credit
 authorizers
negligence
risk management
premium
business interrup-
 tion insurance
casualty insurance
errors-and-omis-
 sions insurance
product liability
 insurance
fidelity bonds
performance
 bonds
workers
 compensation
independent
 insurance agent
direct insurance
 writer

Decisions, Decisions

The other day a little boy and his mom came into Swim World. It was right after opening, and things were pretty slow. Marcia, my boss, was back in the office working on POs, so I helped the woman. She wanted suits for three different teams but didn't really seem to know where to start. We got so involved that neither of us paid much attention to what her son was doing.

In fact, he was trying to climb the accessory shelving unit in the center of the store. Well, it's not designed to take that kind of treatment. It toppled over and took the kid with it. He started to scream at the top of his lungs.

Marcia came running out when she heard the noise. She and the boy's mom got him out from under the shelving. But you could tell his arm was broken. (It was at this funny angle.) By this time, the woman was screaming, too.

Marcia kept her cool. She had me call the rescue squad and tried to calm the woman down—you know, so she could calm the kid down. When the paramedics arrived, they splinted the boy's arm and took him and his mom off to the hospital.

I was still shaking after they left. All I could think about was that the store was going to get sued and it was my fault. Marcia told me to take it easy. She said her insurance company would sort things out.

Boy, I don't think I've ever been so happy to hear the word *insurance*. I started thinking about all the things that could go wrong in a store besides a kid getting hurt. Fire, flood, burglary, shoplifting—and what about employees getting hurt or delivery people? I thought, Marcia's policy must be huge. How did she know what to include? I bet it cost a—and then I realized. What if the insurance company raises her premium because of the accident and she can't pay? What would happen then?

Identifying Business Risks

Did you know that about 30 percent of all business failures are caused by employee dishonesty? Every year crimes like employee theft, burglary, and shoplifting cost businesses billions of dollars, and these costs are rising. What is more, these are not the only risks that businesses face. There are also natural disasters (like tornadoes and floods) and accidents involving both customers and employees.

Such misfortunes are difficult for any business to cope with. Their impact on smaller, newer businesses, however, is especially severe. This is because such enterprises often lack the financial resources needed to deal with the problem or its consequences.

This chapter will identify the major risks that new businesses face. It will also suggest ways to minimize some of those risks. Finally, the chapter will discuss insurance, since being insured is the most common way that businesses deal with risk.

Crime

Crime costs businesses (particularly small businesses) a great deal. In fact, small businesses are 35 times more likely to be victims of crime than large businesses (those with annual sales in excess of $5 million).

Of all businesses, retail enterprises are the most susceptible to crime. This is because so many people pass through them in the course of a business day. As a result, the cost of crime is also highest for retail operations.

Consider an example. Suppose a music store loses a CD worth $15 every day for a year. If the store operates at a 10 percent profit margin, it must sell an additional $54,750 worth of merchandise to make up the loss!

How does a store "lose" merchandise or cash? There are a number of different ways.

SHOPLIFTING. Shoplifting is one of the most common crimes in the retail business. It accounts for about 3 percent of the price of any item.

A shoplifter is anyone who takes an item from a store without paying for it. You would think that shoplifters would take expensive items. However, studies have found that most items taken cost between one and five dollars.

Who shoplifts? About half of all shoplifters are juveniles. A surprising number act on impulse. (In other words, they don't plan to shoplift. They just find themselves in a situation where shoplifting is so easy that they do it.) Many shoplifters are alcoholics and drug addicts. (These are people who can pose a real threat to store employees.) Only a very few shoplifters are professionals who make a career of stealing.

To prevent or minimize shoplifting, a store owner must learn to recognize shoplifters and their peculiar behaviors. Solo shoplifters may act nervous and spend a great deal of time just looking around the store. They may carry large bags or wear bulky clothing in which to hide merchandise. Some shoplifters travel in groups. In these cases, a few group members cause a disturbance while the others take what they came for.

Keep in mind that shoplifters often operate at times of the day when stores are understaffed. To reduce your risk of becoming a shoplifting victim at these and other times, consider these techniques:

- Train your employees to recognize potential shoplifters.
- Keep your store well lit and your display cases low so that you can see your entire operation at a glance.
- Employ two-way mirrors, peepholes, or closed-circuit TV for surveillance.
- Use tamper-proof price tickets or electronic tags, where appropriate.
- Hire a uniformed security guard.

What is the best way to handle a shoplifter if you spot one? The safest approach is to alert a police officer and let him or her apprehend the person. Usually this is done outside the store to make the legal case against the individual stronger.

Although the laws regarding apprehending a shoplifter vary from state to state, in general, the store owner must do the following:

- See the person take the merchandise.
- Be able to identify the merchandise as belonging to the store.
- Confirm that it was taken with the intent to steal.
- Prove that it was not paid for.

Once the shoplifter has been caught, you will need to decide whether or not to prosecute. Keep one thing in mind. If you do decide to proceed with charges, you will be sending a message. You will be telling other would-be shoplifters that such behavior will not tolerated in your store. In so doing, you will be reducing your risk of becoming a shoplifting victim again.

EMPLOYEE THEFT. The Department of Commerce reports that about 75–80 percent of all retail crime is employee theft. One source found that many businesses are losing as much as one-third of their profits to the crime. The cost to the

Many store owners electronically tag more expensive merchandise. How does this hamper shoplifters?

consumer is about 15 percent of the retail price paid.

Employees steal for some of the same reasons as shoplifters. However, trusted employees have access to a business in ways that no shoplifter does. For example, the employee who is considered a workaholic may actually be staying late to steal from the business. Staying late and never taking vacations can be suspect behaviors. This is also true of a sharp change in spending habits or life-style.

Many business owners don't realize that their actions may actually encourage employee theft. Businesses that do not establish policies, controls, security procedures, and penalties are sending a message. They are telling their employees that those who steal will probably not get caught.

To send the right message to your employees, observe the following procedures:

- Control the distribution of keys and other security devices.
- Lock all doors that do not need to be used for entry or exit.
- Watch your trash. (Dishonest employees have been known to place stolen items in the trash to get them out of the building undetected.)

Often business owners are careless about the way they handle cash. Money frequently coming in and going out creates temptation and opportunity for dishonesty. A large number of voided or no-sale transactions, for example, could be a signal that an employee is covering up theft. A good rule is, Don't let one person control a transaction from beginning to end. Instead, have one person handle the funds and another record or account for them.

One of the keys to preventing employee theft is, obviously, to hire honest people. This is not as easy as it sounds. However, if you establish clear personnel standards, you will have a better chance of getting the type of person you want.

When hiring, at the very least use thorough application forms. Ask about an applicant's employment history. Ask for character references. (A character reference is someone who will vouch for the applicant's good character.) Take the time to check the information provided.

Be aware, however, that there are some questions you cannot legally ask. For example, you cannot ask an applicant if he or she has ever been arrested. (You can, however, ask if he or she has ever been convicted of a crime.)

Questions about military, financial, or marital status are prohibited as potentially discriminatory. In fact, you cannot legally ask an applicant's age or address (at least not prior to offering the person a job). All of these areas are seen as matters of personal privacy. As a prospective employer, you can only ask about things that relate to an applicant's ability to do the job.

You do have some other potentially helpful options, however. You can use aptitude and psychological tests. You may also be able to require applicants to take a polygraph, or lie detector, test. (To find out, you should check with an attorney or government representative to determine if such testing is permitted in your state.) Things like these can help you screen out employees who may be more likely to steal.

BURGLARY. **Burglary** is the act of breaking into and entering a home or business with the intent to commit a felony. (A felony is a serious crime, such as stealing.) The problem of burglary is growing, and unfortunately most cases go unsolved.

An entrepreneur's best defense is to minimize his or her risk by selecting a business site carefully. This means considering the overall level of crime in the area and specifically the level of burglaries. It also means selecting a secure building to house your enterprise.

All businesses want honest employees. How can a business owner use the employment application process to screen for this quality?

Your next-best defense is installing high-quality locks and controlling who has access to keys. A good alarm system can also give a business owner more peace of mind.

There are basically two types of alarms—supervised and nonsupervised. With a supervised alarm system, all points of entry to the business are monitored at all times of the day from a central location. A silent alarm alerts police to trouble. With a nonsupervised alarm system, the alarm is activated only when the owner arms it. Again, the alarm may be set to sound at the police station.

Some businesses choose to employ a security guard. He or she patrols the premises during the night and at other times when the business is closed. Hiring a security guard may help to prevent many crimes, not just burglary.

The use of sufficient lighting is another important deterrent to burglars. Many owners leave lights on in their businesses all night. Floodlights in parking lots and on rear entrances can also make it difficult for someone to break in unnoticed.

ROBBERY. **Robbery** is a crime of violence. It involves the taking of property by force or threat. The probability of your being robbed is small compared to other crimes discussed here. However, it is a rapidly growing form of crime, particularly in large metropolitan areas.

Most robberies involve a weapon and a person who is not afraid to use it. Therefore, it is the business owner's responsibility to do what is necessary to protect both employees and customers. This may mean doing exactly what the robber asks, hoping he will take what he came for and leave without harming anyone.

You should, however, attempt to get a good description of the person (or persons) committing the robbery. Note height, hair color, and any distinguishing features or mannerisms. This information will be valuable to the police.

One security measure you might consider is having a safe. That way you can minimize the amount of cash you keep in your register (a

When it comes to security, being discrete is not necessarily the best policy. What security device is in use here, and why is it so obvious?

robber's likely target). An even more valuable security measure is the use of surveillance cameras. These do not have to be real to be effective. Many store owners have found that fake cameras work just as well. When placed where they can be easily seen by potential robbers, they, too, seem to deter crime.

STOLEN CREDIT CARDS AND BAD CHECKS. Using credits cards or checks to pay for purchases is a major convenience for consumers. To businesses, however, they can be a major source of financial loss. Credit cards are often stolen and used to run up huge bills. Customers often write checks against insufficient funds or on closed accounts.

To guard against such risks, many businesses that accept credit cards use **electronic credit authorizers**. These may be integrated with an electronic cash register or may be separate, small machines. They are connected to a central credit bureau and will verify if the credit card being used is good. Other companies call a central authorization phone number to check on credit.

The benefit of such systems is that they allow you to find out if a card can be used before you make a sale. If so, you will receive an authorization number signifying that the card is good.

On the other hand, the credit card may be turned down. Normally this will only result in some embarrassment for the customer. If, however, you are informed that the card is stolen, you will need to ask for identification. (It is probably best not to confront the individual directly with a theft charge, since you don't know how he or she will react.) At this point, the person attempting to use the card will usually leave. You can then alert the police.

Bad checks represent an even greater problem for businesses. In fact, in recent years business owners have sought legislative relief. Typically, companies have charged a service fee if a customer's check is returned. Since that has not proved a sufficient deterrent, many states have passed laws making the writing of bad checks a crime and imposing stiff financial penalties. (In California, for example, the penalty is three times the face value of the check.) Today, many businesses place signs by their cash registers announcing these penalties as a way of discouraging bad check writers.

Another technique that business owners have used to reduce the number of bad checks they receive is to invest in a check reader. This is a device similar to an electronic credit authorizer. The check reader tells the business owner if the account on which the check was written is still open and has no history of bad checks.

In any case, it is wise to write the driver's license number of the person making out the check somewhere on it. That way, if anything is wrong with the check and the address is not current, you will have a way to track down the individual.

Natural Disasters

Crime isn't the only risk facing a new business. Many owners have lost everything as a result of natural disasters like fires, earthquakes, tornadoes, and floods.

Protecting your business from these risks is difficult. For example, the surest way to prevent flood or tornado damage is to choose a location that does not have a history of such disasters. But that may mean moving to another state! If your business is in an active earthquake zone, you can have your building inspected by a structural engineer and, if necessary, reinforced to withstand a quake. But earthquake-proofing a building can be very expensive.

Protecting your business against fire is easier. You can install smoke detectors and sprinkler systems. When choosing a safe for cash and important documents, you can choose one that is fireproof.

Accidents and Injury

Another risk of great concern to businesses is accidents. Workers can hurt themselves or others on the job. Customers can slip and fall on a company's premises.

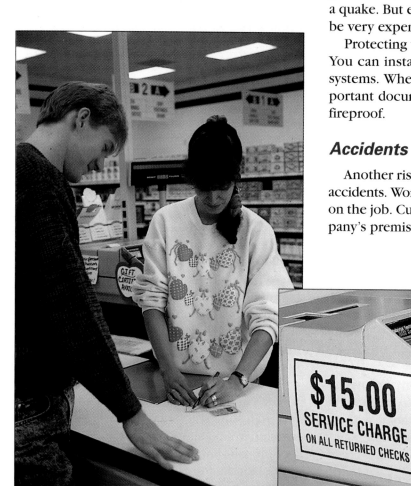

Customers who pass bad checks are a major problem for businesses of all sizes. What preventive measures have been taken in the situations shown here?

Accidents like these can be financially devastating to small businesses. For example, a company can be held responsible for an accident as a result of **negligence**. This is the failure to exercise reasonable care. At the very least under such circumstances, the firm would be required to pay the medical expenses of those injured. It might also have to pay additional amounts awarded by a jury in a lawsuit. Unfortunately for business owners, in recent years the number of such lawsuits has been increasing at a substantial rate. So has the size of the awards.

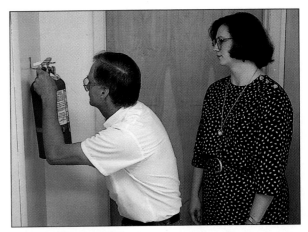

Simply having safety equipment on hand is not enough. What else must a business owner do ensure that it truly reduces risk?

Dealing with Risk

By now it should be clear that you cannot totally protect your business from any of the risks we have discussed thus far. However, there are some things you can do to lessen their impact.

The whole area of how a business deals with risk is called **risk management**. It entails four separate strategies. Most businesses use a combination of these strategies to deal with the risks they face.

Risk Avoidance

When you locate your business in a safe area of town, you are performing risk avoidance. You are attempting to steer clear of crime by shunning environments in which it is more likely to occur. Does your decision guarantee that you will not be the victim of burglary, robbery, or shoplifting? Of course not. But it does reduce your chances from a likelihood to a mere possibility.

Risk Reduction

For risks that cannot be avoided, businesses adopt another strategy. They practice risk reduction.

Many of the procedures and practices recommended in the first part of this chapter are examples of this strategy. Suppose you own a retail store. When you install a sprinkler system, you are attempting to prevent fire from damaging your inventory or destroying your building. You may not be able to avoid the fire, but you can reduce the damage it does. When you place electronic tags on expensive merchandise, you are attempting to discourage theft. You may not be able to eliminate shoplifting, but you can reduce it. You can also reduce the value of the merchandise you lose to it. Risk reduction, then, involves actions you take to reduce both the overall chance and amount of loss.

Every business owner should take these steps to reduce risk:

- Design the work area (whether office, retail space, or manufacturing floor) so that the chances of accident or fire are lowered.
- Hold regular meetings with employees to educate them about the safe use of equipment and the best way to react in an emergency situation.
- Check and service safety equipment (like fire extinguishers and smoke detectors) regularly. Do the same for security equipment like burglar alarms.

- Examine the design of company products carefully, and test them under the most extreme conditions in which they will be used.
- Be sure packaging contains clear instructions for correct use of company products. Be sure it contains equally clear warnings about the hazards of incorrect use.

Risk Transfer

Let's say you have located your new business in a relatively crime-free part of town (risk avoidance). You have installed locks, burglar alarms, and sufficient lighting (risk reduction). Still, you may experience a loss.

How will you cope financially? Most likely, by using the third strategy—risk transfer. You will buy insurance to cover any losses you may incur. You will pay a fee, called a **premium**, to transfer some of your risk to an insurance company.

As a new entrepreneur, you can easily be overwhelmed by all the different types of insurance available. So here, to simplify, we shall discuss insurance for four kinds of business losses that generally require coverage:

- Losses of a business's own property
- Losses arising from lawsuits against a business
- Losses through death of key personnel
- Losses resulting from on-the-job injuries to employees

PROPERTY INSURANCE. This type of insurance covers losses of cash, inventory, vehicles, buildings—in short, all forms of physical property. Businesses usually purchase several different kinds of property insurance. This is because real property (like buildings) and some personal property (like vehicles) are insured separately. In addition, certain risks (like floods and earthquakes) require separate policies.

Thus, a business's standard property insurance policy might protect its premises against burglary, robbery, fire, and water damage. Coverage for the last risk, however, would be limited to damage from storms or broken water mains. It would not include flood damage. If the business had a fleet of delivery vans, they would be protected from all of these risks and more. They would be covered, however, under a separate auto insurance policy.

Businesses can also take advantage of a special kind of insurance to deal with the consequences of property damage. **Business interruption insurance** pays net profits and expenses while a business is shut down for repairs or rebuilding. In other words, the insurance makes up for lost income. This, in turn, allows the business owner to continue making rent, salary, and other key payments.

CASUALTY INSURANCE. Suppose an accident occurs on your business premises—say, a customer or repair person trips and suffers a serious back injury. The result is a lawsuit blaming your business for the accident and demanding payment for medical expenses, lost wages, legal fees, and pain and suffering. To protect your business in this sort of situation, you will need **casualty insurance**.

Casualty insurance also covers the costs of defending your business in court against claims of property damage. For example, suppose your tree-trimming service allows a tree limb to fall through the roof of a nearby garage. The garage owner sues. Casualty insurance would pay the claim.

There are many different types of casualty insurance. For example, companies that do a great deal of advertising often purchase **errors-and-omissions insurance** to protect against lawsuits for mistakes in advertising. Manufacturing firms purchase **product liability insurance** to protect against claims for injuries resulting from use of their products.

Bonding is also a type of casualty insurance. **Fidelity bonds** are a form of insurance that protects a company in case of employee theft. **Performance bonds** protect a business in the event work or a contract is not finished on time or as agreed.

Risk Takers, Profit Makers

Sheri Herrera de Frey and Rick Frey

Spraying crops with conventional chemicals can be expensive, ineffective, dangerous, irresponsible, or just plain illegal. So what's a well-informed farmer to do? Many call Sheri Herrera de Frey. She and her husband, Rick Frey, own and operate Arizona Biological Control (ARBICO). The company is the country's largest supplier of beneficial insects and holistic agricultural services.

Herrera de Frey learned about biological pest control in 1977 when she was earning an MBA at the University of Arizona. After friends told her husband about their business selling fly parasites, he became their Arizona distributor for a summer. That season he earned $75,000—about ten times his teacher's salary. After three years, the Freys embarked full time on their ARBICO venture.

At first, ARBICO simply sold beneficial insects to local farmers. However, they soon outgrew their suppliers and decided to raise their own bugs. Herrera de Frey drew up a business plan and secured a loan. Then she and her husband acquired land from relatives and bought some trailers from acquaintances. As they gained new clients, they added insects to their stock. Today ARBICO offers an entire catalog of sustainable agricultural supplies.

Herrera de Frey's biggest challenge thus far has been educating farmers about the benefits of organic farming. Most in agribusiness only know about chemical strategies. However, Herrera de Frey's arguments for organic farming are plentiful and convincing. She presents chemical farming as a vicious circle. First farmers encourage both plants and pests with fertilizers. Then they destroy both harmful and helpful insects with pesticides. The results are costly to farmers and consumers and unhealthy for those who eat the produce.

Instead of saturating land with chemicals, Herrera de Frey suggests using natural ways to discourage pests. By conditioning soil, using traps, creating barriers, and introducing beneficial insects and organisms, a farmer can raise healthy crops efficiently and safely—and with no side effects for people or land. After harmful insects are controlled, beneficial insects leave as well.

Since its outset, ARBICO has shifted its focus from treating unhealthy crops to maintenance, prevention, research, and education. The Tucson "campus" offers classes and seminars on organic farming, and clients typically cut 40–60 percent of their farming costs. So for those who understand Herrera de Frey's approach, biological pest control doesn't just make sense. It also saves dollars.

LIFE INSURANCE. Imagine the loss a new business would incur if its creator and owner died unexpectedly. The financial loss would only be part of it. However, financial compensation is about all that could be offered in such circumstances. For this reason new businesses frequently buy life insurance for the key people in the business.

The insurance pays the business a certain amount of money in the event of an insured person's death. This amount is the face value of the policy on which the business has been paying premiums. Among other benefits, the amount paid allows the business time to make a decision about replacing the key person. It does this by offsetting some of the losses that may occur because of work delays during the transition.

WORKERS COMPENSATION. This type of insurance is mandatory. In other words, a business owner is required by law to make contributions to the state workers compensation plan.

Workers compensation provides medical and income benefits to employees who are injured on the job. Job-related illnesses are also covered. Employees need only file a claim with the compensation board to have their medical bills taken care of. (There is generally a waiting period for income benefits.) The total amount of the compensation is based on a fixed schedule. The schedule considers the wages or salary of the employee, the seriousness of the injury, and whether the injury is permanent or not.

In some states, workers compensation premiums are a major financial burden for small businesses. The program is supposed to free such firms from the threat of employee lawsuits. (Workers who accept benefits under the program are barred from suing their employers over their injuries.) However, in some states premiums are so high that they are forcing small companies out of business. As a result, for many businesspeople, workers compensation costs have become a key indicator of a state's attitude toward business in general.

Risk Retention

As noted earlier, risk transfer is the principal strategy that businesses use to cope with risk. In some instances, however, it is impossible for a company to transfer a business risk. Either the firm cannot get insurance or is unable to afford the policies that are offered. In these circumstances, if the firm is to do business, it must self-insure. In other words, the owner must put aside a certain amount of money every month to help cover the costs should a loss occur. This strategy is called risk retention.

Gathering Insurance Information

Clearly, then, as a new business owner you will have many decisions to make about risk management. To cope with the complexities of the area, you might want to consult with an insurance professional. Insurance agents are experts trained in advising businesses (among others) on their total insurance package.

Selecting an Insurance Agent

Before talking to an agent, you should define the risks that your business will face. Also, by talking to your local business development agency or SBA, you can probably find out about the types of insurance you are required to carry in your state. Then when you talk to the insurance agent, you will be speaking with some knowledge of the needs and requirements for your business.

There are basically two types of agents. An **independent insurance agent** works with several insurance companies and is usually local. Having your agent in the community in which you do business has the potential advantage of

An experienced insurance agent can be especially helpful to a new business owner. Why?

providing you with faster service. Typically these agents offer very competitive rates. In addition, some specialize in such areas as bonding and liability insurance for certain types of businesses. (Construction, which is very risky to insure, is an example.)

The other type of agent is the **direct insurance writer**. This agent works for one particular insurance company. Business owners generally buy life and automobile insurance through direct agents.

No matter what type of agent you choose, be sure that he or she is someone you are comfortable with. Just like your attorney and your accountant, your insurance agent is a key component of your start-up team and a valuable source of information.

Recording Your Data

The decisions you make about risk management will affect many aspects of your business. They will no doubt play a role in selecting a site, determining hours of operation, and hiring employees. You may therefore find yourself

recording risk-based observations in most sections of your business plan notebook.

In the end, however, their presence will be most obvious in the financial section. There you will record cost information about insurance—either policy premiums or funds you voluntarily set aside. These figures will eventually be incorporated into some of the pro forma financial statements you prepare for your business plan.

Entrepreneur's Bookshelf

To learn more about the subjects discussed in this chapter, consider reading these books and articles:

- "Crime Prevention for Small Business," *Small Business Reporter* (Vol. 13, No. 1, 1988)
- *Hands-On Financial Controls for Your Small Business* by Cecil J. Bond (© 1991)

Chapter 16 Review

Recapping the Chapter

- The major risks facing a new business are crimes, natural disasters, and accidents and injuries.
- Crimes that especially affect business are shoplifting, employee theft, burglary, robbery, and the use of stolen credit cards and bad checks.
- The management of risk involves four basic strategies—risk avoidance, risk reduction, risk transfer, and risk retention.
- Buying insurance is a risk transfer strategy.
- A new business will probably need property, casualty, life, and workers compensation insurance.
- There are two types of insurance agents—the independent agent (who works for many insurance companies) and the direct insurance writer (who works for only one company).

Reviewing Vocabulary

1. Associate each of the following vocabulary terms with a *risk management* strategy. Then, in one or two sentences, tell how the term relates to the strategy.

   - burglary
   - robbery
   - electronic credit authorizers
   - negligence
   - premium
   - independent insurance agent/direct insurance writer

2. Describe the risks that each of the following kinds of insurance are designed to protect businesses against.

   - business interruption insurance
   - casualty insurance
   - errors-and-omissions insurance
   - product liability insurance
   - fidelity bonds
   - performance bonds
   - workers compensation

Checking the Facts

1. Why is the impact of crime greater for small businesses than large businesses?
2. Which type of business is most susceptible to crime? Why?
3. What are three ways to prevent employee theft?
4. What other risks does a new business face besides crime?
5. Why should you use a fireproof safe?
6. What does casualty insurance protect your business against?
7. When you buy insurance, what are you paying for?
8. Describe how the strategy of risk retention works.

Thinking Critically

1. Compare and contrast shoplifting and employee theft in terms of who commits these crimes and how they affect a business.

Chapter 16 Review

2. What is the difference between credit card fraud and writing bad checks? If you were a store owner, how would you deal with each?
3. You are holding a training session for your employees on how to handle shoplifters. What would you want them to know?
4. Does insurance eliminate risk? Explain why or why not.

Discussing Key Concepts

1. How might businesses other than retail be susceptible to crime?
2. What are the three most important steps you could take to protect your own business?
3. Use the four risk management strategies to describe how you would deal with the risk of natural disasters in your geographic area.
4. What benefits (besides the one mentioned in the chapter) are there to taking out life insurance on a new business's owner?
5. Describe how you will go about selecting an insurance agent.

Using Basic Skills

Math

1. Preliminary calculations show that this year your business earned profits of $50,000. In past years, however, the firm has lost up to one-third of its profits to employee theft and about 3 percent to shoplifting. Given these figures, how much do you think your profits actually were?

Communication

2. Think about the kinds of accidents that might befall the employees or customers of your new business. Then prepare a presentation on accident prevention in your workplace. Deliver your presentation to your class.

Human Relations

3. You have discovered that one of your most trusted employees has recently been voiding many transactions at the register. You know that this may be a sign of employee theft. How would you handle the situation?

Enriching Your Learning

1. Interview one or two entrepreneurs to find out how they protect their businesses. How do the techniques they use compare with those discussed in the chapter?
2. Write a two-page section for an employee policy manual describing your business's policy on employee theft.
3. Interview an independent insurance agent and a direct insurance writer about the insurance needs of your own business. What types of insurance do they recommend? How do their recommendations differ, if at all?
4. You are planning to open a gift boutique catering to teenagers. For this business, develop a strategy to deter shoplifters. Present it in written form.

Chapter 17
Operations and Staffing

Objectives

After completing this chapter, you will be able to

- identify the basic components of a management plan;
- formulate both operating and personnel policies for a business;
- prepare an organization chart for a business, as well as job descriptions and specifications; and
- judge how many rules, regulations, and policies a business should have.

Terms to Know

policies
rules/regulations
line organization
staff
line-and-staff
 organization
job specification
recruit
piece rate
commission

Decisions, Decisions

Today I got a real shock. I sat down to pay bills and write payroll checks for my car repair business. It didn't take me too long to realize that I wasn't going to have enough money to go around.

And here I thought business was great—I've been swamped with customers. I guess that doesn't make much difference, though, if you're putting out more money for parts and labor than you're collecting for jobs.

Understand, there's nothing wrong with my pricing or my math. People just aren't paying like they should.

You see, when I first opened up, a lot of friends and relatives came in to get work done. If they said, "Can I pay you on payday?" or "Can you wait till the first of the month?" I said, "Sure." (I mean, how can you say no to your friends and relatives?) Well, I guess my two mechanics thought that meant it was okay for everybody to do it. So, they started telling other customers the same thing. And to be perfectly honest, I didn't stop them. They're good guys, so I thought they'd be able to judge people pretty well.

The problem is that those "paydays" and "first of the months" never seem to come around for a lot of people. Now I'm stuck.

I'm pretty sure I can get a loan to tide me over. But I've got to figure out where I should draw the line on this credit thing. I know I've got to extend some credit to stay in business, but how much and who to? And how do I handle it with my customers and employees?

What Goes into a Management Plan?

For the last few chapters, you have been concerned mainly with the physical features of your business. You have considered location, building, equipment, supplies, and inventory. Now it's time to turn your attention to *how* those things will be used—and *who* will use them.

Recall from Chapter 9 that operations and personnel (or staffing) are the two basic parts of a management plan. You develop and present your decisions in these areas in two forms—policies and rules/regulations.

Policies are general statements of intent about how you want your business run. They provide broad guidelines designed to channel management thinking and actions in certain directions. A company may have a policy of promoting safe use of its facilities or of giving its employees paid vacations. From these examples, it should be obvious that policies deal with recurring situations. They are designed to simplify day-to-day management by eliminating the need to make the same decisions over and over again. However, policies are flexible. They do leave room for individual initiative and interpretation.

In contrast, **rules** or **regulations** are statements that require specific actions. They tell employees exactly what they should or should not do. They leave no room for interpretation. "Employees shall wear hard hats in all construction areas" is a rule. So is "All employees shall get two weeks' vacation after one year's service."

Operating Your Business

Do you remember your marketing mix decisions from Chapter 11? When you spelled out your product, price, place, and promotion strategies, you were, in effect, laying the foundations for your operating policies. This section will show you how to build on those decisions. It will take you through the reasoning process that entrepreneurs use to develop some common operating policies.

Note that the policies discussed here are not applicable to all types of businesses. Nor do they represent every kind of policy. The examples provided, however, should suggest other, relevant possibilities to you. You should write these ideas down as they occur. You can then use your list as a starting point for the operations section of your management plan.

Hours of Operation

Recall that hours of operation are part of your place strategy (how you will deliver your product where and when customers want it). You should set your hours to suit your customers. When can they get to your location? When would it be most convenient for you to contact them?

A movie theater, for example, might be open 12 noon–11:30 P.M. on weekdays and 10 A.M.–1:45 A.M. on weekends. These are the hours when substantial numbers of people want to see movies. In contrast, a wholesaler might have much shorter hours. Office hours might be limited to 9 A.M.–5 P.M. weekdays through Saturday because that's when customers tend to phone in orders. Delivery hours, on the other hand, might be longer—say, 6 A.M.–9 P.M.—to accommodate the varying business hours of customers.

Credit Policies

Credit policies are part of your pricing strategy. Recall that pricing is not just a matter of deciding how much to charge for your product. It also addresses how your customers will pay.

Your first credit policy decision will be, obviously, whether or not to offer credit. What you are selling will help you decide. A no-credit policy would be best for businesses that sell low-priced items and consumable goods. That is why convenience stores and fast-food restaurants usually do not offer credit. However, your business may sell big-ticket items, or you may want to encourage customers to buy in large quantities. In these instances, you will want to make your products easy to pay for. That would mean making credit available.

Should you decide to offer credit, you will need to make a number of other decisions. You will have to select the form (or forms) of credit you will extend. You will also have to decide to whom you will offer credit and in what amounts.

KINDS OF CREDIT PLANS. Many businesses accept bank credit cards. Since the bank that issues the card (not the customer) pays the bill, there is less risk for the merchant in this form of credit. As discussed in earlier chapters, however, this limited risk has a price. Bank card issuers take a percentage of each charged sale as a collection fee.

Some businesses offer charge accounts. With this form of credit, the business gets the full purchase price plus a finance charge (a form of interest). However, the business will have to pay all the costs associated with collecting on these accounts. It will also have to assume all the risk of nonpayment.

Installment plans are another type of credit. They are usually offered when the price of a good or service is too high for customers to pay all at once. Customers who use such plans make a down payment at the time of purchase and regular payments thereafter until the purchase price is paid. For the business offering this form of credit, the costs and risks are similar to those for charge accounts.

Financing sales through a bank is a final form of credit. It is usually reserved for sales of very

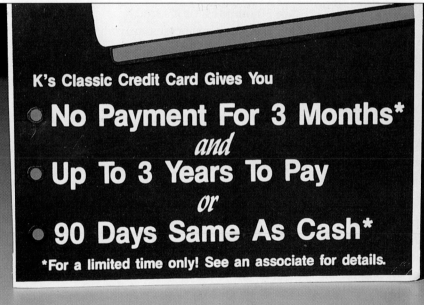

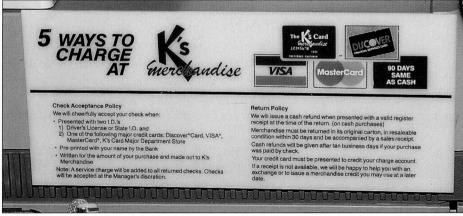

Credit policies come in many forms. Briefly state the policies behind these signs and/or ads.

expensive goods, like new automobiles. With this form of credit, the business gets its money more quickly. The customer, however, can be inconvenienced by delays at the time of purchase.

THE THREE C'S OF CREDIT. Most businesses that do offer credit have standards to determine who is eligible to receive it. The formula that many use is known as the three C's of credit. Here are its components:

- *Character.* Has the customer demonstrated responsibility in paying bills? You can find this out by contacting a credit bureau. Credit bureaus rate people who have been granted credit. Good credit ratings go to those who pay their bills on time. Poor credit ratings are assigned to those who don't.
- *Capacity.* Based on the customer's income and expenses, does he or she have the ability to pay? You can find this out by asking credit applicants to report their income and monthly expenses on your credit application.
- *Capital.* What are the customer's physical and financial assets? Again, you find this out by asking on your credit application.

Ordinarily how much credit you extend to individual customers will also depend on the three C's. You will probably set generous limits for those with higher incomes, good credit ratings, and substantial assets (a home or savings accounts). You will probably set lower limits for those of more modest means. You will probably not extend credit at all to those with bad credit ratings.

Return/Rework Policies

You may choose to have a return or rework policy. This means that your business will guarantee the quality of the goods you sell or the services you provide.

A fair policy regarding replacements, refunds, or repairs will help maintain customer goodwill. You might, for example, want to consider something like "If we didn't install it right, we'll fix it." "Money back guaranteed, no questions asked" is a return policy that could cost you more. You may have to adopt it, however, in order to be competitive.

Delivery Policies

Whether or not to deliver would be another part of your place strategy. For some service businesses, delivery policy can be the key to success. You are probably familiar with Domino's Pizza. Its original delivery policy, the one on which it built a national reputation, promised "Delivery in 30 minutes, or it's free."

For other businesses, as well, delivery policies can be crucial. Retailers who sell big-ticket items like refrigerators risk losing sales if they don't deliver. Wholesalers may have to promise prompt delivery in order stay competitive.

Once you decide to offer delivery, there are other aspects of the policy to consider besides speed. One is whether or not to charge for the service. You might also consider limiting the area in which you deliver.

Other Customer Service Policies

There are too many other service policies to go into each in detail. However, we have listed a number of them below for your review. Look them over and, if any seem applicable to your business, add them to your list.

- *Handling complaints.* Some businesses use the policy "The customer is always right."
- *Servicing what you sell.* If something you sell stops working, will you fix it or help your customers get it fixed?
- *Courtesy to customers.* Some businesses have their clerks ask departing customers, "Did you find everything you were looking for?"
- *Shopping climate.* Your business may have a policy of maintaining certain lighting or housekeeping standards.

Once you have a list of essential policies in hand, you should expand it into formal statements. How can writing out policy statements help you run your business?

- *Provision of rest rooms.* Will these be open to the public or locked and usable by customers only on request?
- *Response time.* Some businesses advertise, "All orders filled within 48 hours of receipt."
- *Warranties.* Manufacturers usually guarantee the materials and workmanship that go into their products.

Employee and Customer Safety

As you learned in Chapter 16, the financial consequences of on-site accidents can be devastating for small businesses. To reduce their liability in such circumstances, businesses often do two things as a matter of policy.

First, they train their employees in safety practices and procedures. At a minimum, such training usually emphasizes the use of protective gear, the safe operation of equipment, and emergency procedures in the event of a mishap. It would most likely be backed up by signs posted throughout the workplace.

As a matter of policy, businesses also give their customers similar warnings. Signs frequently advise customers to stay out of certain areas

Risk Takers, Profit Makers

Lisa Parr

It's not hard to sell a carousel animal. Immediately after Lisa Parr first placed one in the display window of her Chicago studio, she heard the screech of tires followed by the eager knocking of curious passers-by. To restore a carousel animal, however, is a completely different matter. The necessary dedication and craftsmanship have limited the number of carousel animal restorers in the United States to fewer than ten. Of them, Lisa Parr is one of the best.

Like most other specialized antique restorers, Parr never trained specifically for her vocation. Some of her previous jobs included restoring sports cars; repairing and conserving antiques; and teaching studio art, Latin, and history. However, when the Germantown, Philadelphia, native founded Old Parr's Carousel Animals in 1982, everything fell into place. Each occupation has been useful in her restoration of carousel animals for museums and collectors.

Parr began restoring carousel animals because no one else could restore one properly. She began by doing research. To this day, she carefully studies archival pictures, old factory records, and each animal so that she can maintain the integrity of its original design. Emphasizing accuracy, she uses no modern tools or epoxy—just chisels, glues, and paints—to return each animal as closely as possible to its original state.

The precision of her craft has been an ongoing challenge for Parr. Because each step requires forethought and every animal is different, restoration can take from several weeks to several months. Fortunately, Parr's clients share her zeal for authenticity and are understanding. They know that she always sticks to time and price estimates and guarantees a quality restoration.

Parr's unending quest to provide museum-quality restoration for a reasonable price has involved making some adjustments. In advertising, she has learned to be patient about results. Clients may not respond to a daily ad for months. She has learned that having a staff speeds up operations but entails surrendering control. Today she usually works alone, although she does enjoy teaching her techniques to students. She also allows collectors to bring animals to her in addition to tracking them down herself. In these ways, she keeps fees competitive, maintains quality, and ensures the customer's—and her own—satisfaction.

(Authorized personnel only). They warn of dangerous conditions (Stairs slippery when wet). They remind customers not to use certain facilities (like elevators) in emergencies.

Staffing Your Business

In the second major part of your management plan, you will need to address staffing. Recall from Chapter 9 that this means, among other things, preparing three types of documents. You will have to design an organization chart, write job descriptions, and provide resumes for yourself and others in key positions.

You will make your staffing decisions based on how many and what kinds of employees you need. Of course, if you intend to have a one-person operation, this portion of your management plan will be minimal. For many types of businesses, however, it is unlikely that you will be able to do all the work yourself. If you plan to have even one or two employees, you will have to discuss staffing at greater length.

Types of Organization

Your first task in the staffing area is to design an organizational structure for your business. The easiest way to do this is to develop an organization chart. This is a diagram that includes all the jobs that need to be done in your enterprise and shows how they are related to each other.

What guidelines should you use in this process? Try to keep in mind that the structure you design should help you delegate responsibility, authority, and work. Also, try not to think of each job as a full-time employee. Stay open to other possibilities. For example, some jobs (particularly staff positions) can be contracted out to consultants. They may also require only part-time employees.

There are several types of business organization. Here we will discuss only the two most common.

LINE ORGANIZATION. Suppose that all of your employees will be involved in producing or distributing your product. You would use **line organization**. Figure 17–1 illustrates this type of structure. It shows the various levels of positions, with you (as owner) at the top. Those who report and are directly responsible to you are in the middle. Those who report and are responsible to them are at the bottom.

LINE-AND-STAFF ORGANIZATION. Suppose, however, that your operation will be large enough for you to hire **staff**. This term is often used for employees in general. But technically it refers only to those who provide support for production and distribution people. (Examples of staff might include those involved in bookkeeping or personnel activities.) For this type of enterprise, you would use **line-and-staff organization**.

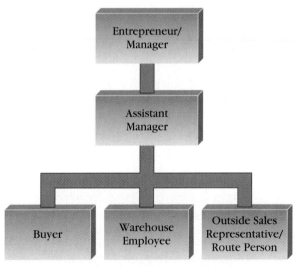

Line Organization Chart

Figure 17–1 *This organization chart depicts the structure of a small wholesale business. The horizontal placement of each position shows its level of authority—top manager, middle manager, or employee. What do you think the lines show?*

Line-and-Staff Organization Chart

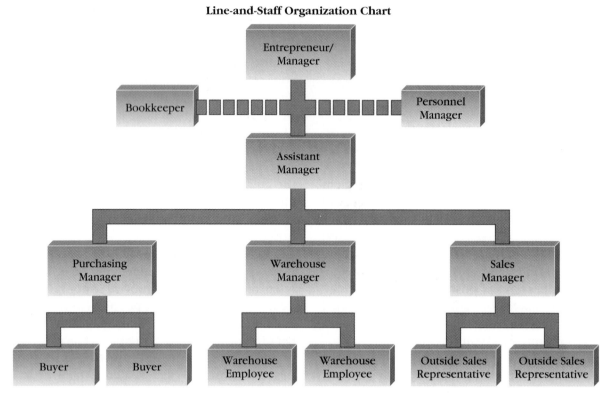

Figure 17–2   Here is the same wholesale business as shown in Figure 17–1 after some growth has taken place. How are the positions connected by solid lines different from those connected by broken lines?

Figure 17-2 provides an illustration. In many respects this second chart looks similar to the first. There are, however, more positions and more levels of authority. The key difference, though, is the *broken* line used to tie in the bookkeeper and the personnel manager. That line is a visual device used to distinguish staff from line personnel.

Job Descriptions, Specifications, and Resumes

For each position in your organization chart, you will need to write a job description. This is a statement describing the nature of the job and its duties and responsibilities. (See Figure 17-3.)

For each job description, you should then write a second statement—a **job specification** (Figure 17-4). This document spells out the abilities, skills, educational level, and experience needed by an employee to perform the described job. Think of it as a kind of want ad.

Finally, you should provide resumes for yourself and others you expect to be involved in the business. These resumes should outline the skills and experience each person will contribute. By comparing them with your job descriptions and specifications, you will be able to recognize gaps in your organization's staffing. These are the areas in which you will need to look for outside assistance.

Personnel Policies and Decisions

At this point, however, you are not quite ready to begin an active search for employees. First, you need to think about the kind of people you want. Then you have to decide how to find them.

EMPLOYEE STANDARDS. The people you hire will in large measure determine what customers and clients think of your company. They will be the face of your business, the voice, and its reputation for quality. That is why many entrepreneurs take the time to establish policies regarding the kind of people they will hire.

For example, your policy may be no more than the statement "Our organization will strive to hire only the best people." Who are the best people? That will depend on the type of business you have. For a retail operation, you may want very social individuals; for a bookkeeping service, people who are detail oriented; for a custom carpentry business, people who share your high standards of quality.

These kinds of traits should be set out in your policy statement. Other personnel decisions that you make will reflect this policy.

RECRUITING. You can **recruit**, or attract, prospective employees by many means. Classified ads, state and private employment agencies, school and college placement offices, union hiring halls, and word-of-mouth are just a few. You should use the recruitment method that you feel will best reach the type of applicants you want.

SCREENING. In order to select the employees you want from the applicants you attract, you will have to carry out a screening process. This can involve a whole series of procedures.

Often the first screen used by businesses is an application form or resume. Either one will help you see how well an applicant matches up to your job specification. Those who don't fit your requirements can be eliminated from consideration immediately.

If you like what you see on the application or resume, you can invite the person in for an

---

**Inside Sales Representative
Electronic Supply Company**

Job Description

Objectives:
- To provide all customer service functions to people or firms placing orders by telephone or in person at one of our wholesale outlets.
- To complement the efforts of outside sales personnel in identifying, qualifying, and developing new business or additional business with existing customers.

Duties:
- Respond to quotation requests.
- Perform order entry.
- Acknowledge receipt of customer orders.
- Expedite orders.
- Provide product information.
- Follow up on vendor sales leads and other vendor requests.
- Perform other duties as assigned.

Responsibilities:
- Handle an average of 20-30 regular customers.
- Accept 20-50 telephone calls per day.
- Enter 10-30 orders per day.
- Visit selected customer facilities once per month.

Figure 17–3   A job description is divided into three parts—objectives, duties, and responsibilities. Characterize the type of information provided under each of these headings.

**Inside Sales Representative
Electronic Supply Company**

Job Specification

Education: High school graduate.

Experience: One year in electronics supply or related field preferred.

Knowledge: Basic knowledge of electronic equipment, components, and terminology. Able to operate a computer.

Skills: Good interpersonal and communication skills required to deal with customers both in person and on the telephone. Basic computer literacy with some knowledge of spreadsheet software desirable.

Figure 17–4   A job specification converts a job description into a set of qualifications. Compare Figure 17-3 with this one. What is the source of each qualification listed here?

Guidelines for Effective Interviewing

1. Define what you are looking for before the interview.

2. Conduct interviews in private. Don't use a panel of interviewers.

3. Put the interviewee at ease. Treat him or her as an equal.

4. Ask general background questions first, more specific questions later.

5. Encourage the interviewee to talk. Be a good listener.

6. Don't cut off the interviewee's answers but interrupt when necessary to pursue a key point.

7. Confirm key observations several times during the interview.

8. Provide an opportunity for the interviewee to ask questions.

9. Observe how the interviewee conducts him- or herself. Give special attention to attitude or outlook.

10. Look for what the interviewee will bring to the job.

11. Cover all of your areas of interest in enough depth to be able to make a sound decision.

Figure 17–5 Interviewing is probably the most valuable form of screening employers have at their disposal. Based on these guidelines, how would you plan for an interview?

interview. An interview can provide you with more insight into the applicant's qualifications. You can also learn about his or her interpersonal and communication skills, if those are important to the job.

Study Figure 17-5. It provides some guidelines for conducting effective interviews. You might also go back to Chapters 12 and 16 to review the kinds of questions that you should *not* ask.

In addition to interviews, you may want to consider testing. Tests are used to evaluate an employee's intelligence, aptitude, achievement, interest, personality, and honesty. Recall from Chapter 12, however, that any tests you use must be related directly to the type of performance expected on the job.

Finally you may ask for character references. By checking these, you can gain some knowledge of the applicant's personal qualities. Contacting former employers would be especially helpful. You could learn about the person's past job performance and determine if the former employer would rehire the individual.

PAY AND BENEFITS.   In order to attract and maintain the kind of employees you want, you will have to do two things. First, you will have to pay a competitive wage or salary. This means paying a rate that is similar to the rates offered by other businesses with similar employee needs. Second, you will have to offer competitive employee benefits.

There are several ways to figure pay. One way is to pay wages based on the amount of time the employee works. You could, for example, pay an hourly rate or a flat salary per week, month, or year. Another way to pay is based on productivity. Productivity pay could be either a **piece rate** (so much per unit produced) or a **commission** (a percentage of sales). You will probably choose the way you pay based on what is standard for your industry.

There are many kinds of employee benefits. Some are required by law. These include the employer's contribution to social security, unemployment compensation, and workers compensation. Optional benefits include things like paid vacations, paid sick leave, health and life insurance, pensions, and child care. Companies offer benefits in conjunction with pay as a way to attract and keep good employees.

As you consider the benefits you will give your employees, you will want to keep their cost in mind. Typically benefits for an employee run between 20 and 40 percent of salary. So, if you pay an employee $1,700 a month, the cost of benefits for that employee will be between $340 and $680 a month *more*.

As you can see, when you decide how much and in what way to compensate your employees, you will be committing yourself to a major business expense. This projected cost will figure heavily in the financial statements you prepare for your business plan.

TRAINING AND DEVELOPMENT.   After you make your hiring decisions, your new employees will have to be trained. Unless yours is a highly technical business, this early training will be given on the job—and *you* will be the trainer.

As your operation grows, you may need to hire a specialist to handle your training needs and the long-term development of your employees. You also have the option of contracting with outside consultants to provide these services.

Developing Policies for Your Management Plan

By now it should be obvious that there are many different policies, rules, and regulations that you will have to consider for your management plan. How can you be sure that you won't miss any that are vitally important to your business? By using this three-step procedure:

- If you haven't already done so, make a list of the policies you've read about here that may be applicable to your business.
- In your mind, go through a typical business day, and note any situations that could require additional policies.
- Write a policy statement to address each of the situations you have identified.

As you work your way through these steps, remember that the intent of a policy is to *simplify* day-to-day management. Therefore, try not to let your policies (and your rules and regulations) get out of hand. Too many can limit your flexibility. Restrict your policy statements to situations in which they will eliminate the need to make routine decisions. Use rules and regulations only where they are absolutely necessary (for example, in areas like health and safety, fundamental fairness, and customer relations).

Organizing and Using Your Data

The policy statements and job documents you have been developing in this chapter should be kept in the management section of your business plan notebook. If they are especially lengthy, when you do your actual business plan, you may want to move them. You can simply reference them in your management plan and place the documents themselves in the appendix.

Some small portions of the materials you have developed in this chapter may be distributed to other notebook sections. For example, some of your operating policies may influence your business description. Certainly your projected costs for employee salaries, benefits, and training will have to be noted in your financial plan section.

Be careful when recording figures in your financial section to distinguish between start-up and operating expenditures. For example, you might think that money spent for training and development would automatically go into your operating costs. However, in order to have capable employees available to you on opening day, you may have to train some of them *before* you open.

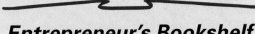

Entrepreneur's Bookshelf

To learn more about the subjects discussed in this chapter, consider reading these books:

- *Starting Right in Your New Business: All the Information You Need to Start Your First Business or Your Next* by Robert Clements and Wilferd F. Tetreault (© 1988)
- *The New Venture Handbook: Everything You Need to Know to Start and Run Your Own Business* by R. E. Merrill and Henry D. Sedgwick (© 1987)

Chapter 17 Review

Recapping the Chapter

- The two basic parts of a management plan are operations and staffing.
- Operating policies for a business include hours of operation and credit, return/rework, and delivery policies.
- Before you staff your business, you should develop an organization chart, define the duties and responsibilities for each position in that chart, and set policies regarding what kind of employees you want.
- Decisions affected by your staffing policy involve ways to recruit, screen, compensate, and train your employees.
- You should not have so many policies, rules, and regulations that they limit your flexibility in managing your business.

Reviewing Vocabulary

Briefly describe how the terms in each pair differ from each other.

- policies—rules/regulations
- line organization—line-and-staff organization
- job specification—job description
- recruit—screen
- piece rate—commission

Checking the Facts

1. How does establishing policies simplify the day-to-day management of a business?
2. Credit policies are a part of which marketing strategy?
3. What is an organization chart?
4. How does writing job descriptions, job specifications, and resumes help to determine staffing needs?
5. List four methods of recruiting prospective employees.
6. What are the two basic ways to figure pay?
7. What parts of your business plan will be affected by operational and staffing decisions?

Thinking Critically

1. A management plan includes information on operations and staffing. Should it include anything else? If yes, what else? If no, why not?
2. Study the marketing strategy decisions you made back in Chapter 11. What operating policies emerge from those decisions?
3. Think through all aspects of your proposed operation. What policies other than those based on your marketing mix can you identify a need for?
4. What kind of organization chart would be most appropriate for your beginning operation? Why?

Discussing Key Concepts

1. What policies, if any, should every business have? Why?
2. What is the best way to get information to prospective employees about job openings that you have? Defend your choice.
3. When would you use all of the procedures described in this chapter—applications, resumes, interviews, tests, and reference

Chapter 17 Review

checks—for screening applicants? When would you use just one of these procedures or a combination of them? Explain.

4. Would your prospective business be better off trying to get and keep employees with an attractive pay and benefits package? by hiring part-time people to carry out all or most of the job duties? by contracting out all or most of the work you need done? Why?

Using Basic Skills

Math

1. After screening all applicants, you hire the best candidate at a salary of $18,000 per year. Your benefits package normally amounts to about 25 percent of an employee's base salary. How much will your new employee's compensation add to your monthly operating expenses?

Communication

2. Do the following for your projected business:

- Design an organization chart.
- Write job descriptions for each position in the chart.
- Write job specifications for each job description.

Using your chart as a visual aid, present your personnel plans to the class.

Human Relations

3. You're thinking about how to interview prospective employees for your new business. You suddenly realize how easy it would be to ask (unintentionally, of course) questions that might be construed as discriminatory. If you did accidentally ask such a question during an interview, how would you deal with it?

Enriching Your Learning

1. Obtain policy handbooks from several businesses, including at least one from a business in your field. Compare and contrast them.

2. Arrange an interview with a business owner in your selected field. Get his or her reaction to the organization chart you developed in the Communication activity above. Make clear that this would be your beginning organizational structure. Record the business owner's suggestions. *Note:* If you are employed in your selected field, carry out the interview with your employer.

3. Try to get a realistic feel for what pay and benefits for your potential employees will cost your business.

- Gather information on current salaries and wage rates for the kind(s) of positions you will need to fill. As sources, use newspaper ads, state employment services, and personnel agencies.
- Contact the IRS, state tax office, and other appropriate agencies to obtain information regarding employer costs and withholding requirements.

Chapter 18
Promoting Your Business

Objectives

After completing this chapter, you will be able to
- distinguish preopening and ongoing promotional plans,
- select the promotional mix for a given business,
- tell how to determine promotional costs for a start-up business, and
- identify the principal approaches you can use to carry out your promotional plans.

Terms to Know

image
public relations
preselling
campaign
promotional
  channels
specialty items
prime time
news release
premiums
sweepstakes
rebates
cooperative
  advertising

? Decisions, Decisions

When I first thought about starting my business, I had this picture in my mind of what a landscaping company ought to be. What I visualized was a company that would come to your house or business, get your ideas about how you wanted your place to look, and lay out a design for you. Then they'd install sod, shrubs, trees—whatever—to turn your ideas into reality.

What I found out, though, was that a lot of different businesses that do just one part of the job call themselves landscaping companies. They may only move dirt or cut grass or lay sod, but they're still landscapers.

I guess those kinds of companies are okay for people who need the one service they provide. But it's certainly not what I have in mind, and I don't think it's what my potential customers have in mind either. When I went out to different neighborhoods to get some reactions to what I wanted to do, a lot of people were interested. They said they'd been hesitant to call landscapers because they didn't know what they were going to get. They felt they couldn't be sure of the service or the quality.

It looks like one of my biggest hurdles is going to be to establish the right image for my business. I certainly don't want people to mix my company up with those other outfits. I definitely want to create the impression that I can do a complete, attractive, high-quality landscaping job. Now the question is, How can I get my prospective customers to see my company that way?

Finalizing Your Promotion Strategy

Early in the entrepreneurial process (Chapter 11), you roughed out a promotional strategy as part of your preliminary marketing plan. Recall that that plan included the four P's of marketing—product, price, place, and *promotion*. Recall further that your promotional options included advertising, publicity, sales promotion, and personal selling.

In this chapter, we will give you more detailed information about promotion so that you can finalize your promotional strategy. We will examine the types of promotional plans you will need to develop for your business. We will take you through the process of selecting the right mix of activities to promote your product. We will discuss how you budget for promotion. And finally, we will suggest some ways to carry out your promotional ideas.

Drawing Up Promotional Plans

Since your business is new, your promotional strategy will have to include two kinds of plans. To start, you will need a plan to lay the groundwork for your opening. You will need another, different plan to support your operation once it is under way.

Preopening Plan

To ensure that you have money coming in as soon as you open your doors, you must promote your business beforehand. In other words, you must have a preopening plan.

The objectives of such a plan usually include the following:

- Establishing a positive image
- Letting potential customers know you are open for business
- Bringing customers in (or having them contact your business)
- Interesting potential customers in your product rather than your competitor's

ESTABLISHING AN IMAGE. Of these objectives, probably the most complicated is establishing a positive image. Your company's **image** consists of all of the beliefs, ideas, and impressions that people have of your business. It is, in effect, your company's personality.

When you start your business, you start with a clean slate. You can project whatever image you want. How? Through public relations. **Public relations** is an umbrella term that covers any activity designed to create goodwill toward a business.

Public relations efforts can be aimed at customers, employees, suppliers, or the community at large. In the early stages of your business, however, you will probably be targeting most of your efforts to your potential customers. Here are a few things you could do to create a positive image:

- *Set high standards for your business.* Federal Express promises to deliver all packages on time and supports that pledge with a money-back guarantee.
- *Know what your customers want.* IBM surveys its customers, sales representatives, and engineers every 90 days.
- *Design your products to satisfy customers' needs.* AT&T designs its telephones to withstand virtually any kind of abuse.

- *Satisfy your customers even after the sale.* During the peak Christmas travel season, executives at Delta Airlines help baggage handlers. This enables Delta customers to receive their luggage promptly when they arrive at their destinations.

Think about what these practices and examples suggest. The businesses involved provide quality products and are customer-oriented. In the business world, both are reputations worth having.

TIMING YOUR PROMOTIONAL EFFORTS. A good rule of thumb is to begin your promotion at least six weeks prior to your opening. Promotional efforts should then intensify as you near your opening date.

In some types of businesses, these efforts would be capped off with a grand opening. In others, a party or reception for prospective customers and even local dignitaries might be appropriate.

Ongoing Plan

Once your operation is under way, you will need an ongoing promotional plan to help you maintain and build sales. Some of the objectives for this plan will parallel your preopening objectives. For example, once you have established a positive image for your business, you will need to maintain it. Other objectives, however, will be new, added to help you presell your goods or services. (**Preselling** is influencing potential customers to buy from you before contact is actually made.)

Objectives for ongoing promotional plans usually include the following:

- Explaining major features and benefits of your products
- Communicating information about sales
- Clearing up questions and concerns in customers' minds
- Introducing new goods or services

A planning calendar is a useful tool for laying out your promotional schedule, or what activities you will use when. What other kinds of information might it be helpful to pencil in?

Depending on the type of business, you may choose to develop ongoing promotional plans seasonally (every six months), quarterly, monthly, or weekly. When shorter (weekly or monthly) plans are used, they are usually based on quarterly or seasonal plans.

For your new business, then, you should start with quarterly or seasonal plans. Then you should rough out monthly plans to estimate your promotional expenditures. (You will need these figures for your pro forma financial statements.)

Promotional Plan Format

You can use the same format for both your pre-opening and ongoing plans. Both can be organized around either independent or related activities or a combination of the two. Related activities would have a similar theme and thus constitute a **campaign**.

For each activity in your promotional plans, you should provide the following information:

- Brief description
- Specific media placement
- Submit dates
- Scheduled date of run or release
- Number of runs, copies, or items
- Costs
- Rationale and any other pertinent notes

Selecting Your Promotional Mix

Promotional mixes vary considerably. Part of the reason for this lies in the distinctive needs of different types of businesses. For example, someone who makes office machine components might use direct mail to contact manufacturers and then follow up with personal selling. A produce store, on the other hand, might use local newspapers to advertise specials, lighted signs to draw customers in, and attractive displays to promote purchases. Even within the same business, however, promotional mixes can vary greatly. Consider the cosmetics field. Revlon concentrates heavily on advertising while Avon focuses on personal selling.

You do not have to use every promotional option in your promotional mix. It is likely, though, that you will use more than one. To help you identify the techniques with the greatest potential for your business, you should keep three things in mind:

- *Target market.* Earlier in the entrepreneurial process, you identified your target market. Since that time, however, you may have narrowed, expanded, or otherwise refined your idea of who your potential customers are. You should therefore take some time now to refocus on your target market, to reestablish them as your principal point of reference. You must match your promotional options to this group. As you consider each choice, ask yourself, How effective will this promotional option be in reaching and communicating to my target market?

- *Promotional channels.* Just as there are established channels for the physical distribution of certain products, there are also established lines of communication for them. Think—when you want to know what's playing at the movies, where do you look? Most likely, in the newspaper. Of course, that doesn't mean you shouldn't look for new **promotional channels.** Such channels might give you an edge over your competition. It is important to remember, however, that existing channels evolved because they were effective in reaching their intended markets.

- *Costs.* You should try to put together a combination of activities that will give you the best results within the limits of what you have to spend. What *do* you have to spend? At this point you can only know in the broadest terms. Do you have thousands of dollars or hundreds? As standards go, this one is not very specific. But it is a starting point that will keep you from committing yourself to options you can't possibly afford.

To make a wise selection of promotional activities for your business, you should be aware of all the possibilities each form of promotion presents. This section is designed to give you that awareness. It discusses your choices in detail.

Advertising

Recall that there are two types of advertising media—print and broadcast. Print media include newspapers, magazines, direct mail, outdoor advertising, directories, and transit advertising. Television and radio are broadcast media.

NEWSPAPERS. Businesses spend nearly one-third of their advertising dollars on newspaper ads. For small enterprises the principal advantage of such ads is their ability to attract local business. They can do this because they provide extensive coverage in a selected geographic area. In addition, newspaper ads are flexible. (Changes in ad copy can usually be made up to 24 hours before printing.) They generate sales almost immediately, and they cost relatively little.

Newspaper ads have disadvantages, too. A paper's total circulation is likely to be much larger than your target market. (In effect, you will be paying to attract people who won't be interested in your product.) There is also a chance that your ad won't stand out since newspapers carry so many ads. Finally, newspaper ads have a limited life. Think of how quickly the average reader disposes of a newspaper once it has been read.

There are, of course, ways to get around some of these disadvantages. You could, for example, place your ads in a local newspaper with a more narrowly defined readership. To ensure that your ad will stand out, you could pay more for a special placement. Newspapers often offer variable rates based on when (day of the week) and where (which section) the ad will run. (See Figure 18-1.)

MAGAZINES. Many general interest magazines, such as *People*, *Time*, and *Life*, give businesses the opportunity to reach extremely large national audiences. At the same time, some of them produce regional editions. These allow advertisers who market their products in, say, only the South to limit their exposure and cost.

Advertising Rate Card

Advertising Rates			
FREQUENCY CONTRACTS			
Short-term Contracts (13 weeks)			
Separate day insertions and space for 13 or more times with a minimum of one ad per week.			
Col. In.	Tues.–Sat.	Mon.	Sun.
1	$16.06	$18.26	$18.94
Annual Contracts			
Weekly Bulk (minimum of 52 weeks) Minimum space used in one week.			
Col. In.	Tues.–Sat.	Mon.	Sun.
1	$15.46	$17.66	$18.34
5	15.05	17.25	17.93
10	14.90	17.10	17.78
20	14.62	16.82	17.50
40	14.38	16.58	17.26
Monthly Bulk (minimum of 12 months) Minimum space used in one month.			
Col. In.	Tues.–Sat.	Mon.	Sun.
35	$14.72	$16.92	$17.60
50	14.59	16.79	17.47
100	14.35	16.55	17.23
200	14.11	16.31	16.99
300	13.98	16.18	16.86
Yearly Bulk Minimum space used in one year.			
Col. In.	Tues.–Sat.	Mon.	Sun.
150	$15.16	$17.36	$18.04
250	14.98	17.18	17.86
500	14.74	16.94	17.62
750	14.59	16.79	17.47
1000	14.50	16.70	17.38

Figure 18–1 Newspapers, magazines, and other media prepare printed summaries of their advertising rates and will mail them to prospective advertisers on request. According to this chart, how much would it cost you to run a 4-inch ad in the Sunday paper if you had a short-term contract?

Specialty magazines like *Sports Illustrated*, *Glamour, Rolling Stone, Good Housekeeping*, and *Photography Today* present businesses with a similar opportunity. By narrowing the national audience to those with particular interests, they simplify the advertiser's task of targeting a special market.

Businesses that sell to other businesses are likely to advertise in trade rather than consumer magazines. Like specialty magazines, trade magazines target specific markets, such as woodworkers, booksellers, or retailers. If such magazines exist for your field, you have probably already encountered them in researching your business.

Magazine ads are likely to be more expensive than newspaper ads and must be submitted 6–8 weeks in advance. However, they have one attractive feature that more than makes up for these disadvantages—longer life. Magazines of all types are often kept for long periods of time. This increases the probability that people will read them—and the ads they contain.

DIRECT MAIL.   Direct mail is an increasingly popular method of advertising. It includes sales solicitation letters, catalogs, coupon books, brochures, and circulars delivered directly to the mail boxes of potential customers.

Direct mail allows you to do two things at once. You can cover a wide geographic territory and at the same time direct your mailings to a specific target market—say, outdoor enthusiasts. Lists of potential customers can be purchased or obtained from a variety of sources. For example, businesses that already have mailing lists for their customers (such as catalog houses) often sell those lists.

Direct mail does have some major limitations. Probably the most significant is suggested by a term often substituted for direct mail—namely, junk mail. Unsolicited mailings are often thrown away without ever being opened—let alone read. This is something worth thinking about when considering the direct mail option, especially since current mailing costs are so high.

OUTDOOR ADVERTISING. This category includes permanently placed billboards, painted signs, and neon displays. It also includes the smaller, movable signs used at the business location.

The principal advantage of such outdoor displays is that they expose their messages to large numbers of people who pass them daily. Unfortunately, the eye appeal of such signs seldom lasts. After the first few viewings, people tend to ignore them. In addition, because of the large size of permanent billboards, many communities have restricted their use.

DIRECTORIES. The yellow pages of the local telephone directory offer a relatively inexpensive form of advertising. The major advantage that directory ads have over other forms of advertising is their longer life. People keep and refer to phone books as long as they are current, which is usually about a year. Note, however, that this advantage can become a disadvantage should your address, telephone number, or advertising message change midyear. The change will not be reflected in the directory until its next printing.

TRANSIT ADVERTISING. Advertising panels placed in public transportation have an obvious and unique advantage. They reach a captive audience! Their principal disadvantage is just as obvious, however. They are restricted to areas where public transportation is available.

OTHER PRINT MEDIA. There are other kinds of advertising that you might not think of as print media. Putting your business's name and address on **specialty items** like pens, caps, and T-shirts is one. Such items, if used regularly by people, can serve as a constant reminder. There is no guarantee, however, that your specialty items will fall into the hands of potential customers. It is also unlikely that they will be very widely distributed.

TELEVISION. Television is a form of broadcast media. It is the second-most-popular form of advertising (after newspapers). Businesses spend fully one-fourth of their advertising dollars on TV ads. They are willing to do so because television reaches such a large portion of the population.

The main advantage of television advertising is that it lets people see your product as well as hear your message. It can also be used to reach audiences of various sizes, from mass national audiences to those within selected major market areas. It can even be used to reach smaller, local markets through cable channels.

Cost is the biggest obstacle to the use of television advertising. Ads are expensive to produce, and the charges for air time are steep. Rates vary according to the time of the day, with the **prime time** hours of 7–11 P.M. being most expensive. This is because the television audience is at its largest during those hours.

RADIO. Radio advertising is another form of broadcast media and is especially effective for local advertising. It is also an economical way to reach a large number of people.

Radio's major advantage is that it allows the advertiser to target both a geographic area and an audience. To do so, however, requires choosing the right radio station. Today, most stations specialize in a particular market, such as country music, rock, easy listening, or news and talk. Fortunately, the stations themselves can tell you about the demographics of their listeners. You can then use that information to select the station that will best reach your target market.

As with television, rates for radio advertising vary according to the time of the day. "Prime time" for radio is usually during the early morning and late afternoon when people are driving to and from work.

Publicity

You probably remember that publicity is the placement of newsworthy items about a company or product in the media. What constitutes "newsworthy"? You might be surprised.

WHAT'S NEWSWORTHY? Consider an example of how publicity worked for one new venture. When Xavier Roberts created his Cabbage

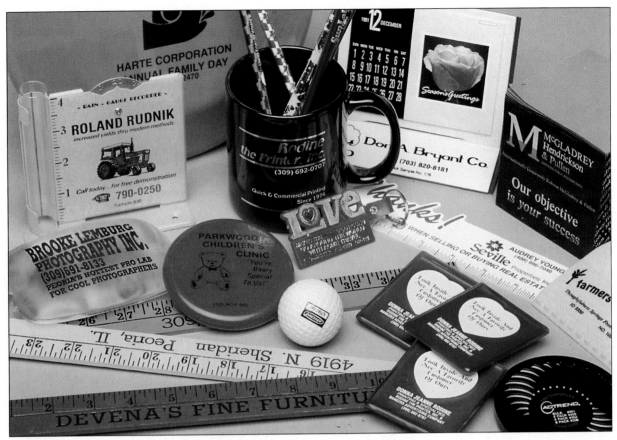

Businesses use specialty items to keep their names in the minds of potential customers. Judging from the selection shown here, what types of items are ideal for this purpose?

Patch Kids, he also developed a whimsical story about where the dolls came from. He set up a "hospital" where people could come and "adopt" his dolls. The concept caught the attention of the press. As a result, Roberts and his dolls were the subject of at least 150 articles in the company's first year alone.

Suppose you don't have an original concept like Xavier Roberts. You can still get publicity for your business in a number of more conventional ways.

Community involvement, for example, is a rich source of publicity. Some companies donate money, equipment, or personnel to local schools. Others participate in environmental cleanups or beautification programs. Still others sponsor events for charity.

Today, especially, such activities can help communities accomplish things they might not otherwise be able to do. For example, several years ago Eppie's Restaurants in Sacramento, California, started a kayak/bike/foot race marathon. Eppie's Great Race, as it was called, was designed to support the local drug abuse program. Today the race is a community institution. It has grown to some 2,000 participants and raises over $40,000 annually. Which do you think would do more for your company—having its name associated with such an event or spending thousands of dollars on advertising?

Risk Takers, Profit Makers

Craig Scheak

Craig Scheak launched Greylag Artist Multiples in 1988 in conjunction with artist Lynda Barry's ascent to critical and cult-level stardom. After Barry's first book came out, Scheak printed her unique "Poodle with a Mohawk" illustration on T-shirts to sell at bookstores. They were a hit. Since then, Greylag has continued promoting Barry and other non-mainstream artists through apparel.

Despite growing up in a family of entrepreneurs, Scheak didn't plan on running a business. While attending the University of Washington, he booked concerts, promoted records, and practiced journalism. The Seattle resident later became a graphics art representative, organizing business matters for artist friends. From these enterprises, he learned promoting, marketing, and design skills. He also made and kept friendly contacts at such places as *The Rocket* newspaper, where he met several artists whose works he would later use.

Eventually, Scheak settled on a job in a Seattle bookstore. It was at the bookstore in 1980 that he became acquainted with Lynda Barry. Recognizing the powerful appeal of Barry's work and perceiving an untapped market, Scheak worked out a T-shirt agreement with her. Book and shirt sales proved to be complementary, and Greylag was born.

As a purveyor of T-shirts with unique prints, Scheak's main objective is to provide a high degree of quality. He doesn't offer a variety of colors or custom fits or sizes. He simply guarantees a distinctive design and a superior T-shirt. It's a strategy that has generated steadily rising profits in the face of rising competition.

However, Scheak keeps Greylag's success in perspective. Recognizing the finicky tastes of his limited-but-loyal market, he keeps in touch with retailers. They let him know how people respond to new designs. He also ensures the best possible relationship with artists by simply leasing images, not demanding first or exclusive rights. This way, the artist loses no rights, Scheak gets topnotch designs, and everyone is happy.

Since the addition of Marilyn McCormick Scheak in 1991, Greylag has been a husband-and-wife, home business endeavor. The Scheaks are both proud of their business's record of providing extra exposure and extra income to low-profile artists. Indeed, their mailing list now reaches 10,000 very interested people. So, if you meet a person wearing a T-shirt adorned with David Boswell's "Reid Fleming, the world's toughest milkman," you'll know. You'll have found someone on Greylag's list.

HOW TO GET NOTICED. In a world of celebrities and sensational news events, you cannot just sit by and hope your efforts will be noticed. You have to call attention to yourself and your enterprise. There are a number of ways you can do this.

- *Write news releases.* These are brief news stories that you send to the media. Figure 18–2 shows the format of a **news release**.
- *Write feature articles.* Because you are an entrepreneur, you probably have expertise in some field. Using that expertise, you can write a feature article for publication. Choose a newspaper, magazine, or newsletter that reaches your target market.
- *Submit captioned photos.* You can take photos of your company's new products, facilities, or employees and write brief explanations to accompany them. Then you can send them to the media.
- *Call a press conference.* This is a public meeting called with the news media for the purpose of making a major announcement.
- *Seek interviews.* These are private meetings with individual representatives of the news media. You could schedule an interview to discuss some aspect of your company's operation or to offer your expert opinion as background for a related story.

A MATTER OF CHANCE. The most obvious advantage of publicity is that its placement in the media is free. In addition, because it is not company sponsored, publicity is often seen by viewers or readers as being more credible than advertising.

There is a downside to publicity, however. As a businessperson releasing publicity, you have no control over when, where, or how the story will be printed or aired. Sending out a news release does not guarantee that a newspaper or television station will use it. It's a matter of chance. But you really do have nothing to lose by trying and a great deal to gain if the item is used.

NEWS RELEASE

DATE: MARCH 12, 1995

TO: BUSINESS EDITORS

FROM: YIKES! BIKES! Bicycle Shop
         Earl Brown, Owner

RE: Grand Opening

On Saturday, May 6, 1995, YIKES! BIKES! will hold its grand opening. Disc jockey Bruno Reneaux from radio station WJZ will be broadcasting live from 12:00 noon to 4:00 p.m.

The store opens at 10:00 a.m., and there will be a free drawing every hour. The first 100 customers will be eligible to win a Nova 4000 mountain bike.

Our new store is located at 1331 Front Street in the newly restored River Front Warehouse. YIKES! BIKES! is a new concept in bicycle retail. Not only do we sell state-of-the-art, currently manufactured bicycles. We also sell beautifully reconditioned classic bicycles. And we'll repair any bicycle in almost any condition.

Store hours will be Monday–Saturday, 10:00 a.m. to 6:00 p.m., and Sunday from 12:00 noon to 5:00 p.m.

Figure 18–2 *A news release should always answer these key questions: Who? What? Where? When? Why? How does the above example measure up to this standard?*

Sales Promotion

Sales promotion involves the use of incentives or interest-building activities to stimulate traffic or sales. It is most often used to enhance the effectiveness of other promotional tools.

Examples of sales promotion include the following:

- *Displays.* Window, showroom, point-of-purchase, and exterior displays all increase buyer awareness. While many displays are designed in-house, others (particularly in retail businesses) are put together by manufacturers and wholesalers. These prepackaged displays may come with instructions for assembly or be set up by supplier representatives.
- *Premiums.* **Premiums** are anything of value that a customer receives in addition to the

good or service purchased. They include coupons and gifts placed inside product packages. Premiums can be used to attract new customers or build loyalty among existing customers.

- *Sweepstakes and Contests.* Sweepstakes and contests are games used by businesses to get customers thinking and talking about what the company has to offer. **Sweepstakes** like those run by Publishers Clearing House are simple games of chance. Contests, on the other hand, require the customer to do something in order to win.
- *Rebates.* Automobile manufacturers have made **rebates** (or returning part of the purchase price) popular in recent years. Such discounts, however, can be used by many other types of businesses.
- *Samples.* Free trial-size packages are particularly useful in introducing new products. Such samples can be distributed by mail, door-to-door, or handed out in retail stores. Soap manufacturers, food packagers, and publishers are some of the businesses that have successfully used this technique.

Sales promotions have the inherent advantage of being able to catch and hold customer interest—at least in the short run. On the downside, some types of sales promotion are expensive. Also, bringing them to an end can result in some customer disappointment.

Personal Selling

The types of promotion we have talked about thus far—advertising, publicity, and sales promotion—are all nonpersonal ways of selling. One of the most common ways that businesses sell their products, however, is through personal contact with customers or clients.

Personal selling is most important when customers need detailed information and assistance. For example, suppose a customer is considering the purchase of a complex or expensive item

(like machinery, a large appliance, or real estate). In such a situation, the personal involvement of a salesperson would help to ensure that the customer's needs were satisfactorily met.

The main advantage of personal selling is, of course, the personal attention that it affords customers. The disadvantages are primarily related to expense. The number of potential customers a salesperson can call or wait on is limited. Thus, the use of personal selling may actually require several salespeople. It may also mean that specialized training is needed and, in the case of outside sales, that expenses must be reimbursed.

Budgeting for Promotion

How much are you going to spend on promotion? It's a question you might think you should have answered earlier, before you considered your promotional mix. Indeed, in an established business, where you had experience with a previous promotional plan and sales figures to work from, that's what you would have done. With a new venture like yours, however, you have no prior plan or sales figures. You must arrive at an estimate in another way.

Cost Out Promotional Activities

At this point, you have some idea of what your mix will be. Now you must find out how much it will cost.

You can obtain advertising rates directly from media sources (radio stations, newspapers, etc.). Their sales representatives can quote you prices and supply you with rate charts. Standard Rates and Data Service, a publisher of media rates, is another information source you might try.

Sales promotion items are unique. So, to figure their costs you must either estimate them yourself or contact whoever is going to produce the promotional piece for you. Let's say you are

Personal selling would be an important part of the promotional mix of most retail businesses. Why would it be especially important here?

thinking about having a sweepstakes. You would contact a printer who could print sweepstakes cards and ask for a quote.

Publicity your business gets from community or other events will not cost you anything. However, the event itself probably will. Don't forget to figure in those costs if you are planning to use this option.

Finally, if you chose to use an agency or consultant to handle all or part of your promotion, you will need to budget for the necessary fees. Using an agency is discussed in more detail a little later.

Note that you will not include personal selling staff and sales training in your promotional budget. These costs, if you have them, will be included in your operating expenses.

Compare Industry Averages

After you have accumulated quotes for all the parts of your proposed mix, you can calculate its cost. Your next step, then, would be to contact trade associations, business publications, the SBA, or business owners in the field. From them you can find out the industry average for promotional expenses. The figure is usually expressed as a percentage of sales.

Make Final Adjustments

The industry figures will provide a standard against which to measure your original mix estimates. If differences between the two figures are large, it will be a signal to you to reexamine and make appropriate adjustments to your mix. If the differences are insignificant, you probably have a realistic budget and mix.

You might be tempted to use the industry average as a starting point for figuring your promotional budget. This is not a good idea because such figures can be misleading. They don't take into account such factors as nature and size of operation, location, availability and cost of media, and nature of potential customers.

Let's say the industry average for your field is 15 percent of sales, and you estimate your sales will be $10,000 per month. If your estimate of the cost of your promotional mix is much more than $1,500 per month ($10,000 x .15), you might want to reconsider your promotional budget. But you will have to exercise some judgment here. It may be that there are peculiarities in your circumstances that justify such a difference.

Newspaper Ad

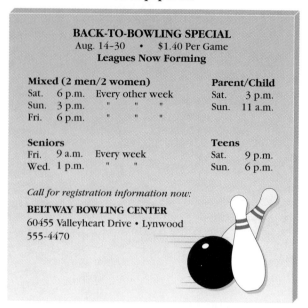

Figure 18–3 *Ads need not be designed by advertising professionals. Do you think you could have written the copy for this ad? How might you have acquired the illustration?*

Carrying Out Your Plans

When it is time to put your promotional plans into action, there will be a great deal to do. You will have to prepare and place your ads, publicity, and sales promotion pieces. If personal selling is part of your mix, you may also need sales training.

Before you begin, you should ask yourself a key question. Can I do this myself, or should I hire someone to do it for me?

Doing It Yourself

As you put together your promotional budget, you may find that you really have no choice in this matter. There may not be enough money to hire a professional *and* carry out the activities you need to reach your target marget. This is true for many new entrepreneurs. In these circumstances, the design of your ads and other promotional items will have to be a do-it-yourself proposition.

This doesn't necessarily mean that your promotional materials will be ineffective or even unprofessional. Many of the ads you see in your local newspaper (like Figure 18–3) are done by small businesspeople themselves. The same is true of the commercials you hear on radio and the flyers you find stuck in your door. They are the proof that business owners can do an excellent job of communicating their message to potential customers.

Getting Help

Your other alternative is to get professional help for some or all of your promotional activities. The cost of professional help can vary greatly. It can extend from a no-fee arrangement to a sizeable percentage of your promotional budget, depending on the services you receive. The source of the help can vary, too.

MEDIA. All of the major advertising media—television, radio, newspapers, and magazines—have advertising departments. The people who work in these departments make their living from selling advertising. To encourage sales, they will often help you do the ads or commercials you run with them. In some instances, they may even do them for you.

MANUFACTURERS AND SUPPLIERS. Sometimes you can get your suppliers or the manufacturers of goods you sell to share your advertising costs. This arrangement is called **cooperative advertising**. For example, suppose you are a retailer and feature the products of a manufacturer in one of your ads. That manufacturer may be willing to pay all or part of the cost of the ad.

Some types of sales promotion can also be done as joint efforts. For example, if you are a manufacturer, you might provide retail outlets with displays to set your products apart. Training for personal selling is another area of possible collaboration. Some manufacturers may be willing to give you and your staff some training to help you sell their products.

AGENCIES. Advertising agencies can handle all phases of your advertising. They can do everything from writing the copy and creating the artwork to choosing the media and producing the ad or commercial. Nearly all television ads as well as those in national magazines are produced by professional agencies.

For their services, advertising agencies charge a substantial fee. Consider an example. Agencies typically receive a 15 percent discount on the price of an ad for placing it with, say, a television station. However, the agency charges the sponsor of the ad the full amount. So, if the full price of the ad is $200,000, the agency only pays $170,000 for it ($200,000 x .15 = $30,000; $200,000 – $30,000 = $170,000). However, the agency still bills its client $200,000. The $30,000 difference is its fee. Because of such high costs, agencies tend to be used more by large rather than small companies.

Organizing and Using Your Data

Any notes you have made for your preopening and ongoing plans should be kept in the marketing section of your business plan notebook. These notes would include such things as your promotional schedule, media contacts, copy and rough layouts for print ads, and scripts for commercials. Any materials you've collected, like rate cards, should be kept in the section folder. Your cost data, of course, would be recorded in your financial plan section. Preopening promotional costs would be added to your start-up figures. Ongoing promotional expenses would be included in your operating costs.

Entrepreneur's Bookshelf

To learn more about the subjects discussed in this chapter, consider reading these books and articles:

- *How to Promote, Publicize, and Advertise Your Growing Business* by Kim Baker and Sunny Baker (© 1992)
- *The Frugal Marketer: Smart Tips for Stretching Your Budget* by Nancy Croft Baker and J. Donald Weinrauch (© 1989)
- "Improving Your Small Organization's Image" by Richard T. Cole, *Public Relations Journal* (June 1989)
- "Put It in Print" by Shelby Meinhardt, *Entrepreneur* (January 1989)
- "Public Relations Through Community Involvement," *Managers Magazine* (October 1988)
- "The Most Common Mistakes in Selling," *Personal Selling Power* (October 1988)

Chapter 18 Review

Recapping the Chapter

- The promotional strategy for your new business should include both a preopening plan (to lay the groundwork for the opening) and an ongoing plan (to maintain and build sales once the operation is under way).
- The activities in your promotional mix should be selected for their effectiveness in reaching your target market. You should also stay within the broad limits of what you have to spend and strongly consider using established promotional channels.
- Determining the promotional costs for a start-up business involves three steps: (1) getting price quotations for each of the promotional activities you have selected, (2) comparing the total amount to the industry average, and (3) making any needed adjustments.
- When it's time to carry out your promotional plans, you can either do it yourself or get help from media representatives, ad agencies, or manufacturers and suppliers.

Reviewing Vocabulary

Write one or two paragraphs answering the question posed by the case study at the beginning of the chapter. Use at least ten of the following terms:

- image
- public relations
- preselling
- campaign
- promotional channels
- specialty items
- prime time
- news release
- premiums
- sweepstakes
- rebates
- cooperative advertising

Checking the Facts

1. What are the four main types of promotion?
2. Why is a preopening promotional plan important to a new business?
3. Why should you refocus on your target market before selecting your promotional activities?
4. Is it possible to have a promotional mix that consists of one technique? Explain why or why not.
5. What kind of audience is radio particularly effective in reaching?
6. What is the biggest advantage of publicity? the biggest disadvantage?
7. Give two examples of sales promotion devices.
8. Name one source of advertising rate information.

Thinking Critically

1. Which is the most cost-effective of all the promotional options? Why?
2. Should preselling your products be a goal of your preopening advertising plan? Why or why not?
3. Is it possible to have more than one "best" promotional mix? Explain.
4. Consider this statement: "The promotional budget should be established before the promotional mix is determined." Is this a good idea for a new business? Why or why not?
5. Can promotion done by a small business owner be as effective as promotion done by professionals? Why or why not?

Chapter 18 Review

Discussing Key Concepts

1. Review the promotional options described in this chapter. Which would be the most effective in reaching and communicating to your target market(s)? Why?
2. Choose three ads that you have recently seen or heard. For each answer the following questions:

   - What do you think is the ad's purpose?
   - Who is the target market?
   - What image is the company trying to project?

3. What is the image you want people to have of your business? Why would that be the right image for your venture?
4. Which would be the most effective approach for you—doing your own promotions or hiring an agency to do them for you? Why?

Using Basic Skills

Math

1. An advertising agency you have hired receives an 18 percent discount on ads it places with magazines. If the agency bills you $1,900 for a series of magazine ads, how much did it pay for them?
2. You have put together a newspaper ad whose dimensions are 1 column by 12 inches (or 12 column inches). You want the ad to run every week during your first quarter of operation. The newspaper has given you three options:

   - A series of single runs at a rate of $19.69 per column inch
   - A 13-week contract requiring that you run the ad 13 times in 13 weeks at a rate of $16.06 per column inch

   - A "bulk rate" contract requiring you to purchase a minimum of 150 column inches a year at $15.16 per column inch

   Which is your best option in terms of cost?

Communication

3. Write a news release announcing the opening of your new business. Make the news release about one page in length.

Human Relations

4. You would like to maximize your promotional dollars by featuring in your ads a particularly attractive line of products that you plan to carry. To the best of your knowledge, the manufacturer of the line has never done any cooperative advertising. How would you convince them that entering into a cooperative advertising arrangement with you would be to their advantage?

Enriching Your Learning

1. Contact the media you plan to use for advertising your business. Obtain information regarding their rates and the services they provide.
2. Contact trade associations, business owners in your field, or other appropriate sources to determine average promotional expenditures as a percentage of sales in your particular type of business.
3. Write a summary of the promotional mix for your business, including a rationale for your decisions. Present your summary in a report to your class, and ask for their input.
4. Develop your business's preopening plan. Include a discussion of your promotional mix and your budget, as well as a grand opening.
5. Design an ad campaign for the first three months your business is open. Describe what kind of advertising you will use and why.

Chapter 19
Record Keeping

Objectives

After completing this chapter, you will be able to
- explain the importance of keeping good business records,
- describe the choices that need to be made to set up a record-keeping system,
- identify which records should be kept daily and weekly,
- discuss the importance of the statements that should be prepared monthly, and
- decide who should keep the records for your business.

Terms to Know

fiscal year
cash basis
accrual basis
accounts payable
accounts
  receivable
disbursements
debit/credit
ledger
aging
cash flow
  statement
balance sheet
accounting
  equation
equities
assets
liabilities

? Decisions, Decisions

Yesterday my brother, Steve, came home from college. He just graduated with a degree in accounting. Whenever he's home, we talk nonstop—about everything.

Of course, right now for me Health Food in a Hurry is everything. That's my business. I'm in the middle of all my start-up planning, and frankly it's all I can think about. I guess that's why I got carried away. I just started pouring out all these details about how I was going to run the place and how I was pretty sure I had the money I needed to start.

That's when Steve brought me down to earth—fast. I'd said the magic word—*money.* And he said, "Have you set up your books yet?"

Frankly, I thought that was down the road quite a ways. So, I tried to laugh him off. I said, "You mean my cookbooks?"

Steve was not amused. He said, "No, I mean your journals. You know—your financial records." He sounded really surprised. He said I was so careful about planning everything else. Why wouldn't I plan my record-keeping system?

Then it was his turn to talk nonstop. First he gave me all these reasons why it was important to keep good records. Then (and here's the scary part) he began listing all of the different types of records I'd need to keep. There must have been hundreds of them!

Okay, I'm exaggerating. But there were dozens of them. So, you tell me—where am I supposed to find the time to keep all these records? I mean, it's a *small* business—just me and one other person. I know Steve meant well, but I've been in shock ever since we talked. Can't I get by with a lot less record keeping?

Why You Need to Keep Records

Businesses today operate in a very dynamic environment. Change is swift and constant, largely because it can come from so many sources. Your customers as well as your competitors can be located down the street. They can also be located halfway across the country—or halfway around the world.

Unfortunately, many new entrepreneurs find themselves unable to respond to the shifting demands of such a marketplace. Why? Because at any given time they don't know the status of their own businesses. That ignorance derives mainly from poor record keeping. In fact, after inadequate management, most of the major causes of business failure are directly related to faulty record keeping.

The purpose of record keeping is to keep the owner and others informed about the state of a business. Things like cash flow, sales, inventory, production, taxes, and payroll must be watched closely. Good record keeping is the only way to do that.

In this chapter, then, you will read about how to set up a bookkeeping system. You will also learn how to keep track of important business information on a daily, weekly, and monthly basis.

How to Set Up a Record-keeping System

Before you can set up a record-keeping system, you must make some basic decisions. What you decide will be dictated by the specific needs of your business.

Choose a Fiscal Year

The first thing you need to do is decide on a financial, or fiscal, year. A **fiscal year** is a 12-month period that can end on the last day of any month. Your business will pay its income taxes based on the fiscal year you select.

A fiscal year may be different from a calendar year, which runs from January 1 to December 31. However, it must be the same 12-month period year after year. Once you have chosen your fiscal year, you cannot change it without approval from the IRS.

How do business owners choose a fiscal year? Often they look for their best quarter, the one in which they are likely to have their highest sales. Suppose a business's sales are at their peak in July. The owner may want to set up a fiscal year so that July falls in the fourth quarter. The object, of course, is to finish the year with revenues trending upward. That is why retail stores often use a calendar year as their fiscal year. Christmas is usually their biggest season.

Choose a Cash or an Accrual Basis

Next you need to choose whether to record income and payments on a cash or an accrual basis. If you use a **cash basis**, you record your income when it is received and your expenses when they are paid. (This is the same system you use with a personal checking account.) Since this is the easiest method, it is generally used by smaller businesses with no inventories.

If inventories are a big source of income for your business, however, you are required by the IRS to use an **accrual basis**. This means you record income when it is *earned* and expenses when they are *incurred*. In other words, what you are really recording is the right to receive income and the obligation to pay expenses at some future date. For example, suppose you sell an item but give the buyer 90 days to pay. With an accrual basis, you must record the sale on the date of the transaction even though you have received no payment.

Businesses that use the accrual basis will use terms like *accounts payable* and *accounts receivable*. **Accounts payable** are those expenses you have incurred but not yet paid. Sales taxes payable, for example, are moneys you have collected but not yet paid to the state. **Accounts receivable** are those sales that have been made but not yet paid for. If your business offers credit, your customers can buy now and pay later. Such sales result in accounts receivable.

Choose a Single- or Double-Entry System

The third and final decision you must make concerns how you will enter items in your records. Should you use a single-entry or a double-entry system? There are advantages to each.

The single-entry system is the easier of the two. That's why it is used by many start-up businesses. You simply record the daily flow of income and expenses. Then at the end of the month, you prepare a summary of the month's receipts and **disbursements** (or payments). The problem with this method is that it does not balance itself. In other words, your one entry for each item cannot be checked against another entry.

To avoid this problem, most businesses use a double-entry system. This means that you enter each income or expense item twice—as a **debit** to one account and a **credit** to another account.

Journal Entries

DATE	ACCOUNT	ACCT. #	DEBIT	CREDIT
March 7	Rent Expense	51	1 4 2 5 00	
	Cash	12		1 4 2 5 00
March 8	Purchases	58	10 5 0 0 00	
	Accounts Payable	23		10 5 0 0 00

PAGE NO. 2

Figure 19–1 *A journal is a daily record of a business's transactions. What evidence is there that the keeper of this journal uses double-entry accounting?*

If you are using this system and your books don't balance, you know that you've made a mistake. (Most likely you've either forgotten to make an entry or written in an incorrect amount.)

It is beyond the scope of this text to discuss double-entry accounting in any detail. As you can probably tell from even a brief description, however, it is a valuable business tool. To learn more about it, you might want to consider taking a basic accounting course.

Daily Record Keeping

The best way to stay abreast of how your business is doing is by keeping records on a daily basis. This procedure has other advantages as well. It makes it more likely that you will catch errors when they occur. It also virtually assures that you will not find yourself playing catchup at the end of the month.

The kinds of records you will keep will depend on the decisions discussed in the previous section. For example, businesses that operate on a cash basis are most likely to use a single-entry system. Thus, their daily record keeping will be fairly simple. Businesses that operate on an accrual basis, however, are more likely to use a double-entry system. Their daily record keeping will be more complex.

Using Journals

The daily record keeping of a double-entry system uses books called journals to record business transactions. The size and scope of your business will determine what kind of journals and how many you use.

A very small business, for example, may use just one journal to record all of its daily transactions. This would be a general journal. Figure 19–1 shows two transactions recorded in such a journal. On March 7, cash was spent to pay the rent. On March 8, inventory was purchased on account (or with credit).

Eventually a business may find that using one journal is not sufficient to keep track of all of its transactions. At that point, the business will set up separate, special journals. These are the special journals most often used:

- *Sales journal*—for all sales on account
- *Cash receipts journal*—for all cash (and checks) received
- *Cash disbursements journal*—for all payments made in cash or check form
- *Purchases journal*—for all purchases on account

Using a Summary of Sales and Cash Receipts

Those businesses that have regular, daily sales will want to keep a daily summary of sales and cash receipts. They should keep this type of record whether they are using a single- or double-entry accounting system.

The summary serves two important purposes. First, it allows you to see at a glance your total daily sales. Second, it allows you to verify the total of your cash receipts.

Figure 19-2 shows a sample summary. You may not need all of its entries. However, you will have something under each of its three main headings.

FIGURING CASH RECEIPTS. The cash receipts section lists cash sales, collections on account, and miscellaneous receipts. What this breakdown acknowledges is that in addition to cash from sales, you may also receive cash from other sources. You may receive payments by mail, refunds or rebates, and other miscellaneous cash. (Miscellaneous receipts are items that you don't normally receive during a day's business. You should attach a memorandum for these to your summary so that you will remember what they were.)

COUNTING CASH ON HAND. The cash on hand section of the summary shows the actual amount in the register broken down into coins, bills, and checks. It also includes the opening cash fund, which for many businesses doubles as a petty cash fund.

Petty cash is used to purchase things that are too inexpensive to write a check for. If you take money out of petty cash for a purchase, you should leave a slip stating the amount you took and its purpose. Thus, if the petty cash fund has a balance of $100 and you take $10 to buy supplies, there should be $90 in cash and slips totaling $10.

At the end of the cash on hand section, you should calculate the amount of cash you will deposit in the bank at the end of the business day. To do this, you subtract the opening cash fund total from the amount in the register.

Once you have your deposit figure, you can then use it to verify your cash receipts total. The two figures should be equal. If they are not, look for a mistake.

If your cash deposit is more than your receipts, ask yourself these questions:

- Did you record all transactions?
- Did you record a transaction for less than the correct amount?
- Did you give a customer too little change?

If the amount you are going to deposit is less than your total receipts, ask yourself these questions:

- Did you record an amount higher than the correct amount for a transaction?
- Did you give a customer too much change?
- Was money taken from the register without recording it?

Summary of Sales and Cash Receipts
January 20, 19– –

Cash Receipts

Cash sales		$2,160.85
Collections on account		160.35
Miscellaneous receipts		69.77
Total Cash Receipts		$2,390.97

Cash on Hand

Cash in the register		
Coins	$ 75.31	
Bills	780.00	
Checks	1,635.66	
Total Cash on Hand		$2,490.97
Less opening cash/petty cash fund		
Petty cash slips	$ 20.55	
Coins and bills	79.45	
Petty Cash Fund		100.00
Total Cash Deposit		$2,390.97

Sales

Cash sales		$2,160.85
Credit sales		465.39
Total Sales		$2,626.24

Figure 19–2 A summary like this one tells you your total daily sales. How and where?

RECORDING SALES. The final section of the summary tells you your total daily sales. It does this by adding together both cash and credit transactions. This procedure also makes it possible for you to see exactly how much of your business credit sales account for as opposed to cash. Your register, depending on its sophistication, may keep track of this information for you.

Weekly Record Keeping

Other record keeping should be done weekly. In these instances, the purpose is clearly to simplify end-of-the-month calculations.

Posting to a Ledger

As noted earlier, journal entries are usually made daily. Businesses using journals and a double-entry accounting system will also post (or transfer) those journal entries to a ledger.

A **ledger** is a collection of all the accounts of a business. Examples of accounts include cash, sales, accounts receivable, and sales tax payable.

Recall that a journal contains what is basically a list of transactions. When you post those transactions to a ledger, you are actually posting them to specific accounts. This allows you to see all that is happening in each of those accounts.

Look at the ledger account of cash in Figure 19–3. It shows the posting of the first journal entry from Figure 19–1. You can see that the cash account had a debit balance of $14,390. Then, the account was credited $1,425. (In other words, the rent payment was subtracted, although the calculation was not shown.) At that point, the account had a debit balance of $12,965.

You should post your journal entries to a ledger as often as necessary to keep your accounts up to date. However, posting weekly is probably often enough for a small business. That will allow you to examine your business's accounts weekly. And that, in turn, will give you a good, ongoing feel for how your business is doing.

Keeping Track of Payments

Keeping track of the bills that your business must pay is important. Some of these are regular monthly bills, such as rent, telephone, and utilities. By reviewing weekly which of these bills are due, you can be sure they are paid on time.

Other bills are payments to suppliers for either inventory or raw materials. Recall that suppliers often offer discounts for early payment.

Ledger Entry

DATE	ITEM	J.R.	DEBIT	DATE	ITEM	J.R.	CREDIT
march 1	Balance	G1	14 3 9 0 00	March 7		G2	1 4 2 5 00

ACCOUNT *Cash* — ACCOUNT NO. 11

Figure 19–3 Journal entries are posted to various accounts in a ledger. What is this account's name? Since the rent payment was credited to this account, which account do you think was debited? How do you know?

Aging Table

Customer	Amount	Current	31–60 days	61–90 days	Over 90
K. Brown	40.55	40.55			
J. Greenberg	120.54		120.54		
T. Blackburn	395.00		395.00		
G. White	59.45				59.45
Percent of Total	100%	6.6%	83.8%		9.7%

Figure 19–4   *Aging your accounts receivable can tell you how promptly your customers are paying. If this table were for your business, would you be pleased or not? Explain.*

(You learned how to calculate these back in Chapter 5.) Keeping track of supplier bills on a weekly basis will enable you to take maximum advantage of these discounts.

After you have written a payment check, you should mark the invoice on which it is based *Paid*. You should keep that invoice, along with all the supporting documents for the transaction. That way there will be no risk of your paying the bill twice.

Aging Amounts Owed to You

Keeping track of what people owe *you* is also important. You will want to know who is slow in paying and who pays promptly. One way to do this is by setting up an aging table. In this case, **aging** means categorizing a customer's account by the length of time since the bill was incurred.

Figure 19-4 shows how to do this. First you list all of your customers in a column. Then across the top of the page you write column headings such as Current, 31-60 Days, 61-90 Days, and so on. You note the status of each customer's account by marking the amount owed in the appropriate column. Immediately you will be able to see how many people have owed you money for long periods of time. That information will help you make better decisions in the future about credit terms for individual customers.

Keeping Payroll Records

If you have employees, you must keep accurate payroll records. In Chapter 5 you were introduced to payroll journals and the calculations they involve. Recall that you need to figure how much to pay and how much to withhold for such things as taxes. In fact, this is the journal that provides the information you need to report and pay taxes to the state and federal governments.

Payroll journal entries must be made as often as you pay your employees. This can mean once a week, once every two weeks, or twice a month.

Keeping Up with Taxes

In Chapter 12 you learned about several of the other taxes that your business is responsible for paying. These included sales tax, federal unemployment tax, and business income tax. Keeping track of collections or withholding for these taxes on a weekly basis is a safeguard. It assures that you will have the money you need to meet your tax obligations when they are due.

Maintaining Other Records

Besides financial records, there are some others you will want to maintain. Exactly what they are and how often you update them will depend on the type of business you own.

Here is a short list of records that most businesses have:

- *Insurance.* Record the types and amounts of insurance you carry. Include policy numbers, premiums, and payment dates.
- *Maintenance.* Record all maintenance work performed on plant and equipment. Include dates, costs, and type of service or repair.
- *Quality control.* Monitor complaints about product quality. Keep track of returns and repairs.
- *Inventory.* Track changes in inventory. Note items and quantities sold, purchased, and currently in stock.
- *General office records.* Keep documentation for all business transactions. Retain invoices, purchase orders, contracts, and business correspondence.

You might want to make a similar list for yourself. Then you could refer to it on a weekly basis as a reminder to stay current on the indicated records.

Monthly Record Keeping

Certain records you keep should be updated on a monthly basis. In many instances these updates will result in prepared statements. However, if you have faithfully done your daily and weekly record keeping, these statements will not be difficult to compile.

Preparing a Cash Flow Statement

The **cash flow statement** is one of the most important statements you create at the end of each month. The statement describes the flow of cash into and out of your business.

Cash flow is so important for one reason—you cannot pay your expenses with profits. You can only pay them with cash. Hence, a business cannot survive without a positive cash flow.

The cash flow statement is a working tool for the entrepreneur. It shows you what you need to know your about your cash status on a regular basis.

The statement is very simple to construct. It follows this pattern:

$$\begin{array}{r} \text{Cash receipts (inflows)} \\ - \text{ Disbursements (outflows)} \\ \hline \text{Net cash flow} \end{array}$$

If you look closely at Figure 19-5, you can see this underlying pattern. The business took in $23,000 (its receipts). It spent $16,620 (the total of its disbursements). This left a net cash flow of $6,380.

Preparing a Profit and Loss Statement

Recall from Chapter 5 (Figure 5-1) that a profit and loss statement is also called an income statement. It compares revenues and expenses over a

Cash Flow Statement March 31, 19--		
Cash Receipts		$23,000
Disbursements		
Equipment	$12,000	
Cost of goods	2,500	
Selling expense	200	
Salaries	700	
Advertising	130	
Office supplies	20	
Rent	500	
Utilities	90	
Insurance	170	
Taxes	70	
Loan principal and interest	240	
Total Disbursements		16,620
Net Cash Flow		$ 6,380

Figure 19–5   *If a business has more money coming in than going out, it has a positive cash flow. If it has more money going out than coming in, it has a negative cash flow. Which situation does this statement illustrate?*

specific period of time to see if the business has made a profit. It is usually prepared monthly as well as annually. Basically, it shows the following:

$$\begin{array}{r} \text{Revenues} \\ - \text{ Expenses} \\ \hline \text{Net income (or loss)} \end{array}$$

Recall, too, that the profit and loss statements for different types of businesses may vary in format. For a service business you would simply subtract expenses from revenues. For retail and wholesale businesses, however, you must first compute the cost of goods sold.

Now you may be thinking, how is this different from the cash flow statement? The income statement includes more than just cash. Cash moves through a business only after it is received. In contrast, the profit and loss statement begins with sales, for which you may not have received payment.

Preparing a Balance Sheet

A **balance sheet** tells an entrepreneur what his or her business is worth at a given time (here, at the end of the month). It is based on the **accounting equation**. That equation states that a business's assets are equal to the financial rights people have in those assets. These financial rights are called **equities**, and they may belong to the owner or to others who have invested in the business.

The equation looks like this:

$$\text{Assets} = \text{liabilities} + \text{capital}$$

Assets are all those things of value belonging to a business. **Liabilities** are what is owed to others. Capital is the owner's equity.

Look at Figure 19–6. The first section shows the assets of the company, including cash, accounts receivable, and inventory. The second section shows the business's liabilities. These include accounts payable and notes payable (or long-term loans). The last section can be

Balance Sheet March 31, 19––		
Assets		
Cash	$10,745	
Accounts receivable	868	
Inventory	5,799	
Supplies	433	
Total Assets		$17,845
Liabilities		
Accounts payable	$ 3,444	
Notes payable	5,705	
Total Liabilities		$ 9,149
Capital		
Joseph Conrad		8,696
Total Liabilities and Capital		$17,845

Figure 19–6   A balance sheet shows how much a business is worth and how much of that amount actually belongs to the owner. In this case, who is the owner, and how much of the business's worth is his/hers free and clear?

called capital or owner's equity. It is what's left over after liabilities are subtracted from assets. It reflects the owner's financial rights to the business.

You may be wondering where you get the information listed on the balance sheet. If you use the double-entry accounting system, each item listed on the balance sheet reflects the balance of each of your ledger accounts. If you use a single-entry system, you must fill in the blanks based on your records. For example, you know how much cash is in your checking and savings accounts. You know how much you owe on your business loan. When you subtract what you owe from what you own, you get your owner's equity.

Again look at Figure 19–6. Assets are $17,845. Liabilities are $9,149. Capital (or owner's equity) is $8,696. If you insert these numbers in the accounting equation, it looks like this:

$$\begin{array}{ccc} \text{Assets} & = & \text{liabilities} + \text{capital} \\ \$17,845 & = & \$9,149 + \$8,696 \end{array}$$

Risk Takers, Profit Makers

Stephen and Bob Arndt

Returning home to Connecticut from their respective colleges in 1986, Stephen and Bob Arndt prepared for their usual part-time job. They stripped and painted houses. But then two things happened to change their plans. First, they learned that the city of Fairfield was taking bids on stripping a historical building, the Old Academy school. Then they discovered an innovative paint-stripping technique. As a result, they wound up launching a full-time business—Arndt Brothers Industries, Inc.

The stripping method, called Peel Away, was patented by Michael Brailsford in England in 1981. Peel Away involved coating a painted surface with a thick, water-based mixture. Then the coating was covered with a laminated cloth and allowed to dry. When the cloth was removed after 24 hours, the mixture and paint came off with it, leaving a clean surface.

Before the Arndts got involved, Peel Away had been used primarily by homeowners on small surfaces like chairs and window panes. However, the Arndt brothers recognized the product's potential for commercial and industrial use. With help from Brailsford, they modified the paste and adapted spraying machines for large surfaces.

It was this modified procedure that won them the contract for the Old Academy building. And it was wildly successful. It stripped at least 20 coats of paint in a single application and revealed graffiti carved more than 100 years before!

Although the Arndts barely broke even with their first job, it enabled them to fine-tune their system and supplied them with invaluable experience and publicity. With $10,000 borrowed from their parents, they parlayed their first job into a manufacturing business producing Peel Away for such edifices as the Baltimore Washington Monument and the Texas A&M ROTC dorms.

Peel Away itself has proved to be as environmentally sound as it is effective. In many older urban areas, lead-based paint is a major hazard to young children. Peel Away is an ideal way to remove it. The paste-and-cloth technique traps most of the dangerous lead particles and prevents them from escaping into the environment. Any that remain on the stripped surface are rinsed away with water that is recycled and purified.

Now based in Milford, Connecticut, Arndt Brothers Industries, Inc. is the sole manufacturer and supplier of Peel Away in the United States. With advice from their father and the SBA, the Arndt brothers have nurtured their company from a garage partnership into an eight-person manufacturing business. Meanwhile, Peel Away is only becoming more profitable—to the Arndts and the environment.

Reconciling a Bank Statement

Once a month you will receive a statement from the bank that describes the status of your business's checking account. The bank may also return your canceled checks.

When you receive this statement you should reconcile, or balance, your checking account right away. This allows you to verify that neither you nor your bank has made any errors in record keeping. It also tells you how much cash you actually have available for business purposes.

Balancing a checkbook is not a difficult process *if* you have been careful throughout the month in entering your transactions. You begin by arranging your canceled checks in numerical order. Then you follow the steps specified on the form provided by your bank to help with the reconciliation process. Usually they include the following:

- *Step 1—Write the bank statement balance on the first line of the reconciliation form.* This is the figure you will be trying to bring into line with your checkbook balance.
- *Step 2—List any outstanding deposits on the appropriate line and add them to the balance.* Outstanding deposits are those that have not yet been added to your account.
- *Step 3—Compare the canceled checks or those checks listed on your statement with your check register or check stubs.* Check off all items that have been returned to you or listed as paid. These represent amounts that have been subtracted from your account.
- *Step 4—List any outstanding checks on the appropriate line and subtract them from the balance.* Outstanding checks are those you have written that do not yet show on your statement. They represent money you have paid that has not yet been removed from your account. The result of these calculations is the adjusted bank balance.
- *Step 5—Compare the balance from your checkbook to the adjusted bank balance.* The two figures should be the same.

- *Step 6—If there is a difference, go back and check your work.* Be sure that all of your calculations are correct. Verify that all checks and deposits have been accounted for somewhere in the reconciliation. Finally, be sure that you have recorded all service charges in your register and subtracted them from your checkbook balance.

Balancing a Petty Cash Fund

If your business has a petty cash fund, you will need to balance it monthly. This fund is a fixed amount that a business owner sets aside to pay for things that are too small to be paid by check.

Each time money is withdrawn from the petty cash fund, a receipt should be prepared. The receipt should show the amount removed and the purpose for which it was spent. Thus, at the end of the month, the amount of money left in petty cash plus the total of the receipts should equal the fund's fixed amount.

Paying Federal Tax Deposits and FICA

At the end of each month, you will need to create records that show that all federal tax deposits for payroll withholding have been made. You will also need to record that FICA and state taxes have been paid. If you are late in making these payments, your business can be assessed penalties and interest. This can be extremely costly.

Who Should Do the Record Keeping?

By now you must be thinking, How am I going to keep all of these records and still find time to run my business? That's a good question. Fortunately, there are a number of good answers.

First you can hire a Certified Public Accountant, or CPA. A CPA is a licensed accounting professional. He or she can help you set up your books, fill out forms, prepare financial statements, and do your taxes. Be aware, however, that this is an expensive option. Also, owners who employ CPAs often fail to stay in touch with the financial side of their businesses because "the accountant is handling it."

Another alternative is to hire a bookkeeper to do the forms, journal entries, and payroll. If you choose this option, however, you will still probably need a CPA. This is because you should have your books checked (or audited) by someone who is licensed at least once a year, preferably at tax time.

A third option is to hire an employee whose sole job it is to take care of the books. Often a part-time person will be sufficient in the early stages of the business.

Finally, you do have the choice of keeping your own books. Many entrepreneurs do this, especially when their businesses are just getting started. They say that it gives them a real feel for how things are going.

Doing your own books is not as difficult as it used to be. Today there are all sorts of materials to help. There are standardized packages available from office supply stores and computer programs like Quicken®. Just be sure that whatever method you choose results in a record-keeping system that is easy to understand, simple to use, and accurate.

Right now, all of this may seem a monumental task. Remember, though—record keeping is the life's blood of your business. Do it regularly and faithfully. Keep up, and you'll remain in control.

Record Keeping and the Business Plan

Think back to Chapter 9, to the kinds of financial statements needed for a business plan. An entrepreneur must be able to estimate *cash flow*, *profit and loss*, and the look of his or her *balance sheet* at the end of one year. Back in Chapter 9 that language may have seemed mysterious. Now, however, it should be familiar.

The statements you will need for your business plan are simply pro forma versions of those you will prepare monthly for your own business. They are the key statements that will keep you apprised of your business's condition. They will tell you whether you can pay your bills, how profitable your enterprise is, and whether its net worth is growing. This is also just the kind of information potential investors would want. And in your business plan, you will give it to them— in estimated form.

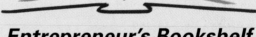

Entrepreneur's Bookshelf

To learn more about the subjects discussed in this chapter, consider reading these publications:

- *Financial Record Keeping for Small Stores,* SBA Small Business Management Series, Stock No. 045-000-00142-3
- "Running Out of Money," *Venture* (January 1986)

Chapter 19 Review

Recapping the Chapter

- Keeping good business records ensures that an entrepreneur will always be well informed about the status of his or her enterprise.
- To set up a record-keeping system, an entrepreneur needs to choose a fiscal year, select a cash or an accrual basis, and decide whether to use single- or double-entry accounting.
- Records that are kept daily are journals and a summary of sales and cash receipts.
- Records that are kept weekly include ledgers, bills to be paid, amounts owed to you, payroll, taxes, insurance, maintenance, quality control, inventory, and general office records.
- Monthly, an entrepreneur should prepare a cash flow statement that will tell how much cash is available, a profit and loss statement that will show if the business has made a profit, and a balance sheet to show the net worth of the company.
- An entrepreneur can do his or her own record keeping or hire someone else to do it—a CPA, a bookkeeper, or a full- or part-time employee.

Reviewing Vocabulary

1. It could be said of each pair of terms below that they are different but the same. Explain how.

   - fiscal year—calendar year
   - cash basis—accrual basis
   - accounts payable—accounts receivable
   - debits—credits
   - ledger—journal
   - cash flow statement—balance sheet
   - liabilities—owner's equity

2. For each of the following terms, write a sentence that shows you understand the term's meaning.

   - disbursements
   - aging (accounts)
   - accounting equation
   - equities
   - assets

Checking the Facts

1. What factor usually determines a business's choice of a fiscal year?
2. Which basis for recording income does the IRS require you to use if inventory is a big source of income for your business?
3. Why would you use more than one journal to record transactions?
4. Which financial statement helps a business owner determine how much his daily bank deposit will be?
5. What is the accounting equation?
6. What is the procedure for balancing a petty cash fund?
7. What are the steps in reconciling a bank statement?

Critical Thinking

1. Would you use a cash or an accrual basis for recording the income of your business? Explain why.

Chapter 19 Review

2. You are using an aging table like the one shown in Figure 19-4 to track your accounts receivable. How would you react to the following results? What would you do about them?

- The Over 90 column accounts for half the money you are owed.
- The 61–90 Day column accounts for 85 percent of the money you are owed.

3. Which takes more knowledge and skill to fill out—a journal or a ledger? Defend your choice.

Discussing Key Concepts

1. Why would a cash flow statement be more useful to a new venture than a profit and loss statement?
2. Why is it important to keep accurate inventory records?
3. Are there any records you might want to keep that were not mentioned in the chapter? Describe them, and explain why you think they would be helpful.
4. Is it possible to keep too many records? Explain.

Using Basic Skills

Math

1. A service company had the following transactions in one month:

Service sales:	Credit	$15,000
	Cash	6,000
Expenses:	Credit	$ 6,000
	Cash	7,000

For that month, compute the firm's (a) revenue, (b) expenses, and (c) net income.

Communication

2. You would like to hire a part-time book-keeper for your new business. Write a news-paper want ad for the position. Keep in mind your business's needs.

Human Relations

3. Your new bookkeeper is causing you some problems. Even though he works hard and seems to stay on top of the bookkeeping, you are finding too many errors in his work. How would you handle the situation?

Enriching Your Learning

1. Contact two local business owners about how they keep their records. Choose two different types of business, such as one manufacturing firm and one retail establishment. If you can, find out how they chose their fiscal year. Also, try to determine which basis they use—cash or accrual—and why.
2. Recall the continuing saga of Swim World and Marcia, the owner. Suppose you have been hired by Marcia to design a record-keeping system for her business. Outline the components of that system based on what you have learned in this chapter. What are your recommendations to her?

Chapter 20
Financing Your Business

Objectives

After completing this chapter, you will be able to

- discuss the difficulties entrepreneurs face obtaining capital in today's economy,
- describe the financial statements needed for a business plan and their purposes,

- distinguish equity and debt sources of financing,
- explain what potential investors and lenders look for in a business plan, and
- draft a business plan that will serve both present and future needs.

Terms to Know

current assets
fixed assets
current liabilities
long-term liabilities
depreciation
angels
venture capitalists
line of credit
trade credit
bootstrapping
factor
collateral
executive
  summary

Decisions, Decisions

Remember when I told you I had the money to start my new business, Health Food in a Hurry? Well, I was exaggerating a bit. I really do have some of the money—I've saved up $5,000 from working summers and weekends. But I know I'm going to need more.

I've been gathering cost data all along, and I can save some money if I work out of my parents' home to start. But I'll still need equipment, supplies, a separate phone line—not to mention a delivery van. And what about my living expenses until the business starts making money?

Okay, so it's not news that a new business needs some financial help. But how do I go about getting that help? What do I need to do?

Small Business Financing and the Economy

Financing a start-up venture today can seem an impossible task. For one thing, today's entrepreneur faces the results of the 1980s savings-and-loan crisis. Banks have become wary of lending to businesses unless they are well established, with a good cash flow and numerous assets. By definition, new ventures do not meet these requirements.

Today there is also less money available from certain kinds of investors. These are the people who lost money in the early 1990s when the real estate market collapsed and recession sent many businesses into bankruptcy.

You may be thinking, then, that starting a new business now may not be such a good idea. This is not true. During hard times many people realize that they need to take charge of their lives and their livelihoods. More businesses are conceived and started in times like these than in any other.

Today, however, entrepreneurs cannot afford to make many mistakes. They must understand the economic climate in which they operate. They must have a solid grasp of the financial structure of their own businesses. And they must know where and how to get investment capital. These things will give them the edge that they need to succeed.

How to Organize Your Financial Data

For the last ten chapters, you have been collecting information for your business plan. Much of that information has had a financial, or cost, component. Now you must take all of the figures you have gathered and present them in such a way that they encourage lenders and investors to help finance your business.

This section will focus on how to organize your costs and figure the amount of money you

business is putting his or her money at risk. If the business is successful, the investor may make an excellent return. If the business fails, however, he or she may lose everything invested.

There are many forms of equity financing. Here are a few that you might tap for your new business.

PERSONAL SAVINGS. The number one source of start-up capital for new businesses is an entrepreneur's own personal savings. The U.S. Department of Commerce reports that 67 percent of all new businesses were started without borrowing any money.

There are other reasons why an entrepreneur should contribute at least 50 percent of the start-up capital. By doing so he or she maintains control of the business. Also, most investors want to know that an entrepreneur has enough faith in an enterprise to risk his or her own money before investors risk theirs.

FRIENDS AND RELATIVES. Entrepreneurs often rely on friends and relatives for additional sources of funds. People who believe in you are more likely to invest in your business than are strangers.

However, you should be cautious. Many entrepreneurs warn never to borrow money from family and friends if you want to stay on good terms with those individuals. You should consider carefully whether the relationships you are relying on can survive should the business fail and the invested funds be lost.

PRIVATE INVESTORS. Private investors are nonprofessional financing sources who tend to invest in the region in which they live. Sometimes they are called **angels** because of the help they give new businesses. They often become involved in start-up financing and usually take on one or two new businesses a year.

Angels are not easy to find because they usually prefer to keep a low profile. The most common way to find them is through networking in your community. There are also some nonprofit organizations that have established networks of angels. You can find out about them by contacting the Venture Capital Network in Durham, New Hampshire.

You should be very careful about choosing private investors. Investigate other things they have invested in. Also, be sure to put the terms of the deal in writing and have an attorney check it.

PARTNERS. More and more entrepreneurs are not going it alone. By taking on a partner with compatible skills, you will not only be able to share the responsibilities of the business but also the costs.

You might want to reread the section in Chapter 8 on partnerships, their advantages and disadvantages. A partnership agreement should also be put in writing and reviewed by an attorney.

VENTURE CAPITALISTS. **Venture capitalists** are individuals or firms that invest capital professionally. In other words, making money through investments is their job, the way they make a "profit." This is in contrast to private investors, who invest capital more as a sideline.

Venture capitalists tend not to be good sources of start-up capital for small businesses, mainly because they are relatively expensive. They usually want a significant interest in a company and a very high return on their investment. They also require financial projections for up to five years. (This is because they usually take their cash and profits out of the business at that point.) Venture capitalists are probably a better source of money for businesses that are already established.

Some states, however, offer state-sponsored venture capital funds. These states are more interested in using the funds to create jobs rather than to get a specific return on their investment. Check with your local economic development corporation for help in locating such funds.

Debt Sources

Sources of debt capital are far more numerous than sources of equity capital. With debt financing, an entrepreneur borrows money and has to repay it with interest.

Risk Takers, Profit Makers

John Sortino

John Sortino loves teddy bears. He loves teddy bears so much that he left a secure, well-paid job to sell them from a pushcart on the streets. Today, after ten years of making and selling bears, Sortino's devotion is paying off. As the president of the Vermont Teddy Bear Company, he now sells $12 million worth of bears worldwide—and he still loves them.

Sortino started sewing bears shortly after his son, Graham, was born. Dismayed by how many of his son's stuffed animals were manufactured outside the United States, he decided to do something about it. For two years, Sortino developed prototype bears. Then, in 1983, he quit his job, filled a peddler's cart with bears, and hit the streets of Burlington, Vermont.

Fueled by his passion to make the best bears in the world, Sortino endured many meager years. He sold only 200 bears in his first year—about $8,000 worth. But because he sold bears first-hand, he could easily adapt. The quality of his bear design gradually improved, and so did sales.

Sortino also developed the financial side of his company. With help from the SBA, he created a business plan. Based on it, he got a low-interest development loan from the state of New York. In 1985, he started wholesaling to small specialty stores and larger department stores. By 1988, Sortino had retired his cart.

Still, in 1989 Sortino wasn't satisfied by the $500,000 the Vermont Teddy Bear Company reaped. General retailers just didn't handle his bears properly, he felt. In a last-ditch effort to lift bear sales to their full potential, Sortino began advertising "Bear-Grams" on New York radio. Customers called a toll-free number to have the world's best bears delivered anywhere.

New Yorkers responded fervently. Now Boston, Chicago, and Philadelphia are also Bear-Gram hot spots.

Since the introduction of Bear-Grams, the Vermont Teddy Bear Company has expanded significantly. One hundred skilled employees now sew bears at home. Another 120 work at the colorful Shelburne factory, which encourages craftsmanship and creativity from its workers. No time clocks dictate working hours, and music always plays. Visitors even come to tour the facility.

The Vermont Teddy Bear Company now sends basic, seasonal, and custom bears to a growing number of bear lovers around the world. Vermont Teddy Bears are even listed in the 1988 *Catalog of Best American Products.* But regardless of his fortunes, Sortino is sure to keep hugging his teddy.

When an entrepreneur raises capital by borrowing, he or she retains full ownership of the business. However, the loan must be carried as a liability on the firm's balance sheet.

BANKS. Banks used to be the primary source of operating capital, or the money that businesses use to support their operations short term. The usual form that such capital took was a line of credit.

With a **line of credit**, a bank agrees to lend a business a certain amount of money at a certain interest rate. The company can then borrow against that credit line as its needs dictate and pay back the money on a regular basis.

Today, banks are far more conservative in their lending practices. They are not inclined to lend to businesses unless they are well established. Thus, the chances of your getting start-up capital or even a line of credit are slim.

After your business is up and running, banks may make some types of financing available to you. For example, you may be able to borrow money using your business's assets as security for the loan. If you don't pay back the loan, the bank can take these pledged assets.

What kind of assets can you use as security? One possibility is your inventory. Another is your accounts receivable. To use the latter as security, you discount them. In other words, you don't borrow against their full value but only about 55–80 percent of it.

TRADE CREDIT. Some businesses use **trade credit** as a source of short-term financing. The term describes a situation in which you get credit from within your industry or trade.

For example, suppose you purchase goods from a supplier on 30–90 days of credit, interest-free. This means that you would have the use of your money for at least an extra 30 days. You would also have the goods you need for either manufacture or resale. If your customers pay promptly, they could provide you with the money you need to pay your bill.

COMMERCIAL FINANCE COMPANIES. Commercial finance companies offer a viable, though more expensive, alternative to commercial banks. Finance companies are less conservative than banks, so they typically take more risk. Consequently, they charge more for the money they lend.

Finance companies usually require some form of security for a loan. Many times this security is the entrepreneur's home, but they may also accept receivables and inventory.

SMALL BUSINESS ADMINISTRATION. You can also go to the SBA for a loan. If the SBA approves your request, it will use a commercial bank to process the loan and release the money. But it will guarantee repayment of up to 90 percent of the loan should your business fail. The guarantee assures the bank that it can only lose that portion of the loan that is not guaranteed. Sometimes the SBA does lend public funds directly. Generally, however, these loans cannot exceed $150,000 and are currently made only to veterans and handicapped persons.

Check also for Small Business Investment Companies (SBICs). These companies are licensed by the SBA to provide equity and debt financing to young businesses. They invest about twice as often in start-up ventures as do venture capitalists. Each SBIC is privately owned, and their requirements depend on the area of the country and the industry.

The SBA has also established Minority Enterprise Small Business Investment Companies (MESBICs). They provide funding to businesses whose ownership is at least 51 percent minority, female, or disabled.

Budget cuts have severely affected the SBA's ability to guarantee loans. However, it is still an avenue that should be explored by entrepreneurs.

Bootstrapping

In the current business environment, most entrepreneurs are finding it necessary to use some very creative techniques to get their businesses off the ground. Collectively, these techniques are called bootstrapping.

Bootstrapping involves operating as frugally as possible, cutting all unnecessary expenses. Often this means getting by by using as few resources of your own as you can. Instead you use other people's or other businesses' resources.

For example, when you bootstrap you hire as few employees as possible. (Employees are generally the greatest single expense a business has.) Instead you use workers from temporary services. That way you do not have to cope with employee tax and insurance payments. The temporary service does that.

Bootstrapping can also mean leasing anything you can rather than buying it. That way your money is not tied up in equipment or a building. With leasing you won't have to make a down payment, and the costs are spread over time.

Other bootstrapping techniques include getting suppliers to give you longer terms and customers to pay in advance. They may also involve selling your accounts receivable to a **factor** (an agent who transacts business for another person). The factor pays you cash and charges a fee of 1 or 2 percent on each account, plus interest on the cash advance. The factor also assumes the responsibility of collecting the accounts receivable.

When investment money is scarce, businesses must be creative about finding resources for start-up. How might this enterprise employ the technique of bootstrapping?

How to Obtain Financing

Once you have identified your potential financial sources, you need to be sure that what you say in your business plan meets their criteria. Recall that your plan should not be written for your use alone. It must address the very specific needs of your financial sources.

What Venture Capitalists Look For

As an entrepreneur your goal is to have your business survive over the long haul. However, the goal of the venture capitalist is to achieve a long-term capital gain through investment and then cash out. You can see from the outset that you and the venture capitalist do not have the same goals.

When venture capitalists do invest in start-up companies (and that isn't often), they are looking for high-growth firms. What is "high growth"? They want a 30–50 percent return on their investment. Using a simple example, suppose venture capitalists give your business $50,000 for five years. At the end of that period, they will want to receive their investment back plus an additional $15,000–$25,000.

Primarily, venture capitalists look for a business with a good management team. They firmly believe that a good team can take a mediocre product and make it successful. But a mediocre team cannot necessarily take even a good product and build a successful business.

Understand that the process of obtaining funding from venture capitalists is a slow one. They will examine every facet of your enterprise. Therefore, don't ever go to a venture capitalist when you are desperate for money.

What Bankers Look For

Do you remember the three C's of credit discussed in Chapter 17? They were character, capacity, and capital. Recall that they were standards designed to help small business owners select credit customers.

Bankers, however, rely on *five* C's to determine the acceptability of a loan applicant. (Because banks lend such large amounts of money, their requirements are greater than others who give credit.) The banks' five C's include the original three plus two more—collateral and conditions:

- *Character.* The bank needs to believe in the character of the entrepreneur and the people with whom he or she is associated. Like venture capitalists, bankers recognize the importance of a good management team.
- *Capacity.* Recall that capacity means the customer's ability to pay in view of their income and obligations. In a sense, then, capacity is another word for cash flow. Banks look for businesses with a sufficient cash flow to pay back any loan that they might grant.
- *Capital.* Banks place a strong emphasis on whether a business has a stable capital structure. This means that they look for businesses that don't have too much debt.
- *Collateral.* Banks are more likely to lend to businesses with **collateral**. They want to know what things of value they can claim if a business does not repay its loan.
- *Conditions.* Banks will consider all of the conditions of the environment in which the business will operate. Business conditions include potential for growth, the amount of competition, the location of the business, and even the form of ownership.

To be considered for a commercial bank loan, you and your business will need to score very high on all of the five C's.

What Private Investors Look For

Private investors prefer manufacturing, energy and natural resources, and some service businesses as investment opportunities. They tend to avoid retail businesses because such enterprises have a higher failure rate, and private investors tend to be conservative.

On average, these investors would like to get ten times their investment at the end of five years from a start-up venture. Like bankers and venture capitalists, private investors look for a strong management team.

How to Finalize Your Business Plan

With your pro forma financial statements, you arrive at the last step of the information gathering process you began back in Chapter 9. Once you complete those statements, you will know if you can make your business a reality. You will know how much it will cost you to start up your operation. You will have some idea how much you can earn in your first year and at what rate. And you will have some definite expectations about what your company will eventually be worth. In short, you will know a great deal that will convince you of your prospects for success. And once you are convinced, you can set about writing the document that will convince others.

The last step before drafting your business plan is preparing your pro forma financial statements. Why wait so long? Why not do them earlier?

Prepare Your Draft Plans

If you have been taking notes systematically and keeping them in your business plan notebook, organizing your writing should not be a major problem. In fact, by now you may find yourself so familiar with the various aspects of your business that you can write spontaneously, referring to your notes only for details.

You will probably put most of your efforts into the business description and the three component plans—marketing, management, and financial. There are no hard-and-fast rules for the contents or organization of these. That will depend on the nature of your business and the requirements of those who will read your plan. For example, you might want to break out your market analysis as a separate section if it is especially important to your business or a potential capital source.

Create an Executive Summary

Whether you are seeking capital or potential partners, there is one extra business plan component that you will surely need. It is called an **executive summary**.

You prepare the summary *after* you have written your business plan. Essentially it is a brief recounting (no more than two pages) of the key points contained in the major sections of your plan.

Why do you need an executive summary? Think about the people to whom you are likely to present your plan—bankers, potential investors, potential partners. They are all people who probably see a great many business plans. Now think about the typical business plan. Most are fairly substantial documents, often 40 or more pages long. Under these circumstances, unless your business concept is inherently interesting, it is unlikely that your plan will be read all the way through. To get this kind of attention, you will need a hook, something to grab the reader's attention and make him or her *want* to read the entire document. That is what an executive summary is for—selling your idea to others.

Update Regularly

There is one last point to remember about business plans. As an entrepreneur with a new business, you need to think of your business plan as a *living* document. It is never really completed as long as your business is growing. Keeping it in a flexible format (in a loose-leaf binder, for example) might help to remind you that you should return to it often.

At a minimum you should review and revise your business plan on an annual basis. (When your business is very young, a review every six months is probably a good idea.) Remember, your business plan is one of your most important entrepreneurial tools. If it is updated regularly, it will keep you and your business on track to success. It will also require that much less work should you have to submit it to new lenders or investors in the future.

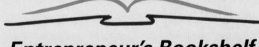

Entrepreneur's Bookshelf

To learn more about the subjects discussed in this chapter, consider reading these books and articles:

- *Venture Capital Handbook* by David Gladstone (© 1988)
- "A Business Plan That Grows with You!" by Jeffrey Lever, *Venture* (December 1988)
- "Business Plans: Myth and Reality" by Roger Thompson, *Nation's Business* (August 1988)
- "Digging for Dollars," *The Wall Street Journal* (February 24, 1989, p. R25)

Chapter 20 Review

Recapping the Chapter

- Financing a start-up venture today is more difficult because the 1980s savings-and-loan crisis and recession have made lenders and investors more cautious and conservative.
- The financial statements needed in a business plan are the pro forma summary of start-up costs, pro forma cash flow statement, pro forma income statement, pro forma balance sheet, and the personal financial statement.
- Equity sources of financing involve giving up some ownership in the company. Debt sources of financing involve borrowing money and paying it back with interest.
- Once you have identified potential financial sources, you need to make sure that what you have said in your business plan meets their criteria. Banks look for evidence of the five C's (character, capacity, capital, collateral, and conditions). Venture capitalists and private investors look for a strong management team and a good return on investment.
- A business plan is a living document that should be reviewed and revised on at least an annual basis.

Reviewing Vocabulary

For each of the following terms, write a sentence that describes what role the term might play in financing a start-up business.

- current assets
- fixed assets
- current liabilities
- long-term liabilities
- depreciation

- angels
- venture capitalists
- line of credit
- trade credit
- bootstrapping
- factor
- collateral
- executive summary

Checking the Facts

1. What is the first step in organizing financial information for your business plan?
2. How do you figure how much cash you will need to start your business?
3. What kind of costs will you use to prepare a pro forma income statement?
4. Name five sources of equity funding.
5. How do banks and finance companies differ in the way they lend money?
6. Describe the five C's of credit that bankers use to judge a loan applicant.
7. What is an executive summary? When and why is it prepared?

Thinking Critically

1. How does studying your industry help you determine sales estimates?
2. If you wanted to retain as much control of your business as possible, what sources of financing would you consider? Why?
3. What advantages does equity financing have over debt financing?
4. Why does a venture capitalist look for a good management team when considering investments?

Chapter 20 Review

Discussing Key Concepts

1. What kinds of start-up costs will your new business have?
2. From which financial sources within your community do you think it would be most difficult for new businesses to raise start-up capital? Explain.
3. Which source of financing do you think is most promising for your new venture? Why?
4. How would you go about looking for a private investor to provide funds for the start-up of your business?
5. How might you use bootstrapping to help your new business get off the ground?
6. Why should you think of your business plan as a living document?

Using Basic Skills

Math

1. You have estimated your start-up costs to be $6,500. You project that for the first six months your ongoing operating costs will be $4,300 and your personal expenses will total $8,200. You have saved $12,780 to put toward your new business. How much money will you need to borrow?

Communication

2. Your Aunt Elizabeth has seemed very interested in your new business idea. You believe she might consider investing in it. Write out what you would say to convince her to give you $5,000 for a 10 percent interest in the venture.

Human Relations

3. Your Aunt Elizabeth has agreed to the above proposal. Now that you have started your business, you realize you need another $3,000. How do you handle this situation? Will you go back to your aunt or approach another investor? Would you consider a debt source? Give your reasons.

Enriching Your Learning

1. Develop a set of financial statements for your business. Include a pro forma cash flow statement, income statement, and balance sheet for the first three years of operation. Also, prepare a personal financial statement.
2. Obtain a loan application from a local bank. Fill it out to the best of your ability. Then, with a list of questions about things you don't understand, go back to the bank and get answers. *Note:* Be sure you ask how the bank deals with applicants under the age of 18.
3. Research sources of financing other than banks in your community. Write a 3–5 page report on your findings.

Managing and Expanding Your Small Business

Chapter 21
Managing Your Operation

Objectives

After completing this chapter, you will be able to

- recognize the dual roles of a small business owner;
- identify the management functions, leadership style options, and skills needed to manage a small business;
- discuss what makes an excellent manager; and
- explain the purpose of a working management plan.

Terms to Know

manager
strategic plans
tactical plans
operational plans
quality control
  programs
situational
  management
time management
conceptual skills

Decisions, Decisions

My preschool business has been open six weeks. So far I've been able to handle all of the little problems that have come up. But today I realized a big one has kind of evolved without my noticing it.

My teachers have been doing a good job seeing to it that the kids are fed and dressed and napped and taken care of. The problem is that they're not doing anything else.

We have a curriculum that we mapped out. But as nearly as I can tell, no one's using it. That can't continue. We're a preschool, not a day care center. People are paying good money for our service. If we don't deliver what our name promises, we could go out of business in a hurry.

I've got to handle this, and I've got to do it quickly. But this is the first time I've had to act like a "boss." What do I say? How do I go about it?

Running and Growing Your Business

Once you open the doors of your business, you will begin to wear two hats instead of one. On the one hand, you will continue to wear the hat of the entrepreneur. The emphasis of this role, though, will shift from starting your business to growing and expanding it.

Your second hat will be that of **manager**. In this capacity, you will coordinate the people, processes, and other resources of your operation on a day-to-day basis. You will do this to achieve your principal objectives—profitability and survival.

Of course, you could hire someone to manage your business. You would still have to oversee the operation yourself, however. For this reason and because your operation will be small, you will most likely do it yourself.

In this final Unit of the book, you will examine both your new role as manager and your changed entrepreneurial role. This chapter will focus on the overall management of your business.

Chapters 22–27 will treat the management of specific areas. Chapter 28 will deal with how to expand and grow your business.

Carrying Out Your Management Role

As a manager, you deal with many different kinds of situations, often at the same time. On any given day, you might take charge of getting out an order that has been bogged down, review sales figures so you can revise your budget, and represent your company at a civic meeting. Or you could handle a dispute between two employees, interview a job applicant, and patch up relations with a dissatisfied customer. At other times, you might spend the whole day negotiating a contract or revising short-term plans.

So how do you prepare to manage these seemingly overwhelming situations and still produce a product? First, you sort out in your mind what it is that managers do when they are managing and how they go about it. Second, you determine what approach to management is most effective for you. Third, you determine which skills you will rely on and how to develop them. This is the process we will talk about in this section.

Performing Management Functions

When managers are managing, they use a series of activities called management functions to meet their objectives. These functions include planning, organizing, directing, and controlling and are exercised in essentially that order. (If it doesn't seem that way, it's because business owners deal with multiple objectives, each of which may be at a different stage.)

PLANNING.   The first step in managing is planning. When you plan, you determine your business's objectives—or specific desired results—and how you are going to reach them.

You will use three kinds of plans. You will begin with broad, long-range goals and with each successive plan narrow them to the specifics of objectives.

- *Strategic plans.* **Strategic plans** map out where you want your business to be in 3–5 years. Usually they don't include a specific target date.
- *Tactical plans.* **Tactical plans** focus on a period of one year or less. They consist of specific objectives with target dates. Tactical objectives make strategic goals a reality.
- *Operational plans.* **Operational plans** address short-range objectives for the implementation of tactical plans. These plans also include policies, rules and regulations, and budgets for the day-to-day operation of the business.

Let's see how these three plans work together. Suppose your strategic plan is to double your production capacity within the next four years. One of your tactical plans might be to complete a new plant, which will increase output by 25 percent,

by March of next year. Your operational plans would include a request for bids to be sent out to contractors for the proposed plant.

Planning is an on-going process. Strategic and tactical plans must be reviewed at least once a year. Operational plans are done for much shorter periods, such as monthly, weekly, and daily.

Changes in the political scene, technology, and the economy may dictate unscheduled review and revision of plans. If you are a manufacturer, for example, a new zoning ordinance may put a damper on your expansion plans. Or, if you are a retailer, the announcement of a new subdivision near your store could change your promotional plans.

ORGANIZING.   To carry out your company's plans, you will have to organize people, equipment, materials, and other resources. You will try to put together a combination that will help you reach your objectives.

This means, among other things, deciding what jobs need to be done and setting up an organizational chart that includes them. You will then have to hire and train new employees to fill these positions and assign authority and responsibility to your new hires.

DIRECTING.   After you have organized your people and resources, you will direct them to accomplish the objectives you have planned for. This part of managing entails guiding and supervising your employees, often one-on-one, while they work.

Directing is carried out by communicating directives, assignments, and instructions to your employees. It also includes motivating employees to perform satisfactorily and providing effective leadership.

CONTROLLING.   The final step in managing is controlling. This is the process of comparing your expected results (your plans) with actual performance. If things aren't working as they should, then you will take corrective action.

How do you compare your plans with what is actually happening? You can use your budget by comparing budgeted costs with actual costs. You

It is almost inevitable that the new small business owner will supervise employees him- or herself. Why?

can also use personal observations and **quality control programs**. (The latter are checks built in to the production process to make sure products meet certain standards.)

What do you do if there are any significant differences between what you planned and what actually happened? You must take steps to correct the problem. Notice, however, that the emphasis is on *significant* differences. You cannot afford to try to control every little difference.

Corrective action can take several forms. You may decide to replace input (people or other resources) or change the control process. You may put preventive measures in place to keep things from going wrong in the future. Finally, you may decide to revise your performance objectives.

Adopting a Leadership Style

Leadership style—the manner in which you approach your management responsibilities—was identified above as a major factor in the directing function. The question you have to answer is, Which leadership style is best for managing my business? In general, you have three choices:

- *Power-oriented Style.* Managers who use a power-oriented style try to maintain total control over their whole operation. They alone make decisions. Suggestions from employees are not sought or even well received. When making assignments, power-oriented managers specify exactly what is to be done and how. They are generally reluctant to share authority and responsibility with employees.

- *Routine-oriented Style.* Managers who use this style are primarily concerned with keeping the operation running smoothly rather than accomplishing other goals. They tend to avoid authority and responsibility. They may make job assignments or provide support, but they don't ordinarily get directly involved with the actual operation. Their major purpose is to provide information and guidelines.

Risk Takers, Profit Makers

Allene Graves

Allene Graves has always found ways to make a profit. After high school, she arranged travel groups so that she could go on free trips. When she was a young girl, she did chores for her neighbors. And before that, she ran a lemonade stand. Maybe that's why she wasn't troubled when the law firm she worked for folded in 1987. She was glad to leave a job that offered little satisfaction and no future. For her, the firm's misfortune was an opportunity to start her own business. With limited experience as a temporary and no outside help, the Washington, D.C., native launched her own temporary service—The Answer Temps, Inc.

What Graves lacked in specific training and preparation, she made up for with determination and perseverance. Using money collected from unemployment, she paid for an answering service and began looking for temps through ads and recommendations. Then she contacted clients for whom she had previously done temp work. One of them became her first customer.

Graves worked triple time during her business's infancy. In addition to tending the business during office hours, she did marketing during her lunch breaks. And she interviewed new temps on evenings and weekends. Fortunately, as her working hours piled up, self-financing proved to be a more than adequate motivator.

Having no outside funding, Graves used her credit cards to start The Answer Temps. For six months, she lived from hand to mouth, meeting her payroll with credit. Fortunately, her hard work paid off. After six months, she turned a profit. Her company now employs over 600 temps and serves numerous businesses and district and federal government agencies.

Graves attributes her success to several factors. She cites personal drive as the main reason for The Answer Temps' prosperity. Her trial-and-error methods have worked, she believes, because she has remained focused on her goal. She also credits experience and ongoing education.

Now that The Answer Temps is an established moneymaker, Graves is seeking new challenges. She co-owns a gas station with her brother and is also involved with community-related projects. Undoubtedly, Graves will continue to find new business opportunities. And for each one, she will also likely find an Answer.

Some managers encourage employee suggestions. In a situation like the one shown here, what might be the advantages of such a policy?

- *Achievement-oriented Style.* Managers who are achievement-oriented are open to and seek out employee suggestions and ideas. They use this input to make decisions, identify problems, and find solutions. Achievement-oriented managers are concerned about getting the job done and are willing to share authority and responsibility in order to do so.

All three of these leadership styles are effective—in different situations. The power-oriented approach can be effective in very large, cumbersome organizations. It also works well in situations where employees are untrained, inexperienced, or involved in a crisis situation. Routine-oriented management is most appropriate in situations that call for the supervision of well-established work processes. Middle management in a large corporation would be an

example. Achievement-oriented leadership is most effective where a manager is dealing directly with employees who are turning out work.

An achievement-oriented approach is most appropriate for a small business. There will be times, however, when you may have to adopt one of the other approaches, at least temporarily. For example, you may have to take on a power-oriented approach if you are at risk of losing a major customer because an order will not get out on time. Or you may have to become routine-oriented for a time in order to stabilize a part of your operation, like office procedures.

Good managers are able to use whichever approach their circumstances dictate. This is called **situational management**. Making the adjustment from one style to another is not difficult, particularly if you regard situational management as a supplement to your basic approach.

Exercising Management Skills

To carry out your management activities successfully, you will draw on a specific set of skills. Some of these you already possess. Others can be gained through education and training. All of them can be refined with practice and experience.

HUMAN RELATIONS. Managers with good human relations skills are considerate, fair, and attentive when dealing with others. These are the skills that a manager needs to interact effectively with employees, customers, and suppliers. These skills are also key ingredients in a manager's ability to lead and motivate employees and are closely tied to communication skills.

Skills in human relations are generally considered to be the most important of all management skills. No matter how large your operation gets to be, you will rely heavily on these skills.

COMMUNICATION. As you know, communication is a foundational skill. It is essential to your effectiveness whether you are planning, organizing, directing, or controlling. You must be able to communicate to employees what you have in mind or what you want them to do, or it won't happen. You learned specific communication techniques for managing as well as creating a business in Chapter 4.

MATH. The ability to perform business-related math computations is also a foundational skill needed by managers. This skill is important in managing daily operations, evaluating business performance, and in making long-range projections. The specific math techniques you will need for managing your business are among those you learned in Chapter 5.

PROBLEM SOLVING AND DECISION MAKING. Managers use the foundational skills of problem solving and decision making frequently. Sometimes, they use them to carry out planned actions. Other times, they use them to handle situations that must be dealt with immediately. Chapter 6 provided you with some basic techniques for dealing with both types of situations.

TECHNICAL SKILLS. Technical skills involve using the tools, equipment, procedures, and techniques critical to your business. In the retail of big-ticket items, they would include mastery of the selling process. In food service, they would include the preparation of food. In manufacturing, they would include the ability to operate complex machinery. These skills would ordinarily come from your prior education and training.

As your business grows, you may turn the management of technical aspects of your business over to supervisors you hire. However, in the early stages—especially in a small business—many of your management functions will require a knowledge of how things work.

TIME MANAGEMENT. Managers are busy people. At any one time, they will have many projects and activities going, all in various stages of completion. In addition, they will have to accomplish a multitude of objectives in a limited period.

Under these circumstances the skill of **time management**—the process of allocating time effectively—can have a big impact on successful management. Figure 21-1 lists some time management techniques that can be useful to managers.

Time Management Suggestions for Managers

1. Set and prioritize your goals.
2. Delegate work to others whenever possible.
3. Plan to spend blocks of time on specific activities that will help you achieve your goals.
4. Schedule your activities on a planning calendar.
5. Schedule your most important work for times (mornings, evenings, etc.) when you do your best work.
6. Group your activities for most efficient time use.
7. Handle or eliminate interruptions so they will take up as little time as possible.

Figure 21–1 Study the time management techniques listed here. Why do you think they would be especially valuable to a new business owner?

CONCEPTUAL SKILLS. Conceptual skills are those skills that enable a manager to understand an enterprise as a whole, to see the relationship among its parts, and to visualize its future. As a small business owner and manager, you will make day-to-day decisions against the backdrop of the bigger picture. It is your conceptual skills that will enable you to appreciate how these decisions will affect your business's future. Your conceptual skills will also help you make the big decisions, such as when and how to expand your business.

Using Principles of Management Excellence

In order to be a really good manager, you should pay particular attention to a few key points. These are the keys to management excellence, according to managerial researchers Thomas Peters and Robert Waterman in their book *In Search of Excellence*. Their eight principles, paraphrased below, hold true in successful small businesses as well as large companies.

Excellent managers do the following:

- They take action, doing something rather than analyzing plans to death.
- They listen to their customers and put themselves in their customers' shoes.
- They encourage their employees to act independently and be innovative, to treat the business as if it were their own.
- They stress the human side of management.
- They instill commitment to the business's values and objectives by keeping in touch with all employees.
- They keep the business focused on what they do best.
- They keep their organization simple, flexible, and efficient and don't overstaff.
- They keep their operations under control and an eye on detail.

Developing a Working Management Plan

When you developed the management plan for your business plan, you set up your pre-opening staffing and day-to-day operating guidelines. You will now have to expand that initial plan into a working management plan.

You will need to add any policy decisions you have made about your operation that are not in your initial plan. These could include decisions about insurance (how much coverage was purchased and from which agency) or banking (planned balance level and which bank).

Your budget will be part of your working management plan. This management tool will be a major factor in making operating decisions and will be discussed in greater detail in Chapter 24.

Your working management plan will also include your tactical marketing objectives. These are marketing objectives you plan to reach within one year. They provide the basis for more immediate marketing decisions.

This working management plan will serve as your reference point for making short-term decisions. As your business changes and you revise your long-range goals, you will, of course, adjust your management plan.

Entrepreneur's Bookshelf

To learn more about the subjects discussed in this chapter, consider reading these books:

- *The 7 Habits of Highly Effective People* by Stephen R. Covey (© 1989)
- *Leadership Is an Art* by Max De Pree (© 1989)
- *Think like a Manager* by Roger Fritz (© 1991)

Chapter 21 Review

Recapping the Chapter

- Small business owners have two separate roles—entrepreneur and manager.
- What managers do is plan, organize, direct, and control.
- Leadership styles include power-oriented, routine-oriented, and achievement-oriented and depend on the management situation.
- To manage a business successfully requires human relations, technical, conceptual, and time management skills as well as the foundational skills discussed earlier in the text (communication, math, and problem solving/decision making).
- Excellent managers adhere to some common management principles that include taking action, listening to customers, and encouraging independence and innovation among employees.
- A working management plan serves as a guide for day-to-day operation of a business.

Reviewing Vocabulary

1. Define the term *manager* in your own words. Then write a sentence for each of the following terms that explains how a manager would use them.

   - strategic plans
   - tactical plans
   - operational plans

2. Write a paragraph that describes how a manager uses each of the terms below.

   - situational management
   - time management

- conceptual skills
- tactical marketing objectives
- quality control programs

Checking the Facts

1. What is different about the entrepreneur's role after a business opens?
2. Which management function occurs first, second, and so on?
3. What do managers do as part of their organizing function?
4. When is the power-oriented leadership style most effective?
5. Which of the skills managers need is usually considered to be the most important?
6. How do excellent managers regard customers?
7. What kind of marketing objectives would be included in the working management plan?

Thinking Critically

1. Do small business owners ever wear their entrepreneur's hat and manager's hat at the same time? Explain.
2. How does planning involve objectives?
3. Can the controlling function be used to prevent problems? How?
4. Compare the power-oriented leadership style with the achievement-oriented style.
5. If you are working, analyze your manager's leadership style. Which of the three styles presented here do you think he or she uses? Give your reasons.

Chapter 21 Review

Discussing Key Concepts

1. Describe how you will use a working management plan in your new business.
2. Why do you think excellent managers encourage employees to treat the business as if it were their own?
3. Which of the skills needed to be a good manager do you feel you possess (although you may need work to on them a little)? How will you improve those skills? How will you attain the skills you don't yet have?

Using Basic Skills

Math

1. You have decided that you will take corrective action only if an expense goes over budget by 10 percent. The amount you budgeted for long-distance telephone calls was $350. When you receive your phone bill, you find that long distance expenses were actually $395. What is the difference between your budgeted and actual expenses in dollars? as a percentage? Would you take corrective action? Why or why not?

Communication

2. Locate and read an article on managing small businesses, management functions, leadership styles, skills needed for management, or outstanding managers. Write a summary of your article. Present your findings to the class.

Human Relations

3. You have given your employees detailed directions on how to carry out a new procedure. Everybody seems to understand. A few days later, one of your employees explains, with great pride, how well he's making the new procedure work. As he talks, you realize he is doing it absolutely wrong. How should you handle the situation?

Enriching Your Learning

1. If you are employed, observe the activities of your manager for a one week period. Record what he or she did at the end of each day. At the end of the week, make a chart categorizing each activity as planning, organizing, directing, or controlling. *Note:* Put things that were clearly nonmanagement in nature in a separate category.
2. Identify a small business owner and manager who is recognized as having outstanding success in your community. Interview this individual regarding the things he or she considers most important in managing a business. Prepare an oral report based on the interview and focus on the eight principles of management excellence cited in the chapter. How does your interviewee measure up?

Chapter 22
Purchasing, Inventory, and Production Management

Objectives

After completing this chapter, you will be able to

- describe how effective management of purchasing, inventory, and production can affect a business's profits;

- identify the kinds of choices purchasing management deals with;
- discuss the purpose of inventory management; and
- list the three basic functions of production management.

Terms to Know

trade discounts
shrinkage costs
obsolescence
  costs
lead time
usage rate
safety stock
Gannt charts
PERT diagrams
critical path
quality circles
productivity
automation

? Decisions, Decisions

When I started my business, Prestige Party Planners and Caterers, I didn't expect to get a big job so quickly. But today this out-of-town couple came in and gave me a huge advance. It seems their daughter goes to college here, and she's planning on getting married as soon as she graduates. She wants to have the wedding here, and they want me to plan and take care of everything. And I mean everything!

Somehow within the next six weeks, I've got to hire a band, plan and prepare one meal for 75 people and another for 250, arrange for places for the rehearsal dinner and reception, decorate, get the cake designed and made, and order flowers. I've also got to arrange for housing for out-of-town guests and coordinate the outfitting of the wedding party. And, of course, they want a limo and a lot of other extras.

Fortunately, I do have decorations and some of the other basic things in stock. Ordering and getting the food prepared shouldn't be a problem either. That's our strong suit—although we've never put together meals for this many people before. I hope I order enough. On the other hand, I guess I could get stuck if I order too much.

My big problem, though, is how to organize it all. I've never done anything this big or complicated before. Where do I start? What comes before what? How can I make it all come together at once? I wonder if there's some secret formula for planning this out so I don't make a mess of it?

Purchasing, Inventory, Production—and Profit

How you manage the purchasing, inventory, and production of your business will have a big impact on your profits. By making effective management decisions in these areas, you can save a great deal of money. For example, a decrease of $2,000 in purchasing or inventory costs will show up as a net profit of $2,000. In many businesses, it would take five times that amount in sales to generate the same profit.

Purchasing Management

When we talk about purchasing in this chapter, we are talking about buying inventory, not supplies or equipment. (Planning for those purchases was discussed back in Chapter 13.) Our focus here is on purchasing products for resale or the materials to create such products.

Purchasing management is primarily of concern to retail, wholesale, and manufacturing businesses. Service businesses, however, may also have some interest in it. Only extractors have a minimal concern with the area.

Purchasing decisions can make the difference between the success or failure of an enterprise. If that seems extreme, consider how much money is invested in such purchases. Manufacturers spend up to 50 percent, wholesalers up to 85 percent, and retailers up to 70 percent of every dollar they take in on inventory. Even service businesses spend as much as 10 percent of their sales for materials that go into the services they create.

Managing purchases effectively should be a high priority for an entrepreneur. It involves making a number of basic choices.

Purchasing mistakes can cost you your business. How?

Selecting the Right Quality

There is a rule of thumb for determining the right quality of inventory to purchase. It is the same for any business. You should buy the products or materials that match your needs. If you are a manufacturer of shelving for businesses, for example, you should buy materials and fasteners that are durable. If you buy a lesser quality, your products might not hold up. If you are a retailer dealing in moderately priced footwear, then that is the level of product you should buy for resale. If you buy high-priced, exclusive products or budget footwear, your customers will go elsewhere to find what they want.

Buying the Right Quantity

How much inventory should you buy? You should purchase the amount needed to maintain your chosen inventory levels. (Deciding on inventory levels is considered inventory management and will be discussed later in the chapter.)

Timing Your Purchases

Buying at the right time means timing your purchases so that your money and storage space aren't tied up any longer than necessary. It can also mean buying to take advantage of economic conditions. For example, if prices are beginning to rise sharply, it may be best to stock up before they go any higher. Or if the economy is in the middle of a recession, that would be the time to keep purchases to a minimum. Making timely buying decisions like these requires that you stay in touch with what's going on in the economy.

Choosing the Right Vendors

You may recall from Chapter 13 that locating vendors (those businesses that will sell you inventory) is not a difficult process. Choosing the right vendors, however, will require a number of thoughtful decisions on your part.

NUMBER OF VENDORS. Should you buy from just one vendor or from several? There are advantages and disadvantages to both approaches.

By buying from a single source, you are more likely to get individual attention and better service. If your orders are large enough, you may even be able to get quantity discounts. The big disadvantage of this approach is that if the vendor suffers a catastrophe (like a fire, strike, or bankruptcy), you may have trouble finding an alternate source. If you use more than one supplier, you reduce this risk. But you also lose the attention and discount opportunities.

To get the best combination, consider using one supplier for 70 to 80 percent of your purchases. Spread the other 20 to 30 percent of your business among several other vendors.

RELIABILITY. Is the vendor able to deliver enough of the products or materials you need, when they are needed? If deliveries are late, or inadequate, you can lose sales and customers.

DISTANCE. How close (or far away) is the vendor under consideration? The cost of transporting products or materials can be a major expense. You are also more likely to get better service from a local vendor. Finally, coordination problems are easier to deal with when the vendor is local.

SERVICE. What services will the vendor offer? You should inquire carefully. Will sales representatives call on a regular basis? Do they know the product line? Will they assist you with layout planning, setting up displays, or solving production problems? If there is equipment involved, can they repair it? Will they make unscheduled deliveries in an emergency? What is their return policy? What other appropriate assistance can they provide?

Getting the Right Price

You may shop several different vendors to determine who offers the best price. In some instances, particularly when orders are large, those prices may be negotiable. That doesn't mean, however, that the lowest price is the right price. You also have to factor quality and service into your decision. If the quality isn't what your customers expect or if the products or materials aren't delivered when they are needed, you can lose more than you gain.

Purchase discounts can also be a factor in the prices you arrive at with vendors. Depending on where you are in the channel of distribution, you may be able to take advantage of trade, quantity, or cash discounts.

Trade discounts are discounts off the suggested retail prices that manufacturers grant to wholesalers and retailers. For example, a manufacturer might give discounts of 50 percent

to wholesalers and 40 percent to retailers. Manufacturers offer these discounts as a way to reward and recognize other channel members for their role in getting the manufacturers' products to consumers.

Quantity discounts are discounts that vendors make available to buyers for placing large orders. Cash discounts allow buyers to deduct a percentage of the purchase amount if payment is received within a specified time.

Following Up on Purchases

Purchasing management doesn't stop with the placement of your order. Recall from Chapter 5 that when you receive a shipment, you should check the purchase order against the invoice. Verify the identity, quality, and condition of your order. If there is anything wrong either with the shipment or on the invoice, you should report this to the vendor immediately. Keeping a close eye on incoming shipments will keep you from paying for somebody else's mistakes.

If you are a retailer or wholesaler, marking information like size, cost, and selling price on the merchandise is also purchasing management. Manufacturers or service businesses will only need to do marking when the grade or source of material has to be identified.

Effective managers also follow up on the performance of their purchased inventory. Retailers and wholesalers follow up on complaints and returns. Manufacturers and service businesses follow up on the performance of materials used to make their products or perform the services they provide.

Inventory Management

The purpose of inventory management is to find and maintain inventory levels that are neither too small nor too large. Too little inventory can result in lost sales, lost customers, and even interruption of your operation. It can also lead to frequent reordering. This, in turn, leads to increased ordering costs resulting from the time and energy it takes to place the orders.

Too much inventory, on the other hand, results in costs that are not always recognized but are very real. These costs can add as much as 25 percent to the cost of your inventory. They include the following:

- *Financing costs*—the interest expense you pay to borrow money to purchase inventory
- *Opportunity cost*—loss of the use of money tied up in inventory
- *Storage costs*—the amount spent on renting or buying the space needed to store the inventory
- *Insurance costs*—the amount spent to insure the inventory on hand
- **Shrinkage costs**—money lost when inventory items are broken, damaged, spoiled, or stolen
- **Obsolescence costs**—money lost when products or materials become obsolete while in inventory

Finding the right levels of inventory requires inventory planning. Of course, there is no way to find and stay at exactly the ideal inventory level. Inventories are constantly changing, and the "right" inventory level will shift with changes in demand and season. Through careful planning and control of your inventory, however, you can strike a profitable balance between too much and too little.

Once you have established your inventory levels, you'll need to implement controls to maintain them. These controls should be designed to help you (1) keep track of your inventory and (2) reorder the right amounts to keep the levels where you want them.

Planning Inventory

Planning inventories to achieve a balance between too much and too little involves answering two questions:

- How many months supply should be on hand?
- How much of an investment in inventory would that represent?

The fact that a business has a relatively small inventory does not necessarily put it at a disadvantage. Why?

CALCULATING SUPPLY AND COST. Recall from Chapter 5 the concept of stock turnover rate. Within your industry there is an average stock, or inventory, turnover rate. This is the average number of times the inventory is sold out during the year for a specific industry. For example, men's clothing stores have an average inventory turnover rate of 3; restaurants, 22; and some chemical manufacturers, as high as 100. Trade associations in your field can provide you with turnover rates for your type of business.

To find the number of months supply you should keep on hand, divide your industry's average inventory turnover rate into 12 (the number of months in a year). If, for example, your industry's average rate is 4, this would be the calculation:

$$\frac{12}{4} = 3 \text{ months' supply}$$

Notice that if you apply this calculation to the restaurant average of 22, you get .54, or about a half month's supply. Obviously, businesses like restaurants that depend on a constant supply of fresh inventory would reorder frequently.

Now that you have estimated how much inventory you should have on hand, you need to figure how much that should cost you. To do this, divide the cost of goods sold for your forecasted annual sales by the average inventory turnover rate for your industry.

Let's say you forecast sales for the coming year to be $100,000 and your cost of goods sold is 75 percent of sales. Using an average inventory turnover rate of 4, your calculation would be as follows:

$$\frac{\$100,000 \times .75}{4} = \frac{\$75,000}{4} = \$18,750$$

Thus, you should keep three months of inventory on hand at a cost of $18,750.

Notice that this example implies that there is one set of calculations for the entire inventory. In reality, you will probably have to do calculations for different product lines or types of materials that may have different turnover rates. Each will require separate calculations.

USING INDUSTRY AVERAGES. The average inventory turnover rate for your industry is useful in another way. You should compare it with your *actual* inventory turnover rate (the calculation in Chapter 5). The number of turnovers you have in a year compared to the industry average is a good indication of how successful you have been in managing your inventory.

Of course, you want to try to turn your inventory over as fast as possible. However, if you are too far ahead of the industry average, it could be a signal that your prices are too low. A lower-than-industry average would indicate you have your inventory tied up in slow-moving merchandise or material.

Keeping Track of Your Inventory

Keeping tabs on how much inventory you have in stock is the first step in controlling your inventory levels. When your business first gets under way, you may be able to keep track of your inventory by just looking at what you have. As your business grows, however, you will probably have to switch to one of the more structured inventory control systems. As a cross-check against any of those systems, you will also have to do a physical inventory count.

VISUAL INVENTORY SYSTEMS. To use this inventory control system, you visually inspect your inventory of products or materials. You look at how much you have on hand and compare it to what you want to have on hand.

It is a simple and quick method of determining your current inventory level. Unfortunately, it is also easy to miss some potential shortages. The system usually works best where sales are steady, you personally handle inventory, and items can be obtained quickly from suppliers. A visual inventory control system would be very appropriate, for example, for a small produce store.

PERPETUAL INVENTORY SYSTEMS. Under this system, a running count is kept of the items in inventory. Although there are several kinds of perpetual inventory systems, the basic process is the same in all of them. As inventory is sold, it is subtracted from the inventory list. As new inventory comes in, it is added.

How do businesses keep track using this system? Businesses that move products or materials in and out of warehouses or storage facilities record additions and deletions as inventory is received or shipped. For retail businesses, when items are received they are added to the inventory, then tagged or ticketed before being placed on the sales floor. Inventory reductions are tracked by tabulating tags or tickets from sold items.

If a perpetual system is used consistently, it gives an accurate picture of inventory at any point in time. Problems arise, however, when stock is moved in or out without being recorded. A perpetual system can also be very expensive. For example, a convenience store owner would have to spend a great deal of time, and therefore money, to use a perpetual inventory system on every item in stock. The system works best with big-ticket items that have to be continually monitored.

Some of the disadvantages of this system in retail operations have been offset by computerized cash registers. They do everything a regular cash register can and at the same time maintain an up-to-date inventory count.

PARTIAL INVENTORY SYSTEMS. The partial inventory control system is really a combination of systems. In this system, a perpetual inventory would be maintained only for those items that account for a large share of the company's sales. Less structured procedures would be used to keep track of the rest of the inventory.

JUST-IN-TIME (JIT) INVENTORY SYSTEMS. The JIT system shifts most of the keeping track of inventory to the vendor. By arranging with suppliers to deliver inventory just before it is to be used, stocks are kept at a minimum. For many manufacturers, this can provide a very effective control. For other types of businesses, particularly retailing, it could lead to disaster.

PHYSICAL INVENTORY COUNT. No matter what type of inventory control system you use, you will need to conduct periodic physical inventory counts. Errors can occur in visual estimates or in recording additions or reductions to inventory. Items can be removed from stock and not recorded. Merchandise or materials can be lost, stolen, or go bad. A physical inventory enables you to get your books back in line with the amount you actually have in stock.

Taking a physical count also allows you to evaluate how effective your inventory control system is. Suppose your perpetual inventory system says you have 450 of something in stock, but your physical count shows only 200. That means your perpetual system isn't working very well.

Physical inventory counts usually involve two employees. One counts and calls out the item and number. The other records the count on a tally sheet.

Physical counts can be done often (the case when a JIT system is used) or as infrequently as once a year. If you plan to take a physical inventory count yearly, you can keep your counting costs down by getting your inventories as low as possible before the count. In retail this is often done through special year-end sales.

Reordering

To keep inventory levels where you want them, you must decide when and how much to reorder. The makeup of your inventory will dictate the reordering system that you use.

Products or raw materials that are inexpensive, used often, and easy to get, should be reordered periodically. That means that enough would be automatically reordered to bring inventory up to predetermined levels. Nuts and bolts needed by a manufacturer, for example, might be replenished every 60 days. Baked goods needed by a restaurant would be restocked daily.

Most retail and wholesale businesses physically count their inventory at least once a year. Why do you think employees doing the count usually work in pairs?

Inventory that is not suited to periodic reordering must be reordered in some other way. You must project your inventory needs. To do this, consider three key questions:

- *What will be the gap in time between placing an order and receiving the delivery?* This is called **lead time**.
- *How quickly will the inventory be used in a given period of time?* This is known as the **usage rate**.
- *How much safety stock will be needed?* **Safety stock** is the cushion of products or materials that keeps you from running out of inventory while you're waiting for an order to be delivered.

There are some complex formulas available for determining both the timing and the quantity of reorders. Although these formulas may have applications to mass production or retail chains, they are not of much use to the small businessperson.

The specific method of reordering you use is not important as long as you approach the matter systematically. You should plan your inventory, order and reorder in accordance with your plan, check to see how well your plan has worked, and make any necessary adjustments.

Production Management

The way a business manages production has a great impact on its profitability. When a business owner makes decisions about production, he or she is making decisions that directly affect product quality, level of output, and costs.

Of course, not all businesses produce goods, but production management can be applied to all types of operations. This area of management is, however, especially important to manufacturing, service, and extraction businesses.

Production management has three functions. The first is to acquire the resources needed to create a business's products. The second is to plan how to convert those resources into products. The third is to make sure that the products produced meet the standards set for them.

The first function, acquiring resources, was discussed in the purchasing and inventory management sections. Here, we will focus on the second and third functions, planning production (scheduling) and meeting standards (quality control). We will also address other production management considerations, such as productivity, automation, and maintenance.

Scheduling

Businesses plan production by making schedules. These schedules describe each activity that must be completed to produce goods or services and estimate how long each activity will take. There are two widely used graphic scheduling techniques.

GANNT CHARTS. **Gannt charts** show the tasks to be performed on the vertical axis and the time required for each on the horizontal axis. In Figure 22–1, for example, individual orders are listed vertically. If you follow across, solid bars span the period over which each order is scheduled to be produced. Broken bars indicate actual production activity.

These charts are generally used for scheduling routine production activities or the beginning and ending dates of concurrent projects. They are not, however, particularly suitable for scheduling complicated projects.

Although Gannt charts may seem simple, they are very helpful. They force you to think through the steps involved in getting a job done and to estimate the time needed for each part of the job. They also provide a means of tracking actual progress against planned activities once the project is under way.

PERT DIAGRAMS. PERT stands for Program Evaluation and Review Technique. **PERT diagrams** are useful for scheduling complex projects or processes that are one-time operations. You might use a PERT diagram, for example, to plan the steps in building a house or manufacturing a specialized piece of equipment.

To use the technique, first identify the project's major activities. Then, arrange the activities on the diagram in the order they occur and add arrows to connect activities that must occur in sequence. Finally, estimate the time necessary to complete each activity and indicate the time on the diagram. Figure 22–2 illustrates PERT scheduling.

The path through the diagram that takes the longest is called the **critical path**. Activities on this path dictate the shortest time in which the project can be completed. A delay in any of these activities can delay the whole project. By focusing on completion of critical path activities within the designated time, you can control the project.

Gannt Chart

Order Number	Quantity	January 4–8	11–15	18–22	25–29	February 1–5	8–12	15–19	23–26	March 1–5	8–12	15–19	22–26
100	1,000	▬▬	▬▬	▬▬	▬▬								
101	1,500			▬▬	▬▬	▬▬	▬▬	▬▬		▬▬			
102	1,000				▬▬	▬▬	▬▬	▬▬	▬▬				
103	700								▬▬	▬▬			

Key: ▬▬▬ Scheduled Time
▬ ▬ ▬ Progress

Figure 22–1 *Gannt charts make it easy to compare planned work (solid lines) with actual progress (broken lines). If you were looking at this chart on February 26, for example, Order 100 would be completed and 102 would be on schedule. Where would Orders 101 and 103 be?*

PERT Diagram

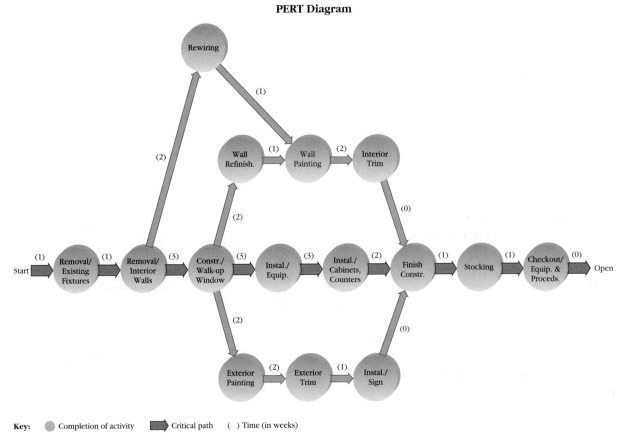

Key: ● Completion of activity ▶ Critical path ( ) Time (in weeks)

Figure 22–2   This PERT diagram lays out the process of remodeling a building for use as a food carry-out business. What is the minimal amount of time required for the completion of the project?

Controlling Quality

Quality control is the process of making sure that the goods or services you produce meet the standards you set for them. You can set standards for appearance, performance, and consistency. If you run a frozen yogurt store, for example, your customers will expect the same quality and quantity every time they buy a sundae. Using quality control, you can make sure they get both.

The specific standards you set for your business will reflect the market segment you are targeting. Customers who want high quality are willing to pay more if they are sure they can get it. Customers who are primarily concerned with low prices will expect reasonable—but not particularly high—quality.

How do you achieve quality control? There are two major ways.

QUALITY CIRCLES.   **Quality circles** are groups of employees who meet to solve problems regarding product quality. Although this approach has received attention for its use by large manufacturers (such as Ford), the concept can work just as well in small operations.

INSPECTION.   You can also inspect your products to control quality. If you do, you must decide whether to perform the inspection during the job or afterwards. Which you choose will depend on what you produce.

If you manufacture complex machinery, for example, you will probably inspect it at several stages of the production process. That way, you

Risk Takers, Profit Makers

Steve Klassen

After leaving college in 1988, Steve Klassen fled Los Angeles and moved to Vail, Colorado. There he divided his time between working at various jobs and snowboarding in the famous Colorado powder. After a while, though, Klassen decided it was time to find a direction—and devoted himself entirely to snowboarding. By 1991, he owned and operated the Wave Rave snowboard shop in Mammoth Lakes, California. He had also earned enough points riding on the Professional Snowboarding Tour of America to be crowned its overall champion.

Initially, though, Klassen had a difficult time finding financial backers for his shop. It wasn't that he lacked experience. He had been an avid snowboarder for nearly ten years. He had participated in a college-level entrepreneurship program. He had valuable retail experience in Vail and connections with a successful shop owner in Boulder. The problem was not with Klassen. It was with snowboarding. Few people were willing to invest money in a still-emerging sport. Finally, after exhausting all his other alternatives, Klassen got financial support from personal sources. A friend in Vail and his elementary school gym coach supplied him with $68,000 in start-up money.

After settling in Mammoth, Klassen launched Wave Rave by attending the annual ski industry trade show in Las Vegas. There he met and did business with manufacturers of snowboards and accessories. He set up shop carefully, creating appealing displays and purchasing any items related to snowboarding. However, while Klassen could oversee his shop's setup, stock, and goals, he couldn't control the weather.

Little snow during the winter of 1990–91 meant financial hardship for everyone in Mammoth Lakes. For young businesses, however, it was especially crippling. One Mammoth snowboard shop folded, but Wave Rave endured, thanks to Klassen's shrewdness. He cut less profitable peripheral items (such as skateboards). Then, he beefed-up popular inventory, increased space for snowboard rentals, and intensified local advertising.

Today Klassen has nearly paid off his start-up debts and is enjoying profits. He attributes Wave Rave's good fortune to his being well informed on business matters—and passionate about his sport.

Klassen still carves up the slopes whenever he gets a chance. For him, it's the best of all worlds—a resort town with expansion in the works, an exciting winter sport with increasing popularity, and a business positioned to take advantage of both. Klassen is looking forward to a long—and hopefully stormy—relationship.

can catch and correct defects before the product is completed. If you provide a service, like dry cleaning, a final inspection would be more appropriate.

You must also decide if each and every product should be inspected or just a representative sample. Cost is the determining factor here. If you are in the business of building mobile homes, inspection of each product would be relatively inexpensive. In contrast, if you make chocolate chip cookies, you could only afford to check selected batches.

Although quality control does take time and there is cost involved, you should view it as a way of ensuring customer satisfaction. Viewed in that light, quality control offers a way to reduce product defects and increase revenue over the long haul.

Managing Other Areas of Production

Productivity, automation, and preventive maintenance are additional areas of production that should be managed effectively. These areas are important to all businesses.

PRODUCTIVITY.   **Productivity** is a measure of how much your business can produce. It is expressed in terms of the rate of output per worker per unit of time. For example, a tool and die operation might have productivity rate for machinists of 35 units per day.

Businesses use productivity rates to measure employee performance. The salesperson who sells $50,000 of merchandise a month is more productive than one who sells $40,000. Obviously, if you can increase productivity, your company can make more money.

One of the ways to increase productivity is through increased employee efforts and concern. Quality circles (discussed above), company incentives, and motivational programs can increase employee productivity. A second approach to increasing productivity is through automation.

AUTOMATION.   **Automation** is the use of machines to do the work of people. It will probably not be part of your early operation because it is expensive. Eventually, however, you may want to automate certain functions in order to cut production time, reduce errors, and simplify procedures. Many businesses find that automating certain manufacturing and clerical jobs is particularly useful.

MAINTENANCE.   Eventually every machine will break down. Such a breakdown can mean lost sales and even the shutting down of an entire assembly line. You can see, then, that the maintenance of machinery is a key factor in production management.

There are three basic ways to manage maintenance. One way is to organize your production process so that when one machine is down, the work can be shifted to other machines. A second way is to build up inventories at each stage of the production process. That way, other machines can continue to run as long as the inventory holds out. The third approach is to do preventive maintenance. This means fixing machines before they break down. The advantage of this approach is that *you* control when the machinery will be down.

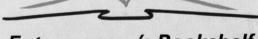

Entrepreneur's Bookshelf

To learn more about the subjects discussed in this chapter, consider reading these publications:

- *Modern Inventory Operations* by J.V. Young (© 1991)
- *Purchasing for Owners of Small Plants*, SBA Pub. No. MP17
- *Buying for Retail Stores*, SBA Pub. No. MP18

Chapter 22 Review

Recapping the Chapter

- Effective management of purchasing, inventory, and production can reduce costs and, therefore, increase profits.
- Purchasing management involves buying inventory of the right quality, in the right quantity, at the right time, from the right vendors, and at the right price.
- The purpose of inventory management is to find and maintain inventory levels that are neither too small nor too large.
- Production management has three functions—(1) obtaining the resources needed for production, (2) planning the steps to convert those resources into products, and (3) making sure that the products produced meet the standards set for them.

Reviewing the Vocabulary

Define each of the following vocabulary terms in your own words. Check your definitions against the chapter's.

- trade discounts
- shrinkage costs
- obsolescence costs
- lead time
- usage rate
- safety stock
- Gannt charts
- PERT diagrams
- critical path
- quality circles
- productivity
- automation

Checking the Facts

1. What is the rule of thumb for determining the right quality of inventory to purchase for your business?
2. What are four considerations when choosing vendors?
3. What is a trade discount?
4. What can happen if there is too little inventory?
5. What costs may result from too much inventory?
6. What are the two questions that must be addressed in inventory planning?
7. When does a visual inventory control system work best?
8. Which scheduling technique would be most useful for complex projects?

Thinking Critically

1. Compare the advantages and disadvantages of buying from one vendor or several.
2. How do you use stock turnover rate to determine how successful you've been in managing inventory?
3. What is the difference between a visual inventory system and a physical inventory count?
4. Why is quality control important?

Discussing Key Concepts

1. As your selected business grows, what inventory control system will be most useful? Why?

Chapter 22 Review

2. Why do you think a JIT inventory control system could be disastrous to a retail business?
3. Where and how could Gannt charts or PERT diagrams be useful in your selected business?
4. Describe how production management can be applied to each of the five types of business—retail, wholesale, service, manufacturing, and extraction.
5. What quality control measures would be most appropriate for your type of business? Why?

Using Basic Skills

Math
1. You are the owner of a business in a field that has an average yearly inventory turnover rate of 6. You have forecasted sales of $240,000 for the next year. The cost of your inventory is 70 percent of your selling price.

   - How many months supply of inventory should you keep on hand?
   - What would be the average dollar value of your inventory investment?

Communication
2. Write or telephone trade associations in your selected field to determine average inventory turnover rates.

Human Relations
3. You have received a shipment from your main vendor, and it lacks several key items that you ordered. You noted the shortage on the delivery sheet and called the vendor to let him know. To your surprise, his reaction implies that you are trying to take advantage of him. He insists that everything was there when the order was shipped. What is the best way to handle the situation?

Enriching Your Learning

1. Interview a manager in your selected field regarding the following:

   - Purchasing and inventory practices and procedures
   - Common purchasing and inventory problems
   - How he or she handles or prevents the most common purchasing and inventory problems

2. If you are employed, arrange with your employer to participate in the next physical inventory that is carried out. If you are not employed, arrange with a businessperson in your selected field to assist in his or her next physical inventory.

Chapter 23
Human Resource Management

Objectives

After completing this chapter, you will be able to

- explain why employees are especially important to small businesses,
- distinguish the staffing procedures of on-going and start-up businesses,
- describe how managers can influence and motivate employees,
- identify the benefit to managers of delegating responsibility, and
- suggest ways to handle some special human resource dilemmas.

Terms to Know

developmental
  activities
educational
  activities
cost-effective
Theory X
Theory Y
hygiene factors
motivating factors
job enlargement
job enrichment
management-by-
  objectives
performance
  evaluation
delegate

Decisions, Decisions

This is really frustrating. Either I have to figure out how to get these three guys fired up, or I have to hire some employees who are excited about what they're doing. I've got all these customers wanting their cars repaired, and this bunch just plods along. I never got this far behind when I was working by myself.

For what I'm paying them (not to mention the benefits they're getting), they ought to be doing twice as much work as they are.

But nothing seems to make a difference. I've done everything I can think of from yelling and screaming to threatening to fire them. Sometimes it seems to do some good, but it doesn't last.

Actually, I think they're just lazy. I wonder why nobody said anything when I checked their references. They all got pretty good reviews from their former employers.

Maybe it's me. Is there something I don't know about getting employees to produce? If there is, I've got to find out what.

People—Your Most Important Resource

Of all the resources a business has to work with, people are the most important. This is particularly true in a small business where the performance of each employee has a major impact on the company's overall performance.

How well you manage your employees will determine how well they carry out their duties. It will also determine how enthusiastic they are about their work.

Staffing Your Business

In Chapter 17 you read about how to staff your business. The steps discussed included recruiting, screening, offering adequate pay and benefits, and providing training and development.

At that point, you were concerned with filling your *initial* staffing needs. But those same steps also apply to your ongoing operation. Here we will discuss some aspects of each step that come into play only after a business is under way.

Recruiting

Once your business is in operation you will have to replace employees who leave for one reason or another. You will also want to add new employees as your business grows.

Ongoing businesses have access to some additional forms of recruitment that start-up businesses do not. These are referrals from current and former employees, walk-ins, recruiting from within, and recruiting from competitors. The last two sources require some additional discussion.

RECRUITING FROM WITHIN. Your best candidates might be right under your nose, ready for a different job assignment or promotion. There are several advantages to recruiting from within. You already know the employee's work habits.

Your recruiting costs are kept down. The procedure minimizes disruption of your operation. Finally, it can motivate other employees to work harder for future promotions.

Internal recruiting also has a few disadvantages. One is that it can cause ill will if other employees feel that they are just as qualified and deserving of promotion. The procedure also limits opportunities for bringing "new thinking" into the company.

RECRUITING FROM COMPETITORS. Hiring employees away from the competition likewise has some advantages. The biggest one is that your new hires already have the skills to do the job. They also come with insights into your competitor's operations.

On the downside, recruiting from competitors can start a costly cycle of raiding each other's personnel. In some instances, it may also cost less to train someone with no employment history in the field. An experienced worker may have to be "untrained" before he or she can be retrained in your company's procedures.

Screening

Recall the screening procedures you used for hiring people to get your business started. They

Whether you recruit from within or from outside, you will probably still want to screen all of your applicants with an interview. Why?

included reviewing applications, conducting personal interviews, and making reference checks. As your business grows, you will use the same devices for hiring additional employees.

One thing will be different, however. You will be able to involve others in the process. For example, you may include the potential employee's immediate supervisor.

Pay and Benefits

The compensation package you established at start-up should be reviewed periodically. It should always include the benefits required by law. But now that your business is up and running, you may want to add benefits you weren't able to offer initially. You may also need to upgrade different parts of the package to be competitive. For example, you may consider offering pensions, profit sharing, or bonuses.

Be aware, however, that expanding your benefits is not just more expensive. It will also increase your management responsibilities. Businesses that offer pensions, for example, are subject to the Employee Retirement Income Act. The act regulates pension plans to ensure that eligible employees do, in fact, receive their pensions. This means that you will have to manage the investment of pension fund moneys to meet the standards of the act. You will also have to handle more government paperwork.

Training and Development

The training and development of your employees is likely to be more complex in your growing business. Of course, you will continue to provide training for new hires. But you should also use training to improve the job performance of current employees.

To this end, you will want to add two types of activities to your training and development plans—developmental activities and educational activities. **Developmental activities** prepare employees—primarily managers, including yourself—to lead the company into the future. **Educational activities** prepare employees for moving up in the organization.

Your training and development program should be the result of a planned process. That process should include four steps.

DETERMINE YOUR NEEDS. This first step involves figuring out your immediate, intermediate, and long-range training and development needs. For example, are too many products coming off the line that don't meet standards? Or are too many customers leaving without buying? Both situations could indicate the need for more employee training. Do you and your other managers lack strategic planning skills? That would indicate a need for developmental activities. Will you want to have key employees ready to move into management positions as you expand in the coming year? That would indicate a need for educational activities.

DESIGN YOUR PROGRAM. Once you figure your needs, you will have to decide just how you are going to meet them. Will you put together a program yourself or designate someone else to do it? Because of the size of your business, it may already be apparent that training and development will need the undivided attention of a specialist. That could mean hiring a full-time employee, contracting with a consultant, or some combination of the two. The local chapter of the American Society for Training and Development (ASTD) can help you connect with a consultant.

Suppose you decide to handle training and development yourself. With your list of needs in hand, you can design your training and development program around them. Figure 23–1 describes some of the techniques you can use.

IMPLEMENT YOUR PROGRAM. If a training and development program is to make a difference in your organization, two things must occur. First, you have to provide the resources (like time and money) for the program. Second, you have to follow up to make sure that what is learned through the program is actually implemented on the job.

Training and Development Techniques

Technique	Description
On-the-job training	Employees learn the job on the job site under the direction of their manager or an experienced employee.
Vestibule training	Training takes place at a location away from the job that is equipped to simulate the actual work site.
Classroom teaching	Lecture, discussion, case studies, role playing, and other traditional classroom techniques are used to provide knowledge and problem-solving skills needed to perform the work.
Coaching	Employees receive ongoing instruction and feedback regarding job performance from their manager.
Mentoring	Employees receive one-on-one assistance from an established employee to help them get oriented within the organization and develop their potential.
Job rotation	Employees are moved from one job situation to another to provide them with a variety of job experiences and/or an understanding of the total operation.
Conferences and seminars	Several trainees or employees meet off the job with experts to learn how to deal with specific concerns or to exchange ideas.

Figure 23–1 The training techniques available to a manager extend far beyond classroom lectures. Which techniques could be considered learning by experience? Which ensure individual attention?

EVALUATE YOUR PROGRAM. After your training and development program has been put in place, you should evaluate it to see if it has been effective. This means figuring out whether or not the program's objectives have been achieved. For example, did sales improve?

You will also want to figure out if the program is **cost-effective**. This means calculating whether or not the increased productivity exceeds the cost of the training. In other words, did sales improve enough to pay for the program?

Evaluating the effectiveness and cost-effectiveness of training efforts is fairly easy.

Risk Takers, Profit Makers

Kristin Thomson and Jennifer Toomey

Ever wonder how records are made? Kristin Thomson and Jennifer Toomey did. Curious about record-making and motivated by her love for straightforward, sincere music, Toomey started Simple Machines with Brad Sigal in 1989. Together they planned to release six 7-inch compilation records. But by the second release, Sigal had left and Thomson had joined. Since then, Toomey and Thomson's swift success has turned the Arlington, Virginia, upstarts' humble diversion into serious business.

Simple Machines' fortunes stem from Thomson and Toomey's willingness to act on their beliefs—whether they pertain to politics, music, or business. The two met while activists with Washington, D.C.'s Positive Force, a volunteer youth group committed to improving society through constructive action. Both had played in numerous bands, organized shows, and known supportive people involved with music. From those experiences, they gained the knowledge, poise, and practical skills necessary for their enterprise.

With encouragement and advice from their friends at Dischord, Merge, and other small record companies, Thomson and Toomey put together their first 7-inch compilation in their kitchen. Their goals were modest—to offer quality products at a fair price and to treat everyone involved like people, not business instruments. A dozen releases later, their formula has proved to be both ethical and economical. They work with established bands like Jawbox as well as new bands like Pitchblende. And their listeners span the globe.

Simple Machines' constructive philosophy pervades all of its operations. When they sent the *Lungfish* LP to the record plant for mastering,

they also sent cookies to separate their job from the rest. When Simple Machines sends merchandise to mail order customers, they include a personal note. And when Simple Machines receives demo tapes they can't use, they return a pamphlet they wrote telling the sender how to release his or her own records. In short, they treat others as they themselves would like to be treated.

Thomson and Toomey's plans aren't so simple any more. In addition to their vinyl agenda, they now champion cassettes as a reemerging medium for do-it-yourselfers. Their latest project is a 7-inch-of-the-month club. Each record is organized around a theme, usually an unconventional view of significant dates and holidays. Such rising goals and expectations confirm two things about Thomson and Toomey. They love a challenge—and they love what they're doing.

Developmental and educational activities, on the other hand, are long-term investments and not as easy to isolate. You will have to judge for yourself whether or not they were effective.

Motivating Your Employees

Getting suitable employees and training them for the job is only the beginning of effective human resource management. The biggest challenge is leading, influencing, and working with them to maximize their productivity on the job.

Motivation plays a large role in managing employees. Motivating employees means getting them excited about their work. There are no guarantees, but when employees are excited about what they are doing, they tend to perform better and be more productive.

A key factor in your ability to motivate your employees is leadership style. A second factor is communication. If employees are to accomplish the goals and objectives you envision, you've got to communicate them clearly. You also have to provide clear feedback along the way so your employees know if they are on track.

How Do Managers Influence Motivation?

Whether managers know it or not, the decisions they make and the way they treat their employees affect employee motivation. There are many theories about how this works. Two in particular are relevant to small business managers.

WHAT MANAGERS ASSUME. One idea is that what a manager *assumes* about his or her employees will affect their motivation. This concept, advanced by Douglas McGregor in his book *The Human Side of Enterprise*, identified two alternative sets of assumptions managers make. He called one Theory X and the other Theory Y.

Managers who make **Theory X** assumptions believe the following:

- People do not like work and try to avoid it.
- Managers have to push people, closely supervise them, or threaten them with punishment to get them to produce.
- People have little or no ambition and will try to avoid responsibility.

In contrast, managers who make **Theory Y** assumptions hold these views:

- Work is natural to people and is actually an important part of their lives.
- People will work toward goals if they are committed to them.
- People become committed to goals when it is clear that achieving them will bring personal rewards.
- Under the right conditions, people not only accept responsibility but also seek it out.
- People have a high degree of imagination, ingenuity, and creativity, all of which can be used in solving an organization's problems.
- Employees have much more potential than organizations actually use.

As you can imagine, managers who use Theory X assumptions don't motivate employees very well. Still, there may be situations in which such assumptions are appropriate. You will probably find, however, that for small businesses Theory Y assumptions are more accurate.

HYGIENE FACTORS VS. MOTIVATING FACTORS. The research of Frederick Herzberg supports another idea about what motivates employees. For a long time most managers thought that money was the principal motivator. According to Herzberg, and others, this is not so.

Herzberg concluded that things like compensation, working conditions, and fair company policies only motivate in the short-run. (Think of how long you were motivated by the last raise you got.) The real value of such things lies not in motivating employees but in keeping them from getting dissatisfied. In this sense, they function

Study this work situation. What do you think are the hygiene factors influencing the workers shown? the motivating factors?

much like good health habits, such as brushing your teeth. They don't make things better, but they do keep them from going bad. For this reason, they are sometimes called **hygiene factors**.

According to Herzberg's theory, the really effective **motivating factors** in the workplace are achievement, recognition, responsibility, advancement, growth, and work itself. Sound familiar? Many of these same concepts are part of Theory Y's assumptions. Both McGregor and Herzberg emphasize the value of work, the importance of achievement, and the active assumption of responsibility.

What Can Managers Do to Motivate Employees?

As a manager, then, you will probably want to embrace Theory Y assumptions. You will want to take full advantage of everything your employees have to offer. How will you do this? Here are a few techniques you can apply.

PROVIDE MEANINGFUL WORK. Employees who are motivated by their work relate to it in a special way. They derive satisfaction from it. They take pride in it. To prompt such feelings, a job must be broad enough to be meaningful. It must offer a range of duties and responsibilities.

If your employees' jobs do not fit this description, consider redesigning them. You could add more tasks of the same skill level to them. This is called **job enlargement**. An example would be having a production worker perform an increased number of operations. You could also give employees more responsibility and control. (Here you would be adding elements at a different, higher skill level.) This is called **job enrichment**. For example, give the accounts receivable clerk responsibility for following up on past-due accounts.

INVOLVE EMPLOYEES IN DECISION MAKING. Give them opportunities to make suggestions about where the organization is going and what their role in it will be. This management approach has two positive outcomes. It gives employees a strong sense of purpose. It also allows them to see their own ideas put to work and thus creates a feeling of "ownership." Both lead to enhanced motivation.

There are two specific techniques for involving employees in decision making. One is quality circles, discussed in Chapter 22. Another is **management-by-objectives**. With the latter, employees both set the objectives and monitor progress toward them.

GIVE RECOGNITION. In a work situation, recognition involves the public acknowledgment of an employee's contribution to the business. Each day you will have many opportunities to bestow recognition informally. It may be a simple matter of praising employees when you see them doing a good job. It could involve giving credit to an employee for a useful idea or suggestion.

You can also give employees formal recognition. A letter of appreciation is one example. Presenting plaques or awards at meetings or banquets is another.

When you recognize an employee's contributions, he or she is more likely to continue to perform well. You also increase the morale and motivation of all other employees.

PROVIDE PERFORMANCE EVALUATIONS. A **performance evaluation** is basically a review and evaluation of how well an employee is doing on the job. Formal performance evaluations are usually done once a year, although you may want to give informal evaluations more often.

A formal evaluation is ordinarily done in a private meeting with an employee. At that time, you can let the employee know what he or she has been doing right. You can also use the occasion to help the employee make work-related changes to become more productive.

If they are handled properly, performance evaluations can be highly motivational. They can serve as a basis for pay increases and promotions. Even suggestions for improvement can be presented in a positive light—as something to strive for, a measure of future accomplishment.

REWARD PERFORMANCE. Systems for rewarding performance are used to acknowledge employee achievement. They often rely on financial rewards. Does that contradict our earlier contention that money is a hygiene, and not a motivating, factor? Not really. Money can serve both purposes. As a motivator, it represents both recognition and achievement. Employees use financial accomplishments to compare their value and success with others. Commission salespeople, for example, may view financial rewards as a way of "keeping score."

Your reward system can include things besides money. Other options might be special assignments, job titles, or promotions. These, too, represent acknowledgment and achievement.

Delegating Responsibility

Delegating responsibility is an extremely useful management tool. When you **delegate**, you give an employee the responsibility to carry out some of your work. To use the technique

Letters and plaques are frequently used to acknowledge an employee's outstanding performance. This employer carries the process one step further. How?

successfully, you must give sufficient authority to the employee to get the job done. If you assign the person a project, then he or she must be able to make all the decisions related to it.

Delegation has many advantages. First and foremost, it allows you to concentrate on managing your business instead of being caught up in details of its operation. The technique is also motivational. It demonstrates that you have confidence in your employees and respect for their abilities. Finally, delegation allows you to develop your employees for even greater responsibilities.

Of course, certain conditions have to exist before you delegate responsibility and authority to an employee. The employee must be capable and willing, and you must trust that he or she can handle the job. You also have to be aware that the final responsibility for getting the job done rests with you. These conditions should not discourage delegation but help you match employees with opportunities for delegation.

Dealing with Special Dilemmas

As a manager of people in a business, you will encounter many difficult problems. Many of them will have no clear-cut solutions. In this part of the chapter, we will describe a few of the dilemmas you might face. Our list is by no means exhaustive. It will, however, help you start thinking about how you might handle problems as, or even before, they arise.

Throughout this text, we have stressed the importance of communication, human relations, and problem-solving. These skills will be especially helpful to you in solving the problems associated with human resource management.

Unions and Your Business

As the manager of your own small business, you will probably not find the idea of unions appealing. They do represent some loss of control

Delegating responsibility can make an owner's job much easier. It is also a highly motivational technique. In what sense?

and strain on financial resources. Nonetheless, if you understand why they exist, you will be able to make better decisions about them.

Essentially, unions come into existence when employees believe they aren't being treated fairly. They join unions because the organizations strengthen their ability to bargain for wages, benefits, and job security.

How you decide to deal with unions will depend on your unique circumstances. The role of unions in your type of business and your own philosophy will also play a part. One possibility, of course, is to head off employee concerns by establishing practices of fair treatment and open communication.

Discrimination Based on Gender

In Chapter 12, we described the EEOC and its role in protecting the rights of employees. Recall that one of the factors on the basis of which you may *not* discriminate is gender.

In addition to the EEOC's general guidelines, there are laws and regulations that pertain specifically to discrimination and gender. As a human resource manager, you must be aware of these.

One is the Pregnancy Discrimination Act. This act requires that pregnant employees be treated like all other employees when determining benefits.

The EEOC's sexual harassment guidelines provide another example. They forbid sexual harassment that affects decisions about employment conditions, promotions, and raises.

As owner and manager, you are responsible for seeing that your employees are not subjected to either kind of discrimination. You are also responsible for setting the highest standards of behavior for your employees.

On-the-Job Problems and Employee Termination

You have made every effort to get the right people, thoroughly train them, and motivate them as effectively as you can. However, you may still have some employees who have difficulty functioning in your organization. They may be performing below expectations, or their actions may be contrary to your organization's goals.

When this happens, you should first try to help the individual involved work out or overcome the problem. You may have to show the person how to apply problem-solving techniques to the situation. You may have to come up with a mutually acceptable way to change the person's thinking or actions.

Sometimes the solution will lie in professional counseling or assistance. Your first step in such a case will be to convince the employee of the need for help. Then you will probably have to assist the individual in making contact with the appropriate professional or agency. You should try to handle the situation with as much understanding as possible, but you should also be firm. Make clear that if the person is to continue as your employee, he or she must get help.

In the end, you may find the only realistic way to deal with the problem is disciplinary action. This could include such things as docked pay or termination (firing). Neither situation is easy for anyone involved, and you should try to handle it with as much tact as possible.

Terminations require additional special handling. If possible, schedule the termination process for the end of the day. Give the employee the exact reasons for the action, and explain severance pay and unemployment compensation. You may also want to help the person find another job, one more suited to his or her skills. Keep in mind that the way you handle the situation can have an impact on your relationship with your other employees.

Not all of the problems you will deal with are brought on by employees. Incidents occur both in and out of the job setting that are beyond both your and their control. For example, you may find it necessary to terminate an employee because of a drop in business rather than something the person has done. Those circumstances call for special sensitivity on your part.

Entrepreneur's Bookshelf

To learn more about the subjects discussed in this chapter, consider reading these books and articles:

- *Second to None: How Our Smartest Companies Put People First* by C. Garfield (© 1991)
- *People, Common Sense, and the Small Business* by Patricia Tway (© 1992)
- "When Managing Gets Tough—How to Handle Difficult Employees" by R. Williams, *Black Enterprise* (March 1992)

Chapter 23 Review

Recapping the Chapter

- People are a business's most important resource. They are especially important in small businesses where each employee has a major impact on the business's performance.
- Staffing a business, whether ongoing or start-up, requires the same steps—recruiting, screening, setting pay and benefits, and providing training and development. The ongoing business, however, has more options and personnel to work with—and more demands upon it.
- Managers influence employees through assumptions about them and use of motivating factors.
- In order to motivate employees, managers can (1) provide meaningful work, (2) involve employees in decision making, (3) give recognition, (4) provide performance evaluations, and (5) reward performance.
- Delegating responsibility expands an owner's ability to manage in the workplace.
- To handle human resource dilemmas, a manager needs good communication, human relations, and problem-solving skills.

Reviewing Vocabulary

1. Write a sentence for each pair of terms below. In each sentence, use the terms in a way that shows you understand the difference between them.

- developmental activities—educational activities
- Theory X—Theory Y
- hygiene factors—motivating factors
- job enlargement—job enrichment

2. Write a paragraph or two explaining how you think *management-by-objectives* might operate in the workplace. Include the following terms:

- performance evaluation
- delegate
- cost-effective

Checking the Facts

1. What are the advantages of recruiting from within?
2. Why is it important to review your compensation package periodically?
3. What is the purpose of developmental activities?
4. What are Theory X assumptions? Theory Y assumptions?
5. Name two motivating factors.
6. How does involving employees in decision making motivate them?
7. What is the value of formal performance evaluations?
8. When you delegate responsibility to an employee, who has the final responsibility?
9. What should be your first course of action in dealing with employees who have on-the-job problems?

Thinking Critically

1. Compare the advantages and disadvantages of recruiting from within and from a competitor.
2. Describe why you might not expand the benefits you offer employees.

3. Review the motivating techniques and the Herzberg theory in the chapter. How do the techniques relate to the motivating factors? Which techniques use which factors?
4. Explain how money can be used as both a hygiene factor and a motivator.

Discussing Key Concepts

1. Visualize your selected business at the end of six months of operation. What training, development, and education needs will you have? Describe them.
2. Would you provide training that was effective but not cost-effective? Explain why or why not.
3. Do you think most employees are like those described by Theory X or Theory Y? Why?
4. What do you think motivates employees better than anything else? Give your reasons.
5. Do you agree with the sequence of options given for dealing with on-the-job problems? Why or why not? Are there other options?

Using Basic Skills

Math

1. Errors by your telephone sales staff are costing you about $9,000 per year. These costs include unproductive delivery costs because of incorrect addresses or directions, misquotes, spoiled product, and lost sales from alienated customers. Sending your four telephone salespeople to a telephone sales training seminar will cost $500 each for registration. Travel and lodging costs will be another $625 each. Their salary and benefits will add up to $125 per day for each

employee for the four days they will be gone. Temporary replacement costs will be $1,500. Will the training be cost-effective?

Communication

2. Locate and read an article on motivating employees. Compare the article's conclusions with what you read in this chapter. Summarize your findings in a brief paper and share them with the class.

Human Relations

3. Several of your warehouse employees have complained to you that they don't want to work with Todd, your warehouse supervisor. They say he is abusive, obnoxious, and sometimes downright mean. A few have even threatened to quit. All of them try to avoid work situations where Todd is directly involved. The problem is compounded by the fact that Todd is one of your oldest and most trusted employees. How will you handle the situation?

Enriching Your Learning

1. Interview a businessperson in your selected field regarding the following:

   - His or her training, development, and education needs
   - How he or she provides training, development, and education for employees and managers

2. If you are employed, observe and note the techniques that your manager (and other managers in the business) use to motivate employees. Which techniques are the most effective? Which are the least effective? Share the results of your observations with the class.

Chapter 24
Financial Management

Objectives

After completing this chapter, you will be able to

- identify the documents you will need to do financial planning,
- describe how to analyze your business's finances,

- understand why financial analysis and management should be done regularly, and
- discuss how to manage your business's finances effectively.

Terms To Know

ratio analysis
working capital
variable costs
fixed costs
cash budget
capital
  expenditures

Decisions, Decisions

I always heard that if you want your business to be successful, you've got to put your profits back into it. That made sense to me. So, I did.

My trenching business was going pretty well this past spring. I had a chance to get contracts to dig trenches for three small utility companies around here. I figured it was my big break.

I had to have more equipment to do the work, though. So, I took all the money I could out of the business and sank it into another backhoe and truck. I even hired two more employees.

Well, I got the contracts—all three of them. The equipment is just what we needed. My crews and I are working seven days a week, 12 hours a day, and we're right on schedule. From the outside, it probably looks as though the company is really doing great.

Somehow, though, when I put all that money back into the business, I didn't think about the expenses I'd have before I got any payoff. Now, I've got a payroll to meet, payments to make, and I don't get paid until the job is done—two months from now!

How did I get into this fix? More important right now, how do I get out of it?

Financial Statements— A Second Look

Back in Chapter 20 you put together your pro forma income statement, balance sheet, and cash flow statement for the start-up of your business. You should understand, however, that those documents can do more than help you borrow money. They are also the financial plans for operating your business. They provide blueprints for you to follow as you make day-to-day financial management decisions.

Analyzing Your Finances

As part of your business's record keeping, you will periodically have to prepare similar documents that show your *actual* performance. By analyzing these documents, you will gain an understanding of your business's financial situation. There are two ways to use such documents for financial analysis.

Comparing Financial Statements

One way to analyze your financial condition is to compare completed statements on a regular, predetermined schedule. How often will depend on the needs of your business, but it may be quarterly, semiannually, or annually.

You will use current and past income statements and balance sheets. By comparing these, you will be able to identify trends, major variations in performance, and problem areas. If these trends are inconsistent with your goals, they signal the need for further investigation or change.

By comparing current and prior income statements, you can see any unusual upward or

Income Statement (Year 1)

Lopez Electronics
Income Statement
Year Ended December 31, 19- -

Revenue from Sales

Gross sales	$1,750,000	
Less sales returns and allowances	15,000	
Net Sales		$1,735,000

Cost of Goods Sold

Beginning inventory	$ 695,500	
Purchases	846,000	
Total goods available for sale	$1,541,500	
Less ending inventory	388,000	
Total Cost of Goods Sold		1,153,500

Gross Profit on Sales $ 581,500

Operating Expenses

Salaries	$ 190,000	
Advertising	133,000	
Sales promotion	2,000	
Travel and entertainment	5,200	
Depreciation—store equipment	8,000	
Miscellaneous selling expenses	1,500	
Rent	15,000	
Depreciation—delivery equipment	5,000	
Depreciation—office furniture	1,200	
Utilities	4,500	
Insurance	40,000	
Telephone	2,200	
Miscellaneous general expenses	2,000	
Total Operating Expenses		409,600

Net Income from Operations $ 171,900

Less interest expense   24,000

Net Income Before Taxes $ 147,900

Less federal income taxes   40,950

Net Income After Taxes $ 106,950

Figures 24–1 and 24–2 By comparing income statements for successive years, you can pinpoint problem areas. For example, the firm whose statements are shown here and on the next page increased sales but still suffered a loss of income. Why? Name some of the items responsible.

downward trends in your sales, cost of goods sold, or operating expenses. For example, look at Figures 24-1 and 24-2. Notice that even though net sales have increased, net income after taxes is down. By comparing both statements, you can see which expenses have increased and caused the lower income.

Comparing your current balance sheet with previous balance sheets can also show you how well you are doing. Is your net worth (owner's

Income Statement (Year 2)

Lopez Electronics
Income Statement
Year Ended December 31, 19- -

Revenue from Sales

Gross sales	$1,845,750	
Less sales returns and allowances	16,500	
Net Sales		$1,829,250

Cost of Goods Sold

Beginning inventory	$ 388,000	
Purchases	1,218,000	
Total goods available for sale	$1,606,000	
Less ending inventory	376,000	
Total Cost of Goods Sold		1,230,000

Gross Profit on Sales $ 599,250

Operating Expenses

Salaries	$ 203,200	
Advertising	152,950	
Sales promotion	2,150	
Travel and entertainment	10,500	
Depreciation—store equipment	8,000	
Miscellaneous selling expenses	1,600	
Rent	15,000	
Depreciation—delivery equipment	5,000	
Depreciation—office furniture	1,200	
Utilities	4,800	
Insurance	42,000	
Telephone	2,250	
Miscellaneous general expenses	2,200	
Total Operating Expenses		450,850

Net Income from Operations $ 148,400

Less interest expense   28,000

Net Income Before Taxes $ 120,400

Less federal income taxes   40,150

Net Income After Taxes $ 80,250

equity) increasing or decreasing? What about assets and liabilities? For example, suppose your total assets increased but your owner's equity stayed the same. A quick look at the liabilities section would probably reveal that you've taken on more debt to pay for the additional assets.

You can also compare your balance sheet with the balance sheets of similar businesses. This would show you how well you're doing in relation to other businesses.

Calculating Ratios

Another way to analyze your financial condition is to compare certain numbers from a balance sheet or income statement. You do this by performing calculations designed to show the relationship between the two figures. This kind of analysis is called **ratio analysis**, and it, too, should be done regularly.

The meanings of various ratios can be interpreted. For some ratios, there are commonly accepted standards throughout the business world. Other ratios are meaningless unless they are compared with industry standards. You can find these industry standards through trade associations and published materials. The latter include Dun & Bradstreet's *Cost of Doing Business* and Robert Morris Associates' *Annual Statement Studies*, both often found in public libraries.

There are ratios that could be calculated for every combination of items on the two statements. Since many of those have limited application in everyday management, we will present only a few key ratios here.

CURRENT RATIO. The current ratio is the ratio between current assets and current liabilities. These numbers are found on a balance sheet. (See Figure 24-3.) The current ratio indicates a company's ability to pay its bills. It is determined as follows:

$$\frac{\text{Current assets}}{\text{Current liabilities}} = \text{current ratio}$$

$$\frac{\$596{,}000}{\$288{,}900} = 2.06 \text{ to } 1$$

A current ratio of 2.06 to 1 means that you have a little more than two dollars of current assets for every one dollar of current liabilities. A current ratio of 2 to 1 is usually considered enough to give a company a comfortable amount of capital to carry out its operations.

WORKING CAPITAL. Businesses also use a **working capital** calculation. (This figure is technically not a ratio.) It shows in dollars the capital a firm has to carry out its daily operations. You use the same numbers from the current ratio calculation, but you subtract current liabilities from current assets:

Current assets	$596,500
– Current liabilities	288,900
Working capital	$307,600

DEBT RATIO. The debt ratio measures the percentage of total dollars in the business provided by creditors. These numbers also come from a balance sheet. (Again, see Figure 24-3.) The debt ratio is calculated as follows:

$$\frac{\text{Total liabilities}}{\text{Total assets}} = \text{debt ratio}$$

$$\frac{\$450{,}900}{\$741{,}800} = 61\%$$

This means that you are in debt for 61 percent of your assets.

Business owners usually prefer to have a high debt ratio. This would mean that others, such as creditors and suppliers, were financing the business. You, as owner, would not be using any more of your own money than necessary. On the other hand, if you need to borrow money, creditors usually prefer that you have a moderate debt ratio.

NET PROFIT ON SALES. This ratio uses numbers from an income statement. It indicates how effectively and efficiently the company is being managed. It shows the number of cents on each sales dollar that is left after all expenses and income taxes are paid. It is figured as shown below:

$$\frac{\text{Net income after taxes}}{\text{Net sales}} = \frac{\text{net profit on}}{\text{sales ratio}}$$

$$\frac{\$\ 106{,}950}{\$1{,}735{,}000} = 6.16\%$$

Whether or not this is a good ratio for you depends on how it compares to other companies in the same field. If the figure is lower than the average, it could mean that your prices are set too low. It could also mean that your costs are unusually high. Or it could mean a combination of the two.

Lopez Electronics
Balance Sheet
December 31, 19– –

ASSETS

Current Assets

Cash		$ 45,500	
Accounts receivable	$162,000		
Less allowance for bad debt	5,500	156,500	
Notes receivable		6,000	
Inventory		388,000	
Total Current Assets			$596,000

Fixed Assets

Delivery equipment	$120,000		
Less accumulated depreciation	30,000	$ 90,000	
Furniture and store equipment	$ 79,000		
Less accumulated depreciation	23,200	55,800	
Total Fixed Assets			145,800
Total Assets			$741,800

LIABILITIES

Current Liabilities

Accounts payable	$147,000	
Notes payable	78,000	
Salaries payable	15,900	
Income taxes payable	48,000	
Total Current Liabilities		$288,900

Long-term Liabilities

Mortgage payable on equipment	$ 70,000	
Note payable	92,000	
Total Long-term Liabilities		162,000
Total Liabilities		$450,900

OWNER'S EQUITY

Rene Lopez, Capital	290,900
Total Liabilities and Owner's Equity	$741,800

Figure 24–3   You use figures from a balance sheet to compute current ratio. Suppose total current assets for this firm had been $335,000. What would have been its current ratio? What would this have said about the company's financial condition?

OPERATING RATIO.   This ratio shows the relationship between each expense on the income statement and sales. It expresses what percentage of sales dollars the expense is using up. To calculate the operating ratio for any given expense, you use the following formula:

$$\frac{\text{Expense}}{\text{Sales}} = \text{operating ratio}$$

For example, if sales for the month were $10,000 and the monthly rent $1,000, then the lease expense would represent 10 percent of sales:

$$\frac{\$\ 1,000}{\$10,000} = 10\%$$

If that percentage is higher than what is considered average in your field, it could mean that you are spending more for your lease than you should.

Managing Your Finances

Financial analysis helps you see where there may be problems with your plans or operation. It can tell you whether or not your business's goals are being met. It cannot, however, solve your problems.

To do that, you as a business owner must know how to manage your finances effectively. You must know how to plan for profits and manage your cash flow, capital expenditures, and taxes.

Planning for Profits

Profits don't just happen. The owners of successful businesses plan for them. This is a process that involves four steps.

FORECASTING SALES.   To begin profit planning, you have to forecast sales. As an ongoing business, you will have sales records on which to base your projections. You can also use the current rate of sales growth in your field or the rate of growth of the Gross National Product. Then you would adjust your forecast based on other economic factors, such as inflation or recession.

Consider an example. Suppose that in your industry sales have been up 5 percent per year for the last three years and inflation rates have

stabilized at 2 percent. This is how you could forecast sales, if you had sales last year of $300,000:

$$5\% + 2\%\ =\ 7\%$$
$$.07 \times \$300,000\ =\ \$21,000$$
$$\$300,000 + 21,000\ =\ \$321,000$$

EVALUATING PROFIT POTENTIAL.   If you are satisfied with your forecast, you would need no other adjustments to your profit planning. However, you may want to improve your profit picture.

One way to do this is to increase sales revenues by going after additional market share. This would mean making some changes in your marketing mix. For example, you may feel that you can increase your profits by adding new products, increasing prices, or increasing advertising.

You may be absolutely right, but you have to consider that every change has a cost connected with it. And sometimes that cost is more than the change is worth. Therefore, before you make the decision to jump in, you have to evaluate the profit potential of the move.

One approach to evaluating profit potential is to use a variation of the break-even analysis you were introduced to in Chapter 5. The variation shows how many units of product must be sold in order to make a profit based on the marketing mix change:

$$\frac{\text{Fixed cost}}{\text{Selling price} - \text{variable cost}} = \frac{\text{break-even}}{\text{point}}$$

Variable costs are the expenses associated with operating a business that change with each unit of product produced. Examples are the materials used for production, wages, and utilities. **Fixed costs** are the expenses that don't change with units produced. Examples of these would be insurance, licenses, and rent.

Consider a situation that uses the formula. Suppose you have a business that manufactures light recreational equipment. You have read about a potential market in manufacturing portable backboards for three-on-three basketball street tournaments. That is right down your

Fixed and variable costs are key elements in determining a business's profit potential. What are some of the fixed and variable costs this operation incurs?

alley. The article predicts sales of 100 units in your region. You believe you can sell the backboards for $250 each. The materials, labor, and other variable costs will be about $150. Because you will have to buy a couple of pieces of equipment, your fixed costs will be $5,000. Here is the calculation you would make:

$$\frac{\$5,000}{\$250 - \$150} = \frac{\$5,000}{\$100} = 50 \text{ units}$$

The break-even point is 50 units. This means that if you sell 50 units, you will cover all your costs. For every unit over 50, you will have $100 ($250–$150) going toward profit. If competition or other factors would limit your sales to less than 50, adding the product would have no potential for profit. Also, if you had to spend $10,000 or more for fixed costs, there would be no potential for profit. You would have to sell more than 100 of the backboards to increase profits, and that would exceed the predicted sales.

This type of analysis could be used to evaluate the profitability of any change in marketing mix. New advertising campaigns, additional salespeople, and costs related to changes in location or remodeling are all examples.

CONTROLLING COSTS. The other route to increasing your profit margin is to control costs.

All of your variable costs are controllable. However, you would only want to control those expenses that are "out of line." Those are costs that might be especially high or low when compared with your past records or with other companies in your field.

Look back at how to calculate operating ratios. Those ratios show how much of your sales dollars are being spent for each expense. If there is a big difference between your costs and the costs of others in your industry, you need to investigate further. Chances are you can improve profits by making a cost control adjustment.

Recall, too, the operating ratio example from earlier in the chapter. The percentage of lease expense when compared to sales was 10 percent. If others in your industry are only paying 5 percent, you may have a larger facility than you need. Thus, you could reduce costs and improve profits by changing locations. Suppose, however, that others are paying 15 percent. This might mean that you could increase profits by paying more for a better location. This would be especially true if you were a retailer.

In other instances, using your previous experience might give a better comparison. Let's say, for example, your shipping costs double over the previous year. You may be able to increase your profit by finding another trucking contractor or leasing your own trucks.

BUDGETING. The final step in planning for profit is preparing budgets, or the financial plans for your business. Budgets are where you put the information discussed in this section.

At the beginning of each planning period, you should prepare a pro forma income statement and balance sheet and any other budgets you may need. As an ongoing business, you will have the financials from your previous operating period to build on. You will make adjustments to those statements based on the sales forecasts, new profit projections, and cost control changes you have developed. These updated financial projections will comprise the master budget for guiding you through the period.

Managing Cash Flow

Managing your business to maximize profitability is not your only financial management concern. It is entirely possible, and not uncommon, for a business that is growing and profitable to fail. The reason? Sometimes such businesses simply run out of cash.

Profits are often "plowed back" into new inventory and equipment and expanding facilities. As a matter of fact, this is often considered an admirable approach to building a business. The problem, however, is that you can't pay employees, lenders, or suppliers with profits you've reinvested. You've got to have cash. In other words, you've got to manage your cash flow so that you have enough on hand to meet your obligations when they come due.

USING A CASH BUDGET. A **cash budget** like the one shown in Figure 24–4 is very similar to a pro forma cash flow statement. There are,

	MONTH 1			MONTH 2			MONTH 3		
	EST.	ACT.	DIF.	EST.	ACT.	DIF.	EST.	ACT.	DIF.
Cash Budget For Quarter Ending _____									
Projected Cash Receipts									
Cash sales									
Collections on accounts receivable									
Other income									
Total Receipts									
Projected Cash Disbursements									
Purchases (raw materials, merchandise)									
Advertising									
Dues, subscriptions, licenses									
Insurance									
Interest									
Legal and professional expenses									
Office supplies									
Payroll taxes									
Rent									
Salaries									
Sales taxes									
Telephone									
Travel and entertainment									
Utilities									
Notes payable									
Other _____									
_____									
_____									
_____									
Total Disbursements									
Net Cash Increase (Decrease)									

Figure 24–4   The format of a cash budget differs from a cash flow statement in that it has room for three separate entries for every month instead of one. What is the purpose of such an arrangement?

Cash Budget Summary
For Quarter Ending _____

	MONTH 1			MONTH 2			MONTH 3		
	EST.	ACT.	DIF.	EST.	ACT.	DIF.	EST.	ACT.	DIF.
Estimated beginning cash balance									
Plus net cash increase (or minus net cash decrease)									
Estimated ending cash balance									
Necessary cash balance									
Short-term loan needed (if cash is less than amount required)									
Cash available for short-term investment (if cash is greater than amount required)									

Figure 24–5   This form can be used to summarize the outcomes of your financial planning. Study its entries. If you used such a form during a quarter, would you have an entry for every space on every line? Why or why not?

however, two major differences. First, your projections for the cash budget will be based on past operating records instead of estimates. Second, the format of the cash budget is slightly different. To start, it has three columns to show estimated cash flow, actual cash flow, and the difference between the two. Also, the cash budget format can show cash flow projections at the bottom or on a separate summary form.

Cash budgets may be for a year in advance. However, they are more typically done for three-month periods.

With a cash budget, you can plan to meet cash needs by making sure there is enough money on hand when it is needed. You can also anticipate and get ready for shortfalls. Let's say your budget indicates that at the end of the month you are going to have $6,000 less cash than you need. You have time to make arrangements for short-term financing. On the other hand, if you see ahead of time that you're going to have a sizeable cash surplus, you can figure out how to put the money to work for you. These are the options highlighted by a cash budget summary (see Figure 24-5).

IMPROVING YOUR CASH FLOW. There are certain areas in a business operation that have more room for improving cash flow than others. Some of those are described below, along with some steps you can take to make improvements.

- *Tighten up your credit and collections.* If you extend credit to customers, be sure you can collect. If a customer goes past due, follow up immediately.
- *Take advantage of credit terms.* Pay your bills on time, but take all of the time that is available to you. You may also be able to improve your cash flow by negotiating better terms.
- *Manage inventory carefully.* As we discussed in Chapter 22, excess inventory can tie up your cash. If inventory doesn't sell, then cut prices and turn it back into cash.
- *Put cash surpluses to work.* When you temporarily have more cash than you need, consider investing it. Although the returns on such short-term investment will not be great, they will add to your cash flow over time. Of course, these funds should only be invested

Risk Takers, Profit Makers

Gary Wong

Skeletons in the closet have been known to ruin people's careers. For Gary Wong, comic books in the closet provided one. At 28, Wong rediscovered his 16-year-old collection of comic books. His ensuing attempts to update the collection developed into a home business and eventually became a thriving neighborhood retail store.

Although Wong always wanted to operate his own business, he never trained specifically to sell comic books. At first, he studied to be a dentist like his father. However, he was never really set on it. Only a few units shy of meeting the requirements for dental school, he withdrew from the University of Southern California. The next semester, he enrolled in the university's entrepreneur program from which he graduated in 1987.

The whole time he had been in school, Wong had also been instructing tennis at the Hillhurst Tennis Center in the Los Feliz area of Los Angeles. By observing and working within that service business, Wong learned firsthand the importance of promotion, communication, and networking. He also became accustomed to working seven-day weeks and fine-honed his salesmanship by selling his ideas and methods to his students. But in 1992, after 11 years of tennis, he needed a break.

It was during that break that Wong found his old comic books in a closet. He began updating his collection by buying other people's collections. At conventions, he acquainted himself with fans, dealers, and the whole comic book business.

After profitably dealing comic books at conventions and from his garage, he began surveying local shops. He studied product selection and layout and listening to the advice of owners. Then he reviewed his school notes on business plans and cash flow and invested his savings in his own store.

Wong promoted heavily. He placed flyers in book stores, video shops, and other hangouts. He also advertised in local and school newspapers. Once he had customers in the shop, he knew return business and good word-of-mouth would follow. In February 1992, the Comic Connection opened its doors.

Wong's specialty—selling hot comics at reasonable prices—practically guarantees satisfying and retaining customers. His biggest challenge is determining which titles will be in demand in future months and ordering accordingly. To keep up on trends, Wong attends at least one convention a month. He also stays in touch with his suppliers to ensure that he gets the comics he wants. Seriously pursuing connections like these allowed the Comic Connection to break even its first month. Continuing to pursue them has allowed the business to run a profit every month since.

where the cash can be retrieved on short notice.

- *Keep your payroll under control.* Contracting work out or hiring part-time people may cost less than keeping a complete staff of full-time employees.
- *Cut expenses.* Try to avoid excess spending. You may be tempted to buy expensive company cars or have your offices redecorated when the money is rolling in. But keep in mind that the bills may not be far behind.

Planning for Capital Expenditures

Effective financial management also includes planning for **capital expenditures**. These are long-term commitments of large sums of money to buy new equipment or replace old. They are major purchases for your business for which you should plan far in advance of actual need. If you don't, making such purchases could disrupt your other financial plans.

How do you plan for capital expenditures? First, you must decide if your business is, in fact, able to pay for the equipment. You should also consider the revenue it will generate and how long it will take to pay for itself. And you should avoid excessive investment—buying more or better quality than you need.

When you plan for a capital expenditure, you are planning for a future purchase. You will probably have to pay for some of it yourself and borrow the rest. So, planning will mean saving a certain amount of money. You will also want your debt ratio at a point attractive to lenders. This could mean paying off some debts before incurring any new ones.

Managing Taxes

We discussed your legal obligations to pay taxes in Chapter 12. However, there are some additional tax considerations that relate to financial management:

- *Try to time income so that you can control the year in which it is taxed.* For example,

you may be able to time certain sales for the beginning of the upcoming year to defer taxes to that year.

- *Time your deductions.* During high income years, you should identify costs that can be deducted during that year, rather than in following years when income may be lower.
- *Choose the depreciation method that is most beneficial to you.* "Most beneficial" is a matter of time and circumstance. New businesses, for example, often have more to write off than they have in income. So, it is better to spread your write-offs out over as much time as possible.
- *Claim research and development expenses.* You may not have many of these early in your operation, but you should be aware that they are deductible. Expenses such as new product research and studies that improve production would fall into this category.
- *Keep records of all expenses.* Any honest expense is deductible, but it is up to you to keep the records.
- *Keep up to date on tax laws.* Tax laws change every year. Frequently they change in a way that affects your profits. Therefore, staying on top of the changes is an important part of your financial management.

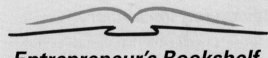

Entrepreneur's Bookshelf

To learn more about the subjects discussed in this chapter, consider reading these books:

- *The Entrepreneur and Small Business Problem Solver* by William A. Cohen (© 1989)
- *Cash Traps* by Jeffrey Davidson and Charles Dean (© 1992)
- *Surviving the Credit Crunch of the 1990s* by L. Woltjen (© 1989)

Chapter 24 Review

Recapping the Chapter

- The same financial statements you used in your business plan—income statement, balance sheet, and cash flow statement—can help you with financial planning.
- You can analyze your business's finances by comparing completed financial statements and calculating certain ratios.
- Analyzing and managing your business's financial position on a regular rather than random basis helps you spot problems in advance and plan ways to cope with them.
- Managing finances effectively includes planning for profits and managing cash flow, capital expenditures, and taxes.
- Profit planning begins with sales forecasting.
- A business can fail—even if it is growing and showing a profit—if it runs out of cash.
- Capital expenditures should be planned for well before they are needed.
- To a certain extent, you can manage taxes to enhance your financial position.

Reviewing Vocabulary

Write a paragraph that describes how you would use each of the following in the financial management of your operation.

- ratio analysis
- working capital
- variable costs
- fixed costs
- cash budget
- capital expenditures

Checking the Facts

1. How frequently should income statements and balance sheets be compared with previous similar documents?
2. What kinds of things can you learn about your business by comparing current and past income statements?
3. You want to compare ratio analysis results for your business with other businesses. Where can you get such information?
4. What does a current ratio indicate?
5. What does debt ratio measure?
6. Name the growth rates you would use to forecast sales.
7. What kind of costs can be controlled to increase your profit margin?
8. How is a cash budget different in format from a cash flow statement?
9. What are three ways to improve your cash flow?
10. Why is it important to keep up to date on tax laws?

Thinking Critically

1. Why would creditors want you to have a moderate debt ratio?
2. How is the break-even analysis formula in this chapter different from the one you learned in Chapter 5? How are the two alike?
3. The chapter cites only two ways to improve profits (increasing market share and controlling costs). Why? Are there other ways? What are they?
4. What is the difference between controlling costs to improve profits and the steps that can be taken to improve cash flow? Explain.

Chapter 24 Review

Discussing Key Concepts

1. How often should financial statements be prepared? Why?
2. Is cutting costs most often the best cost control strategy for improving profits. Why or why not?
3. What is the ideal way to improve cash flow? Explain.
4. Is it ethical to try to minimize your business taxes? Why or why not?

Using Basic Skills

Math

1. You are the owner of a restaurant with a small dance floor. For the past year, you have had a band on Saturday nights and have drawn an average of 80 couples. Many regulars have told you that you could increase business if you enlarged the floor. That remodeling would cost $12,000. You calculate that each couple spends about $30, and your variable cost for each bill is $25. By enlarging the floor, you also figure you can increase business to 90 couples. You are concerned, though, that dance bands in operations like yours only seem to go strong for a couple of years. How long would it take you to break even? (Assume 90 couples would come every Saturday night.) Would enlarging the floor be a profitable move?

Communication

2. Write a trade association in your selected field to obtain industry averages for important ratios.

Human Relations

3. Since you opened your business, you have had a very loose credit policy. In order to improve your cash flow, you have decided to tighten up considerably and are asking all of your customers to pay within 30 days. One of your best customers gets irate at that request and threatens to do business someplace else. How should you handle the situation?

Enriching Your Learning

1. Obtain sets of financial statements, preferably from your field, for two consecutive accounting periods. Analyze any changes that occurred between the two periods, and apply the ratio analysis techniques with which you are familiar. Draw conclusions and make "decisions" based on your analysis. Write a brief summary.

   If you are employed, ask your employer to review old financial statements for two consecutive periods with you. Determine what your employer looked for, what conclusions he or she came to, and what decisions he or she made based on those conclusions.
2. Interview an accountant who prepares taxes for small businesses. Ask him or her what most small businesses should do to have the best possible tax situation. Also, ask about any new tax laws that may be pertinent to your industry. *Note:* If you haven't talked to an accountant before, find out about the services he or she provides to small businesses. Ask what he or she would recommend for your operation. Inquire about the cost of those services as well.

Chapter 25
Computers in Small Business Management

Objectives

After completing this chapter, you will be able to
- list the advantages of using computers in small business management,
- discuss some of the problems associated with business use of computers,
- describe three different approaches to computerizing a business,
- name the major types of application software and explain what they do, and
- identify some sources of computer equipment.

Terms to Know

computer integrated manufacturing (CIM)
hardware
software
computer viruses
electronic bulletin boards
microcomputers
time-sharing
computer terminal
spreadsheet
cells
database management
modem
graphics software

Decisions, Decisions

I knew something was up the minute I saw that big smile on Marcia's face. She had the look of someone who'd made a big decision and was totally thrilled with it.

"Congratulate me," she announced. "I've decided to give up messy paper record keeping. I am going to computerize Swim World!"

For Marcia, that *was* a major decision. I knew she'd been thinking about it for a while. She never really complained about all the paperwork and calculations. To her that was just part of doing business. But I could tell she was having trouble keeping up as the business grew.

Computers seemed to be the only way out, but Marcia had no experience with them. She didn't have one of her own and

she'd never taken a computer course in school.

I told Marcia that I'd be glad to help in any way I could. I *have* taken a course and even used computers in a few of my classes. But, of course, that was personal use. For a business, Marcia's into kinds of equipment and software that I've only read about. I told her, though, I'd sure like to learn.

Marcia laughed and said, "As if you had a choice! For the next few weeks, you're going to hear about nothing else."

Then she gave me a demonstration. She rattled off a whole list of questions she was mulling over. "For a business this size, what kind of computer do I need? How do I want to use it? What equipment do I need to go with it?" In other words, what does she need to know about everything computer?

Benefits of Computers

There is hardly any part of your life that is not touched by computers. When a store clerk sweeps one of your purchases across an optical scanner, he or she is recording information on a computer. When you dial a telephone number, a computer makes the actual connection. When you ask an automated teller machine to check the balance in your account, you are interacting with a computer.

But what has this increased use of computers meant to entrepreneurs? How has it simplified—

or complicated—the way they do business? That is the focus of this chapter.

Better Information

To many people, the greatest benefit of computers is the access they provide to large amounts of information. However, it is not how much information computers can provide that is important. It is what they can *do* with it.

Quite simply, computers can provide *better* information. They can screen data according to the needs of the user, condense it, and present it in a usable form. What is more, computers can do all of this much more quickly than human beings.

Better Internal Controls

If business data is input regularly and accurately, a computer can provide a variety of up-to-date status reports at the push of a button. An example was cited earlier. Grocers use electronic scanning devices to input product data into their main computers. This enables them to know at all times the exact status of their inventory.

Computer integrated manufacturing (CIM) allows manufacturers even more control. With computers they can measure production at every step of the manufacturing process. They can regulate the speed at which products are produced. They can closely control the size and timing of deliveries from suppliers. They can even monitor and control quality.

Better Use of Personnel

The incredible speed of computers permits entrepreneurs to set up their most monotonous tasks to be handled by computer. Tasks such as accounting, calculations, sorting data, and generating form letters can be done in a matter of minutes, even seconds, by a computer. This ability to take over the monotonous tasks of a business frees up the entrepreneur and his or her employees for more important duties. For the new business owner, it can also mean hiring fewer employees to do clerical work.

Better Sales

Increasingly business owners are coming to realize that computers have a significant role to play in generating revenues or sales. Salespeople gather very important information every day—sales leads, competitor pricing, customer service ideas. Unfortunately, much of this information is lost because it is not recorded and shared.

Recognizing this, some businesses now provide their salespeople with access to computers to record what they see and hear. This information, once entered in a firm's computer system, can be analyzed and used to make future decisions about marketing strategy.

Problems Associated with Computers

The wealth of experiences you have had with computers has probably influenced your feelings about them positively. But some people still resist them for a variety of reasons.

Expense

One of the most common reasons businesspeople give for not computerizing their businesses is cost. This is a valid consideration. Although computers have come down in price significantly, they still constitute a major expense for a small business.

Why? Mainly because you can't buy just a single piece of **hardware**, or equipment, called a computer. At a minimum, you must also buy **software** (the programs that run the computer) and a printer. You may also want special features like a color monitor (or screen), additional disk drives, and increased memory. For a business computer, you will also probably want to purchase a maintenance contract. All of these things can add substantially to the cost of a computer.

Resistance from Employees

Today many employees fear that they will be replaced by computers. Should you decide to computerize your business, you might want to take steps to alleviate any such anxiety on your employees' part. Include them in the decision-making process. Help them to feel that computers will make their jobs easier or more interesting. Finally, emphasize that by learning to use a computer they will be adding valuable new job skills to their resumes.

Other employees may be concerned with potential health risks sometimes associated with computer use. These include such things as headaches, muscle aches, and eyestrain. You and

Computer System

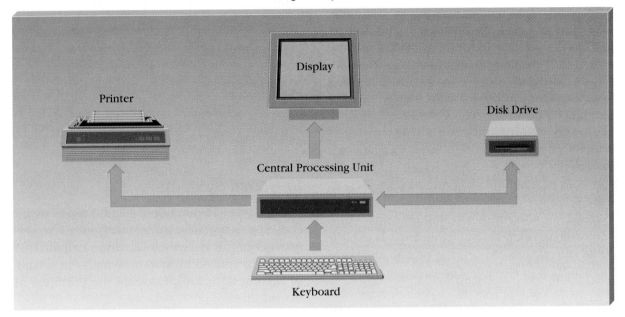

Figure 25–1   Computers are expensive because the purchaser must buy a system rather than just a computer. For example, all of the components shown here are part of a typical desktop computer setup. Which component do you think could most accurately be described as "the computer"?

your employees both can avoid such problems by observing a few simple precautions:

- Take frequent breaks.
- Look away from the computer screen periodically.
- Use adjustable furniture and antiglare screens.

"Garbage In, Garbage Out"

This is an old saying among computer enthusiasts. Put simply, it means that the quality of information you put into a computer determines the quality of information you get out.

You have probably heard businesspeople or their employees try to explain away a mistake by saying it was "a computer error." You should recognize such a comment for what it is—an excuse. Most "computer errors" are the result of human errors (omitting data, entering it incorrectly, or failing to remove inaccurate data). Since most computers can't talk to defend themselves, however, they make very convenient scapegoats.

As both a businessperson and someone who has grown up with computers, you should be aware of the limitations of this approach. Just as you are more computer literate than past students, so are your customers. They will readily see through your blaming a machine for your own shortcomings or those of your employees.

System Failures

Computers do, however, have their own weak points. As an entrepreneur potentially dependent on a computer, you should be aware of them.

When a computer suddenly stops working and you can't access any of its information, we say that the system has "crashed." The condition has a number of causes. Power outages can shut down the computer out of sequence, crippling it. Power surges, a burst of enormous power in the electrical system, can overload its circuits. And then there are **computer viruses**.

Just as live viruses invade human cells and destroy them, computer viruses invade the memory (or stored data) of a computer and destroy it. Basically they are hidden commands that tell a computer to erase its own files. How do computer viruses "invade"? Always with some help from the computer user. Usually they enter a system hidden on a data disk or buried in software programs taken from **electronic bulletin boards**. (Bulletin boards are services that computer users can access through telephone lines and from which they can obtain a variety of software programs free.)

How can you protect yourself against computer system failures? The simplest way is to back up all of your records on tape or disk and store them in another location. Another technique is to have a backup power source, such as a battery. Finally, you can use a computer "vaccine." These are programs that detect and destroy any viruses present on a disk or in a computer system.

Computer Crime

When computers became a major industry, some people took their computer creativity and applied it in illegal ways. Computer criminals developed ingenious ways of accessing computers and stealing or altering information. Other individuals used computers as a means of revenge. Disgruntled employees would erase thousands of hours' worth of work when they left their jobs or were fired.

How can you protect your business data from computer criminals? The simplest and least inexpensive way is to secure your computer with a key. This locks the machine and prevents an unauthorized user from starting it. You can also secure important data by using a password and telling only those people who need access to the data what that password is. Finally you can employ one of the security programs now available. These scramble the data in a file so that it is unreadable to anyone who doesn't have the code needed to unscramble it.

Your Hardware Options

Computerizing your business is not just a matter of walking into a store and picking out the personal computer of your choice. Having your own computer is one option, but there are others. You should consider all of them before making a final decision.

In-House Systems

An increasing number of small businesses are choosing to purchase **microcomputers**, or personal computers as they are often called. This means that the entire system, which can usually sit on a desktop, is located on the premises of the business.

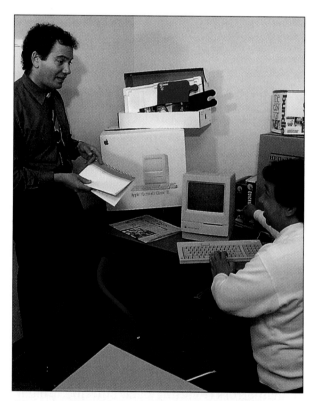

Many small business owners start small when they computerize. They rely on a single personal computer installed at their place of business. What is this arrangement called?

Risk Takers, Profit Makers

Richard Kilby

Watching the company one works for go down the drain can be a disheartening experience. For Richard Kilby, however, it was inspiring. As the production manager for a small printing operation, he had a good view of the financial mismanagement that led to its failure. And he knew he could do better.

So, at 22, Kilby borrowed $10,000, rented the back room of a Raleigh bookstore, and established Barefoot Press. What started as a one-man, part-time operation now consists of eight employees, fills a 6,500-square-foot shop, and serves clients across the country.

Kilby's first step in founding Barefoot Press was research. He pored over business texts, concentrating on case histories. He also took advantage of free counseling from the city's small business and technology development center. After determining how much business would be necessary to keep his enterprise alive, Kilby purchased a small press and began accepting jobs.

In the early years, Kilby managed his business conservatively. He made up for having little capital by working around the clock and living modestly. Starting lean also kept spending in check. And he was sure not to overextend his own or his customers' credit, as his previous employer had done.

At first, many of Kilby's clients were friends. A member of the underground publishing scene, he printed music fanzines and alternative magazines. Through these, he attracted the attention of independent record labels, which he recognized as a growing market. (They also paid in advance and didn't require immediate turnaround). Today, about 40 percent of Barefoot Press's business is 7-inch record sleeves, CD packaging, cassette J-cards, and small posters for maverick companies such as Merge, Allied, Jettison, and Simple Machines.

The remainder of Kilby's business is general commercial work, but even those relationships are uncommonly personal. Barefoot Press strives to understand each customer's business and provide solutions. At times, Kilby or other staff members attend clients' research and development meetings to offer market and product advice as well as to identify printing needs. This way, Barefoot Press satisfies what Kilby calls a "personality niche."

Kilby's personal approach to business also applies within the print shop. Uncomfortable with playing the autocrat, he stresses teamwork and allows his staff flexible hours. In turn, they work conscientiously, communicate well, and attend frequent meetings. Such dedication, cooperation, and support have empowered upstart Barefoot Press to succeed in the face of well-heeled competition.

An in-house system has the advantage of being available whenever you need it. You have total control over how the system is used and who uses it. The disadvantage is that you must purchase all of the equipment and train people to use it.

Following a few simple steps will help you arrive at the in-house computer solution that will be the best for your business:

- *List all of the activities that your business performs.* These might include bookkeeping, market research, and inventory control.
- *Prioritize the listed activities.* Place those that most need to be computerized at the top of the list, those that least need to be computerized at the bottom.
- *For each task to be computerized, figure out what information is needed and in what form.* For example, you may need correspondence, mailing lists, customer and supplier accounts, and sales or quality control data. Your format possibilities might include text, table, graph, or accounting statement.
- *Determine which software will give you the information you need in the form that you need.* To find objective evaluations of software, consult computer journals like *Personal Computing*, *Byte*, *PC*, and *PC World*. Be sure that the software you choose is easy to use and has good support from the manufacturer.
- *Select a computer system that can run the software you have chosen.* Also, look for a system that has the capability to expand as your business grows.
- *Integrate the computer system into your business.* Teach employees how to use the system to advantage. Keep backup (or paper) copies of everything until you are certain that there are no problems with the system.

Service Bureaus

A service bureau performs all of the functions that you would do on your in-house computer. You simply supply them with the data that goes into the computer, such as checks, journal entries, and invoices. The service bureau enters the data and returns the output in the form you want. What this means to you is that you don't have to purchase a computer system or train employees in its use. However, you do lose some flexibility and control over the computer output.

Before choosing a service bureau ask yourself the following questions:

- *Does the bureau have a good reputation in the community?* Does it maintain confidentiality?
- *What other businesses does the bureau serve?* How do they compare in size, purpose, and organization with your own?
- *Is the bureau reliable?* Can it produce the documents as quickly as you need them? Does it have a backup strategy for computer failures?
- *Is the bureau financially sound?* Will it be in business for a long time?
- *What are the bureau's rates?* How do they compare in the long run with owning the computer system and hiring employees to run it?

Time-sharing

Time-sharing is a third possibility. It involves linking up with a source computer owned by another company. That company could be in the time-sharing business, or it could simply share space with you in the same building. In either case, you merely rent a **computer terminal** (monitor and keyboard) and access the main system by telephone. You pay only for the time you actually use the computer.

In considering this option, ask yourself the following:

- Are there security devices available so that no one else can access your files?
- Are the rates such that it actually costs less to time-share than to purchase the rest of the system? (Remember, under this option you still need an employee who can run the computer. Also, the rent on the terminal can run $50–$150 or more per month.)

Most small businesses can use software designed for the vast majority of computer users. This store is featuring a package with such broad appeal. What is it designed to do?

- Does the source computer firm have backup software to protect against computer failures?

Your Software Options

Recall that software is the program that tells the computer what to do. You have basically two routes you can take when choosing software. You can purchase popular programs designed to meet the needs of the vast majority of businesses. Or you can have programs custom designed to meet the unique needs of your business. Here we will consider programs of the first type.

Word Processing/ Desktop Publishing

Word processing software is probably the most popular application software in use today. It allows a business to create all of its basic documents, from letters to invoices to contracts. The most popular of these programs allows the user to see on the computer screen exactly what will be printed on the page.

Word processing software works basically like a typewriter—with one key exception. It automatically wraps text to the next line so that you don't have to hit a return key within paragraphs. It also allows you to make corrections, move text, and format pages before printing out.

Documents produced in this way can be saved on disks for both reference and reuse. This means, among other things, that a business can generate form letters and mailing lists, merge the two, and create hundreds of letters from one original.

More advanced word processing programs allow you to create documents in the same way that publishers do. You can insert pictures and graphs into text and set up pages with columns, just like those in newspapers and magazines. You can even create professional-looking brochures and other promotional materials.

Spreadsheets

Spreadsheet software offers a real advantage to bookkeepers, accountants, and business owners who do their own record keeping. A **spreadsheet** is simply a grid of rows and columns, similar to an accountant's note pad. You use it by inserting numbers, formulas, or words in the boxes, or **cells**, that make up the grid. What makes a spreadsheet so valuable is that if formulas are used, you don't have to do any calculations. The computer does them automatically.

A spreadsheet also allows you to do "what if" analysis. For example, suppose you have the following data on a spreadsheet:

Employee	Salary
A	$20,000
B	$19,000
C	$30,000
D	$25,000
Total	$94,000

Now suppose that you want to know the effect of increasing A's salary to $22,000, B's to $23,000, and C's to $34,000. If in the Total cell you have placed a formula that tells the computer to add the column, when you make the changes the total will automatically be recalculated.

Having done pro forma financial statements, you can no doubt appreciate what a powerful tool this is. If your business wants to consider the effect on profits of various scenarios, the spreadsheet is the most efficient way to do it.

Database Management

If you can picture a file cabinet with all of the files organized inside, then you have a good idea of what a **database management** program does. It allows you to work with several files at once, modifying them and moving them around. Database programs are often used to store client or customer information and mailing lists.

Database software allows you to perform the complex sorting and screening functions mentioned earlier. For example, you can ask your computer to find all customers whose annual purchases exceed $5,000. Or you can ask it to find all vendors in a certain geographic area.

Many programs also allow you to transfer information from a database management program to another program, such as a spreadsheet or word processor. In this way, you can create a report that has both text and data in a table format.

Accounting

While you can take care of all of your accounting needs with a word processor and a spreadsheet, some businesses prefer to have special accounting-only software. This software has ready-made ledgers, journals, inventory control sheets, and financial statements. All you do is enter data in the form that the program requires.

Advanced accounting packages automatically make follow-up entries for you. For example, if you enter information into the journals, it is automatically entered by the computer into the general ledger and the appropriate financial statements. Advanced accounting programs can even write checks and reconcile your business's bank account. Features like these are more than time-savers. They allow you to obtain a clear picture of your business's financial status whenever you wish.

Communications/Electronic Mail

Communications software allows your computer to talk to and interact with other computers, even at a great distance. It does so by using telephone lines and a special piece of equipment called a **modem**.

If yours is a business with locations spread over a wide geographic area, you can use communications software to set up an electronic mail system. One business that relies heavily on such a system is Mrs. Field's Cookies. Every store has a computer terminal that is connected by modem to the main system. Founder and owner Debbi Fields uses that system to send information to and get instant feedback from her employees in every part of the country. In this way, she maintains control over the quality and productivity of every store.

Having communications software also allows you to access large databases such as CompuServe and The Source. These databases have a wealth of information, everything from newspaper articles and stock market quotations to online shopping networks.

Project Management

For businesses that have a project orientation, such as construction or product development firms, project management software is a real help. Using graphics, such a program can set up a time line for a project showing all the steps, the time each takes, and the cumulative costs. It can even prioritize the tasks and flag those that are behind schedule or running over budget. These

Graphics software gives computer users the capability to draw on their monitors. What sort of illustration is the user preparing?

kinds of functions are important to businesses whose profits depend on how quickly and close to budget they finish projects.

Graphics

Many spreadsheet programs include graphics capabilities but only to the extent of bar charts, pie charts, and line graphs. This is sufficient for most business purposes. However, if you frequently do presentations to clients, newsletters, or your own advertising and promotion, you may want to consider **graphics software**. This is a program that allows you to draw and produce pictures in a variety of colors and styles. You can even create overhead transparencies or slide show presentations right on your computer.

Very advanced computer-assisted design (CAD) programs allow you to design products on your computer screen and look at them from any angle. You can even use such a program to animate your design.

Where to Buy Your Computer Equipment

The first place that people think of when they want computer equipment is usually a local retail store. In fact, most computers *are* sold through retail outlets. The reasons for this are simple. Retail stores are easily accessible. There you can see various kinds of computers and software in action and get advice from people who are knowledgeable. You can even find someone to install your computer and contact later if you have any problems. However, you will pay more for all of these advantages.

The next-most-popular source for computer equipment is mail order. You can purchase virtually anything you need from a catalog and have it shipped directly to your business. Ordering through a catalog can save you up to 50 percent on the price. However, you receive no technical support, and you will have to set up the system yourself.

There are two other sources you might want to check. You could buy from the manufacturer directly or from a computer discount outlet. Both options can save you money.

Entrepreneur's Bookshelf

To learn more about the subjects discussed in this chapter, consider reading these books and articles:

- *Computer Wimp No More* by John Bear (© 1992)
- *Your First Computer* by Alan Simpson (© 1992)
- "Computers That Turn a Profit," *D & B Reports* (July–August 1987)
- "When Computerization Fits Just Right," *In Business* (July–August 1987)
- "How to Get the Best Deal from a Computer Dealer," *Inc.* (November 1987)
- "How to Buy the Best PC," *Nation's Business* (January 1988)

Chapter 25 Review

Recapping the Chapter

- Using computers in small business management has the advantages of providing better information more quickly, better internal controls, better use of personnel, and better sales.
- Some problems often associated with computerizing a business are the expense, resistance by employees, computer system failures such as those caused by viruses, and computer crime.
- You can computerize your business by purchasing an in-house system, using a service bureau, or contracting for a time-sharing arrangement.
- The major types of application software are word processing, used to create text-based documents; spreadsheets, used to create financial statements and make projections; and database management, used to organize and modify files.
- Computer equipment can be purchased through retail stores, by mail, directly from the manufacturer, or from computer discount outlets.

Reviewing Vocabulary

Write a sentence for each term below explaining how it is related to either *software* or *hardware*.

- computer integrated manufacturing (CIM)
- computer viruses
- electronic bulletin boards
- microcomputers
- time-sharing
- computer terminal
- spreadsheet
- cells
- database management
- modem
- graphics software

Checking the Facts

1. How can computers provide better internal controls for a manufacturing business?
2. How can computers be used to generate sales for a business?
3. Why are employees sometimes resistant to the use of computers?
4. Explain the meaning of this statement: Garbage in, garbage out.
5. Name two things that might cause a computer system to crash.
6. What can a business owner do to improve the security of his or her computer system and data?
7. Describe four things you should do before buying an in-house computer system.
8. How is communications software used?

Thinking Critically

1. Why is the use of computers becoming so important to small businesses?
2. "To err is human—but to really foul things up, it takes a computer." Do you agree or disagree with this statement? Explain your answer.
3. Explain how you think computers could help in carrying out the following activities:

   - Inventory management in a retail business
   - Quality control in a manufacturing concern
   - Projecting sales in a wholesale operation

Chapter 25 Review

4. Which should come first for a business—the computer or the software? Explain.
5. Explain the difference between a service bureau and a time-share arrangement.
6. How do spreadsheet and database software differ from each other?
7. Assume you are Marcia, the owner of Swim World. What areas of the business would you computerize and why? What are the first five questions you would ask a computer salesperson?

Discussing Key Concepts

1. Computerizing your business will mean laying off several employees. Will you still do it? Why or why not?
2. Suppose your employees are resisting your plan to computerize your business. How would you handle the situation?
3. Given their advantages and disadvantages, which of the various sources for computer equipment would be the best for you?
4. People seem willing to deal with some computers (ATMs, for example) but not others (automated answering services). What do you think accounts for the difference?

Using Basic Skills

Math

1. Your business uses form letters to notify regular customers of upcoming sales. In one morning, you can type 3 such letters from scratch. If you use a computer and a word processing program to save the letter and just replace the name and address on each, you can produce 12 letters in the same time. If you also use database software to merge your customer mailing list with the form letter, you can produce 54 letters. Describe the effect of computer technology on your rate of production:

   - How does your word processing rate compare with your typewriting rate?
   - How does your plus-database rate compare with your word processing rate?
   - How does you plus-database rate compare with your typewriting rate?

Communications

2. You are starting a business to manufacture a new kind of bicycle. Compose a letter to a local computer store explaining your needs and asking the manager to prepare some suggested equipment for next Friday when you will visit the store for a demonstration.

Human Relations

3. Suppose you suspected that one of your employees was accessing and changing files on the company computer. How would you handle the situation? How would you prevent it from occurring again?

Enriching Your Learning

1. Assume that a representative of a computer manufacturer is scheduled to speak to your class. List four questions you would ask.
2. Research two different computers from two different manufacturers (Apple and IBM, for example). Be sure the machines you choose are similar in terms of their capabilities. Write a three-page report comparing and contrasting the two systems.
3. Visit a computer software outlet and ask for a demonstration of one of the kinds of software discussed in this chapter. Review the software for the class based on what you learn.

Chapter 26
Marketing Management

Objectives

After completing this chapter, you will be able to

- explain why marketing management is important to a business,

- identify a new and valuable source of marketing information,
- analyze changes in marketing mix, and
- describe what is involved in preparing a new marketing plan.

Terms to Know

private brand
kiosks
consumer pretests

? Decisions, Decisions

Business was great when we first started. My wife had been making these monogrammed stuffed bears as a hobby. Then she began selling them to people to give as gifts. Pretty soon we had a little plant set up with employees and all, and we were selling to stores all over the state. It seemed that as long as we could turn out stuffed bears, people would buy them.

Then all of a sudden sales took a nose dive. We had no idea why. Up until then, we'd been doing most of our selling by sending catalogs to potential outlets. But with sales in such bad shape, I thought I'd better get out on the road and call on our customers in person.

It didn't take long to find out the problem. Almost every store I went into had somebody else's bears—different designs and shapes, but bears just the same. And they were lower priced.

Well, we were able to get back some of our customers by giving bigger discounts, but it really cut into our profits. Now we have to figure out how to get the business back where it was. We're going to have to answer a lot of hard questions. For example, how can we find out what our customers want now? Should we try to come out with new products? Do we have any alternatives? How can we price competitively and still make a profit? Is there a better way to get the products out? a better way to sell them?

Actually, even if we do figure all this out, I'm still going to feel uneasy. We got caught flat-footed once. How do we keep from getting caught that way again?

Why Marketing Management Is Important

You can't assume that the target markets, customer demands, and competition you identified in starting up your business will remain the same. Markets will change. Customer buying habits will change. Conditions in your business environment will change. What you've got to do is stay on top of all these changes. If you don't, you can lose customers and miss opportunities.

Do you remember the marketing concept? It states that if a business is to succeed and make a profit, it must focus all of its efforts on satisfying its customers. This concept should also be the guiding principle for your day-to-day, ongoing marketing decisions.

In this chapter, we will again look at market research and review your marketing mix. Our focus, however, will be on managing these as ongoing activities.

Continuing Your Market Research

Suppose you are the owner/manager of a tape and CD store. The items that are moving fastest this week may not even be on the charts in a month. To stay profitable, you must keep up with what's going on in your market. The basic tool for doing that is the same one that helped you define your market in the first place—market research.

You were introduced to market research and its techniques in Chapter 10. But now that you have an ongoing business, you have a valuable new source of information—your customers.

Current and former customers are a very useful source of primary information. You can gather information from them in two ways—through surveys and through focus groups. You can take a survey by mail, phone, or personal interview. You might, for example, send a mailing to customers asking their preference for and suggestions about some of the services you offer. You can organize some of your customers into a focus group. They can meet and give you feedback on, say, your product lines.

You can also make use of the wealth of secondary information that is available through your operation. Your own accounting records and sales receipts can give you up-to-date information on expenses and what's moving and what's not. Your suppliers can often provide information on trends and activities that affect your marketing decisions.

Another useful idea is to set up a file of newspaper, magazine, and trade publication articles that pertain to your operation. These articles can range from reports on trends and population shifts to features on new production, financial, or marketing procedures.

As a general rule, collect any information that might affect or be useful to your operation. Information about customer interests, what's going on in your market, or conditions in your business environment will be particularly helpful.

Ongoing market research should be done continually. It will provide you with much of the background you need for your marketing decisions. It will also give you cues when there is a need for more structured and detailed market research.

You can rely on this sort of informal research as the basis for much of your information gathering. However, you will need to plan to review regularly the information you collect. If you don't set the time aside, it will be lost to other things demanding your attention.

At some time, you may want more sophisticated or extensive research conducted for your business. If so, you can consider contracting with a professional market researcher. These services are available, for a fee, to small businesses as well as large corporations.

Reviewing Your Marketing Mix

Ongoing market research provides you with the information you need to monitor your marketing plan. By being aware of what's happening in your market, you can make changes in your marketing strategies (the four P's) as necessary. In this section, we will look at the kinds of changes businesses often have to consider in their product, price, place, and promotion strategies.

As you read about these changes, remember that they have a cost. Before you make any of them, you should always calculate that cost.

Possible Product Changes

Concerns about product strategy are the same for both start-up and ongoing businesses. What goods or services should you offer? How will your products be different from your competitors' products? What can you do to make sure customers can identify your products? The only difference is that now you will be making decisions about existing products rather than projected ones.

You should remember that a change in any one of your products could affect your other products. For example, a change might stimulate sales through increased traffic or cause a loss of sales

Risk Takers, Profit Makers

Paul Van Doren

Some top athletic shoe companies focus on stars, paying high-profile athletes millions of dollars to endorse their latest models. Orange, California-based Vans targets the streets. By offering basic styles, casual comfort, and long-lasting quality, Vans appeals to everyone, from scholars to skateboarders.

Paul Van Doren, the founder of Vans, grew up in the athletic shoe business. He advanced from sweeper to vice-president at a factory in Boston. After a year at a new plant in California, however, he got tired of working for inept supervisors and making money for retailers. So, he quit to go into the shoe business for himself.

Van Doren designed a basic canvas shoe with rugged soles. He planned to sell his shoes through his own stores at sensible prices. In 1966, he and three friends founded the Van Doren Rubber Company.

The first years for Van Doren were hectic. When the first store opened across the street from the original plant, it had display models but no stock—just empty boxes. Van Doren took orders, then made shoes to be picked up later that day. But on the first afternoon, he didn't have exact change. So, he handed over the shoes and asked to be paid later. (Each customer did in fact return with the money.) Today every Vans store carries stock, but they still fill custom orders in 19 days or less for little or no extra cost.

With hard work and long hours, the Van Doren Rubber Company grew rapidly. To sell enough shoes to keep the factory running, a new store opened every week. From Monday to Sunday, Van Doren would find a store, sign the lease, remodel the facility, install racks, fill inventory, and then hire and train a manager. Today 70 outlet stores serve Southern California, and 4,500 retailers serve the country.

Only once has Vans' development snagged. Following the huge success resulting from exposure in the 1980 film *Fast Times at Ridgemont High*, Paul Van Doren stepped down from management. But without his guidance, Vans overdiversified. Offering American-made shoes for soccer, skydiving, and every other sport proved to be costly. By 1983, Vans was bankrupt. Van Doren returned to refocus the company. Now it's bigger than ever.

After 25 years, Van Doren's original shoe design and the company's strategy remain intact. Vans is still based in Orange, and the manufacturing process has changed little. Richard P. Leeuwenburg, who has been CEO since 1988, has instilled the Van Doren operation with new vigor by increasing Vans' marketing nationwide and establishing a second factory in San Diego. Like its shoes with their thick waffle soles, Vans is now geared for a long and sturdy life.

through negative consumer reaction. You should always consider those kinds of effects before making any decision to change your products or product lines.

ADDING PRODUCTS.   Before adding products to your line or adding lines, ask yourself these questions:

- *Is there sufficient demand to add the new product?* A few people may have expressed interest, but remember—you've got to sell enough to break even.
- *Is the product consistent with your current business?* It may be a good idea for somebody's operation but not for yours.
- *Will it compete with your current products?* It may sell very well. But if it takes away an equal amount in current sales, what's the point?
- *Is it the best use and application of your economic resources?* Can your money, labor, and facilities be better used by putting them to work in connection with another product line or another part of your marketing mix?

ELIMINATING PRODUCTS.   One reason to eliminate a product is because it isn't selling.

Coffee company Maxwell House added this item to its product lines. Was it a good addition or not? Explain.

Sometimes businesspeople are slow to take such action, thinking they can *make* the item sell. But not cutting the product can lead to a build up of inventory and financial losses. By not cutting it, you may be using sales and/or production efforts unwisely.

Another reason for eliminating products is to simplify your line of goods or services. This allows you to focus on the things you do well. However, you should also consider whether or not a broader range of products is necessary to compete.

CHANGING PRODUCTS.   Changing the style or design of your product, if the changes are consistent with customer demands, can give you a competitive edge. For example, you may make changes to keep in step with current fashions. You may also improve your products by taking advantage of the latest technology.

However, changing your product may affect your prices and distribution. Timing, too, must be considered. You want your offerings to be up to date, but you don't want to be ahead of the market.

CHANGING BRANDS, PACKAGING, OR LABELS.   If you manufacture products under a variety of brand names, you may want to consolidate them all under one brand. This could help to build a brand preference among customers. Or, if you carry other people's brands for resale, you may be able to sell more by offering your own **private brand**. (These are products packaged with your name on them.)

You might want to change packaging and labels to enhance the attractiveness, interest, and salability of your products. You might also change your packaging for environmental reasons. For example, in an effort to reduce waste, some manufacturers are using less packaging. Other businesses are using a type of packaging that is more degradable in landfills. Because so many consumers are concerned about the environment, these kinds of changes could make your product more appealing.

Many businesses have changed their product packaging in response to environmental concerns. In this case, what is the product, and how has the packaging apparently been altered?

REVISING GUARANTEES AND SERVICE POLICIES. Improving or adding guarantees or service policies may help build customer confidence and increase sales. Particularly with big-ticket items, these guarantees and policies can make the difference in a sale. Of course, you must be capable of providing the additional guaranteed services.

Possible Price Changes

Coming up with your original pricing strategy was a complex process. What is more, once you have established prices, ways of changing them are limited. Nonetheless, you must attend to this strategy continually to make the most of your opportunities.

PRICING FOR PROFIT. As you know, profit or loss is determined by the relationship between your selling price and your costs. This fact of business life will, from time to time, cause you to consider adjusting prices as a way to increase profits. You could increase prices or lower prices to increase sales volume.

If you are thinking of doing either, you must consider two factors. First, are your products' prices elastic or inelastic? Recall from Chapter 2 that a price is elastic if a small change in price causes a significant change in demand. A price is inelastic if a change in price has little or no effect on the demand. Second, what are your competitor's prices? These questions must be examined before making your final decision.

REACTING TO MARKET PRICES. As part of your ongoing market research, you will want to keep an eye on current market prices for your products. If you are in a competitive market and prices fall, your customers can get away from you quickly if you don't lower your prices to stay competitive. If prices are on the rise, you have two choices. You can raise prices similarly and increase your profits. Or you can choose to keep prices lower and create customer goodwill by not taking advantage of the situation.

REVISING TERMS OF SALE. Since how a customer pays is part of pricing, revising terms of sale is another way to make changes to your pricing strategy. You could make purchases easier by changing your credit policies. You could implement or revise trade, quantity, or cash discounts. You might choose to offer leasing or consider arranging financing for customers with an outside lender. Whether or not any of these options would be useful will, of course, depend on the nature of your business.

Possible Place Changes

When you make changes in your ongoing place strategy, they will most likely be in the areas of location, layout, and availability. To some extent, you may also make changes in your channels of distribution.

IMPROVING LOCATION. As your business grows, you may look for ways to improve your location. You could extend it by using **kiosks**, or stands, on street corners or in malls. With some businesses, you could "take your location to the customer" through mobile units.

You might also want to consider more permanent and substantial changes. You might add outlets or branch operations. You could change your base location to be more accessible to customers. Because these are more permanent steps, however, they would have to be coordinated with your plans for growth.

REARRANGING LAYOUT. You may also want to rearrange the physical layout of your operation. For retail and some service businesses, this change can enhance sales. Adding or expanding parking or access to your business can do the same. If you are a manufacturer, wholesaler, or extractor, you might reorganize how your goods are physically distributed. This could increase your capability to serve your customers and, thus, increase sales.

INCREASING AVAILABILITY. Availability is generally the easiest adjustment you can make in

Changes in a business's place strategy can take many forms. What has this restaurant apparently done?

your place strategy. It can also be the most effective because it makes it possible for your customers to do business with you.

Let's say, you have a tutoring service. Presently it is open until 5:00 P.M. on weekdays. You can increase your availability and business by staying open in the evenings and on Saturdays. Consider another example—you supply food to restaurants. You may choose to change your delivery schedule to match your customers' needs better. These are both ways of increasing availability.

CHANGING CHANNELS OF DISTRIBUTION. The type of business you have and where you are in the channel determine the choices you have here. If you are in a manufacturing business, you have some control over channel decisions. You can continually look out for ways to improve your channel choices. For example, you could choose a more direct channel with fewer intermediaries.

Businesses that are at other points in the channel have more limited options. If you are a retailer or wholesaler, you could look for product sources that can deliver more effectively and efficiently. You could also look for alternatives in that part of the channel where you do have some control—between you and your customers.

Before you make any change in channels, you should look at the new channel, keeping in mind three questions:

- What effect will the new channel have on your sales volume and stability?
- What effect will it have on your gross profit?
- What effect will it have on your operating costs?

Possible Promotion Changes

Although the promotion strategy is a part of the marketing mix, it is often treated separately. In fact, decisions made about promotion make up a promotion plan apart from the marketing plan.

Here we will look at the kinds of changes you might have to make in sales management. We will look at short-term changes, such as choosing salespeople, using advertising dollars more effectively, and stimulating sales. Then we will look at long-term planning.

Remember, as you make changes in one part of your promotion mix, you may affect other parts of the mix. Sometimes you will make changes in combination and sometimes in isolation. In either case, you should always consider their impact on the rest of the promotional mix.

GETTING THE RIGHT SALESPEOPLE. Choosing the right salespeople is critical. Recall from Chapter 18 that personal selling helps to ensure that a customer's needs are satisfactorily met. Compare this to the marketing concept, and you can see how good salespeople help a business make a profit.

When you need to add salespeople, use the following guidelines:

- *Hire people who understand selling.* Such people know that selling is less a matter of getting customers to buy and more a matter of helping them make good buying decisions.
- *Hire people who have the personality traits needed to sell successfully.* Those traits include being people-oriented, enthusiastic, sincere, tactful, and positive. To be effective they must also be good listeners, good communicators, and problem solvers. Courtesy, empathy, perceptiveness, and poise are valuable traits, too.

MAKING THE MOST OF YOUR ADVERTISING DOLLARS. Advertising is expensive—especially if you're not getting results. So, if something isn't working, you'll want to change it as quickly as possible.

Most advertising problems stem from using ineffective media and/or timing. You can find out if your advertising is working by using some market research techniques that can give you quick feedback.

One technique uses **consumer pretests**. With this procedure, a panel of consumers evaluates an ad before it runs. Another technique asks a group of consumers for their reaction after they have seen or heard an ad. You can also get feedback on your advertising from your customers, or by watching for whether or not sales are generated by the advertising effort.

You might also choose to use advertising researchers, like Arbitron Ratings Company. They can provide you with the numbers and demographics of viewers, listeners, or readers for different media.

STIMULATING SALES. Regardless of how well you have thought out your promotional plan, you may at times find that sales are not moving at the pace you had planned. You need a jump start to get them rolling again. More salespeople would not likely help in this situation.

Nor would more of the same advertising or other promotional activities you are currently using.

You could, however, use sales promotions. Recall that these are displays, premiums, sweepstakes and contests, rebates, and samples. Adding such things to your promotion mix is often effective because they give people an incentive to buy and build interest in your products. In fact, they are most often used to enhance other promotional tools. And they can be put in place quickly.

LONG-TERM PLANNING. To do long-term planning for your promotion, you should begin by reviewing your plans on a regular schedule. This may be as often as quarterly or semiannually.

You will start with your sales forecast for the upcoming period. From this forecast, you can arrive at a promotional budget necessary to support that level of sales.

One way to ensure that you get the most from your advertisements is to pretest them on consumers. How do you think this technique might work?

Next, decide on a revised promotional mix. As with your original mix, you want the best possible combination of personal selling, advertising, publicity, and sales promotion for your business.

When deciding, you will have several resources to draw from. This includes your market research, previous plans, and recent short-term decisions. The new experience you are gaining will also give you an idea of what works and what doesn't. For example, you may not know exactly how much advertising is enough, but you'll have a sense of how much is too much or too little. And you will have a knowledge of the market and your competitors' strategies.

Once you've determined your mix, you can prepare a new promotional plan. Use the format presented in Chapter 18 to detail out your plan for the upcoming period.

Revising Your Marketing Mix and Plan

As you make changes to each of your marketing strategies, you will probably create the need to make changes in your other strategies. Let's look at an example.

You are the operator of a "no-frills" driving range. You decide to upgrade your facility by covering the tee areas where your customers hit the golf balls. This would be considered a change in product. Then, you would probably consider changing your price strategy to pay for the improvement. You would certainly want to advertise to let the golfing public know about your improved facility. This change in promotion strategy could generate more business. And, you would now have the capability to stay open during bad weather in the summer and even in the winter. This would be a change in availability, which is part of the place strategy.

Ideally, as you change one strategy, you will change the others. In reality, however, it often doesn't work that way. Because owners are so busy with other business activities, they often do not make all the changes as quickly as would be profitable. Or the most effective changes are not made at all.

Regularly scheduled review and revision of your marketing plan can remedy this situation. It can provide an opportunity to identify and make strategy changes that should have been made but weren't. It can also ensure that your new tactical plan objectives are incorporated into the plan.

Making long-term changes to your marketing plan is much like making long-term promotion plans. You should review and revise on a regular schedule (at least annually). A regular review ensures that your marketing mix is as effective and efficient as possible and that your new tactical plan objectives are implemented. You should also use all the resources available to you. These include market research results, previous plans, recent decisions, and, of course, your own business experience.

After you have reviewed your marketing strategies and changed your marketing mix to meet new challenges, you will have a new marketing plan. This plan can then be used to guide your marketing decisions for the upcoming period.

Entrepreneur's Bookshelf

To learn more about the subjects discussed in this chapter, consider reading these books:

- *Marketing on a Shoestring* by J. Davidson (© 1988)
- *Market Smarts* by Allan J. Magrath (© 1988)

Chapter 26 Review

Recapping the Chapter

- Marketing management is important to a business because it provides a way to keep up with changes in markets, customer buying habits, and business conditions.
- In an ongoing business, you have a valuable additional source of primary information—your customers.
- Changes in one marketing mix strategy (product, price, place, and promotion) often impact one or more of the other strategies. In addition, every such change has a cost attached to it.
- To update your marketing plan, you should (1) review it regularly, (2) look at recent research and decisions, and (3) make changes to meet new challenges.

Reviewing Vocabulary

Write a sentence describing a marketing management situation for each term below.

- private brand
- kiosks
- consumer pretests

Checking the Facts

1. Why must you keep up with the changes in your market?
2. Name two market research techniques that are especially useful for gathering information from current and former customers.
3. What is the first question to ask when you are deciding whether or not to add new products to your line?

4. What can you do to prices to increase profits?
5. Where can adjustments be most easily made to the place strategy?
6. Why is it important to take quick action on advertising that isn't working?
7. What are the two reasons for at least annual revision of your marketing mix and plan?

Thinking Critically

1. How does the marketing concept affect day-to-day marketing decisions?
2. Review the start-up marketing decisions you made in Chapter 11. How do they compare with the ongoing marketing decisions presented here? How are they different? Are there any similarities?
3. How does not raising prices when market prices are rising create customer goodwill?
4. Compare the traits needed to be a successful salesperson with the traits of the three leadership styles described in Chapter 21. Also, compare them with characteristics needed to be a successful entrepreneur from Chapter 3. What conclusions can you draw? Explain.

Discussing Key Concepts

1. Come up with a product that you might add to your business. How might this new product affect your other strategies?
2. With your proposed business in mind, design a one-page customer survey. How often would you conduct this survey? Who would you give it to? What questions would you ask?

Chapter 26 Review

3. How would the elasticity of your products' prices affect your decision to change them?
4. Let's say you own a small retail store that sells wicker furniture, baskets, and handicrafts. Sales have been very slow this fall and you want business to pick up for Christmas. The only promotion you've done is advertising in two of the local newspapers. Design a new promotion strategy for the upcoming fall quarter.

Using Basic Skills

Math
1. You are the owner of a bicycle shop. Recently, you decided to sell a new style of bike that, with the suggested retail price, would give you a gross profit of $150. After three weeks you have sold ten of the new bikes and are thinking about whether or not to add the line permanently. The problem is that every new bike you sold was to someone who came in looking for a regular bike. You estimate that gross profits from the ten sales you "lost" would have been $75 for four of the bikes, $125 for four others, and $200 each for two "superbikes." Should you add the new bikes permanently to your selection?

Communication
2. As the owner of the wicker and handicrafts store described above (Discussing Key Concepts, Item 4), make up a flier to announce your new sales promotions.

Human Relations
3. You are going to add a salesperson to service current customers and call on new prospects. An employee, who has been with you for the past year and has done an excellent job as a stockperson, tells you that he's really interested in the job. You would like to give him an opportunity, but he doesn't appear to have the traits to be successful in sales. How should you handle the situation?

Enriching Your Learning

1. Interview the manager of a market research firm to find out what services the firm could provide that would be useful to your business. Also, find out how much their services would cost.
2. If you are employed, interview your employer or marketing manager about the following:

   - *Ongoing market research conducted by your company.* What procedures are used? What kind of data do they gather? How do they use it in making marketing strategy decisions?
   - *Marketing strategy decisions.* What kind of decisions most frequently have to be made? Which are the toughest? Why? How often do they update the marketing plan?

   If you are not working, interview the owner or marketing manager of a company in your selected field.

Chapter 27

Social and Ethical Responsibility

Objectives

After completing this chapter, you will be able to

- explain what constitutes socially responsible conduct in business,
- discuss the responsibilities that businesses have toward their customers and the environment,

- describe some situations in which businesses often find themselves facing ethical decisions, and
- suggest a procedure for developing a formal code of ethics.

Terms to Know

philanthropy
proactive
ethics
bribes
dumping
conflict of interest
norms

Decisions, Decisions

You're not going to believe this. I'm 18 years old and going to graduate from high school this year. I don't have a job yet, but yesterday I received a credit card in the mail. It has my name on it and a credit limit of $1,000. Are these people crazy or what?

I took the card to school and showed it to my entrepreneurship teacher. She used it to start a discussion. The gist of it was how businesses entice people like me into spending money we don't have.

The class came up with all sorts of examples. You say you're "unlucky." You've had a few accidents and a couple of tickets. Never mind—one company will get you insurance. You say you just declared bankruptcy. Never mind—another company will give you credit. You say you'd just love to drive that luxury car, but you don't have the luxury income to go with it. Never mind—it's yours to lease for just $149 a month.

Nowhere that you can see or hear is there any mention of how much you're going to pay all totaled. Take the car example. They tell you in the fine print that you have to put $5,000 down to get the $149 rate. *And* you have to lease the car for five or six years. Some deal!

Fact is, though, that there are probably lots of people out there uninformed, desperate, or just plain foolish enough to take them up on it. Actually, I have to admit that I toyed with the idea of using my new line of credit to buy a new amp for my guitar. But I knew I'd have no way of making the payments. I know a trap when I see one.

What I want to know is, How can companies make those kinds of offers? Is that a responsible way to do business?

What Is Socially Responsible Conduct?

The history of this country is rich in stories of legendary entrepreneurs like J. P. Morgan, John D. Rockefeller, and Andrew Carnegie. While some of these men were considered ruthless in business, they all felt a responsibility to give something back to society.

Morgan gave books and numerous works of art to libraries and museums. (His own library was turned into a famous research institution by his son.) Rockefeller gave away over a half billion dollars in his lifetime. Much of the money went to foundations that even today fight hunger, disease, and similar conditions. Carnegie established over 2,800 libraries as well as the Carnegie Institute for scientific research. He also financed the construction of New York City's famous concert hall, Carnegie Hall.

Today, however, social responsibility in business is more than a matter of **philanthropy**. It has to do with the way you conduct your enterprise on a daily basis.

Social responsibility means that a business acknowledges that it has a contract with society. That contract implies a number of duties. These include making safe, good-quality products, treating customers right, and operating honestly. Socially responsible companies tend to improve the quality of life for everyone. They also inspire loyalty in their employees and customers.

Your Responsibility to Consumers

Responsibility to consumers is the most frequently mentioned social responsibility that businesses have. As a socially responsible business owner, you will have to do more than provide your customers with the products they want. You will have to provide those products at fair prices. You will also have a duty to inform your customers and protect them from unsafe products.

It would be nice to think that businesses are self-motivated to do such things. Unfortunately, that has not been the case. Today much of what business is doing to protect consumers is the direct result of two forces—the consumer movement and government regulation.

The father of the consumer movement is Ralph Nader. He began by focusing on unsafe automobiles and branched out to other areas where he felt consumers were being treated unfairly. It is perhaps a measure of his success that today automobile companies go out of their way to emphasize in their ads the very issue Nader started with—safety. Other movement institutions like Consumers Union, which tests and evaluates products, have had a comparably dramatic impact on product quality.

Government regulation has also brought about changes in business conduct. Laws like the Truth-in-Lending Act, discussed in Chapter 12, ensure that businesses fully inform customers about purchases. Others, like the Fair Credit Billing Act, specify how quickly businesses must respond to consumer complaints.

After more than two decades of such "encouragement," businesses today often go out of their way to do more than is expected for their customers. Even though the regulatory climate has changed (moving back toward deregulation), businesses persist in their new habits. The proof is in what many businesses today acknowledge is their most important competitive tool—customer service.

Your Responsibility to the Environment

Have you noticed how many companies are also using advertising campaigns that are environmentally oriented? Oil companies are showing how they protect species of birds. Chemical companies advertise how they can protect crops without poisoning the environment with pesticides. Companies that formerly distributed products in spray containers now advertise pump containers that emit no fluorocarbons into the atmosphere. As with safety-oriented ads, these ads too are evidence of an established trend.

Like consumerism, the trend toward environmental concern has its roots in a movement going back more than 20 years. As a result of that movement, the Environmental Protection Agency (EPA) was established. It was charged with implementing and enforcing environmental statutes. Today, for example, the agency makes sure that businesses properly dispose of hazardous wastes. This is a task so serious that the penalties for failing to comply include imprisonment.

Environmentalism has also been reinforced by the media and the public in general. Both are very hard on any business that pollutes the environment in a massive or dramatic way. As an example, consider the public furor over the Exxon Valdez oil spill in Prince William Sound in 1989. The company's slow response and reluctance to take full responsibility seriously damaged its image.

Today many companies have learned from Exxon's mistakes. They have adopted a **proactive** policy on the environment. In other words, they have set about establishing a record of sound environmental decision making in advance of any problems. And they have aggressively promoted their efforts. For example, another oil company, Amoco, used to produce the foam containers for businesses like McDonald's. It has since begun recycling foam products and

Today businesses are far more environmentally aware than they were in the past. What is the likely result if they are not?

educating people and communities nationwide on the value of such programs.

What Does It Mean to Be Ethical?

Ethics are simply guidelines for human behavior. They help us decide how to act in certain situations, especially those in which honesty, integrity, and fairness are involved. Ethics set the boundaries for what we believe to be correct and moral behavior.

Businesspeople are sometimes portrayed as ruthless, suggesting that they will do anything for money. Perhaps this stereotype comes from the fact that in a free enterprise system companies *must* make a profit to stay in business. However, most businesses do not earn their profits by unethical means. In fact, many entrepreneurs start their businesses for reasons other than money. They are motivated by things like independence, adventure, and achievement.

Are Everyone's Ethics the Same?

People do not necessarily share the same ethical values. If they did, ethics wouldn't be the issue that it is.

Some employees, for example, feel that it is all right to steal from the company they work for. They take pens, computer disks, paper, and other "insignificant" items. They justify this conduct by saying that "the company owes me this" or "the company can afford it." Other employees abuse their expense accounts by charging their company for items that are really personal.

Employers can be less than honest, too. They may try to avoid taxes by not reporting employee earnings or by hiding money abroad, where the IRS can't find it. They may fail to report or remedy unsafe working conditions.

Risk Takers, Profit Makers

Ben Cohen and Jerry Greenfield

Ben Cohen and Jerry Greenfield wanted to do something for a living more fun than driving a cab and working as a lab technician. They decided to make ice cream. Of course, at the time, they had no idea how ice cream was made. So, in 1978 they invested five dollars in a correspondence course, and shortly thereafter began producing Ben and Jerry's Ice Cream.

Initially, they dispensed their treat from a renovated gas station. Within a year, however, they were distributing it in pint containers to neighboring restaurants and grocery stores. Sales continued to grow as they increased their distribution from one state to the next. Before long Ben and Jerry's Ice Cream had become a national favorite. *Time* touted it as "the best in the world."

From the beginning Cohen and Greenfield wanted to create a socially responsible company. As a part of this commitment, Cohen and Greenfield started the Ben and Jerry Foundation, a nonprofit institution that funds community organizations. The company donates 7.5 percent of its pretax earnings to the foundation each year.

But Cohen and Greenfield have not confined themselves to such behind-the-scenes efforts. They've put their convictions right on and in their products. They've designed ice cream novelties and flavors to support specific social concerns.

For example, their Peace Pops ice cream bars provide information on the label about "1% for Peace," a nonprofit effort to redirect 1 percent of the national defense budget to nonmilitary purposes. Sales of their Rain Forest Crunch ice cream, which uses nuts from rain forest trees, contribute to the preservation of South America's rain forests. Chocolate Fudge Brownie ice cream directly helps train and employ disadvantaged youths from the inner city.

Cohen and Greenfield are equally concerned about how their company's operation affects the environment. For example, the company is researching the possibility of using cellophane from plant cells instead of plastic to wrap some of its products. Plans are also in the works to recycle plastic ingredient buckets by turning them into such things as loose-leaf binders and key rings.

Not all of these efforts have been met with unanimous approval. Some top company managers objected to "1% for Peace" and Peace Pops. They thought supporting such efforts might jeopardize the company's profits. In such instances, Cohen and Greenfield have stuck to their convictions. With their net income growing at an annual rate of 39 percent, they have proved that a company can have a social conscience and its profit, too.

AT SPECIAL RISK—SMALL BUSINESSES.
Unfortunately, small businesses are more likely to do things that are ethically questionable. It is not that their owners or employees are fundamentally less honest. They are just more likely to be under the kind of economic pressures that threaten their survival. The following factors add to their vulnerability:

• Small companies are generally less structured and formal.
• They do not have the resources, such as public relations people and lobbyists, to deal with ethical problems.
• They don't take the time to identify potential ethical problems.

This is not to say that larger companies are immune to ethically questionable conduct. However, they are less likely to be operating in a survival mode. They also tend to be more in the public eye. As a result, they are more careful about how they do business.

WHAT A DIFFERENCE A CULTURE MAKES.
Dealing in international markets presents some especially challenging ethical dilemmas for American businesses. In fact, some businesses have chosen to avoid international markets entirely because of such difficulties. Here are some areas in which different ethical standards may apply abroad:

• **Bribes.** These are illegal payments made to secure special services for a business or special consideration for its products. In many parts of the world, bribes of one sort or another are an accepted part of doing business. It is important, therefore, that you determine your company's policy on giving or taking bribes *before* you begin doing business abroad.
• *Patent or copyright infringement.* Some countries are simply not respectful of patents held by foreign nationals. They force foreign inventors to go to court to enforce their rights. Other countries draw out the patenting process that foreigners must go through. Often

there is a hidden motive behind such tactics. The delay allows their own nationals to familiarize themselves with the invention and then patent similar devices first.
• *Unfair pricing.* **Dumping** is probably the most commonly protested form of unfair pricing. It occurs when a nation sells its products abroad at below cost. It is illegal to dump products in the United States. However, in other countries (notably Japan), the practice is an accepted part of being aggressively competitive. Being aware of such practices will help you evaluate your business prospects realistically, both here and abroad.

Special Problems for Entrepreneurs

Entrepreneurs, by definition, operate in dynamic environments under a great deal of pressure. In such situations, the temptation is great to put aside ethics to meet a short-term obligation or make a short-term gain. Entrepreneurs, therefore, need to be aware of their own ethical values (as well as those of their employees) if they are not to sacrifice the future of their businesses.

One type of ethical problem that businesspeople frequently face is **conflict of interest**. Consider an example. On the 20th anniversary of Walt Disney World in Florida, the company gave free trips to the resort to journalists, securities analysts, travel agents, and convention planners from 35 countries. You can imagine their motivation. The amount of publicity and goodwill the gesture created was immeasurable. However, the gesture also created a conflict for the journalists and Wall Street analysts. Why? Because they are supposed to have an objective point of view. But how could they report anything negative about the Disney Corporation after they had been treated so well by that firm? Their gratitude toward Disney and their responsibility to their readers were in conflict.

What should the journalists and analysts have done? Many would say that they should have turned down the trips. That would have been a sacrifice to most of them, but sticking to your principles often is.

Consider another example. A major university (University A) was up for renewal of a grant to provide a masters degree program in an African nation. They learned that another American university (University B) was willing to pay a bribe to officials in the country to ensure that they got the grant. University A was unwilling to do so. They subsequently lost the grant they had had for a number of years. University A had a firm ethics policy and stood by it. University B apparently had no such policy.

Now, you may be thinking, "But University B won." In the short term, it did. But remember, you are in business for the long term, and your integrity is what will ensure that your customers keep coming back. That is the only way your business will grow and thrive.

Developing a Code of Ethics

Many businesses find that developing a set of guidelines that spells out appropriate business conduct is helpful in situations like those described above. Such collections of guidelines are called codes of ethics.

WRITTEN VS. UNWRITTEN CODES. Codes of ethics can be written or unwritten. Unwritten codes are simply **norms**, or ways of doing things that have come about over time. For example, in your business it may be understood that salespeople do not accept any gifts, except maybe an occasional meal. This rule is not written down anywhere. It is just passed on verbally from one salesperson to another.

Formal, or written codes, usually grow out of unwritten ones. What would prompt a business to reduce long-standing norms to writing? Probably a growing awareness of the potential

Specifying the kinds of gifts (like meals) that company employees can accept from clients or suppliers is a common element in codes of ethics. What potential ethical difficulties do such gifts present?

for misunderstandings. This potential is liable to increase the longer the business is in operation and the more it grows. There may also be an increasing awareness over time that the company has more to lose. Once established, it would have valuable relationships to protect and goodwill painstakingly built up over numerous transactions. All of this could be destroyed very quickly by the careless actions of someone in the company.

HOW TO DEVELOP A FORMAL CODE. Once your new business is up and running, then, it might be wise to find some time to consider potential ethical issues. To develop a set of guidelines, consider these steps:

- *With your employees, brainstorm situations likely to present ethical dilemmas for the company.* If an entrepreneur understands the industry in which he or she is operating, it should be fairly easy to hypothesize about potential ethical problems the business might face. For example, an export company might have to do business in a country where paying someone "under the table" is accepted practice. If the owner understands this, he or she can better prepare employees to deal with the situation.
- *Discuss potential solutions.* Have your employees offer suggestions on how they might handle these situations. (This technique will give you a better sense of their values.) Consider the merits of the various alternatives. Your goal is to achieve an outcome that is more positive than negative for everyone involved.
- *Write a set of general guidelines based on the outcome of your discussions.* The guidelines will probably offer a range of acceptable ways to deal with the types of situations that are likely to occur.

A code of ethics arrived at in this manner can form a basis for decision making in your organization. It can also ensure that ethics are an integral part of the way your company does business.

As part of its code of ethics, one company (Cray Research, Inc.) has its employees use the following question as a standard of conduct: How would I feel if my actions appeared on the front page of the newspaper for my family and friends to see? To get a feel for how such a standard might work, try it yourself the next time you are unsure about what to do in a particular situation. You may find that you want to incorporate this standard into your own personal ethical values— and into your business from the moment you start up.

Entrepreneur's Bookshelf

To learn more about the subjects discussed in this chapter, consider reading these books and articles:

- *The Complete Guide to Executive Manners* by Letitia Baldridge (© 1985)
- *The Courage of Conviction* by Philip L. Berman (© 1986)
- "Public vs. Business Expectations: Two Views on Social Responsibility for Small Business" by James J. Chrisman and Fred L. Fry, *Journal of Small Business Management* (January 1982)
- "Ethical Problems Encountered by U.S. Small Businesses in International Marketing" by Michael A. Mayo, *Journal of Small Business Management* (April 1991)
- *New Venture Creation: Entrepreneurship in the 1990s* by Jeffry A. Timmons (© 1990)
- "Can You Afford to Be Ethical?" The *Inc.* FaxPoll™, *Inc.* (December 1992)

Chapter 27 Review

Recapping the Chapter

- A socially responsible company is one that makes safe, good-quality products, treats its customers right, and operates honestly.
- A business has a duty to protect its customers from unsafe products and misinformation. It also has a responsibility to do business in such a way that the environment is not damaged.
- Businesses often face ethical dilemmas when their economic survival is threatened, when doing business abroad (where ethical practices may differ), and in situations that create conflicts of interest.
- A business owner can develop a formal (or written) code of ethics by (1) working with employees to brainstorm potential ethical dilemmas, (2) discussing how these situations might be handled, and (3) writing a set of guidelines that spell out acceptable solutions.

Reviewing Vocabulary

Demonstrate your understanding of the following terms by providing two examples *not found in your text* for each. Describe your examples in one or two sentences.

- philanthropy
- proactive
- ethics
- bribes
- dumping
- conflict of interest
- norms

Checking the Facts

1. How did the legendary entrepreneurs of American history demonstrate social responsibility in their time?
2. Why have businesses become more concerned about product safety and quality?
3. Name two groups that monitor businesses to make sure that they are not damaging the environment.
4. Why are small businesses more likely to do things that are ethically questionable?
5. Why are large firms less likely to take chances where ethical behavior is concerned?
6. Describe three business practices that are unethical in the United States but may be acceptable abroad.
7. If a code of ethics is not written down, how is it perpetuated?
8. Explain why a business owner might want to develop a formal code of ethics for his or her business.
9. What ethical standard does Cray Research suggest that its employees use to evaluate their conduct?

Critical Thinking

1. What is the difference between social responsibility and ethical responsibility?
2. How do socially responsible firms improve the quality of life for everyone?
3. Think of a company whose advertising is based on how it works to protect the environment.

   - What are the expressed goals of the company?
   - What are the unadvertised goals?

Chapter 27 Review

4. A friend offers to let you copy his new software to save you the purchase price. Would you do it? Why or why not?
5. Suppose you are in the office of a competitor and you notice a sheet of paper on the desk that looks like the numbers for a marketing plan. Your host leaves the room to get you some coffee. Should you look at the paper? What would you do and why?
6. What is the value of developing a written code of ethics?

Discussing Key Concepts

1. Do you believe that most businesses act responsibly toward consumers? Can you think of a company that has not? Describe the company's behavior and the consequences.
2. Should businesses that accidentally pollute the environment have to pay cleanup costs and damages? Why or why not?
3. What effect, if any, does the possibility of monetary gain have on business ethics?
4. Do you believe that you have the "right" to take things like pens, paper, and computer disks from the place where you work? Why or why not?
5. Should American businesses pay (or accept) bribes while operating in countries where bribes are the norm? Explain your answer.

Using Your Skills

Math
1. If your community recycling center will pay you five cents a can for aluminum cans, how many would you have to recycle to earn $20?

Communication
2. You have determined through observation and reports from others that one of your employees has been taking office supplies home for personal use. You feel that it is necessary to express your anger at this practice. Write a memo to your employees explaining why this practice is not acceptable and the effect it has on the company. Include a statement of the consequences of continuing the practice.

Human Relations
3. You have recently decided to begin exporting your product to the former Soviet Union. From talking with other businesspeople, you have learned that it is customary to pay people to get through the bureaucratic maze. What would you do to ensure that your employees handle the situation in a way that is appropriate?

Enriching Your Learning

1. Interview two entrepreneurs, one in a service business and one in a goods business. Find out what unique ethical problems they each face. Then inquire if they have written codes of ethics. (If so, ask for a copy or a description.) Present your findings in an oral report to the class.
2. In a 2–3 page paper, describe a situation in which you faced an ethical problem. How did you deal with it? What helped you arrive at your final decision?

Chapter 28
Making Your Business Grow

Objectives

After completing this chapter, you will be able to

- distinguish intensive, integrative, and diversification growth strategies;

- discuss some of the advantages and disadvantages of expanding a business; and
- describe different sources of funding for expansion.

Terms to Know

market
  penetration
master franchise
  agreement
vertical
  integration
horizontal
  integration
diversification
synergistic
  diversification
horizontal
  diversification
conglomerate
  diversification
private placements
prospectus
public stock
  offering
employee stock
  option plans
  (ESOPs)

Decisions, Decisions

Gee, where did the time go? Would you believe—Swim World's been in business three years now!

It's been tough, but all considered, I think things have gone pretty smoothly. Our target market when we began was school swim teams. We've worked really hard to get the business of all the teams in this part of the state. Right now our market share is about 65 percent, which I think is pretty good.

But Marcia says the business has reached a crossroads. Do we want to remain small and just service the customers we have, or do we want to expand?

Well, you can probably guess what Marcia thinks. No consultations needed—Swim World's gonna grow! The real question is how? Should we try to win more customers from our competitors—you know, capture 85 percent of the market? Should we start selling other kinds of products, like maybe designer swimsuits or beach clothes? Or should we open a second store in another part of the state? How's that for a group of challenging choices?

Timing Your Expansion

If as an entrepreneur you have put together a good team and developed a viable idea, your new business will not remain small for long. A successful business at some point will start to grow.

What choices do you have for expanding your business when it reaches that stage? When you decide that your business is ready, you can choose from among three different approaches.

Using Intensive Growth Strategies

The first approach takes advantage of what are called intensive growth strategies. These provide growth by exploiting opportunities *within a business's current market*.

A business that wants to increase sales to its target customers would consider this approach. It might come by those additional sales in one of three ways.

Market Penetration

Market penetration is simply attempting to increase sales by using more effective marketing strategies within your current market. One way to do this is by getting your customers to use your product more often. Arm & Hammer Baking Soda provides a classic example of this technique. Its manufacturer increased sales by suggesting an additional way to use the product—as a refrigerator deodorizer. Today customers regularly purchase baking soda for both cooking and keeping their refrigerators smelling fresh.

You can also penetrate your market by attempting to attract your competitors' customers. Coca Cola and Pepsi utilized this strategy during their famous "cola wars."

Risk Takers, Profit Makers

Ella Williams

It's a challenge when you're a woman and a minority entering an already competitive and established market. But when Ella Williams founded her own engineering firm, it wasn't for the challenge. It was out of necessity.

Williams started AEGIR simply to pay the bills. With encouragement from her mother, support from friends, and help from the SBA, the Oxnard, California-based entrepreneur now competes with big businesses—and she wins.

Williams laid the groundwork for her enterprise during a 13-year stint in Hughes Aircraft's finance department. There she gained experience in the engineering trade while working as an accountant. She also met Chips Sawyer, who guided her through Hughes' engineering business and encouraged her to start her own.

Williams took his advice. First, she enlisted five engineer friends to commit themselves (and their experience) to AEGIR's roster. Then in 1975 she left Hughes and began promoting AEGIR to potential clients.

For the next two years, Williams raised her daughter, took on temporary work, experienced a divorce, and marketed AEGIR. Meanwhile, she continued her college education, earning extra money by collecting aluminum cans. Her persistence paid off when she won a contract with the Point Mugu naval station. To finish the job, Williams mortgaged her house for $65,000—at 21 percent interest!

Since then, she has found that others have been more willing to employ her company. Because of AEGIR's small size in comparison to other engineering firms, Williams can provide her clients with unusual attention and speed. Good references and a growing clientele have meant growth for AEGIR, even in a shrinking industry.

Despite her prosperity, Williams is not done shaping AEGIR. She's now diversifying it. In addition to serving the defense industry, AEGIR solicits transportation and environmental projects. So far, her strategies have been profitable. AEGIR has three offices nationwide, is establishing a fourth office, and employs 70 people.

While Williams relishes her success with AEGIR, she's already embarking on another entrepreneurial endeavor. To help those who are less fortunate than herself, she's starting Ella's World-Class Cheesecakes, Breads, and Muffins. In this enterprise, children from inner-city Los Angeles will gain work experience and earn college tuition money. Through her new business, Williams hopes to share an attitude instilled in her by her mother—that any goal can be reached by a person who believes in him- or herself.

Finally, you can go after people in your present market who are not using any product like yours. This is done by exposing these nonusers to your product and demonstrating its benefits.

Market Development

Another intensive growth strategy is market development. With this strategy you increase the number of target customers by taking your product to new geographic locations. This may mean opening a branch in another community as well as opening national or international locations.

FRANCHISING. Franchising is one of the most popular ways to expand a business. Recall from Chapter 8 that franchising is selling the right to do business under a company's name. It also includes training the franchisee and providing many types of assistance to maintain quality control. Here we will explore how franchising is used to expand your business's operations.

One of the biggest advantages of franchising is that you can expand your business using other people's money. Potential franchisees pay start-up fees. (Depending on the arrangements, they may also pay royalties on sales.) With fewer banks willing to lend for expansion, this is likely to become an increasingly important source of capital.

Franchising also makes it easier for you to manage your growing organization. With franchising you personally train your franchisees. They, in turn, hire and are responsible for the employees who work for them.

Be aware, however, that franchising may not be the answer to all of your expansion problems. There are some disadvantages to the arrangement. It is virtually like starting your own business over again. You must prepare training manuals, detailed instructions on how to run the business, and a detailed analysis of the market and your competitors. In addition, the costs of setting up the franchise structure are considerable. They may include legal, accounting, consulting, and training expenses.

When you finally have your franchise program going, it may be a very long time before you make a profit. One company in Memphis has sold over 70 franchises but will probably not show a profit for at least another year. In fact, waiting 3-5 years for a profit is not uncommon.

How do you know if your business is appropriate for a franchise program? Consider the following list of questions. Although it does not represent all of the questions you should ask yourself, it can give you some idea.

- *How long have you run the business?* The longer, the better. You will have a clearer understanding of how a successful business should be run.
- *Can your business be systematized and duplicated?* Remember, you must be able to teach your business operations to others. If it is too complicated, the cost and time to train franchisees may be prohibitive.
- *Is your business one that will grow?* Be careful that it's not a fad. To be a good franchise prospect, your business should have a large potential market.
- *Will it be easy to take your product to other geographic areas and other markets?* Generally, seasonal items are not good choices for franchises.

The classified sections of business publications often carry ads for franchises. How appropriate is this business for franchising according to the questions presented above?

• *Can your business generate a high percentage of gross profit?* The production costs for your product must be low enough to ensure a gross profit.

One final caution—setting up a franchise is a very complicated process. Therefore, it is important to get help from attorneys and accountants who have considerable experience dealing with franchises.

INTERNATIONAL EXPANSION. Entrepreneurs who have chosen the franchise route to expansion haven't limited themselves to the United States. Increasingly, they are exploring the options presented by the Pacific Rim, Europe, and the emerging Eastern European countries. Of course, not all international expansions have been in the form of franchises. Some businesses like Calcorn, Inc.'s Popcorn Palace have formed partnerships in Japan and have enjoyed tremendous success.

Today many countries are sending representatives to the United States, looking for businesses that can be adapted to their cultures. Businesses like Dairy Queen, Baskin-Robbins, McDonald's, and Pizza Hut—that have established successful franchises in the United States—are prime candidates for a foreign franchise.

Typically, an American business will sell a **master franchise agreement**. This document gives the franchisee the rights to an entire country. In this way, the franchisor avoids the hassles of starting up in an unfamiliar place.

Expanding into the former Soviet Union has become very popular, but it still has many problems. You need to form a partnership with a company native to the region and go through reams of bureaucratic paperwork. Also, your profits cannot be taken out of the former Soviet Union in the form of dollars. Because rubles have no value outside of Russia, many companies like Pepsi are taking their profit in trade goods.

Product Development

Another way to increase sales to target customers is to develop new and improved products. You have probably noticed many companies advertising "new and improved" versions of existing products. Shampoo, paper towels, toothpaste, and cereal are frequently examples.

You can also develop new packaging and sizing for your product. Recently, for example, detergent manufacturers have begun offering their products in concentrated form. These come in small, compact boxes that are easier to handle.

Many "new" products are simply variations or improvements on old ones. In each of these cases, what is the parent product and how has the manufacturer changed it to appeal to new customers?

Using Integrative Growth Strategies

A second approach to expanding your business relies on integrative strategies. These involve growth *within your industry*. Your business can grow by integrating either vertically or horizontally.

Vertical Integration

With **vertical integration**, a company expands by moving into areas either earlier or further along in its channel of distribution. In most instances, this means taking over either suppliers or distributors or both.

BACKWARD INTEGRATION. If you employ backward integration, you attempt to gain control of the suppliers you use to make your products. Suppose, for example, you are a manufacturer of plastic items. You might want to buy your plastics supplier if the firm is a profitable operation. By doing this, you may be able to cut costs and thus expand your business.

FORWARD INTEGRATION. If you choose forward integration, you attempt to gain control of the distribution systems for your product. You can do this in two ways. First, you can eliminate intermediaries by selling directly to your customers. Second, you can gain ownership of the distributors or dealers of your products.

Horizontal Integration

You can also expand your business by buying up your competitors to increase your market share. This is known as **horizontal integration**.

For example, you may decide to purchase a company that has a product and market compatible with yours. Or you may purchase a troubled company with buildings and distribution channels already established in a new geographic area. That way your product can move into a new geographic market without the expense of locating or constructing new buildings or setting up distribution channels.

Using Diversification Growth Strategies

The third approach to expanding a business involves diversification strategies. **Diversification** means to invest in products or businesses that are different from the products you sell or the business you own. Businesses that have exhausted the opportunities within their present industry or market often use this kind of approach. Diversification strategies, then, (in contrast to intensive or integrative strategies) exploit opportunities *outside a business's market or industry*.

Synergistic Diversification

With **synergistic diversification**, you try to find new products or businesses that are in some way technologically compatible with yours. You may purchase the rights to make a product that is made in a manner similar to your own. Or you may buy another business that is technologically similar.

Consider a specific example. Say, you own a bakery. You may decide to purchase a small gourmet restaurant, figuring that it can be a showcase for your baked goods.

Horizontal Diversification

With **horizontal diversification**, you seek products that are technologically unrelated to yours. However, you want them to be salable to your present customers.

For example, Bell Sports, which manufactures bicycle helmets, has begun selling clothing with the Bell logo as well as other cycling accessories.

The company hopes that if their customers are happy with Bell helmets, they will buy other Bell products as well.

Conglomerate Diversification

If you choose **conglomerate diversification** to expand, you look for products or businesses that are totally unrelated to yours in terms of technology or markets. Why would you want to do that? You may be looking for an enterprise that fills a gap in your own business. For example, suppose your primary business involves a great deal of traveling. You may purchase a travel agency to cut costs and provide convenience. Or you may decide to buy the building in which your company is located for much the same reasons. You could then lease the extra space to another business, thereby becoming a landlord.

Some businesses grow by diversifying. Which path to diversification has this deli business taken? Explain.

Looking at Advantages and Disadvantages

Expansion is a natural outgrowth of a successful business. In an age when consumer tastes and preferences are constantly changing, a business that has expanded and diversified in some way will have the advantage.

However, expansion does bring with it some concerns that shouldn't be overlooked. These involve areas as diverse as management, marketing, finances, and record keeping.

Take the marketing area. When you move from an owner-operated business to two or more additional sites, you lose the close contact you had with your customers. Consequently, it is not as easy to keep apprised of their needs.

In addition, you will need to decide whether to transfer your present business image to the new location or establish a different image. Many times, particularly in retail, an image that works in one community will not meet the needs of another.

In the management area, you will need to decide if your new store or stores will operate independently or be controlled by the main store. Sometimes the main store will control the marketing, accounting, finance, and purchasing functions. This arrangement leaves the branch store to handle mainly its day-to-day operations. (The branch will keep detailed records on its transactions and send this information to the main store on a regular basis.) With expansion also comes the need to hire additional managerial staff. This can be expensive.

Finally, with expansion your record-keeping requirements will become more complicated. You will need to develop an accounting system that can track sales, net income, expenses, and so on at all of your locations. Usually the system that worked when you had only one location will not be adequate to keep track of the accounting at additional locations.

Financing Your Expansion

When financing the expansion of your business, you can look to the same sources described in Chapter 20. These include personal savings, friends and family, venture capitalists, and banks.

As noted in Chapter 20, venture capital is more accessible to businesses financing expansion. However, this does not necessarily translate into easier money in general. Bank financing is becoming less accessible as banks tighten their lending policies in the face of stricter regulation.

One source of financing that becomes available as your business grows is your own positive cash flow. (You learned about this possibility in Chapter 24 when you studied the cash budget summary.) As more cash comes into the business and less cash leaves, the excess can be used to fund expansion—if there's enough.

Normally, however, a fast-growing business requires more cash than it can generate. Therefore, other sources of financing must be considered.

Private placements are a way that companies can sell investment interests in their businesses to sophisticated, private investors. (Sophisticated investors are those who regularly invest and have a clear understanding of the risks involved.) To offer a private placement, you will need to develop a **prospectus**. This is a type of business plan geared toward investors.

Private placements are highly regulated. So, you must get an experienced attorney involved to put one together.

In contrast, a **public stock offering** allows a business to raise money by selling shares of stock in the company. This is accomplished through one of the stock exchanges, like the New York Stock Exchange. To do a public offering, your company should have a documented track record of several years of increasing revenues.

While they are an excellent source of expansion capital, public offerings are costly and time-consuming to put together. This is because of the many legal, accounting, and administrative requirements of the Securities and Exchange Commission. This is the commission that protects the public from illegal or poorly prepared offerings.

Employee stock option plans (ESOPs) are yet another potential source of financing. They have become very popular of late. The ESOP, which is organized by the company, borrows money from a bank or insurance company. It then uses this cash to purchase stock in the company, which it offers to its employees at favorable rates. The stock serves as collateral for the bank note, while the company uses the cash for expansion.

ESOPs are an attractive benefit for a company's workers. What are they for a company's owner(s)?

Entrepreneur's Bookshelf

To learn more about the subjects discussed in this chapter, consider reading these books and articles:

- "How to Expand by Franchising" by Les Rager, *Nation's Business* (June 1989)
- "The Long Road to Franchising" by Ronaleen R. Roha, *Changing Times* (January 1987)
- "Capital: Strapped for Expansion Cash?" by Ellyn E. Spragins, *Inc.* (December 1989)

Chapter 28 Review

Recapping the Chapter

- Intensive growth strategies provide opportunity for growth within your market. Integrative growth strategies give you the opportunity to grow within your industry. Diversification growth strategies provide opportunities outside of the market or industry in which your business normally operates.
- The three basic intensive growth strategies are market penetration, market development, and product development.
- The integrative growth strategies include vertical and horizontal integration.
- Diversification growth strategies include synergistic, horizontal, and conglomerate diversification.
- Expansion often complicates a business's management, marketing, finances, and record keeping.
- Three sources of funding for expansion are private placements, public stock offerings, and ESOPs.

Reviewing Vocabulary

Write two or three sentences describing each of the terms below.

- market penetration
- master franchise agreement
- vertical integration
- horizontal integration
- diversification
- synergistic diversification
- horizontal diversification
- conglomerate diversification
- private placements

- prospectus
- public stock offering
- ESOPs

Checking the Facts

1. What is the difference between market development and market penetration?
2. List three questions you should ask yourself before you consider franchising your business.
3. What is the value to the franchisor of giving a master franchise agreement to the franchisee?
4. What is the purpose of horizontal integration?
5. When you are looking for opportunities outside your current market, what types of strategies might you use?
6. Why would you need a new accounting system if you were expanding to several locations?
7. What is the advantage of an ESOP over other types of expansion financing?

Critical Thinking

1. Your product, a new kind of cereal, seems to have reached a plateau in the growth of its market share. Which growth strategies could you use to increase its sales? Explain.
2. Compare and contrast product development and market development strategies in terms of purpose and growth.
3. Compare and contrast synergistic diversification and horizontal diversification.

Chapter 28 Review

4. Give two reasons for not expanding your business.
5. What are the advantages of a private placement over a public offering for a growing business in need of expansion financing?

Discussing Key Concepts

1. Pick a business with which you are familiar and identify ways to expand it using the three integrative growth strategies.
2. What might be some problems associated with conglomerate diversification?
3. Identify a successful franchise in your community, and discuss why you believe this business was a good choice for franchising.
4. You want to expand an innovative bicycle business internationally. What steps would you take?
5. Keeping your prospective business in mind, which source of financing would you use to expand your business?

Using Basic Skills

Math

1. Your business's revenues in its first six months of operation were as follows: $2,500; $2,800; $3,050; $3,500; $4,200; and $4,900. By what percentage did your monthly revenues grow over the course of this period?

Communication

2. In your local newspaper, locate an ad for a franchise opportunity. Compose a letter to the company asking for specific information about the franchise.

Human Relations

3. You have received a letter from a firm in Japan that is interested in licensing your business to operate in that country. Make two lists for yourself:

   * First, list some things that would be important to the Japanese representative to know about your business.
   * Second, list the things you would want to know about the Japanese company and Japan as a market.

Enriching Your Learning

1. Interview the owner of a business in your community. Find out if he or she has a growth strategy and how he or she determined what strategy or strategies to use. Also, ask the owner if the chosen strategy has been successful. Why or why not? Present your findings to the class.
2. Pick a product with which you are familiar. Assume that you are the owner of the business that produces and markets this product. Develop a market penetration strategy that is different from anything currently being used by the company. Justify your choice of strategy in a short report.

Glossary

abstract words   Words that can take on many meanings. (44)

accounting equation   Equation on which a balance sheet is based: assets = liabilities + capital. (244)

accounts payable   Those expenses that have been incurred but not yet paid for; money owed *by* a business. (238)

accounts receivable   Those sales that have been made but not yet paid for; money owed *to* a business. (238)

accrual basis   A method of recording income and expenses in which income is recorded when it is earned and expenses are recorded when they are incurred. (238)

aging   Categorizing customer accounts by the length of time since the initial bill was incurred. (242)

angels   Coined term used for nonprofessional investors who tend to put their money into local businesses. (256)

appointments   Interior design details; equipment and furnishings such as planters, fish tanks, etc. (189)

assessment   An evaluation to determine one's strengths and weaknesses in a particular area. (31)

assets   All those things of value that belong to a business or an individual. (244)

automation   The use of machines to do the work of people. (287)

balance of trade   Difference between a nation's exports and imports. (24)

balance sheet   Financial statement that tells an entrepreneur what his or her business is worth at any given time. (244)

bootstrapping   Operating a business as frugally as possible, using as few of the owner's resources as possible. (259)

brainstorming   A problem-solving technique that involves the spontaneous contribution of ideas from all members of a group. (74)

brand   The name, symbol, or design used to identify a product. (30)

break-even point   Number of units of a product that, when sold at a given price, covers production costs. (57)

bribes   Illegal payments made to secure special services for a business or special consideration for its products. (345)

buffer   A statement designed to soften the blow of bad news. (46)

burglary   The act of breaking into and entering a home or business with the intent to commit a felony. (196)

business interruption insurance   Type of insurance that pays net profits and expenses while a business is shut down for repairs or rebuilding. (200)

business plan   Document that describes a new business and tells why it is deserving of financial support from lenders and investors. (109)

campaign   A series of related activities designed to bring about a particular result. (223)

capacity   Ability of a person to legally enter into a contract. (145–146)

capital   The buildings, equipment, tools, and other goods needed to produce a product; also, the money used to buy these things. (19)

capital expenditures   Long-term commitments of large sums of money to buy new equipment or replace old equipment. (313)

cash basis   A method of recording income and expenses in which income is recorded when it is received and expenses when they are paid. (238)

cash budget   Financial statement that shows a business's projected and actual receipts/expenses and the difference between the two. (310)

cash flow statement   Financial statement that describes the flow of cash into and out of a business. (243)

casualty insurance   Type of insurance that protects a business from lawsuits arising from a variety of causes. (200)

cells   The boxes that make up the grid in a spreadsheet. (323)

census tracts   Subdivisions of Standard Metropolitan Statistical Areas, each containing 4,000–5,000 people. (169)

channel of distribution   The path a product takes from producer to final user. (134)

claims   Definitions of an invention's components as described in a patent application. (142)

collateral   Things of value that a lender can claim if a borrower fails to repay a loan. (260)

commission   A percentage of sales given in place or as part of a salary. (216)

computer integrated manufacturing (CIM)   Use of computers to measure production at every step of a manufacturing process. (318)

computer terminal   Computer monitor and keyboard. (322)

computer viruses   Commands hidden in software or on a data disk that tell a computer to erase its own files. (319)

conceptual skills   Those skills that enable a manager to understand an enterprise as a whole and visualize its future. (273)

concrete words   Words that have a clear meaning. (44)

conflict of interest   A conflict between the personal interests and official responsibilities of a businessperson doing a job. (345)

conglomerate diversification   Growth strategy in which a business owner looks to acquire products or businesses that are totally unrelated to his or her existing enterprise. (356)

consensus   Agreement among group members. (77)

consideration   That which is exchanged for the promise in a legally binding contract. (145)

consumer pretest   Procedure in which a panel of consumers evaluates an ad before it runs. (26)

contract   A binding agreement or promise to do something. (145)

cooperative advertising   An arrangement whereby the suppliers or manufacturers of goods that a business sells agree to share that business's advertising costs. (233)

copyright   The exclusive legal right to publish and sell an original work of authorship such as a book, movie, musical composition, or computer software program. (143)

corporation   A business that is chartered by a state and legally operates apart from its owner(s). (8)

cost-effective   Economical in the sense that the benefits realized exceed in value what was spent to produce them. (23)

cost of goods sold   Amount paid for inventory sold during a given period of time. (56)

counteroffer   An acceptance of a contract that differs from the terms of the original offer. (145)

criteria   Standards on which judgments or decisions may be based. (75)

critical path   The path through a PERT diagram that takes the longest time; indicates the shortest period in which a project can be completed. (284)

current assets   Cash (or things that can be quickly converted to cash); also, things that are used up in the operation of a business within a year. (254)

current liabilities   Debts due within a short time, usually a year. (254)

database management   Type of software that allows a computer user to work with several files at once, modifying them and moving them around. (324)

debit/credit   The two types of entries used in a double-entry accounting system; each income or expense item is entered as a *debit* to one account and a *credit* to another. (238)

delegate   To give another person responsibility for carrying out some of one's own work. (23)

Delphi technique   Procedure used to obtain consensus among group members who do not meet face-to-face; employs circulation of questionnaires. (77)

demographics   Statistical data that describes markets by criteria such as age, gender, family size, income, occupation, education, race, religion, and/or social class. (10)

depreciation   A tax adjustment made to certain fixed assets to account for the fact that they become less valuable with age. (254)

descriptive research   Type of research done when the problem involves determining the current status of something. (10)

developmental activities   Activities that prepare employees to lead a company into the future. (23)

direct insurance writer   An agent who works for one specific insurance company. (203)

disbursements   Payments. (238)

discount   A reduction in the retail or wholesale price of a particular product. (64)

diversification   Investing in products one does not currently produce or businesses one is not currently involved with. (355)

dividends   Earnings paid to stockholders. (105)

drawn to scale   Drawn according to an established scale of measurement, as ¼ inch = 1 foot. (189)

dumping   Selling one's products abroad at below cost. (345)

economic base   The major source of income for a community. (168)

economics   The study of the decisions (or choices) that go into making, distributing, and consuming products. (17)

educational activities   Activities that prepare employees for moving up in an organization. (293)

elastic   Describes a product for which a small change in price causes a significant change in the quantity demanded. (22)

electronic bulletin boards   Services that computer users can access through telephone lines and from which they can obtain a variety of software programs free. (320)

electronic credit authorizers   Devices that connect stores to a central credit bureau and instantly verify the status of credit cards offered for payment. (197)

employee stock option plan (ESOP)   Employee benefit that provides a company with investment capital and employees with an ownership interest. (357)

enterprise zones   Areas in which businesses are encouraged to locate through the extension of incentives like reduced taxes. (168)

entrepreneur   A person who undertakes the organization and ownership of a business with the intent of making a profit. (5)

entrepreneurial   Of or having to do with entrepreneurs. (5)

entrepreneurship   The process of getting into and operating your own business. (5)

equilibrium price   The price at which consumers will buy all of a product that is supplied, leaving neither a surplus nor a shortage. (2)

equipment   Refers to implements used in a business's operation. (13)

equities   The financial rights owners or investors have in a business's assets. (244)

equity   Ownership. (104)

errors-and-omissions insurance   Type of insurance that protects against lawsuits for mistakes in advertising. (200)

escrow period The length of time for a real estate transaction to go through. (147)

ethics Guidelines for human behavior, especially in situations involving honesty, integrity, and fairness. (343)

exclusive distribution Limits the number of outlets for distribution of a product to one per area. (135)

executive summary A brief recounting of the key points contained in a business plan. (261)

exploratory research Research used to expand knowledge when little is known about a problem. (124)

exports Products one nation sells to another. (24)

facade The face of a building. (189)

factor An agent who transacts business for another person. (259)

factors of production Resources that businesses use to produce the goods and services that people want; land, labor, capital, and entrepreneurship. (18)

feasibility Workability; the quality of being practical or doable. (115)

feedback A receiver's response (both verbal and nonverbal) to a message. (49)

fidelity bonds Type of insurance that protects a company in case of employee theft. (200)

fiscal year The tax year selected by a business (may be different from a calendar year). (238)

fixed assets Assets, such as equipment, that will be used over a long period of time. (20)

fixed costs Operating expenses that do not change with the number of units produced. (308)

fixtures Things attached to a building or thought of as part of it (like ceiling lights and display cases). (158)

focus group interviews Interviews with small groups of businesspeople or potential customers; used as part of exploratory research. (124)

foundational skills Math, communication, and decision skills that entrepreneurs use regularly in setting up and running a business. (37)

franchise A legal agreement to begin a new business in the name of a recognized company. (97)

franchisee The buyer of a franchise. (97)

franchisor The seller of a franchise. (97)

Gannt charts Scheduling charts that show tasks to be performed on the vertical axis and time required on the horizontal axis. (284)

general expenses Expenses connected with the running of a business rather than the manufacture and distribution of its products. (57)

general partners Members of a partnership having full responsibility for management and unlimited personal liability. (103)

goods Tangible products. (18)

goodwill The loyalty and regular patronage of customers. (97)

graphics software A computer program that allows a user to draw and produce pictures in a variety of colors and styles. (325)

gross lease Lease under whose terms a tenant pays a fixed monthly rent while the landlord pays taxes, insurance, and general operating expenses for the premises. (14)

hardware Computer equipment. (318)

historical research Research carried out to explore past occurrences, including their causes and effects. (124)

horizontal diversification Growth strategy in which a business owner seeks products that are salable to his or her present customers but technologically unrelated to those products. (355)

horizontal integration Growth strategy that involves buying up one's competitors in order to increase market share. (355)

hygiene factors Things like compensation, working conditions, and fair company policies, that keep employees from becoming dissatisfied. (295)

hypothesis A tentative assumption made for test purposes. (72)

image The beliefs, ideas, and impressions that people have of a business. (222)

imports Products one nation buys from another. (24)

incentives Advantages, such as lower taxes, offered by communities to attract new enterprises. (168)

income statement Financial statement that shows how much a business has earned or lost during a year; also called a profit and loss statement. (56)

independent insurance agent An agent who works with several insurance companies. (202)

industrial parks Areas within a community that are set aside for industrial uses. (173)

inelastic Describes a product for which a change in price has little or no effect on quantity demanded. (22)

inquisitive Curious; given to asking questions. (34)

intensive distribution Places a product in all suitable sales outlets. (135)

intermediaries People or businesses that move products between producers and final users. (134)

interrelationships The access, arrangement, and flow among all the activities in a building. (181)

inventory Merchandise purchased for resale. (56)

investment The money one puts into a business as capital. (33)

invoice The seller's record of a transaction initiated by a buyer. (61)

job descriptions Documents that detail the duties and responsibilities of company personnel. (110)

job enlargement Adding more tasks of the same skill level to an employee's job. (296)

job enrichment   Adding tasks of a higher skill level to an employee's job, thus giving the employee more responsibility and control. (296)

job specification   Document that spells out the abilities, skills, educational level, and experience needed by an employee to perform a given job. (214)

kiosks   Stands or booths. (334)

label   That part of a package used to present information. (130)

layout   A floor plan. (181)

lead time   The gap in time between placing an order and receiving the delivery. (283)

lease   A contract to use a facility or equipment for a specified period of time. (146)

ledger   A collection of all the accounts of a business. (241)

liabilities   Monetary amounts owed to others. (244)

limited partners   Members of a partnership who are not actively involved in management and whose liability is limited to their initial investment. (103)

line-and-staff organization   Form of business organization used when a company is large enough to hire staff, or people who support production and distribution employees. (213)

line of credit   An amount of money that a bank agrees to lend a business at a certain rate of interest and against which the business can borrow. (258)

line organization   Form of business organization used when all employees are involved in producing or distributing a company's product. (213)

long-term liabilities   Amounts owed for more than a year. (254)

management-by-objectives   Motivational technique that involves employees in decision making by having them set objectives and then monitor progress toward those objectives. (296)

manager   Person who coordinates the people, processes, and other resources of an operation on a day-to-day basis. (267)

markdown   Amount or percentage by which a business lowers its retail prices in order to move merchandise. (64)

market analysis   Research of potential customers, proposed goods or services, competition, market trends, and available suppliers. (110)

marketing concept   States that if a business is to succeed and make a profit, it must focus all of its efforts on satisfying its customers. (119)

marketing mix   The particular combination of product, price, place, and promotion strategies that a business owner uses to reach his or her target market. (110)

market penetration   Growth strategy that attempts to increase sales by using more effective marketing. (351)

market research   Process used to do a market analysis. (122)

market share   A portion of the total sales generated by all the competing companies in a given market. (122)

markup   The amount added to the cost of an item to cover expenses and ensure a profit. (63)

master franchise agreement   Document that gives a franchisee the rights to do all franchisor business in an entire country. (354)

microcomputers   Personal computers. (320)

modem   A special piece of equipment that allows a computer to talk to and interact with other computers over telephone lines. (324)

motivating factors   Things like achievement, recognition, responsibility, and advancement, that encourage employees to better job performance. (296)

negligence   The failure to exercise reasonable care. (199)

negotiation   The process of persuading someone to agree with your point of view in such a way that both of you win. (48)

net income   Result of subtracting a business's expenses from its revenues; also called net profit. (56)

net lease   Lease under whose terms a tenant pays taxes and all operating expenses for a premises in addition to a monthly rent. (176)

news release   A brief news story sent to the media. (229)

niches   Suitable areas for entrepreneurial ventures. (11)

nominal grouping   A decision-making technique in which people acting both individually and as group members make ranked lists of potential solutions to a problem and eventually vote to determine the top choice. (77)

norms   Ways of doing things that have come about over time. (346)

obsolescence costs   Money lost when products or materials become obsolete while in inventory. (280)

odd/even pricing   Employs odd prices ($19.99) to suggest bargains and even prices ($20) to suggest higher quality. (133)

operating expenses   Expenses incurred in operating a business; also, expenses directly related to the manufacture and distribution of a business's product. (56, 57)

operational plans   Plans that address short-range objectives for the implementation of tactical plans. (268)

opportunity cost   Thing sacrificed in order to get another. (19)

organization chart   Chart that presents all the jobs in a business and shows how they are related to each other. (110)

package   The physical container or wrapper that holds a product. (130)

partnership   Form of business in which two or more people are owners and share in the assets, liabilities, and profits. (102)

patent   A grant to an inventor that gives him or her the exclusive right to produce and sell an invention for a period of 17 years. (142)

percentage lease   Lease under whose terms a tenant pays either a percentage of net income or a flat rate plus a percentage of gross revenues. (14)

performance bonds   Type of insurance that protects a business in the event work or a contract is not finished on time or as agreed. (200)

performance evaluation   A review and evaluation of how well an employee is doing on the job. (297)

persistent   Willing to work until a job is done, no matter how long it takes. (34)

PERT diagrams   Scheduling diagrams that show a project's major activities in sequence, with the most time-consuming arranged along the critical path. (284)

philanthropy   The promotion of human welfare through giving. (341)

piece rate   So much per unit produced. (216)

policies   General statements of intent about how a business is to be run. (207)

premium   Fee paid for insurance coverage. (200)

premiums   Anything of value that a customer receives in addition to the good or service purchased. (229–230)

preselling   Influencing potential customers to buy before contact is actually made. (222)

prestige pricing   Employs higher-than-average prices to suggest exclusiveness, status, and prestige. (133)

primary data   Information that is collected for the first time and is specific to the problem being studied. (124)

prime time   For television viewing, 7–11 P.M. (226)

principal   Amount borrowed. (57)

principle of diminishing marginal utility   States that in the face of low prices, consumers will not continue to buy indefinitely. (22)

private brand   Products packaged with the retailer's rather than the manufacturer's name on them. (332)

private placements   A way that companies can sell investment interests in their businesses to sophisticated, private investors. (357)

proactive   Acting in anticipation of future problems. (342)

productivity   A measure of how much a business can produce. (287)

product liability   The legal theory that manufacturers are responsible for injuries caused by their products. (150)

product liability insurance   Type of insurance that protects against claims for injuries resulting from use of a company's products. (200)

product mix   All the products a company makes or sells. (131)

product positioning   Refers to how consumers see products in relation to each other. (130)

profile   Pattern of traits and experiences. (36)

profit   What is left after all the expenses of running a business have been deducted from income. (21)

pro forma   Projected or estimated. (110)

promotional channels   Established lines of communication for certain products. (224)

promotional mix   Combination of advertising, publicity, sales promotion, and personal selling. (137)

prospectus   Type of business plan geared toward investors. (357)

psychographics   Statistical data that describes markets by criteria such as personality, opinions, activities, and interests. (120)

psychological pricing   Employs price to affect customers' perceptions of a product or company. (133)

public relations   Term that covers any activity designed to create goodwill toward a business. (222)

public stock offering   The sale of shares of stock on a stock exchange to raise money for a business. (357)

purchase order   A preprinted form that organizes a purchase so that all essential information is presented simply and clearly. (60)

quality circles   Groups of employees who meet to solve problems involving product quality. (285)

quality control programs   Checks built in to the production process to make sure products meet certain standards. (269)

ratio analysis   Way of analyzing a business's financial condition by comparing certain numbers from a balance sheet or income statement. (305)

rational approach   A series of steps used when making nonroutine decisions to ensure that every aspect of the problem or decision is considered. (72)

rebate   Part of the purchase price returned to the customer. (230)

recruit   To attract prospective employees. (215)

research designs   The several basic ways to structure research studies. (122)

resumes   Documents that summarize education, skills, and work experience of job applicants. (110)

risk management   How a business deals with risk; involves four strategies—risk avoidance, risk reduction, risk transfer, and risk retention. (199)

robbery   The taking of property by force or threat. (196)

role models   People whose attitudes and achievements others try to duplicate. (33)

rules/regulations   Statements that tell employees exactly what they should or should not do. (207)

safety stock   The cushion of products that keeps a business from running out of inventory while it awaits delivery of an order. (283)

sales potential   An estimate of how much of a product a business can expect to sell. (121)

satisficing   Using a solution that suffices for the moment rather than considering all the possibilities. (72)

scarcity   Situation that exists when wants are unlimited but resources are not. (19)

secondary data Market research data collected to explore some problem other than the one under study. (124)

selective distribution Limits the number of sales outlets for a product in a geographic area. (135)

service mark A word, symbol, design, or combination of these that a service business uses to identify itself. (143)

services Intangible (or conceptual) products. (2)

shrinkage costs Money lost when inventory items are broken, damaged, spoiled, or stolen. (280)

situational management The use by managers of whichever leadership style their circumstances dictate. (271)

software The programs that run a computer. (318)

sole proprietor The sole owner of a business—the person who receives its profits and is responsible for its activities and any losses it incurs. (100)

specialty items Items such as pens, caps, and T-shirts imprinted with a company's name and used for advertising purposes. (226)

specialty magazines Publications targeted to people with interests in sports, camping, fashion, and a variety of other areas. (87)

spreadsheet A grid of rows and columns on a computer screen, similar to an accountant's note pad. (323)

Standard Metropolitan Statistical Areas (SMSAs) Geographic areas into which the Census Bureau divides the United States. (169)

start-up costs Expenses incurred in opening a business. (160)

stock Certificates indicating the amount of equity each investor has in a business. (104)

stock turnover rate Frequency with which inventory is sold and replaced over a given period of time. (58)

strategic plans Plans that map out a business's course for the next 3-5 years. (268)

supplies Items that are used up in the operation of a business. (158)

sweepstakes Simple games of chance used by businesses to get customers thinking and talking about what the company has to offer. (230)

synergistic diversification Growth strategy that involves seeking products or businesses that are technologically compatible with one's existing products or business. (355)

synergy Feeling of unity that allows family members working together to achieve more than all of them working apart. (96)

tactical plans Plans that focus on a period of one year or less. (268)

target market The specific market segment toward which all of a business's activities are directed. (120)

Theory X A set of negative assumptions about employees based on the premise that people do not like work and will try to avoid it. (295)

Theory Y A set of positive assumptions about employees based on the premise that work is natural to people and an important part of their lives. (295)

time management The process of allocating time effectively. (272)

time-sharing A way of computerizing a business that involves linking up with a source computer owned by another company. (322)

trade area The region or section of a community from which a business draws customers. (170)

trade credit Credit obtained from within one's industry or trade, usually from one's suppliers. (258)

trade discounts Discounts off suggested retail prices that manufacturers grant to wholesalers and retailers. (279)

trade magazines Periodicals published for specific types of businesses or industries. (87)

trademark A word, symbol, design, or combination of these that a business uses to identify itself or something it sells. (143)

trade shows Exhibitions at which vendors and manufacturers introduce new products and promote established ones. (89)

transferable skills Skills that can be used in many types of businesses. (90)

unique One of a kind. (87)

usage rate The speed at which inventory is used in a given period of time. (283)

variable costs The expenses associated with operating a business that change with each unit of product produced. (308)

vendors Businesses that provide inventory as opposed to supplies. (160)

venture A business enterprise or undertaking involving some degree of uncertainty or risk. (5)

venture capitalists Individuals or firms that invest capital professionally. (256)

vertical integration Growth strategy that involves buying either one's suppliers or distributors. (355)

warranty of merchantability Warranty implied by law whenever something is sold; assures the buyer that the product bought is of at least average quality and fit for the purpose for which it was intended. (149)

workers compensation Provides medical and income benefits to employees who are injured on the job. (202)

working capital Figure that shows how much money a company has to carry out its daily operations. (306)

workstation An area with equipment for a single worker. (183)

zoning laws Laws designating certain areas of a community for residential, commercial, industrial, or public use. (146)

Index